KU-530-029

Contents

I hope that some kind of formal evaluation of the Transmitted Deprivation Programme will be made. It would be a pity (to say the least) not to try to draw some specific lessons from such an enterprise before someone embarks on the next. From here there seems so much that we need to find out about research sponsorship that research on research seems badly needed. No doubt it would be wise to heed Mr Posner's mistrust of the genre and perhaps aim no higher than to record the history of the exercise in a systematic fashion, its aims and achievements, the processes of collaboration and the experience of key participants, while this is still relatively fresh.

(National Archives, Kew, London, MH 166/1518:
Hazel Houghton to P.V. Foster, 8 May 1979)

The Programme of Research into Transmitted Deprivation … would make a fascinating research topic in itself … there is certainly a rich mine for the student of the sociology of knowledge….

It is all there: the growth from a superficially simple idea to a voluminous debate, the definition and redefinition of terms (from cycle of deprivation to transmitted deprivation to intergenerational continuities in deprivation), the interplay of ideology and research that produced such changes (the first two definitions imply pathology, the third allows of structural interpretations), the social construction and reconstruction of the social problem, the development and reification of a concept, and so forth.

(John Edwards, 'Running in families?', *Times Higher Education Supplement*, 26 November 1982, p 16)

Please retain these files for the 25 year period. They are the history of the commissioning of an important and complex set of studies and we are likely to receive requests for documentation of the process of commissioning. We have already received one such query and as the years go by and the work assumes historical importance I would anticipate more requests for the records of the process.

(National Archives, Kew, London, MH 166/1515:
Hazel Canter to Mrs Sutton, 8 October 1985)

FROM TRANSMITTED DEPRIVATION TO SOCIAL EXCLUSION

Policy, poverty, and parenting

John Welshman

First published in Great Britain in 2012 by

The Policy Press
University of Bristol
Fourth Floor
Beacon House
Queen's Road
Bristol BS8 1QU
UK
Tel +44 (0)117 331 4054
Fax +44 (0)117 331 4093
e-mail tpp-info@bristol.ac.uk
www.policypress.co.uk

North American office:
The Policy Press
c/o The University of Chicago Press
1427 East 60th Street
Chicago, IL 60637, USA
t: +1 773 702 7700
f: +1 773-702-9756
e:sales@press.uchicago.edu
www.press.uchicago.edu

© John Welshman 2012
Index © Rowena Gavars 2012
Transfered to Digital Print 2013

British Library Cataloguing in Publication Data
A catalogue record for this book is available from the British Library.

Library of Congress Cataloging-in-Publication Data
A catalog record for this book has been requested.

ISBN 978 1 44730 586 6 paperback

Cover design by Qube Design Associates.
Printed and bound in Great Britain by Marston Book Services, Oxford

Acknowledgements

This book has been a long time in the making and, as ever, numerous people helped with the research for it. Perhaps foremost among them are those researchers and former civil servants who agreed to be interviewed: Tony Atkinson, Richard Berthoud, Tessa Blackstone, Mildred Blaxter, Muriel Brown, Alan Clarke, Frank Coffield, Raymond Illsley, Nicola Madge, Robin Matthews, Geoffrey Otton, Michael Rutter, Adrian Sinfield, Olive Stevenson, Peter Townsend, and Robin Wendt. All were most generous with their time, producing correspondence and other private papers, and in many cases commenting on an earlier article and on draft chapters. John Veit-Wilson was most helpful in giving me access to the private papers of his mother, Harriett Wilson, and even did half of the photocopying. Don Brereton kindly commented on whether my account of the origins of the cycle speech matched his own recollections. Others who offered advice, particularly in the early stages, were Alan Bacon, Virginia Berridge, John Bynner, Andrew Denham, Harvey Goldstein, Hilary Graham, Chris Grover, Peregrine Horden, Ruth Lister, Sally MacIntyre, John Stewart, and Charles Webster. Alan Deacon has been a source of constant encouragement. Originally I had hoped that we might write this book together, and it is a source of disappointment to me that Alan's caring responsibilities meant that he could not take on significant new commitments. His support, again particularly at the outset, was invaluable.

This is primarily a historical study, based not just on published documents and oral interviews, but on extensive archival research. In terms of the last, I would particularly like to thank Melody Allsebrook at the Economic and Social Research Council for her patience in tracking down documents in the archives of the former Social Science Research Council; Pauline Connor at the Department of Health Record Store at Nelson in Lancashire; staff at the Albert Sloman Library, University of Essex; and the staff of the National Archives, Kew, London. Sheridan Westlake, from the Conservative Campaign Headquarters, kindly permitted access to the Conservative Party Archive in the Bodleian Library, Oxford, and to the Keith Joseph papers, and at the Bodleian, Jeremy McIlwane, the Conservative Party Archivist, and Paul Cartwright were also helpful at short notice. The staff on the interlibrary loans desk at Lancaster University Library, particularly Jenny Brine, were unfailingly patient.

The Universities of Lancaster and Leeds and the Social Policy Association funded a workshop held at the University of Leeds in July

2002, to mark the 30th anniversary of the cycle of deprivation speech. Subsequent funding provided through Lancaster University's Research Committee Small Grants Fund, along with a period of sabbatical leave, made it possible to conduct the oral interviews and do additional archival research. Articles exploring aspects of this story have been published in the journals *Benefits*, *Children & Society*, *Economic History Review*, the *Journal of Epidemiology and Community Health*, the *Journal of Social Policy*, the *Political Quarterly*, and *Twentieth Century British History*. Papers on transmitted deprivation have been given at the University of Exeter; the University of Leeds; the London School of Hygiene and Tropical Medicine; St Catherine's College, Oxford; and the University of Bergen, Norway. I am grateful to all those who came to listen, and for their comments. At The Policy Press, I would like to thank Philip de Bary, Emily Watt, Jackie Lawless, Laura Greaves, and my referees, who have made the production of this book, if not the writing of it, so relatively painless. I am grateful to Rose Welshman for her care in transcribing the interviews, and in proofreading. Earlier books have been dedicated to my parents, and to my wife and children. But here I would like to record my gratitude to some of those who have inspired my interest in history, and encouraged my own progress through school and university: Peter Biller, John Bossy, Chris Clark, Richard Fletcher, Noel Orr, Jonathan Powis, Ted Royle, Jim Sharpe, David Thompson, and Charles Webster. I hope they might recognise something of themselves in the following pages.

Abbreviations

ASBO	Antisocial Behaviour Order
BASW	British Association of Social Workers
BCS	British Cohort Study
BHPS	British Household Panel Survey
CASE	Centre for Analysis of Social Exclusion, London School of Economics and Political Science
CDP	Community Development Project
CPAG	Child Poverty Action Group
DES	Department of Education and Science
DHSS	Department of Health and Social Security
DSS	Department of Social Security
DWP	Department for Work and Pensions
ECHP	European Community Household Panel (Survey)
EPA	Educational Priority Area
ESRC	Economic and Social Research Council
EU	European Union
FIP	Family Intervention Project
FIS	Family Income Supplement
FSU	Family Service Unit
IILS	International Institute for Labour Studies
IQ	Intelligence Quotient
JRF	Joseph Rowntree Foundation
LSE	London School of Economics and Political Science
MOH	Medical Officer of Health
MRC	Medical Research Council
NA	National Archives, Kew, London
NCDS	National Child Development Study
NHS	National Health Service
NIESR	National Institute for Economic and Social Research
ODNB	*Oxford Dictionary of National Biography*
ODPM	Office of the Deputy Prime Minister
PSID	Panel Study of Income Dynamics (US)
RCDIW	Royal Commission on the Distribution of Income and Wealth
RMI	*Revenu Minimum d'Insertion* (France)
SEU	Social Exclusion Unit
SSRC	Social Science Research Council
WPTD	Working Party on Transmitted Deprivation

Timeline: from transmitted deprivation to social exclusion

Year	Policy	Publications
1970	June, election of Conservative government Sir Keith Joseph appointed Secretary of State for Social Services	Townsend (ed), *The concept of poverty* Bronfenbrenner, *Two worlds of childhood* Holman, *Socially deprived families in Britain*
1971	July, early discussions between Joseph and Andrew Shonfield (SSRC) Joan Cooper and Geoffrey Otton papers	Oliver and Taylor, 'Five generations of ill-treated children in one family pedigree' Wright and Lunn, 'Sheffield problem families' Blackstone, *A fair start* Ryan, *Blaming the victim*
1972	Rothschild Report on government R&D February, 'Bloody Sunday' March, 1st formal meeting of DHSS and SSRC June, Joseph's cycle speech to the Pre-School Playgroups Association June, convening of Joint Working Party September, Joint Working Party early papers Unemployment climbs to 1 million	Davie et al, *From birth to seven* Rutter, *Maternal deprivation reassessed* Atkinson, *Unequal shares* Townsend and Bosanquet (eds), *Labour and inequality*

1973	April, seminar 'Dimensions of Parenthood', All Souls College, Oxford April, seminar 'Approaches to Research on Transmitted Deprivation', LSE October-November, study trip to the US	Blackstone, *Education and day care for young children in need*
1974	January, start of Research Programme March, election of Labour government Barbara Castle appointed Secretary of State for Social Services SSRC–DHSS, *First report of the DHSS/SSRC Joint Working Party on Transmitted Deprivation* DHSS, *The family in society: preparation for parenthood* DHSS, *The family in society: dimensions of parenthood* October, Joseph's Edgbaston speech	Townsend, 'The cycle of deprivation: the history of a confused thesis' Kellmer Pringle, *The needs of children* Jordan, *Poor parents* Morgan et al, *Five thousand American families*
1975	SSRC–DHSS, *Second report of the DHSS/SSRC Joint Working Party on Transmitted Deprivation*	Marsden and Duff, *Workless*
1976	April, David Ennals appointed Secretary of State for Social Services	Berthoud, *The disadvantages of inequality* Rutter and Madge, *Cycles of disadvantage*
1977	SSRC–DHSS, *Third report of the DHSS/SSRC Joint Working Party on Transmitted Deprivation*	CDP, *Gilding the ghetto*
1978		Wilson and Herbert, *Parents and children in the inner city* Holman, *Poverty* RCDIW, *Report no 6: Lower incomes*

1979	May, election of the Conservative government	Townsend, *Poverty in the United Kingdom*
1980	December, formal end of Research Programme	Coffield et al, *A cycle of deprivation?*
1981		Blaxter, *The health of the children* Sinfield, *What unemployment means* Showler and Sinfield (eds), *The workless state*
1982	Joseph's attempt to abolish the SSRC Rothschild Report on the SSRC	Essen and Wedge, *Continuities in childhood disadvantage* Blaxter and Paterson, *Mothers and daughters* Mortimore and Blackstone, *Disadvantage and education* West, *Delinquency* Brown and Madge, *Despite the welfare state* Donnison, *The politics of poverty*
1983		Brown (ed), *The structure of disadvantage* Atkinson et al, *Parents and children* Ashley, *The money problems of the poor* Fuller and Stevenson, *Policies, programmes and disadvantage* Murie, *Housing inequality and deprivation* Madge (ed), *Families at risk* Berthoud, 'Transmitted deprivation: the kite that failed' Glennerster (ed), *The future of the welfare state*

1984		Triseliotis and Russell, *Hard to place* Murray, *Losing ground* Duncan, *Years of poverty years of plenty*
1986	Joseph, 'Introduction', in S. Smiles, *Self-help* (1859)	Bane and Ellwood, 'Slipping into and out of poverty'
1987		Wilson, *The truly disadvantaged*
1988		Quinton and Rutter, *Parenting breakdown*
1990		Kolvin et al, *Continuities of deprivation?*
1994	Death of Joseph	
1995		Room (ed), *Beyond the threshold* Falkingham and Hills (eds), *The dynamic of welfare*
1996		Paugam, 'Poverty and social disqualification'
1997	May, election of Labour government June, Blair's Aylesbury estate speech August, Mandelson's Fabian Society social exclusion lecture November, CASE–ESRC 'Cycles of Disadvantage' seminar December, Blair's Stockwell speech December, launch of SEU	

1998	SEU, *Rough sleeping* SEU, *Bringing Britain together* SEU, *Truancy and school exdusion* November, Treasury seminar	Lee and Hills (eds), *New cycles of disadvantage?* Giddens, *The third way* Levitas, *The inclusive society?* Leisering and Walker, *The dynamics of modern society* Madanipour et al, *Social exclusion in European cities*
1999	CASE and HM Treasury, *Persistent poverty and lifetime inequality* HM Treasury, *Tackling poverty and extending opportunity* March, Blair's Beveridge Lecture on child poverty SEU, *Teenage pregnancy* SEU, *Bridging the gap*	Byrne, *Social exclusion* Leisering and Leibfried, *Time and poverty in western welfare states* (English translation)
2000		Fairclough, *New Labour, new language?*
2001	Launch of Sure Start	
2002		Hills et al (eds), *Understanding social exclusion* Ghate and Hazel, *Parenting in poor environments*
2003		Le Grand, *Motivation, agency, and public policy* Sennett, *Respect*
2004	ODPM, *Breaking the cycle*	Hills, *Inequality and the state* Lister, *Poverty*

2006	January, Respect Task Force, *Respect action plan* June, work of SEU transferred to Cabinet Office August, Blair's BBC social exclusion interview September, Blair's JRF social exclusion speech HM Government, *Reaching out: An action plan on social exclusion*	Belsky et al, 'Effects of Sure Start local programmes on children and families' Olds, 'The Nurse–Family Partnership'
2007	January, selection of 40 'Respect' zones February, Cabinet Office, Social Exclusion Taskforce, *Reaching out: Progress on social exclusion* April, launch of 53 Family Intervention Projects May, launch of the Nurse–Family Partnership Summer, *Families at risk review*	UNICEF report on child well-being

Preface to the paperback edition

Writing this provides an opportunity to survey developments in policy since 2007, when the book was originally published. How far is it still relevant to the changed policy context of 2012? Initially, under Gordon Brown, Tony Blair's populist Respect agenda seemed much less marked. Instead a new Child Poverty Unit was established – worklessness and low pay were viewed as the biggest direct causes of poverty, and work was seen as offering the best route out (HM Treasury/DWP/DCSF, 2008). While documents still highlighted 'intergenerational cycles of deprivation', there was a genuine desire to engage with academic experts. A day conference in June 2008 was attended by over 100 stakeholders from across government, the third sector, stakeholder organisations, the wider policy and research community, and academia (DWP, 2008a). With the Child Poverty Act (2010), the government sought to enshrine in legislation its 1999 pledge to eradicate child poverty in the UK by 2020 (Child Poverty Unit, 2009).

Nevertheless by November 2009, two million children in Britain lived in households where neither parent had a job, a rise of 170,000 since 2008 (Williams, 2009). Moreover running alongside the debate about child poverty was the drive for welfare reform. What was needed was a welfare system that rewarded 'responsibility', and that enabled people to become 'authors of their own lives'. This included enforcing the obligation to work, moving Incapacity Benefit claimants onto the new Employment and Support Allowance, individual budgets for people with disabilities, and getting more parents into employment (DWP, 2008b). This was amplified by references to 'personalised conditionality matched by personalised support'; almost everyone on benefits should take active steps towards work. The White Paper again used the phrase 'cycle of deprivation', but, with a nod to working poverty, argued that work only offered the best route out of poverty if 'work pays' (DWP, 2008c).

At the local level, the Family Intervention Projects (FIPs) begun in April 2007 continued their work in places such as Blackburn in the North West. Success was measured by a reduction in complaints about families to the police and the council (Hefferman, 2007). In his 2009 conference speech, Gordon Brown said 'family intervention projects work. They change lives, they make our communities safer and they crack down on those who're going off the rails'. Brown vowed to introduce the model nationwide, rehousing and retraining 50,000 of the most 'chaotic' families. The Department for Children, Schools and Families (DCSF) estimated that 2,600 families had taken part in 170 centres since 2007. One mother in the Dundee FIP said that initially she felt the constant monitoring oppressive: 'I thought they were prying on me'. But gradually she began to feel the benefits of it: 'In the end, I didn't feel they were observing me. I felt like it was more like a friend coming up' (Gentleman, 2009).

More generally, Labour MP for Nottingham North, Graham Allan, signalled his intention to turn Nottingham into 'early intervention city', citing the value of projects he had visited in Colorado and New York (Wintour, 2008). A £218m three-year scheme announced in March 2008 indicated children as young as ten could be identified as at risk of becoming criminals and subjected to intensive one-to-one mentoring and training (Curtis, 2008). Taking over as Home Secretary, Alan Johnson in June 2009 sought to revive the focus on antisocial behaviour, admitting the Government had 'coasted' on the issue (Ford, 2009). Meanwhile the Department of Health announced plans to undertake a £4m multi-centre randomised control trial of the Family Nurse Partnership (FNP) begun in May 2007, arguing in the meantime that the FNP could make a 'powerful contribution ... as a preventive and early intervention service for potentially high need, high cost families' (DoH, 2009).

Many of these ideas were shared by the Conservatives, particularly Iain Duncan Smith (Mongomerie, 2008). David Cameron had called for an end to the 'moral neutrality' whereby society refused to distinguish between good and bad behaviour. Cameron said 'of course, circumstances – where you are born, your neighbourhood, your school and the choices your parents make – have a huge impact. But social problems are often the consequences of the choices that people make' (Stratton, 2008). The theme of 'Broken Britain' was a prominent theme of pre-election campaigning for the May 2010 General Election. While Duncan Smith talked about 'dysfunctional families', cut off from the norms of society, others countered by pointing to growing social inequalities. In their election manifestos, Labour said it would expand the FNP and FIPs for the 50,000 most dysfunctional families, while the Conservatives focused on the Big Society instead of big government.

Following the election, there were plans for ministers and advisers to adopt workless families and to volunteer to become family champions. It was estimated there were 120,000 'troubled' families: 50,000 'hard core families with multiple problems', and 70,000 'second tier' problem families who 'disproportionately gobble up resources'. Emma Harrison, social entrepreneur and Chair of A4e, said 'families like that are negative millionaires' (Driscoll and Woolf, 2011). In November 2011, Home

Secretary Theresa May said 1,200 families in which children had already offended would be given intensive one-to-one therapy to stop them turning to crime (Bentham, 2011). Particularly brutal murders involving children, or evidence of wider social unrest, continued to prompt periodic anxiety about social breakdown. Press reporting of the incident in Edlington, Doncaster, where two brothers tortured two boys, had parallels with the James Bulger murder (1993). David Cameron suggested people had to ask deep questions about 'what has gone wrong in our society', while a leader article in *The Times* argued that Britain had 'a depressingly static underclass' (Webster, 2010; *The Times*, 2010). Similarly the riots of August 2011 led to anxieties about 'moral decline', with Cameron arguing gangs were at the heart of disturbances, and the culmination of a 'slow-motion moral collapse' (Riddell, 2011).

Researchers have suggested that while Labour's policy for tackling poverty and disadvantage began well, little changed after 2004. Expenditure on tax credits and benefits flattened out, and progress on reducing worklessness stalled. A decade of economic growth and huge Parliamentary majorities had presented a 'rare opportunity only partly grasped' to restructure society in the interests of the poorest children (Stewart, 2009). Policy experts argued that efforts to reduce child poverty had not taken sufficient account of the 1.4 million poor children who lived in working households (Cooke and Lawton, 2008; Kenway, 2008). It was argued that the FNP was congruent with a new approach to social exclusion, where the most important task was to identify the most 'at risk' households (Dodds, 2009). On the other hand, research found that while women experienced the FIPs in punitive and disciplinary terms, they also had a constructive or positive impact on their lives (Parr, 2011). It was research which pointed to anger and frustration with the way the police engaged with communities as the triggers for the August 2011 disturbances.

But research had little impact on the policy agenda. In December 2011, David Cameron argued that the government was determined to 'get to grips' with England's 'most troubled families'. The relatively small number of families that caused many of the problems in society were characterised by worklessness; poor housing; no qualifications; mental health problems; longstanding illness or disability; low income; and being unable to afford food or clothing. There were said to be 4,500 of these families in Birmingham, 2,500 in Manchester, and 1,115 in Sandwell. Their problems were intergenerational, and they cost the state £9 billion (£75,000 per family). One group in society was living apart from the rest. Cameron promised more targeted support, with the government pledging £448m to 'turn around' the lives of 120,000 families by 2015. Louise Casey was to head up a new Troubled Families Unit, while family workers would identify these families and make sure children got to school on time, and were properly fed (Morris, 2011). Briefly, Emma Harrison was appointed 'families czar' (Simpson, 2012).

In the US, the 'culture of poverty' thesis has begun to stage a comeback, with an upswing in cultural explanations (Cohen, 2010). Certainly in the UK, the resurgence of the discourse of problem or troubled families since 2007 has been striking, as has been the continued emphasis on the FIPs and the FNP. The reasons are the same as those that have ensured the resilience of the underclass concept over the past 130 years. First, the unresolved issue of the relative importance of behavioural and structural factors in the causation of poverty and deprivation. Second, the desire by government to quantify the size of the 'problem', and to devise targeted interventions to tackle it. Third, the economic recession, growing unemployment, and cuts in public spending, which together continue to raise the spectre, both real and imagined, of groups perceived as 'unemployable' or 'cut off' from the norms of the mainstream working class. And fourth, the value of problem families as convenient symbols and metaphors for fears and anxieties whose empirical reality remains unproven (Gentleman, 2010).

Sadly, several people whom I interviewed for the book, or that I met in the course of researching it, have died: Mildred Blaxter (1925-2010), Dennis Marsden (1933-2009), Robin Matthews (1927-2010), and Peter Townsend (1928-2009). Their passing underlines the value of capturing their voices and experiences for the benefit of future researchers and policy-makers.

John Welshman, Lancaster, April 2012.

References

Bentham, M. (2011) 'Young offenders to get personal therapists to keep them from gangs', *Evening Standard*, 1 November, p 6.

Cohen, P. (2010) '"Culture of poverty" makes a comeback', *New York Times*, 17 October.

Cooke, G. and Lawton, K. (2008) *Working out of poverty: A study of the low-paid and the 'working poor'*, London: Institute for Public Policy Research.

Child Poverty Unit (2009) *Ending child poverty: Making it happen*, London: Child Poverty Unit.

Curtis, P. (2008) 'Schools and agencies to spot 1,000 children at risk of turning to crime', *Guardian*, 19 March, p 6.

Dodds, A. (2009) 'Families "at risk" and the Family Nurse Partnership: The intrusion of risk into social exclusion policy', *Journal of Social Policy*, vol 38, no 3, pp 499-514.

DoH (Department for Health) (2009) *The Family Nurse Partnership Programme*, letter, 3 December.

Driscoll, M. and Woolf, M. (2011) 'Ministers to adopt problem families', *Sunday Times*, 21 August, pp 1-2.

DWP (Department for Work and Pensions) (2008a) *Ending child poverty: 'Thinking 2020': A report and think-pieces from the Child Poverty Unit conference*, Working Paper No 56, London: DWP.

DWP (2008b) *No one written off: Reforming welfare to reward responsibility: Public consultation*, Cm 7363, London: The Stationery Office.

DWP (2008c) *Raising expectations and increasing support: Reforming welfare for the future*, Cm 7506, London: The Stationery Office.

Ford, R. (2009) 'We must step up fight against yobs, says Johnson', *The Times*, 22 June, p 11.

Gentleman, A. (2009), 'How do you solve a problem like 50,000 chaotic families?', *Guardian*, 2 November, pp 12-13.

Gentleman, A. (2010) 'Is Britain broken?' *Guardian*, 31 March.

Hefferman, C. (2007) 'Relative calm', *Society Guardian*, 12 December, p 7.

HM Treasury/DWP/DCSF (2008) *Ending child poverty: Everybody's business*, London: HM Treasury.

Kenway, P. (2008) *Addressing in-work poverty*, York: Joseph Rowntree Foundation.

Montgomerie, T. (2008) 'A new party for the poor', *Guardian*, 8 July, p 29.

Morris, N. (2011) '"Problem family" plan starts to fall apart', *Independent*, 16 December, p 35.

Parr, S. (2011) 'Family policy and the governance of anti-social behaviour in the UK: Women's experiences of intensive family support', *Journal of Social Policy*, vol 40, no 4, pp 717-37.

Riddell, M. (2011) 'London riots: The underclass lashes out', *Daily Telegraph*, 8 August.

Simpson, E. (2012) 'Britain's still not working ...', *The Times*, 1 February, pp 4-5.

Stewart, K. (2009) '"A scar on the soul of Britain": Child poverty and disadvantage under New Labour', in J. Hills, T. Sefton, and K. Stewart (eds) *Towards a more equal society? Poverty, inequality, and policy since 1997*, Bristol: The Policy Press, pp 47-69.

Stratton, A. (2008) 'Don't be afraid to say what's right and wrong – Cameron', *Guardian*, 8 July, p 4.

The Times (2010) 'The irresponsible society', 23 January, p 2.

Webster, P. (2010) 'Not an isolated incident but evidence of broken society, says Cameron', *The Times*, 23 January, p 9.

Williams, R. (2009) 'Child poverty grows as 2 million children have no parent in work', *Guardian*, 3 November, p. 15.

Wintour, P. (2008), 'Timely interventions', *Guardian Society*, 30 April, p 6.

Introduction

From the cycle of deprivation to social exclusion

The 35-year period covered by this book is framed by two speeches. The first was by Sir Keith Joseph (1918-94), then Secretary of State for Social Services, in London on 29 June 1972, and was given to the Pre-School Playgroups Association. In the speech, Joseph referred to a 'cycle of deprivation', and voiced a paradox: 'why is it that, in spite of long periods of full employment and relative prosperity and the improvement in community services since the Second World War, deprivation and problems of maladjustment so conspicuously persist?'.[1] He acknowledged that deprivation was an imprecise term. But Joseph had continued: 'perhaps there is at work here a process, apparent in many situations but imperfectly understood, by which problems reproduce themselves from generation to generation'.[2] He did not want to be misunderstood, and there was not a single process. But it seemed that in a proportion of cases, occurring at all levels of society, the problems of one generation reproduced themselves in the next. Joseph argued that the phenomenon of 'transmitted deprivation' – what he had called the cycle of deprivation – needed to be studied, and had become clearer over the previous 20-30 years with rising living standards. A Department of Health and Social Security (DHSS)–Social Science Research Council (SSRC) Working Party on Transmitted Deprivation was established. The large-scale Research Programme that was organised through the Working Party from 1974 was to span eight years. It cost around £750,000 (at 1970s' values), and by 1982 had generated a substantial body of published and unpublished material.

The second speech was by Prime Minister Tony Blair to the Joseph Rowntree Foundation (JRF) in York on 5 September 2006. In August of that year, Blair had signalled a major push on social exclusion, aiming to show the government's determination to tackle 'a hard core underclass' estimated at one million people (*The Independent*, 24 August 2006, p 18). In the JRF speech, the focus was on the bottom 2% in society. Four issues identified as challenges were: halving teenage pregnancies by 2010; supporting children in care; tackling chaotic parenting through the National Parenting Academy, the extension of parenting orders, and a network of family support schemes; and helping benefit claimants with mental health problems (*The Guardian*, 30 August 2006, p 8). In an interview with the BBC, on 31 August 2006, Blair defined those he was talking about variously as people with multiple problems, families where identification and intervention came too late, and hard-to-reach or dysfunctional families. The problems that these families faced were not simply about low income. But the key point was that there was now a belief that it was possible to predict, with reasonable accuracy, those families that were going to be difficult for the future. Action might even be taken pre-birth if necessary as families with alcohol and drug problems were being identified too late. Blair reiterated that more general forms of intervention, such as the Sure Start initiative for pre-school children, had not proved to be a rising tide that would lift all boats, and it was not just a problem of poverty (*The Guardian*, 1 September 2006, p 5).

In the JRF speech itself, Blair's thesis was that 'some aspects of social exclusion are deeply intractable. The most socially excluded are very hard to reach. Their problems are multiple, entrenched and often passed down the generations'.[3] Previously the debate had been divided into two camps – those who argued that the answer was to improve the material poverty of such families, and those who said that the families themselves were the problem – but while for some families material poverty was the root of their problems, for others it was the result of a multiplicity of lifestyle issues. The success of measures to tackle child poverty, reduce unemployment, and improve public services meant that the persistent exclusion of a small minority stood out. Moreover children and families likely to go wrong could be predicted. Overall, where children were involved and in danger of harm, or where people were a risk to themselves or others, it was a duty not to stand aside: 'their fate is our business'.[4] Blair suggested that the debate was about coupling rights with responsibilities, and with acknowledging that both individual agency and structural causes were relevant. Overall, the focus of government policies on social exclusion had moved to a more interventionist focus on those deemed hard to reach in earlier programmes, or what was perceived as a hard core underclass.

This book

Joseph's theme had been that of a hypothesis of a 'cycle of deprivation', while Blair's was that of a new government stance on social exclusion. But despite the passage of 34 years, the fact that one speech was given by a Conservative minister, the other by a Labour prime minister, and inevitable differences in language, the content was remarkably similar. In all of the recent debate, the rhetoric of a cycle of deprivation, and of intergenerational continuities, has been ever-present. However, politicians and journalists appear unaware of the historical resonances of terms such as 'problem families' and 'cycle of deprivation' (*Financial Times*, 11 January 2006, p 2). More significantly, with some important exceptions, academics working in social policy, contemporary history, sociology, and political science have largely neglected the cycle speech and Research Programme. It is true that the language of a cycle of deprivation and intergenerational continuities are recognised as being part of the historical legacy of what we might term the vocabulary of poverty (Gordon and Spicker, 1999, pp 35, 84; Spicker, 2007, p 112). Nevertheless, the notions of a cycle of deprivation or transmitted deprivation are more often dismissed as part of an individual or behavioural strand in the discourse of poverty, interesting in its own way, but of limited usefulness or relevance. Despite their obvious relevance to recent policy initiatives, the many research studies that were published gather dust on library shelves. Thus the impact of Joseph's cycle speech, the direction taken by the subsequent Research Programme, and how New Labour got to this point, are the subject of this book. Its broader themes are those of the relationship between ideology, social science, and public policy, as they relate to the specific themes of debates about policy, poverty, and parenting.

In poverty research, the history of the debate over transmitted deprivation is usually passed over fairly briefly, being located in terms of the deserving and undeserving poor. While recent work has explored parenthood, child poverty, and social exclusion, it has rarely mentioned the 1970s' research, locating its historical roots in terms of Rowntree's 'cycle of poverty' (Utting, 1995, p 33; Ridge, 2002; Adelman et al, 2003; Platt, 2005). This demonstrates how writing on poverty has been concerned with an essentially materialist approach (Gazeley, 2003; Lister, 2004). Recent work on poverty dynamics has acknowledged earlier interest in intergenerational continuities, but again has tended to point to the methodological shortcomings of these studies (Leisering and Walker, 1998b, pp 14–15; Leisering and Leibfried, 1999, p 18). Indeed some of this research has used the studies commissioned as part of the Research Programme to argue that researchers failed to produce evidence that would substantiate the original cycle of deprivation hypothesis (Gordon and Pantazis, 1997, pp 35–6; Gordon and Spicker, 1999, pp 35, 84). A. H. Halsey, for instance, has noted of debates about cycles of disadvantage that 'Sir Keith Joseph had put forward a subcultural version of genetic inheritance theory, but the environmentalists' emphasis on social conditions proved more convincing' (Halsey, 2004, p 98). The studies commissioned as part of the Research Programme have thus themselves been used by those on the Left to discredit the concept of the cycle of deprivation, and by extension the notion of an underclass.

It is this neglected aspect of the history of social science, and of the relationship between government and the research community, that this book sets out to explore. Rodney Lowe has suggested that the task of historians is to work out the balance between the combination of circumstances and individual personality and ideas that together drive social policy (Seldon and Lowe, 1996, pp 166, 176). Its approach is that of the social historian, using archival materials, published documents, and oral interviews to reconstruct the history of the original cycle speech and subsequent Research Programme. The book is organised into three parts, and has three main aims. First, to explain what led Sir Keith Joseph to announce his hypothesis of a cycle of deprivation in June 1972, looking at his own personal background, his earlier interest in problem families, and the particular policy context of the early 1970s. Second, to trace the direction taken by the Research Programme, including relationships between researchers with different disciplinary backgrounds, the stance taken by DHSS civil servants, and the outlook of social scientists in general. Third, to explore the links between the Research Programme of the 1970s and more recent New Labour policy initiatives around child poverty, antisocial behaviour, and social exclusion. The main focus of the book is thus on Britain, although it occasionally looks in detail at the experience of the US, for example at the similarities and differences between the Head Start and Sure Start initiatives on child poverty. In all of this, the aim is to offer a historical perspective on current policy debates, and more specifically to understand why New Labour has returned to the themes of the Research Programme.

Evaluations of the Research Programme

Having noted the neglect of this episode in recent intellectual history, the potential value of such a study has nonetheless been underlined by work from several different perspectives. The cycle of deprivation hypothesis, and the research that was commissioned through the Research Programme, have been explored in passing by earlier writers, concerned in different ways with evaluating the achievements of the Research Programme; the career of Sir Keith Joseph himself; the history of the concept of the underclass; the apparent neglect of agency and behaviour by social policy analysts in the postwar period; and the way that New Labour has returned to these themes. In the final report on the Research Programme, Muriel Brown and Nicola Madge offered some insights into its origins and development (Brown and Madge, 1982a). Nevertheless, as one reviewer noted at the time, their book was essentially a synthesis of the different projects, rather than a study of the Research Programme itself (Edwards, J., 'Running in families?', *Times Higher Education Supplement*, 26 November 1982, p 16).

In the immediate aftermath of the Research Programme, there were few attempts to evaluate its effectiveness. But Richard Berthoud suggested that the hypothesis of transmitted deprivation was a 'sort of burp from a debate about poverty and pathology that had been rumbling on for decades, if not centuries', and the question it implied was fundamental to an understanding of the relationship between individuals and institutions in the social structure (Berthoud, 1983a, p 151). The Programme was an important test of the ability of social scientists to make a contribution to a real debate, and of the newly formed SSRC to bring the social sciences to bear on a question brought to it by outsiders. Berthoud argued that the membership of the Joint Working Party indicated differences in approach to transmitted deprivation. Whereas the SSRC saw it as taking in all the social sciences, the DHSS assumed that it was a problem to do with individuals, and hence the responsibility of the personal social services. Joseph's speech outlined a hypothesis, but in the Research Programme the relationship between poverty and deprivation remained unclear. Berthoud argued that by failing to define deprivation, the Joint Working Party allowed researchers working on the Programme to interpret it as they wished, but also permitted a strong assumption that poverty and personal inadequacy were one and the same (Berthoud, 1983a, p 156). Moreover, the SSRC had little experience of commissioning research, the demand from researchers for funding was weak, the nature of the Programme was unclear, and there was a strong suspicion that the Programme was politically motivated.

Berthoud argued that only one project, by Frank Coffield and colleagues based at the University of Keele, identified the issues fundamental to the deprivation debate and confronted them head on. The other projects 'to a greater or lesser degree ignored, avoided, or skirted around the central question of the Programme' (Berthoud, 1983a, p 160). Yet Coffield's methodology was not appropriate, and his study was more useful in advancing the question than in providing an answer. The two other studies that Berthoud looked at in detail focused on either income poverty (a project by Tony Atkinson, Alan Maynard, and Chris Trinder [1983]), or difficulties of childcare (a project by David Quinton and Michael Rutter [1988]). Berthoud argued that while the first team studied economic questions exclusively, collecting no data on the personal attributes of their sample, the second studied psychiatric questions exclusively, and collected no data on economic position. Berthoud questioned whether the SSRC had launched the Programme and commissioned the research in the most effective way, arguing that the technique 'of declaring the field open and allowing each researcher to plough his own furrow' had not proved satisfactory (Berthoud, 1983a, p 163).

Berthoud argued that because of the way in which the Research Programme had been set up, Brown and Madge as authors of the final report would have to 'make bricks with very little straw' (Berthoud, 1983a, p 164). He argued that they did not take up the opportunity to offer an independent viewpoint, and there was no hint that any of the studies were in any way disappointing. They accepted the failure of the Programme to define deprivation, and used 'deprivation' and 'disadvantage' interchangeably. Berthoud argued that Brown and Madge were similarly cautious on the question of the causes of deprivation, and that their use of the term 'invulnerables' was unfortunate. He wrote that 'if social forces merely alter probabilities, those who "escape" are simply those whose number did not come up, but the term "invulnerable" suggests that they may have had some special armour which protected them from an otherwise inescapable destiny' (Berthoud, 1983a, p 166). The section of the report on policy and practice was too diffuse to be useful, and the final report as a whole said little about intergenerational continuities. Berthoud therefore noted of Joseph's reported scorn for social sciences in general, and sociology in particular, that 'such a blanket condemnation suggests little power of discrimination, but if the contribution to the debate on deprivation made by his most direct critics from the social sciences contributed to his view, one can have some sympathy for it' (Berthoud, 1983a, p 155).

A conceptual stepping stone

Apart from evaluations of the Research Programme, writing on the history of the underclass has sought both to demonstrate that the cycle speech had important continuities with earlier and later underclass discourses, but also to use the evidence from the Research Programme to demolish the validity of the concept as an empirical reality. In particular, John Macnicol's (1987) analysis of the history of the concept of the underclass opened with an account of the cycle speech and Research Programme of the 1970s. He argued that the cycle speech could be seen as a specific product of the rediscovery of poverty, consisting of a combination of reformist social engineering and a conservative 'social pathology' perspective that emphasised cultural deprivation. At one level, Joseph's initiative was part of a broader governmental attempt to push the balance in favour of the social pathology interpretation. Macnicol again noted that the research studies commissioned by the Joint Working Party had produced 'highly sceptical' verdicts on the original concept (Macnicol, 1987, p 294). Focusing in particular on the research by the Coffield team, Macnicol argued that they were unable to unlock the riddle of which behavioural characteristics were pathological, and which were functional or adaptive. The behaviour of the families, for instance, in their approach to time, appeared to disprove the culture of poverty thesis, which had alleged that people focused on the present and gave little thought to the future.

Macnicol wrote more generally that 'in all this painstaking and expensive research, surprisingly little cognisance was taken of the history of the concept' (Macnicol, 1987, p 295). Joseph was unwittingly articulating a perspective that had had a long history. Macnicol argued that:

> The concept of an inter-generational underclass displaying a high concentration of social problems – remaining outwith the boundaries of citizenship, alienated from cultural norms and stubbornly impervious to the normal incentives of the market, social work intervention or state welfare – has been reconstructed periodically over at least the past one hundred years, and while there have been important shifts of emphasis between each of these reconstructions, there have also been striking continuities. Underclass stereotypes have always been a part of the discourse on poverty in advanced industrial societies. (Macnicol, 1987, p 296)

Macnicol wrote that many proponents of the underclass had seen it as '*distinct* from the working class – in effect, a rootless mass divorced from the means of production – definable only in terms of social inefficiency, and hence not strictly a class in a neo-Marxist sense' (Macnicol, 1987, p 299 [emphasis in original]). He outlined three problems of defining the underclass. First that a popular version of the concept had been internalised by ordinary working-class people as the converse of 'respectable'. Second was the difficulty of separating the underclass concept from wider assumptions about the inheritance of intelligence and ability that were common before Intelligence Quotient (IQ) testing was discredited. Third was the fact that the idea of an 'underclass' had also been used by those on the Left to describe the casualties of capitalism, and those suffering acute economic disadvantage (Macnicol, 1987, p 300).

Macnicol linked this earlier history to the underclass debates in the US in the early 1980s, arguing that proponents of the underclass concept seemed only 'half aware of its conceptual flaws and completely ignorant of its long and undistinguished pedigree' (Macnicol, 1987, p 315). He identified five elements in its periodic reconstructions. First, it was an artificial 'administrative' definition relating to contacts with organisations and individuals of the state, such as social workers. In this respect, it was a statistical artefact in that its size was affected by such factors as eligibility, take-up of benefits, and economic factors such as changing levels of unemployment. Second, in order to gain scientific legitimacy, such a definition had to be conflated with the separate issue of intergenerational transmission, typically of alleged social inefficiency. Third, certain behavioural traits were identified as antisocial while others were ignored – a wide variety of human conditions were lumped together and attributed to a single cause. Fourth, the underclass issue was mainly a resource allocation problem. Fifth, Macnicol claimed that it was supported by people who wished to constrain the redistributive potential of state welfare, and was thus part of a conservative analysis of the causes of social problems and their solutions. A final enduring feature of the debate was the frequency with which its proponents had called for more research (Macnicol, 1987, pp 315-16). Sustaining the viability of the concept of the social problem group in the interwar period, for instance, had only been possible by use of a suspect methodology, but it nonetheless had enormous symbolic importance as part of a broader reformist strategy within conservative social thought.

Inspired in part by Macnicol, other writers hostile to the concept of an underclass in the 1990s in Britain drew on the cycle speech and Research Programme. Hartley Dean and Peter Taylor-Gooby, for example, argued that Keith Joseph had proposed a 'variant of the culture of poverty thesis', but that the research commissioned by the Working Party demonstrated nothing of the sort. An intergenerational cycle was frequently broken by individuals and families, there was no single simple explanation of deprivation, and transmission was influenced by many critical chains of events (Dean and Taylor-Gooby, 1992, pp 35-6). Paul Bagguley and Kirk Mann argued that the Research Programme had 'found the idea severely lacking in empirical evidence' (Bagguley and Mann, 1992, pp 121-2). Finally, Alan Walker also noted that Britain's variant on the culture of poverty thesis was the cycle hypothesis. He wrote that Charles Murray's assertion of the emergence of an underclass

–

in Britain in the 1980s was a blend of both cultural and cycle of deprivation elements. Walker again drew on the earlier research to refute Murray's explanation of the underclass, arguing that this approach to poverty had been 'demolished by the overwhelming weight of scientific evidence against it' (Walker, 1996, p 68). Nevertheless, this work has only looked at the cycle speech and Research Programme in broad outline (Welshman, 2002, 2006a).

A cycle of enrichment

Increasing interest in Joseph himself has meant that some limited attention has been directed to the cycle hypothesis; Joseph's speech can be seen to have had both longer-term antecedents and more immediate policy origins. In their biography of Joseph, Andrew Denham and Mark Garnett (2001a) locate the origins of the cycle speech in terms of Joseph's own personal background and family life. They note his happy childhood; his genuine concern with poverty, especially for those with disabilities; his traditional views on the respective roles of parents; and his sense of guilt over his privileged background. They locate the cycle speech within the broader context of Joseph's earlier concern with young people and low-income families, along with wider debates about family planning. They have written that Joseph's reputation for honesty and compassion was reinforced during the 1970-74 period, and in their view perhaps the best illustration was the reception of the cycle speech. While it later drew criticism from academics, the thesis 'proved that Joseph would not remain content with the sticking-plaster solutions which were all that his current Department could offer; his vision penetrated to the roots of social disadvantage, and unlike most politicians he seemed to feel the "undeserved" misfortunes of others like a wound' (Denham and Garnett, 2001a, p 100).

More generally, Denham and Garnett have suggested that Joseph was unusual in the depth of his commitment to poverty and that 'his self-imposed mission to improve the life-chances of children born into poverty inspired a tireless search for solutions to social problems' (Denham and Garnett, 2002, p 194). However, they also note that unless his enthusiasm was tempered by more cautious counsellors, he tended to underestimate the difficulty of effecting beneficial change, and 'to embrace remedies which reduced complex issues to a few simple propositions' (Denham and Garnett, 2002, p 194). Denham and Garnett have acknowledged Joseph's earlier concern with problem families, in the mid-1960s, and they suggest that it was local visits to deprived areas that confirmed his belief in both the existence of a hard core of families, and the persistence of intergenerational continuities. Denham and Garnett argue that Joseph was torn between a desire to reach firm conclusions, and a need to think things through before stating his position. Thus the cycle speech was 'not so much a call for an open debate as an invitation to researchers to find empirical support for ideas which he held already' (Denham and Garnett, 2001a, p 224). They interestingly contrast the cycle speech with the better-known speech made in Edgbaston, Birmingham, in October 1974. This was more apocalyptic in tone and statistically flawed, but was given in the context of a leadership campaign, and consequently received much greater attention. It effectively ended Joseph's chances of ever leading the Conservative Party.

A final coda to this story is provided by Joseph's attack, as Secretary of State for Education and Science in the early 1980s, on the SSRC. It is often suggested that it was Joseph's experience with the Research Programme that fuelled his contempt for social science and for the SSRC, so much so that as a minister he tried to abolish the Council (Berthoud, 1983a, p 160; Timmins, 1995, 2001 edn; Donovan, 2001, pp 179-93; Denham and Garnett, 2002, p 197). The Council had remodelled its committee structure, so that it was based on 'problems', rather than disciplines (Weir, 1981, p 365). However, shortly afterwards, in December 1981, Joseph asked Lord Rothschild to carry out an urgent review of the SSRC's work; this coincided with a £1.1 million (4%) cut in the Council's budget for 1982-83, a cut originally intended by Joseph to be £2 million. This story has been told elsewhere, and need not be repeated here. But the letters that Joseph exchanged with Geoffrey Howe, then Chancellor of the Exchequer, make it clear that he planned to abolish the SSRC. He wrote that Rothschild's brief was to identify what work might be done at the customer's expense; what work could be done by other bodies; 'and whether, if these changes in responsibility were made, there would be continuing justification for the Council's existence' (Weir, 1982, p 11; Flather, 1987; Halsey, 2004, pp 137-41). The letters were leaked to the journal *New Society*, and its writer claimed that Joseph had been 'deeply offended' by the reaction of sociologists and others to the theory of transmitted deprivation, feeling that the SSRC had not taken his idea seriously enough.

Robin Matthews, a former Chair of the SSRC and then Master of Clare College, Cambridge, wrote subsequently that Joseph's suspicions were not that the SSRC was doing its job badly, but were more general in nature. Joseph doubted whether 'research' in the social sciences could reveal anything not apparent to common sense. In the terms of reference given to Rothschild he emphasised the customer–contractor principle as an expression of market philosophy as applied to research, and he suspected that social science academics were predisposed to a particular point of view (Matthews, 1982, p 2). In the event, the SSRC survived the review, since the Rothschild report was overwhelmingly in favour of the Council. Interestingly, Rothschild noted that:

> The need for independence from government departments is particularly important because so much social science research is the stuff of political debate. All such research might prove subversive of government policies because it attempts to submit such policies to empirical trial, with the risk that the judgement may be adverse. It would be too much to expect Ministers to show enthusiasm for research designed to show that their policies were misconceived. But it seems obvious that in many cases the public interest will be served by such research being undertaken. (*An enquiry into the Social Science Research Council by Lord Rothschild*, 1982, p 12, para 3.12)

Rothschild might have had the Research Programme in mind. Nevertheless, while it survived, the SSRC was forced to drop 'science' from its title, being renamed the Economic and Social Research Council (ESRC) and being banished from London to Swindon.

The revival of agency

The need for a study of this kind has been underlined by new thinking in social policy in Britain, which has sought to look more closely at the relationship between agency, structure, and poverty. In the 1970s, commentators such as Peter Townsend stressed the importance of wider structural factors, and were unwilling to admit that either cultural factors or individual agency might have a role to play in determining the response of people faced with unemployment and poverty. Increasingly, however, social policy analysts are coming to concede that the structural focus of social policy in the postwar years – typified by arguably its most influential figure, Richard Titmuss – was in fact a source of serious weakness that subsequently left it ill-equipped to deal with assaults by the Right in the 1980s. It has been argued that research in the social administration tradition has been limited to distributional issues, and has neglected the study of social relations. The effect of this writing has been to refocus attention on the relative importance of behavioural and structural factors in causing poverty and deprivation. In some cases, it has drawn directly on the experience of the Research Programme.

Michael Titterton, for example, argued that the dominant paradigms in the study of social welfare had ignored the role of agency. In the early 1990s, Titterton was a consultant to the ESRC's Human Behaviour and Development Group. He claimed that these paradigms were characterised by a preoccupation with pathological views of health and welfare, and by inadequate conceptualisations of the 'mediating structures' between the individual and wider social forces. The concept of 'coping', for example, showed that there were variations in vulnerability and coping styles, and these were differentiated by gender, age, and social class. Titterton argued that a new paradigm should try to understand people's 'differential vulnerability'; it should examine the different coping strategies that they use; and it should include the people who survive. He called for a new paradigm of welfare, where the focus was on the differential nature of vulnerability and risk among individuals, and their different reactions to threats to welfare. This work should 'generate respect for informal modes of coping and helpseeking, and should create a new sensitivity towards the creative and diverse ways in which people respond to their own problems and the ways in which they help other people to respond' (Titterton, 1992, p 19).

Titterton drew on some of the studies that had been included in the Research Programme, noting that both a literature review by Michael Rutter and Nicola Madge (1976), and the final report by Muriel Brown and Nicola Madge (1982a), had argued that the 'invulnerables' should be studied – those who had somehow overcome the adversity and stress encountered in their life-course. Brown and Madge, for instance, had related the story of three dolls, one made of glass, one of plastic, and one of steel. When each was hit by a hammer, the first broke, the second was scarred, but the third gave off a 'fine metallic sound'. Titterton argued that it was that sound that everyone was trying to investigate. The constitutive nature of the individual coping successfully with an adverse social environment in the course of their lifespan was still 'very much a mystery for social science' (Titterton, 1992, p 3). The factors that accompanied resilience needed to be studied. He argued that there were two reasons why researchers had not responded to Brown and Madge. First, there was an overwhelming preoccupation with a pathological view of health and welfare, and with the problems of 'maladjustment' in society. Second, the conceptual approaches of social scientists, as well as their vocabulary, had become hidebound and limiting. The search for social pathology had led to a neglect of the mediating structures between individuals and wider social forces.

———

Moreover, the fashionable rejection of individual pathologies had left a gap that researchers were struggling to fill. Thus one of Titterton's conclusions was that the 'invulnerables', or those who coped well in adverse circumstances, and the resilience or protective factors that helped to shield individuals in stressful conditions, were fruitful areas for social scientific investigation (Titterton, 1992, p 17).

The revival of interest in human agency in sociological and social policy debates, was also considered by Alan Deacon and Kirk Mann (1999). They noted contradictions in the apparent similarity of developments in social policy and sociology. Agency had been neglected by participants in debates about social policy, empiricism, Fabianism, and Marxism – the poor were rarely active agents of change. Moreover, questions about agency had been not just neglected in the postwar period, but had been consciously dismissed, as a reaction to the individualism of the Charity Organisation Society on the one hand, and the weaknesses of social casework on the other. In particular, the denial of agency was due to the influence of Titmuss, so that 'arguments about problem families or cycles of deprivation were an irrelevance or worse' (Deacon and Mann, 1999, p 418; Welshman, 2004). More recent debates about welfare were more about behaviour than structure, more to do with dependency than poverty. Deacon and Mann characterised these new perspectives as welfare as a channel for the pursuit of self-interest; welfare as the exercise of authority; and welfare as a mechanism for moral regeneration. Overall, they concluded that the revival of agency had created opportunities for a social science that was more sensitive to the activities of poor people, and more representative of the diversity of British society (Deacon and Mann, 1999, p 435).

Research on the 'Americanisation' of welfare debates has also related policy changes to moralism. Alan Deacon (2000) illustrated how US dependency theorists – Charles Murray and Lawrence Mead – pushed issues onto the policy agenda that had been neglected and suppressed in Britain. The void that developed in the US around discussions on race following the publication of the Moynihan Report (Moynihan, 1965) seemed similar to that which emerged in Britain on questions of the importance of behaviour in explanations of poverty. Deacon noted that many British academics remained hostile to the idea of an underclass, and to compulsion in welfare-to-work programmes. He concluded that the 'Americanisation' of welfare had enhanced and sustained a morality that was shared by Blair and Thatcher, but distrusted by Old Labour and One Nation Conservatism (Deacon, 2000). Deacon argued that it was a quasi-Titmuss paradigm or school that dominated social policy from the 1960s. Because it was increasingly preoccupied with the growth of material inequalities and paid less attention to altruism and the quality of social relationships, it also paid less attention to how people's behaviours and activities represented some form of meaningful choice. If Titmuss fiercely rejected any attempt to explain poverty in terms of the failings or weaknesses of the poor themselves, in the quasi-Titmuss paradigm this rejection of individualist or behavioural accounts of poverty hardened and broadened into a more determinist approach that precluded any discussion of such factors (Deacon, 2002a, p 14). Deacon argued that in both the US and Britain, the reluctance and even refusal of the dominant perspectives to debate or even to discuss issues of behaviour or choice created a vacuum that was later filled by conservative ideas about welfare dependency and an underclass.

Deacon (2002a) identified four factors that shaped the quasi-Titmuss paradigm. First was the growing influence on the welfare debate of Marxist political economy, which focused on collective rather than individual action, and paid far more attention to the development of theory. Second, the influence of Anthony Crosland, who did not share Titmuss's moralism, and who believed that people were more self-interested and less inclined to altruism than Titmuss supposed; Crosland made a technical rather than a moral case for equality. Third, the upsurge in unemployment from the mid-1970s, which seemed to exemplify the futility of trying to solve social problems by changing people. Fourth, the growth in inequality in Britain in the late 1970s and 1980s, and the concomitant rise in relative poverty. This reinforced the hostility of the quasi-Titmuss paradigm to attempts to locate the causes of poverty in the behaviour and attitudes of the poor themselves (Deacon, 2002a, pp 23-5). Deacon argued that this hostility was exemplified in the debate about transmitted deprivation. The original challenge to see how discontinuities in cycles of disadvantage could be brought about was not taken up, and the whole scope of the Programme was altered. Explanations of poverty, child health, and even abuse emphasised the uneven distribution of income and wealth, the unequal structure of employment, and the class-related pattern of life chances (Deacon, 2002a, p 26).

Deacon has commented since that explorations of agency are now at the heart of debates about welfare reform. The main question has been how people are able to act independently, and how far their behaviour is constrained by social structures. But this concern with agency has been delayed and belated because it was associated with a moral and judgemental approach to welfare. Thus Deacon suggests that while scholars seek to develop new ways of understanding agency and structure in relation to poverty, debates about welfare continue to be 'preoccupied by the spectre of dependency and the attribution of blame' (Deacon, 2004, pp 447-55). This further underlines how a historical study of the cycle speech and Research Programme is a prerequisite for understanding contemporary debates about child poverty and social exclusion.

New Labour and the cycle of disadvantage

A final factor in drawing attention to the cycle speech and Research Programme has been the way in which the New Labour government, since 1997, has returned to the themes of behaviour, parenting, and the experiences of pre-school children. In 1999, Charles Leadbeater had suggested that Keith Joseph should be regarded as one of New Labour's intellectual godfathers, in part because he attacked the dependency culture associated with long-term welfare benefits, which in his view had helped to create a cycle of deprivation in poor families (Leadbeater, 1999, p 13). Andrew Denham and Mark Garnett agreed, and concluded that the similarity between Joseph's ideas and New Labour was more than a coincidence. Tony Blair had left intact much of the policy framework created under Margaret Thatcher and John Major, and Joseph left an important mark upon that framework. Moreover, in its greatest departures from Thatcherism – its communitarian rhetoric and its declaration of war against child poverty – New Labour was merely echoing the Joseph of the early 1970s (Denham and Garnett, 2001b, p 105). The origins of the cycle speech and the direction of the Research Programme are of interest, as they anticipate so much of the current debate around policy, poverty, and parenting. Pete Alcock, for example, wrote in 2002 that if the cycle of deprivation was a kite that failed 'thirty years later, however, it seems that the kite may have been taken out of the cupboard and dusted off for new trials; and some of the questions raised by Sir Keith in 1972 are now, once again, at the centre of the debate about the causes of poverty and social exclusion, and the strategies by which they can be reduced' (Alcock, 2002, p 177).

There has been interest in the links between New Labour's focus on cycles of disadvantage, the cycle hypothesis, and the Research Programme. It has been claimed that New Labour's policy on child poverty provided a good example of the 'third way' on welfare. Thus the ending of child poverty was often presented less as an objective in itself, and more as a means of reducing inequalities in opportunity. In November 1997, for example, a conference entitled 'New Cycles of Disadvantage' was organised by the Centre for Analysis of Social Exclusion (CASE) on behalf of the ESRC. The aim was to broaden

Treasury links with sociologists and social policy specialists (Lee and Hills, 1998). Alan Deacon suggested from these and other sources that 'New Labour has come to occupy similar ground to Sir Keith, albeit by a somewhat different route' (Deacon, 2002b, p 180).

He identified three broad themes that were common to Joseph and New Labour. First was a belief in the importance of the family as a forum within which children developed moral sentiments and learnt moral practices. Second was the unique importance of what society did to and for children in the first five years. It had been suggested that it was the growing acceptance among policy makers of the proposition that childhood deprivation had longer-term consequences that was probably crucial in assembling the political will to tackle child poverty. Third was the preoccupation with the ways in which disadvantage passed from one generation to another. Nevertheless, Deacon noted that where New Labour suggested that individual behaviour and attitudes had played some part in the perpetuation of poverty across generations, it had been careful to present those behaviours and attitudes as responses or adaptations to adverse circumstances (Deacon, 2002b, p 181). At the same time, there was an important element of conditionality in initiatives such as Sure Start. Overall, Deacon argued that New Labour echoed some of Joseph's arguments alongside other, more divergent ideas, and had broken with the excessive structuralism and determinism that had characterised Centre/Left thinking on welfare for much of the postwar period. Noting that Nicholas Timmins had written that Blair, Brown, and Joseph could sit down and have a sensible conversation, Deacon added that the cycle of deprivation 'would be a major topic in any such conversation' (Deacon, 2002b, p 183).

Other work drew attention to continuities between New Labour's emphasis on cycles of disadvantage and the Research Programme of the 1970s. Deacon argued that New Labour's commitment to the elimination of child poverty reflected in part a growing recognition of the extent to which the opportunities open to people during their lifetime were diminished by the experience of poverty in childhood. He claimed that New Labour's interpretation of the evidence of intergenerational continuities in child poverty drew on and integrated five competing explanations of why such continuities existed. Nevertheless, Deacon suggested that what was new was not the evidence and analyses of the cycle of disadvantage presented to New Labour, but its receptivity to such arguments (Deacon, 2003). He outlined five different explanations of the perpetuation of poverty across generations, and illustrated these by reference to US scholars and commentators. He outlined these as a cultural explanation (Oscar

Lewis); a rational explanation (Charles Murray); a permissive explanation (Lawrence Mead); an adaptive explanation (William Julius Wilson); and a structural explanation (William Ryan). Deacon concluded that New Labour's interpretation of the cycle of disadvantage did recognise the significance of structural factors, but that its rhetoric was closer to the adaptive account, suggesting that behaviours and attitudes had played some part in the perpetuation of poverty, but that they were responses or adaptations to adverse circumstances. However, New Labour's insistence that the creation of new opportunities would not be sufficient on its own reflected the influence of the rational, permissive, and cultural explanations of the cycle of disadvantage. New Labour had an interpretation of the causes of social exclusion that was both structural and behavioural; in Deacon's words, it sought both to 'level the playing field' and to 'activate the players' (Deacon, 2003).

Moreover he suggested that the interplay between the 'situational' and the 'cultural' had been a prime issue in the Research Programme of the 1970s. First, the focus of the Programme had shifted, from a focus on a minority of multiply deprived families, to more general disadvantaging circumstances. Second, even those studies that retained the focus on families provided at best mixed support for the cycle thesis. Third, none of the studies was able to explain why some households and families were able to break the cycle while others were not. Deacon suggested that the majority of academics saw Joseph's research agenda as 'at best a red herring and at worst a distraction from the much more important issue of the generation and persistence of inequalities' (Deacon, 2003, p 132). The final report, by Brown and Madge (1982a), admitted that few of the researchers had responded to the challenge of determining why children disadvantaged in one respect were often not disadvantaged in another.

Methods and sources

The Research Programme is thus viewed increasingly as a useful case study in the way social problems are framed, and of the relationship between politics, ideologies of welfare, and the responsiveness of individuals and organisations to research evidence (Becker and Bryman, 2004, pp 30–3). Deacon has been arguably the main commentator on the links between Joseph and New Labour. Nevertheless, while his approach has been extremely illuminating, it has been based for the most part on published studies, notably the literature review by Rutter and Madge (1976), and the final report by Brown and Madge (1982a). It has not moved beyond these to archival sources and oral interviews, which make it possible to reconstruct the intellectual history of the cycle speech and Research Programme. Moreover, New Labour's subsequent approach to antisocial behaviour and social exclusion, especially from 2006, means that the continuities with Joseph's cycle of deprivation are arguably much greater than in the debates about child poverty.

The cycle speech and Research Programme are coming to be seen as relevant to New Labour's approach to social exclusion, child poverty, and antisocial behaviour. However, while the research has been cited as illustrating the alleged neglect of agency by social scientists in the 1970s, and their corresponding focus on structural factors, neither it nor the cycle hypothesis has attracted systematic analysis. Neither is mentioned in Joseph's entry in the *Oxford Dictionary of National Biography* (ODNB), partly because they have been overshadowed by the Edgbaston speech. Very limited use has been made of internal departmental files, and of oral interviews with civil servants and researchers. In the long run, the cycle of deprivation matters because it has been taken up by New Labour theorists, but in the 1970s it was perceived as a policy failure, interesting in its way, but apparently of limited significance.

Even so, the potential value of a historical approach was recognised by some perceptive commentators at the time, and has been confirmed by more recent developments. Perhaps most interestingly, a reviewer of two of the original studies noted that:

> The programme of research into transmitted deprivation … would make a fascinating research topic in itself … there is certainly a rich mine for the student of the sociology of knowledge.… It is all there: the growth from a superficially simple idea to a voluminous debate, the definition and redefinition of terms (from cycle of deprivation to transmitted deprivation to intergenerational continuities in deprivation), the interplay of ideology and research that produced such changes (the first two definitions imply pathology, the third allows of structural interpretations), the social construction and reconstruction of the social problem, the development and reification of a concept, and so forth. (Edwards, J., 'Running in families?', *Times Higher Education Supplement*, 26 November 1982, p 16)

Organisations and individuals associated with the Research Programme have been more inclined than previously to explore the significance of their involvement. Mildred Blaxter, for example, has provided some personal reflections on her involvement in the Research Programme, locating it in terms of the development of qualitative methods (Blaxter, 2004, pp 55-6). Moreover, the ESRC itself has claimed that the Research Programme was 'landmark research', while conceding that there was a 20-year gap before it was again perceived as relevant, being taken up by New Labour, the Treasury, and reflected in initiatives such as Sure Start (ESRC, 2005, p 17).

The approach taken in this book is that of the social historian, drawing upon and widening a preliminary analysis of the cycle speech and the Research Programme, which itself yielded new insights into the origins of the cycle speech, the stance of civil servants in the DHSS, and the outlook of social scientists (Welshman, 2005). The most obvious products of the Research Programme are the 17 books published in the Heinemann series (1976-90). Although the volume of material is difficult to establish at this point in time, these have been interrogated through archival and unpublished sources. By 1982, the Research Programme had generated 19 studies, four feasibility projects, and 14 review papers, and Brown and Madge list some 37 individual contributors to it (Brown and Madge, 1982a, pp 27, 355-60). An SSRC listing from the ESRC archive at Swindon (the RB series) indicates 35 major projects in 12 subject areas, and includes some 33 original files, 54 research contracts, 18 consultancies, and details of five seminars.[5] Most of the SSRC material has been transferred into 23 DHSS files at the National Archives (NA) at Kew, London, although some documents remain at Swindon. The Kew files thus contain the minutes of the Joint Working Party, correspondence between ministers and civil servants, referee reports on grant applications, and other unpublished reports.

While some of the main actors in the story are now dead (among them Urie Bronfenbrenner, Joan Cooper, Keith Joseph himself, Israel Kolvin, Michael Posner, Alice Sheridan, and Peter Willmott) some 16 interviews were carried out with former civil servants and social scientists, mainly to confirm and supplement the archival materials. Brown and Madge list 24 DHSS and 16 SSRC members of the Joint Working Party in the period 1972-82 (Brown and Madge, 1982a, pp 353-4). Some, although not many, of those contacted refused to be interviewed, some were alive but too ill to be involved, while others felt that they could remember little about either the cycle speech or Research Programme. But of the 16, seven can be characterised as researchers (Richard Berthoud, Tessa Blackstone, Mildred Blaxter, Frank Coffield, Nicola Madge, Adrian Sinfield, and Olive Stevenson); four as SSRC members of the Joint Working Party (Tony Atkinson, Muriel Brown, Alan Clarke, and Michael Rutter); one as a DHSS member

(Geoffrey Otton); three as interested observers of the debate (Raymond Illsley, Peter Townsend, and Robin Wendt); and one as a former Chair (Robin Matthews). In this respect, the methodology underlying the book draws significantly on what has been called 'elite oral history' (Seldon and Pappworth, 1983).

The research has drawn on the Joseph papers in the Conservative Party Archive in the Bodleian Library, Oxford, and the Peter Townsend papers at the University of Essex, while the oral interviews have uncovered further private papers, from Nicola Madge, Muriel Brown, Adrian Sinfield, and Harriett Wilson. Newspapers, particularly *The Times*, have been helpful in tracing the direction taken by the Research Programme, as have been the *SSRC Newsletter* and journals such as *New Society*. The book provides the first systematic analysis of the available archival sources, supplemented by oral interviews with civil servants and social scientists. In so doing, the book fills a major gap in social policy: the history of debates over transmitted deprivation, and their relationship with current initiatives on social exclusion.

Commentators in the US have always been more sensitive to the moral dimension of welfare debates (Deacon, 2003). This is amply borne out in the work of Alice O'Connor, who has suggested that the idea that scientific knowledge holds the key to solving social problems has long been an article of faith in US liberalism, and that this is particularly apparent in the case of the 'poverty problem'. She has argued that poverty knowledge has to be assessed 'as a part of historical trends in ideology, politics, institutions, culture, and political economy' (O'Connor, 2000, p 557; 2001, p 8). Most fundamentally, poverty knowledge:

> reflects a central tension within liberal thought about the nature of inequality – not so much over whether inequality is innate or environmental in origin, but whether it is best understood and addressed at the level of individual experience or as a matter of structural and institutional reform. (O'Connor, 2001, p 9)

She argues that this tension has often been resolved in favour of the individual interpretation. She also outlines what a reconstructed poverty knowledge might look like, drawing on insights from historical analysis to take in the political, ideological, institutional, and cultural (O'Connor, 2001, p 22). O'Connor has set out four dimensions to a reformulation of the poverty problem: to depauperise poverty as a social problem and develop a broader study of political economy rather than a narrow study of the poor; to remove the distorting lens of the culture of poverty and make poverty knowledge a study of broader cultural dynamics; to recognise the limitations of the research industry model much shaped by government funding; and to acknowledge and embrace the inherently political nature of poverty knowledge (O'Connor, 2001, pp 292-4). The links between the cycle speech, the Research Programme, and New Labour's approach to child poverty and social exclusion indicate the potential value of attempting to extend O'Connor's suggestions on assessing poverty knowledge.

Summary: the structure of the book

This book, then, is an intellectual history of the cycle speech and the Transmitted Deprivation Research Programme of the 1970s, exploring their relevance to current policy initiatives on child poverty, antisocial behaviour, and social exclusion. The book is divided into three parts. Part One focuses on Keith Joseph and the cycle speech. The first chapter examines the drafting of the cycle speech within the DHSS, its content and its sources of evidence, and Joseph's continuing interest in the cycle in later years. Chapter Two explores the concept of the cycle in terms of earlier and related ideas. These include Joseph's family background, his genuine concern with poverty, and his interest in problem families; its links with a DHSS Preparation for Parenthood initiative; the broader policy context of the late 1960s and early 1970s, including deprivation, abortion, and family planning; and the influence of debates in the US about the value of early intervention, as in the Head Start programme.

Part Two traces the setting up of the Research Programme, drawing in particular on archival materials, and charts the direction it took. Chapter Three explores the establishment of the Joint Working Party, including its DHSS and SSRC personnel; some of the conceptual difficulties it grappled with; the commissioning of a literature review; and the approach of the Labour government, following its election in March 1974. Chapter Four traces the middle years of the Research Programme, from its formal launch in May 1974 to the publication of the Joint Working Party's Third Report in November 1977, and the commissioning of projects. Chapter Five looks further at the final years of the Research Programme; looks at the stance adopted by DHSS civil servants, who became increasingly sceptical about it; and draws on reviews of the books that were published in the early 1980s, to gauge the reaction to the Research Programme. Chapter Six explores the response of social scientists to the cycle speech and Research Programme, using a collective biography approach to the careers of three of those who were marginal or openly hostile to it: Harriett Wilson, Adrian Sinfield, and Peter Townsend.

Part Three of the book looks more broadly at the cycle speech and Research Programme, and traces continuities over the period since 1972. Chapter Seven explores the influences on New Labour, including the concept of social exclusion, emerging originally from France; the influence of research on poverty dynamics; and the revival of agency. Chapter Eight examines New Labour's focus on a 'cycle of disadvantage' as reflected in the Sure Start initiative for the under-fives, the growing emphasis on antisocial behaviour and problem families; and the new stance on social exclusion as exemplified in Blair's JRF speech in September 2006. The Conclusion draws the earlier themes together. Overall, the argument is that while the cycle speech and Research Programme have been recognised as being relevant to the approach taken by New Labour to child poverty from 1997, these continuities have become even more striking given subsequent efforts to tackle antisocial behaviour and social exclusion.

Notes

[1] Adrian Sinfield papers, 'The cycle of deprivation', 29 June 1972, p 4, para 15. These are currently in the possession of the author. I am extremely grateful to Adrian Sinfield for his generosity in making various papers available to me.

[2] Adrian Sinfield papers, 'The cycle of deprivation', 29 June 1972, p 5, para 17.

[3] www.pm.gov.uk, T. Blair, 'Our nation's future – social exclusion', 5 September 2006 (accessed 6 September 2006).

[4] www.pm.gov.uk, T. Blair, 'Our nation's future – social exclusion', 5 September 2006 (accessed 6 September 2006).

[5] SSRC, 'Transmitted deprivation', in the possession of the author.

Part One
The cycle hypothesis

This part of the book explores the cycle of deprivation speech of June 1972. Chapter One explores its drafting and content; the evidence that Keith Joseph produced in support of it; and the speech in retrospect. Chapter Two traces the longer-term origins of the speech, including the earlier history of the underclass, Joseph's personality and family background, his interest in problem families, its more immediate policy origins, and the influence of experiments with pre-school programmes in the US.

ONE

Sir Keith Joseph and the cycle speech

Introduction

The cycle of deprivation hypothesis is particularly associated with Sir Keith Joseph, and the then Secretary of State for Social Services gave three speeches on this theme in the period June 1972 to June 1973. The first, which was the most interesting and best known, was given on 29 June 1972, at a conference for local authorities organised by the Pre-School Playgroups Association, at Church House, Westminster, London. The second was given in Brighton, on 27 March 1973, at the Spring Study Seminar of the Association of Directors of Social Services. The third, which stressed the links between the cycle and a DHSS initiative called Preparation for Parenthood, was given on 27 June 1973, again at Church House, Westminster, a year after the original cycle speech, at the annual conference of the Pre-School Playgroups Association. As well as these three speeches, Joseph mentioned his theory on numerous other occasions, in radio broadcasts, more minor speeches, and other writings. On 27 September 1972, for instance, he appeared on *Woman's hour*, on BBC Radio 2, where he debated the cycle with Frank Field of the Child Poverty Action Group (CPAG), and Margaret Croucher, a social worker with Family Service Units (FSUs).[1]

The cycle speech has received little attention in general surveys of social policy under the Heath government, and indeed the full text of the speech is not easy to find. Morrison Halcrow, in the first biography of Joseph, noted that the speech went through 11 drafts, and while it failed to hit the headlines, was welcomed by both Left and Right, establishing Joseph as a thoughtful observer of social policy (Halcrow, 1989, pp 51-2). Timothy Raison (1990, p 84) suggests that it illustrates the genuine sense of commitment that characterised the Heath government's social policy, Rodney Lowe (1996, p 210) observing merely that the expansion of nursery and primary schools was designed to break the cycle of deprivation with which Joseph had become increasingly concerned. Nicholas Timmins has written that the cycle speech 'brought forth profoundly different interpretations. To some on the left it looked like an appeal for community action.

To others it appeared to blame the individuals and deny the state's responsibility. To the right it appeared to be a defence of the family. To many it just seemed common sense'. At the time, the speech seemed to 'sum up much of the best of concerned progressivism' (Timmins, 1995, 2001 edn, p 289).

This chapter explores the cycle of deprivation speech, aiming to understand its content and immediate origins. It examines the drafting of the speech within the DHSS; the content of the speech itself; the evidence that Joseph cited in support of it; and the links between the speech and the parallel Preparation for Parenthood initiative. It also traces Joseph's ongoing interest in the cycle in the years after 1972. The argument of the chapter is that the speech was primarily an individual obsession of Joseph's, but that civil servants who had been transferred from the Home Office played a key part in the drafting of it. Moreover, while the speech located the problems of families within the broader context of poverty and disadvantage, the primary focus was on individual behaviour and parenting; Joseph's evidence was mainly drawn from psychiatric and criminological literature. Finally, there is much evidence that Joseph continued to be troubled by the cycle in the years after 1972. Chapter Two explores the longer-term background to and timing of the speech: here the focus is primarily on the content and its immediate origins.

The drafting of the cycle speech

In the election of June 1970, the Conservatives were returned to office and Joseph was appointed Secretary of State for Social Services. The DHSS had been created on 1 November 1968, from the Ministries of Health and Social Security. Its responsibilities included the administration of the National Health Service (NHS) in England, the welfare services run by local authorities, and social security services in England, Scotland, and Wales. These last included schemes for National Insurance, family allowances, and supplementary benefits, which were guided by the Supplementary Benefits Commission, located within the department. The new department was thus a large one, performing the functions of the two former ministries, and organised into numerous divisions. It was housed at the modern Alexander Fleming House, south of the Thames at the Elephant and Castle. Richard Crossman, Joseph's Labour predecessor as Secretary of State for Social Services (1968–70), had pointed out its inconvenience for Westminster and Whitehall, saying that he felt 'exiled' there (Howard, 1990, 1991 edn, p 295).

Civil servants remembered Joseph's arrival at the DHSS. Robin Wendt, for example, his Principal Private Secretary, recalled:

> Joseph certainly came to the department with a reputation for competence and having achieved something. We also knew about his academic background and his role at All Souls College. The one thing that none of us were prepared for was the huge contrast between this apparently high-flying, successful, glamorous Tory minister who came from a very conventional Conservative background … and on the other hand, the extremely modest and occasionally hesitating and diffident and shy, nervous man who sat in his office most of the time, worrying away about some of the social problems he thought he ought to be dealing with … I think he was very torn about wanting to be a minister and wanting to be successful, and on the other hand, feeling a lot of the time, 'What am I doing here? Why is it me? I'm not really cut out for all this.'[2]

Departmental files illustrate that some of the issues concerning the new Secretary of State in his first year were the need for greater expenditure on community services; steps that might eliminate family poverty; and working out how best to reduce child deprivation, with a five-year programme for day nurseries and special help for some groups. Joseph hoped to draw all these into a strategy and bid for resources that were not otherwise available.[3] Other issues included the debate about the 'poverty trap', a term coined by Frank Field, then of the CPAG; the introduction of the means-tested Family Income Supplement (FIS) for low-paid workers; and the Report of the Departmental Committee on the Adoption of Children (Home Office, Scottish Education Department, 1972). In July 1971, John Pater (1911-89), then in charge of the DHSS Local Authorities Social Services Division, noted that the department was committed to producing a paper on areas of social deprivation following a conference the previous November chaired by Professor David Donnison, then Director of the Centre for Environmental Studies.[4]

In his biography of the welfare state, Nicholas Timmins locates the cycle speech and Research Programme within a longer-term perspective. He argues that Joseph was thinking about intergenerational continuities at the same time as he inherited the Children's Department from the Home Office as part of the Seebohm reorganisation of social services (Timmins, 1995, 2001 edn, p 289). In many ways it was a curious period. At one level, the 1969 Children and Young Persons Act was invoking a new era in the treatment of difficult children, dependent on well-qualified and trained Children's Departments. Meanwhile the 1970 Local Authority Social Services Act, which followed the report of the Seebohm Committee (Committee on Local Authority and Allied Personal Social Services, 1968), was abolishing local authority Children's Departments, leading to the establishment of Social Services Departments. Once these reforms had been carried out, the Children's Department itself was transferred from the Home Office to the DHSS, as part of the unifying of local authority Children's and Welfare Departments. Many civil servants were unhappy about the move, leaving the grand Home Office in Whitehall for Alexander Fleming House at the Elephant and Castle.[5]

There is support for the assertion by Timmins. In the early months of 1971, for example, Joseph began to visit approved schools and remand centres, and these experiences confirmed his suspicions that family background was a key factor in deprivation among families and adolescents. He became convinced that 'something in the parental background had virtually doomed these children', and it was not poverty alone; many children survived poverty because the family bonds were strong (Coleman, T., 'Captain of the Second XI', *The Guardian*, 12 November 1973, p 13; Denham and Garnett, 2002, p 196). Joseph's belief in intergenerational continuities was clear. He recalled he was told by one Director of Social Services that:

> we have 20,000 households in this city. Nearly all our problems – delinquency, truancy, deprivation, poverty and the rest – come from about 800 of them. And I think that most of the families have been known to us for five generations. (Cunningham, J., 'The family way', *The Guardian*, 4 June 1973, p 9)

On another occasion, Joseph recalled that he had been told by a social worker that:

> in one particular County Borough there were 800 problem families, and nearly all of them had been known to the social services, the church and other welfare organisations for the previous five generations. (Joseph, K., 'Britain: a decadent new utopia', *The Times*, 21 October 1974, p 1)

—

At the Home Office, the Children's Department had run approved schools, and therefore included the Children's Inspectorate. Joseph's injunction to sort out the family obviously came as a shock to these civil servants who thought of themselves mainly as running approved schools (Timmins, 1995, 2001 edn, p 289). Thus the key people in this enterprise were a handful of senior officials from the former Home Office Children's Inspectorate, notably Joan Cooper (1914-99). Sister of Frank Cooper (1922-2002), himself later a pugnacious Permanent Secretary at the Ministry of Defence, Joan was a former local authority Children's Officer. She was then Chief Inspector at the Children's Department at the Home Office, and subsequently Director of the Social Work Services Division at the DHSS. Geoffrey Otton had also transferred from the Home Office as Head of the Children's Department, subsequently becoming Under Secretary in the DHSS Local Authorities Social Services Division. Educated at Christ's Hospital and St John's College, Cambridge, Otton was a typical civil servant of his generation; as Chair of the Supplementary Benefits Commission, David Donnison was later to find him a talented administrator (Donnison, 1982, p 36). However, Otton later recalled of this point in his career that:

> I discovered almost within a few weeks, that he [Joseph] thought he'd inherited from the Home Office a sort of task force or SAS for improving the family, and he gradually unwrapped for us his own quite passionate convictions about what became known as the cycle of deprivation.[6]

Issues relating to juvenile courts, remand homes, approved schools, and child neglect had been debated by the Ingleby Committee (1960), which had recommended that local authorities should have a duty to prevent child neglect; and that various services concerned with the family should be reorganised (Home Office, 1960, p 154). Subsequently, two White Papers, *The child, the family and the young offender* (Home Office, 1965) and *Children in trouble* (Home Office, 1968), had further explored the potential of preventive work in connection with juvenile delinquency and the family. It has been argued that the White Papers reflected the influence of professional social work thinking, and the growth in power of civil servants at the head of the Children's Department in the Home Office, notably Derek Morrell and Joan Cooper. Anthony Bottoms has argued that they were committed to a 'childcare' view of delinquency, where delinquency was a presenting symptom of a deeper maladjustment; children grew up deviant if they were denied early social work intervention at crisis periods. Along with broader developments in social work, these views were also reflected in the 1969 Children and Young Persons Act, which embodied a move towards voluntary agreements and civil rather than criminal proceedings. In this, the Act reflected a more 'welfare'-oriented juvenile justice system based on classical social work concepts. Again the core of the Act reflected a conjunction of interests and ideology between the Labour Party and those in key positions in social work (Bottoms, 1974, pp 331-3; Clarke, 1980).

Thus the Home Office at least had a long history of involvement in debates relating to juvenile delinquency, the family, and social work. Cooper herself provided a commentary on this period in her later history of the personal social services (Cooper, 1983). Urged on by Joseph, for whom this issue had come to have a messianic appeal, a small group of four or five civil servants began to draft a paper on what was initially called the 'cycle of degradation'. Geoffrey Otton, Joan Cooper, an Assistant Secretary called Bob King, and a Principal named R. R. G. Watts spent hours on it, producing numerous drafts. Otton later recalled that:

> it was very touchy stuff. It wasn't the sort of thing that governments were expected at that time to involve themselves in, and for us, the Civil Service – I'd never done anything like this. I'd come from dealing with crime and immigration and approved schools.[7]

While the speech loomed large from an early stage, Joseph kept on having new ideas, and the drafts went backwards and forwards, getting longer and longer.

Some of the broader work on poverty followed on from initiatives begun under Crossman, in the previous Labour government. In June 1971, for example, Wendt had noted to Mildred Riddelsdell (1913–2006), the Second Permanent Secretary, that Joseph regarded the report of the Steering Group on Poverty as impressive, leading to further work in various directions. These included the need for more knowledge on the dynamics of poverty, its duration, the links with poor management and disability, and the implications for children under five.[8] Wendt noted in July 1971 that Joseph was particularly anxious that more work should be done to discover the underlying causes of social deprivation among children. It was difficult to establish cause and effect, but he asked what research had been done, and how far recreational facilities could improve the lives and prospects of children living in urban areas.

—

Other ideas were to measure the results of services, and to carry out experimental studies of particular areas, where the provision of services was the dependent variable. Wendt hoped by the autumn to circulate a paper drawing attention to gaps in social provision and the need for a programme of research.[9] This is the first mention of a paper on the 'cycle of degradation' in the relevant files.

The recollections of civil servants amplify the archival sources. Subsequently, there were two papers, by Joan Cooper on the 'problem' as seen by the DHSS and some of the ways by which it might be tackled; and by Geoffrey Otton on education and the Preparation for Parenthood initiative. These are undated, but were circulated to social scientists by the SSRC in February 1972, and were probably in existence well before then. Cooper's paper defined the cycle of deprivation as 'the process through which inadequate damaged parents tend to produce under-functioning children who in their turn parent another inadequate or damaged generation'.[10] The relevant factors were seen as including genetic endowment, childrearing practices, family stress, disability, 'hostile environments', and economic and cultural patterns. Cooper argued that there was evidence of a cyclical process, but that the significance of childrearing practices, young parents, and illegitimacy was uncertain. Similarly, it was not clear whether the best strategy would be to concentrate on at-risk groups vulnerable to downward mobility, or on problem family groups already exhibiting pathological tendencies. Cooper therefore recommended that the strategy should be to focus on social development in fairly general terms, and to concentrate on family functioning during the childrearing period; on education for parenthood during adolescence and early marriage; and on research, development, and the evaluation of existing programmes.

Geoffrey Otton, on the other hand, was naturally more cautious, writing that the underlying thesis was 'that there is an observable pattern of transmitted deprivation from parents to children'.[11] It occurred at all levels of society and, however defined, there seemed to be a cyclical process at work, through which problems recurred in families despite a steady improvement in community services. Not all the recurring problems could be attributed to the operation of a cycle – a complex mix of personal, social, economic, genetic, and environmental factors were involved – and generalisation was dangerous. Thus it was a 'very uncertain field', and the DHSS was having to proceed on the basis of assumptions that were open to question. Nevertheless, there appeared to be a broad consensus among social workers and teachers that some kind of cyclical process was at work. Evidence included the case records of children in approved schools; research on problem families; assumptions in the field of education; and evidence on illegitimacy from the National Child Development Study (NCDS). These longitudinal studies appeared to show that the roots of deprivation occurred in early infancy, and while education could not remedy all the damage done during a child's upbringing, it might promote a better understanding of the consequences of future parental behaviour (for example attitudes to illegitimacy and abortion). Education for parenthood might be one way of breaking the cycle.

A paper by Joan Cooper, entitled 'The cycle of deprivation', and dated January 1972, subsequently became the first of the Joint Working Party papers. This is recognisably an early draft of the cycle speech. In this paper, Cooper noted that deprivation took many forms and had many causes: economic factors such as unemployment and poverty; environmental factors such as poor housing and lack of community facilities; personal factors that caused people to be damaged by illness, accident, or genetic endowment; and cultural factors that could affect patterns of childrearing. She had revised her earlier description of the cycle, writing that it 'describes the process through which inadequate or damaged parents tend to produce a significant proportion of under-functioning children who, in turn, become the inadequate parents of yet another generation'.[12] Even with a great improvement in environmental conditions, in terms of abolishing the slums and improving housing, there still remained a major task to disseminate knowledge about the needs of young children, and to modify childrearing practices. Moreover, Cooper claimed that deprived, depressed, or 'under-functioning' individuals and families, who were unable to manage adequately, tended to congregate in areas with their own subcultural lifestyles, where behaviour patterns were shared, and where they felt less open to criticism. In this, Cooper seemed to reflect some of the US literature, for example by Oscar Lewis and Elliot Liebow (Liebow, 1967).

Certainly the influence of the social work lobby on Joseph was recognised at the time. Alan Clarke, for example, then Professor of Psychology at the University of Hull, and later to play a central role in the Research Programme, recalled that:

> He was in the hands of his social work advisers, of whom he had half a dozen I think. I've met some of them, and they would feed him with the normal social work line of a practising social worker: well, the Bloggs family, the grandfather was a criminal, the father is a criminal and young Willy is a delinquent, so you have clear transmission

from grandfather to father to son, and there's not much you can do about it, and that's why there continues to be social problems. They were feeding him this. There would be no mention of escape because they didn't know about it.[13]

Robin Wendt later recalled of the civil servants that:

> When Joseph came up with his transmitted deprivation idea, it was clearly their duty to help him think it through and write his speeches, but I don't think they ever became attached to it in the way that he clearly was and in the way that they in turn were attached to other broader social policies … I suspect there was a bit of scoffing going on in the background.[14]

Nevertheless, it does seem that while the cycle was very much driven by Joseph, the DHSS was supportive, because its civil servants saw the hypothesis as a way to stimulate research on social work services. Indeed this may also explain why they became so disappointed with the Research Programme in the mid-1970s, as we shall see in Part Two.[15] In February 1972, for example, Joan Cooper asked in a memo to a colleague whether 'handicap' might be the cause or a contributory factor in the cycle, and if the DHSS might fund and oversee a research programme in this area. Such a research programme might examine whether the presence of a 'handicapped' member in a family was a causative factor in 'transgenerational' deprivation; the extent to which 'grossly deprived families' were characterised by the presence of 'handicapped' members in the current and previous generations; whether 'handicap' was a precipitatory or contributory factor in determining whether the family prospered; and whether the provision of appropriate services avoided decline or facilitated an escape from 'gross deprivation'.[16]

Joseph circulated early drafts of the cycle speech to friends and colleagues in the spring of 1972. One recipient was Moyra Bannister, wife of Sir Roger, the neurologist and four-minute miler. She agreed with the emphasis on the family, and made practical suggestions for sports centres, playgroups, centres where people might take up hobbies, and the provision of ante-natal courses, noting that 'it is a question of bringing the mediocre up to the level of the best'.[17] Bannister advocated a three-pronged attack that would break the cycle of deprivation by focusing on hospital services that would support mothers through ante-natal care, birth, and post-natal care; attention to children before they went to school; and the last year at school. For his part, Joseph valued her advice, noting to his civil servants that:

> She is to be taken seriously both as Dr Bannister's wife and very much in her own right (daughter of the late P. Jacobson of the IMF) [International Monetary Fund]. Please include her views in the collation and in your considerations.[18]

This enthusiasm was not shared by some. A. M. Lamb, the Deputy Chief Nursing Officer, for example, noted that Mrs Bannister had referred throughout her letter to the 'hospital service' when she meant the health service, noting that she 'appears to be unaware of the health services in the community which are not at present part of the hospital service'.[19]

As we will see in Chapter Three, discussions were already under way with the SSRC about the potential for research, and in addition to these Joseph had made his own overtures to some academics. In an attempt to explore the potential usefulness of anthropological research, for example, Joseph himself met Professors Mary Douglas (1921-2007), Eric Miller, and Clyde Mitchell in May 1972. Douglas, then Professor of Social Anthropology at University College London, knew Joseph personally, and was one of the few social scientists sympathetic to Conservative policy (*Times Educational Supplement*, 10 May 1974, p 1).[20] Joseph wished to develop, over a period of five to 10 years, anthropological approaches to the problems faced by the DHSS, to provide his successors with insights into the causes and symptoms of social problems, which would both reveal what the problem areas were and open up policy options on prevention.[21] In the event, nothing came of this and anthropologists were to play a limited part in the Research Programme.

The content of the speech

By the summer of 1972, the drafting of the cycle speech had been completed; what was needed was a suitable occasion on which to launch the hypothesis. Brian Harrison has observed that while Joseph was not an original thinker, he was interested in ideas, and he had that quality essential for a creative politician: knowing when new ideas are needed, what they are, where to look for them, and how to project them (ODNB, 2004). However, in terms of the last, the cycle speech was unusual in that it was given at a conference for local authorities organised by the Pre-School Playgroups Association, at Church House,

Westminster, London, at 2pm on Thursday 29 June 1972. This was not a politically high-profile occasion. Geoffrey Otton later recalled of the Association that:

> They had operated under the sponsorship of the Department of Education up to this time; and as they were not seen as central to the department's concerns they received a pretty modest government grant. But as DHSS moved into the area of social deprivation and parenting, officials saw that the Association could be a key player. They arranged for it to come under DHSS sponsorship, and increased its grant. And one consequence was that they identified the Association's AGM as a suitable forum for launching the speech.[22]

However, when members of the Association saw the proposed text, they were appalled, seeing the proposals as interfering in other people's lives, demeaning the people who needed pitying most, and treating them as a problem. One of Otton's main tasks, therefore, was to negotiate with the Association, assuring its members that their comments on the draft speech would be taken on board.

Pre-school education had much longer-term origins. A Nursery School Association had been formed in 1923 as a result of the frustration felt at the 1918 Education Act, which had made the *possibility* of the extension of nursery schools a reality. Its aim was to arouse public opinion and extend the provision of maintained nursery schools by the state. The Pre-School Playgroups Association, on the other hand, was concerned mainly with encouraging the growth of playgroups set up by voluntary and cooperative effort. It had been founded much later, in 1961, in direct response to frustration felt by mothers. At this time it was chaired by Lady Plowden (1910-2000), earlier Chair of the Central Advisory Council for Education, and a key influence on the report *Children and their Primary Schools* (Central Advisory Council for Education, 1967). The majority of its members were themselves mothers of young children, women whose experience with pre-school children was sufficiently recent to motivate them to become members. Many were actively involved in the running of pre-school playgroups, defined by the Association as 'a group of from six to thirty children aged two and a half to five years who play together regularly daily or several sessions weekly' (Blackstone, 1971, p 76). Whereas most private nursery schools were set up on a profit-making basis, playgroups usually made small charges to cover or contribute to costs. By September 1965, there were 600 groups affiliated to the Pre-School Playgroups Association, and 950 members; by 1971 the number of affiliated groups had more than doubled. Compared to the Pre-School Playgroups Association, the executive of the Nursery School Association had fewer mothers of young children, and more nursery school teachers.

Joseph said he saw the speech as an opportunity to express his appreciation of the work of the playgroup movement, and also to share some thoughts on what he regarded as intractable problems in society, which bore on the future of family life. While medical provision for children under five was good and improving, less was known about the social and emotional needs of young children. At that time, the main problem faced by the Pre-School Playgroups Association, both its central organisation and its local branches, was a lack of resources. Therefore in the speech, Joseph announced new grants for day nurseries and playgroups under the umbrella of the Urban Programme, since in May 1972 the government had allocated over £1 million for daycare provision for the under-fives. He announced a capital grant of £9,500 and a recurrent annual grant of £45,000, in order to accelerate the provision of playgroups. He saw them as being both an impressive area for voluntary organisation activity, and also an essential social service. Joseph wanted more playgroups, especially in urban areas of need, and 'to see the standards constantly improving while at the same time preserving the essential qualities of family involvement and voluntary service'.[23]

But it was in the second half of the speech that Joseph developed his main theme, noting that the family was under attack, and arguing that family life needed to be strengthened. Joseph voiced a paradox: 'why is it that, in spite of long periods of full employment and relative prosperity and the improvement in community services since the Second World War, deprivation and problems of maladjustment so conspicuously persist?'.[24] He acknowledged that deprivation was an imprecise term. What he meant by it was 'those circumstances which prevent people developing to nearer their potential – physically, emotionally and intellectually – than many do now'.[25] Deprivation took many forms, could be found at all levels of society, and had many and complex causes. Factors might be economic (persistent unemployment and low income); living conditions (bad housing and overcrowding and few opportunities for recreation); personal (illness or accident or genetic endowment); and those that affected patterns of childrearing (children deprived of love or guidance). Deprivation 'embraces many disadvantages, which can occur singly or in different combinations throughout society, and which we see persisting despite all our advances'.[26]

But Joseph continued: 'perhaps there is at work here a process, apparent in many situations but imperfectly understood, by which problems reproduce themselves from generation to generation'.[27] He referred to this as a 'cycle of deprivation'. He did not want to be misunderstood, and there was not a single process. But it seemed that in a proportion of cases, occurring at all levels of society, the problems of one generation reproduced themselves in the next. According to Joseph, social workers, teachers, and others could often be sure that 'a child, because of his background, is operating under disadvantage and prone to run into the same difficulties in his turn as his parents have experienced'.[28] This much was known, and services were already working with the casualties of society – problem families, vagrants, alcoholics, drug addicts, the disturbed, the delinquent, and the criminal. Joseph argued that the phenomenon of 'transmitted deprivation' – what he had called the cycle of deprivation – needed to be studied, and had become clearer over the previous 20-30 years with rising living standards.

Joseph argued that although the cycle was not fully understood 'a number of objective studies do tend to bear out the subjective belief of many practitioners that cyclical processes are at work'.[29] His evidence included intergenerational studies of problem families in Sheffield; research at the Cambridge Institute of Criminology, indicating that a range of adverse social factors were strongly linked with future delinquency; the evidence from the NCDS that Otton had uncovered; research that seemed to show that parents who had been ill-treated went on to ill-treat their own children; and a comparison of the US and USSR that appeared to put England at the bottom of an international league table of parental involvement. Even so, there was a need for research 'to supplement and systematise the many separate studies that are gradually clarifying the causes and characteristics of particular social disorders'.[30] The cycle could not be broken until the mechanisms were understood more clearly, and the DHSS had already been in touch with the SSRC to see if a research programme could be established.

Joseph acknowledged that while deprivation was wider than poverty, there was no doubt that low income played a part, and efforts to combat poverty had to continue. For this reason, he said, the government was increasing the level of benefits, introducing new ones, and improving access to those that already existed. These included FIS, the national rent rebate scheme, and an improvement in income support. Research was also needed into the dynamics of family poverty, the mechanisms and circumstances that led families into poverty, but also its duration and effects, and the forces that enabled some to escape. Much of this was relevant and complementary to research on the cycle.[31] However in the meantime, his remedies were noticeably more limited. Apart from playgroups and services for the under-fives, they focused on family planning, support for parents, and attention to the needs of children. Joseph claimed, for instance, that if effective family planning was more widely practised, the numbers caught up in the cycle would be much reduced. Large family size was correlated with delinquency, low intelligence, and poor reading skills.

Another area for study and action was greater understanding and awareness of child development and the importance of the roles of parents. Inadequate people tended to be inadequate parents, and inadequate parents tended to rear inadequate children.[32] This was what some had termed Preparation for Parenthood. Good parenting relied on understanding the needs of children, and respecting their need for love and guidance. Nevertheless, distinctions between fortunate and unfortunate families cut across income lines and family size; there were 'good parents in poor homes; and bad parents in prosperous homes. There are good parents of large families and bad parents of small families'.[33] Some parents had their own emotional needs, and these had to be met. More generally, to reach those already deprived, there was a role for social agencies, the churches, voluntary organisations, and schools, and for health visitors and social workers.

Joseph ended the speech by arguing that without a healthy family life, a healthy society was not possible; increasingly the focus had to be on prevention. The paradox was that while conditions in general had improved, misery continued unabated; perhaps because much deprivation and maladjustment persisted from generation to generation through a cycle of deprivation. Parents who were themselves deprived in childhood became in turn the parents of another generation of deprived children. He noted that the SSRC had been asked to help with understanding the working of the cycle, and efforts to improve housing and abate poverty had to continue. But the emotional and intellectual deprivation of young children also had to be tackled. There seemed to be a marked contrast between the medical care given to mothers, on the one hand, and, on the other, the lack of effort to prepare mothers and fathers for their role as parents. Joseph proposed to consult widely on Preparation for Parenthood. He hoped that there would be more discussion about these issues, since he wished to see new thinking and new initiatives in this whole area.[34]

Perhaps because of the known unease of the Pre-School Playgroups Association over the content of the address, it was not one of Joseph's better speeches. Geoffrey Otton (who was present) later recalled that:

in a way that was perhaps typical of Sir Keith as a person, I think as he got up to make the speech, he lost his nerve over it, so he hurried through it in a not very rhetorical fashion. And the total delivery was rather flat.[35]

It may be partly because of this, that, while the speech was reported in the main broadsheet newspapers, overall it met with a fairly muted immediate response. *The Times*, for instance, commented in a leader that the personal social services needed to be coordinated, but that:

> Personal and family difficulties, poverty, bad housing, poor school conditions, the sense of living in a decaying area – they all contribute to the feeling of personal hopelessness that drags some people down and starts some children off with such a poor chance in life. All these causes need to be tackled as part of a combined approach to the problems of deprived areas, because deprived areas and deprived people go together. (*The Times*, 30 June 1972, p 17)

As Halcrow later noted, the speech in a modest way established Joseph as a conscientious commentator on social policy issues. It did not arouse anything like the storm associated with his speech in Edgbaston two years later.

The evidence for the cycle

Joseph's speech was in part a call for more research, acknowledging that, while self-evident, the cycle was poorly understood. Nevertheless, he did base his argument on a range of studies that appeared to support his hypothesis. These sources of evidence bear closer examination as they provide insights into the type of literature that Joseph, along with the civil servants who drafted the speech, were drawing upon. Geoffrey Otton recalled how much Joseph was reading at this time:

> he [Joseph] went off on summer holidays with a car full of books, and then would come back and send us all photocopied pages from them and demand commentary on them and so on, so this was taking me, in particular, into very unfamiliar territory.[36]

Joseph's first example of the cycle was provided by the Sheffield problem family studies, which had followed up 120 problem families in 1955,

1967, and 1971. Sheffield was not unusual as a local authority in focusing on problem families in the context of public health provision; what was different was the attempt to do a longitudinal follow-up, and to carry this interest into the late 1960s and early 1970s. Like many Medical Officers of Health (MOsH) at the time, the theme of the problem family was one that Catherine Wright, then Assistant Maternity and Child Welfare Medical Officer, had addressed in annual reports from the mid-1950s. In 1955, for example, she had written that little progress had been made in tackling 'a social problem in which the interplay of poor genetic endowment and a bad environment throws up so many imponderables' (Sheffield Health Committee, 1956, p 106; 1960, p 42; 1970, p 58). Subsequently two social workers were engaged to help 42 families where more intensive support and guidance was felt to be required. In 1955, Wright had reported on 120 families judged by health visitors to be problem families. Investigating the first 100 of these, she suggested that there were three categories of 'established' problem families. Help was necessary in the form of the provision of adequate housing, advice on family spacing and limitation, economic assistance, nursery care for young children, the supervision of adolescents, and practical help and guidance to create a family unit (Wright, 1955, pp 381-4).

Twelve years later, Wright, along with Wilfrid Parry, then Deputy MOH and Deputy Principal School Medical Officer, and John Lunn, Lecturer in Preventive Medicine and Public Health at the University of Sheffield, reported on an attempt to follow up 108 of these families. They had found that what they termed parental immaturity and instability were a frequent cause of family failure, and in extreme cases these failures gave rise to problem families, which were often badly housed, badly organised, and a 'liability to the community' (Parry et al, 1967, p 130). Social failure was handed down through the generations, and the picture created was of children deprived emotionally and materially. Of the families, 84 had had contact with the statutory and voluntary agencies, 81 lived in council houses, 66 still had the same marriage partner, and there was chronic physical disability in 36 households (55%). The poor work record of the fathers was a constant characteristic of problem family households; 59% had had contact with the Ministry of Social Security, and 72% were in arrears with council rents. Parry et al noted that an important change had occurred in the housing situation, and only 13% of the households had little furniture, or would qualify as problem families on this account. The survey confirmed the view of case workers who had lived in the same locality over a number of years that, with the exception of a minority of cases, most families settled down, and could present an outwardly 'normal' appearance. Parry et al concluded that 'these changes show a considerable improvement in respect of housing accommodation and material possessions, but serious problems remain regarding productive employment and the care and education of children' (Parry et al, 1967, p 132).

Four years later, Wright and Lunn reported on the circumstances of the married sons and daughters of 116 of the 120 original families, 835 known descendants, 555 of whom had been traced. They looked particularly at housing circumstances, employment and household possessions, and contacts with social agencies, commenting that 'the number of contacts a family has with certain social agencies provides a useful measure of the extent of their social failure' (Wright and Lunn, 1971, p 315). Wright and Lunn felt that there was no reason to doubt the original designation of the families as 'problem'. The housing and material goods of the second generation were much improved compared to those of their parents, reflecting the general rise in the standard of living. Overall, a third of the original families were average, competent households; a third were already problem families, or in the process of becoming so; and a third were precarious and vulnerable. Their fates depended on the strengths and weaknesses of the personalities of the parents. Wright and Lunn claimed, for example, that fathers who were in irregular work, and were unable to provide adequately for their families, had a 'deadly' effect on their wives, and were damaging to their sons and daughters. These sons were 'wanting in the dominant role' they had to assume when they came to marry, and had poorly paid, undemanding jobs interspersed with periods of unemployment. Most were labourers, drivers' mates, cleaners, scrap collectors, coal baggers, and painters of white lines. Wright and Lunn argued that these intergenerational continuities demonstrated the importance of access to contraception (Wright and Lunn, 1971, p 320).

Leaving aside the weakness of the problem family literature for the moment, Joseph's second example came from research concerned with child delinquency. At the Cambridge Institute of Criminology, Donald West (1969) had sought to measure personal and family disturbance of the kind usually thought to foster delinquency, and, in light of relationships between personal background and misbehaviour, to see what factors were most prevalent. He found that more parents had serious marital problems, were of unstable and deviant personality, and were careless or perverse in their methods of childrearing. West wrote that 'dull, ineffectual and unstable persons may be expected to sink to the lowest level and hence to suffer from poor housing, low incomes and large unplanned families. They may also produce poorly socialised children who will carry the same features into the next generation' (West, 1969, p 136). West was interested in those factors, such as above-average intelligence, that might protect some individuals from becoming delinquents. Parental pathology, in the form of unsuitable discipline, unfortunate attitudes towards children, and deviant personalities, was remarkably concentrated among the 'socially handicapped' group. However, he noted that family income was also effective in identifying a 'problem-prone' minority. Overall, West suggested that basic social and economic factors appeared to outweigh personal and psychological factors in the backgrounds of future juvenile delinquents. Thus West concluded that 'personal inadequacies and external handicaps reinforce each other in these unfortunate families', and instead of trying to answer the question of which came first, it might be more useful to ask at what point the 'vicious circle' could be broken (West, 1969, p 149).

West had used the metaphor of a circle, and Joseph's advisers augmented this evidence with studies of particular localities by psychiatrists. North-East Wiltshire, an area with a population of around 200,000, had been the first place in the country to set up child abuse registers and procedures. From the 1950s, the MOsH and Children's Officers had noted families in which children were at continued risk of violence from their parents. J. E. Oliver, a Consultant Psychiatrist, later used this data to explore the problem of battered babies by interviewing as many living relatives as possible from the maternal and paternal sides of these families. With Audrey Taylor, a Senior Medical Social Worker, Oliver suggested that explanations of why parents ill-treated or neglected their children were likely to be superficial unless backed up with an understanding of the parents when they themselves were children. Oliver and Taylor claimed to have found evidence of five generations of ill-treated children, and they suggested that the family pedigrees that they had drawn up were representative of others in the locality. They wrote of one that 'the families described in this pedigree contain numerous members who suffer from mental illness, profound disturbances of personality and degrees of subnormal intelligence' (Oliver and Taylor, 1971, p 479).

The emphasis on intergenerational continuities and family planning was stressed in later publications. In 1973, Oliver, along with Jane Cox, a sociologist and Research Social Worker, wrote that in that part of Wiltshire:

---

a few kindreds have absorbed the energies of disproportionate numbers of professional people to little avail. Distress and social dependency within these kindreds is perpetuated through the generations, with certain lines at serious risk of continuing the pattern. (Oliver and Cox, 1973, p 90)

Subsequently, Oliver reported on attempts to identify all the families in the area in which there was a pattern of two or more generations of child maltreatment and multi-agency involvement. Oliver claimed to have found 147 families and 294 maltreated children. He concluded that at least 10% of the total child abuse and neglect cases were accounted for by parents who had severe personality disorders and/or criminal tendencies, and who themselves came from families with serious mental and social problems over two, three, or more generations (Oliver, 1985, p 489).

Joseph had noted that a comparison of the US and USSR appeared to put England at the bottom of an international league table of parental involvement with children. This was *Two worlds of childhood* (1970, 1972 edn), by Urie Bronfenbrenner (1917-2005), then Professor of Psychology at Cornell University in the US. The book compared the 'concern of one generation for the next' in the USSR and the US, looking at socialisation in the family, pre-school centres, children's groups, classrooms, schools, neighbourhoods, communities, and the nations as a whole. Bronfenbrenner argued that in the USSR, children's collectives constituted the basic structures in all Soviet programmes designed for the care or education of children, and while children's groups existed in the US, they were more fluid, and relatively independent of the adult society. He noted in passing that England was the only country that exceeded the US in the willingness of its children to engage in antisocial behaviour, writing that 'England is also the only country in our sample which shows a level of parental involvement lower than our own, with both parents – and especially fathers – showing less affection, offering less companionship, and intervening less frequently in the lives of their children' (Devereux et al, 1969; Bronfenbrenner, 1970, 1972 edn, p 116).

More generally, Bronfenbrenner concentrated on families and children's groups, and highlighted the value of the US Head Start programme. He argued that it was the withdrawal of the family from its childrearing functions that was the major factor that threatened a breakdown of the 'socialisation process' in the US (Bronfenbrenner, 1970, 1972 edn, p 152). The process had first been noticed among the families of the poor, and it was organisations such as Head Start, which involved parents and other community members again in the lives of their children, that could revitalise the socialisation process. Parents were included on the advisory boards of programmes, and meetings for parents, where staff made presentations, were an important feature. Neighbourhood centres were an important part of any comprehensive educational programme. Bronfenbrenner argued that 'what is called for is greater involvement of parents, and other adults, in the lives of children, and, conversely – greater involvement of children in responsibility on behalf of their own family, community, and society at large' (Bronfenbrenner, 1970, 1972 edn, p 166). It was to neighbourliness, civic concern, and devotion to the young that the US had to look if it was to rediscover its moral identity as a society and a nation.

This was a complex mass of material, including follow-up and longitudinal studies, generated by researchers whose backgrounds included public health, psychology, psychiatry, and criminology. Least was said about the NCDS, which was the most recent piece of evidence, but which also linked patterns in child development to the country's economic and social structure, along with government policy (Davie et al, 1972, pp xv-xvii). Joseph interpreted the evidence as suggesting that second generation problem families could be produced at an alarmingly rapid rate; a range of adverse factors was associated with future delinquency; and parents who were ill-treated when they were young went on to ill-treat their own children. Moreover, children in working-class families, particularly those with semi-skilled and unskilled fathers, were disadvantaged from birth; and it was a lack of parental involvement that lay at the heart of the malaise in US society, and by implication in England, so that what was called for was greater involvement of parents and other adults in the lives of children.[37] As we shall see in Chapter Six, this evidence was subsequently picked over by social scientists hostile to the cycle of deprivation hypothesis.

The cycle speech in retrospect

While the speech met with a muted response at the time, Joseph was to remain interested in poverty and the cycle of deprivation. When he saw the draft first report of the Joint Working Party, in the summer of 1973, for example, he wrote to its then Chair, Robin Matthews, that:

> I have read the report with interest and admiration. I know it represents much hard work and I am greatly indebted to you personally for the lead you gave as Chairman and to you and your distinguished colleagues for the very valuable

contribution which your report makes. I recognise that the conceptual difficulties were considerable and synthesising the vast amount of relevant literature was a formidable one. I am impressed and encouraged that you have found it possible to present such a thorough report at this stage.[38]

In July 1975, he asked the SSRC if he might see any material that had emerged on the cycle, especially Michael Rutter's literature review.[39] The concept of the cycle continued to feature in Conservative Party documents on children and deviancy, with plans to transfer responsibility for all children to the DHSS, and to correlate such sources as court registers, school attendance records, and data on maladjustment with factors that characterised families caught up in the cycle.[40] Joseph himself made unsuccessful approaches to the Joseph Rowntree Social Service Trust and the Nuffield Foundation for funding for studies on children and pre-school education.[41]

Nevertheless, through the 1970s, as Britain's economic problems worsened, Joseph's correspondence became increasingly dominated by letters from the directors of small companies concerned about the problems of British industry. His outlook by the mid-1980s is illustrated in his 'Introduction' to Samuel Smiles' *Self-help* (Joseph, 1859, 1986 edn). Joseph noted that the reproductive process was clearly very powerful, although one that was not fully understood, and he had come to the conclusion that there was a cycle process at work. In his Gilbreth Lecture, given in 1979, Joseph recalled: 'that seemed to me to prove that which I had asserted, that there is a cycle' (Joseph, K., 'The class war', *The Guardian*, 18 July 1979, p 7). In this situation, he became exasperated with the direction taken by the Research Programme. His book *Equality* (1979), for example, co-written with Jonathan Sumption, opposed the redistribution of wealth and was critical of Tony Atkinson's emphasis on equality; Atkinson, then a Professor in the Department of Political Economy at University College London, had been one of the main researchers in the Research Programme (Joseph and Sumption, 1979, pp 21-8, 47-52, 84). Moreover, when the final report on the Research Programme was published (Brown and Madge, 1982a), Joseph, as Secretary of State for Education and Science (1981-86), asked whether he might discuss its policy recommendations with its authors.[42]

It is often suggested that it was Joseph's experience with the Research Programme that fuelled his contempt for social science and for the SSRC, so much so that he tried to abolish the latter (Berthoud, 1983a, p 160; Timmins, 1995, 2001 edn; Donovan, 2001; Denham and Garnett,

2002, p 197). Denham and Garnett suggest more generally that Joseph remained interested in the cycle of deprivation, and affected by his experiences with the Research Programme. His concern with the cycle, for example, played a part in his reluctance to introduce education vouchers in the early 1980s, believing that some parents would lack the means to exercise real choice. Joseph was intellectually attracted to a scheme of education vouchers because he wanted to give every parent in the country the same freedom of choice as the relatively wealthy (Denham and Garnett, 2002, p 197). But he argued that badly educated themselves and transmitting their lack of ambition to their children, parents in the lower classes would fail to make the effort. Instead the state should pour resources into these 'sink' schools, in an effort to try to recruit the best teachers. More equitable tax treatment of parents with dependent children might break the cycle of deprivation, and voluntary organisations could contribute to the bringing up of children (Joseph, 1990, pp 11, 14).

Apart from these implicit criticisms, Joseph occasionally hinted at his disappointment with the Research Programme. In his pamphlet *The importance of parenting* (1991) Joseph alluded to the preference by Michael Rutter and Nicola Madge for the phrase 'cycles of disadvantage', and he claimed of the cycle of deprivation that 'no-one denied the thesis'. He argued that the quality of parenting was not necessarily linked with low income, and recommended research to show the relative effectiveness of different methods of helping people become 'good enough' parents (Joseph, 1991, pp 5, 9, 13; Denham and Garnett, 2001a, pp 369-73, 379, 421, footnote 31). From the perspective of the House of Lords in the early 1990s, Joseph continued to offer support for the Home-Start charity that had been set up in response to his cycle speech. Founded by Margaret Harrison, it was based on the idea that volunteers should befriend families, providing more intimate assistance to those struggling to bring up children (Denham and Garnett, 2001a, pp 225, 373, 421; 2002, p 197). The wheel had come full circle, and, disappointed with the SSRC and irritated by social scientists, Joseph had turned his back on the state, and gone back to the solutions offered by voluntary organisations.

Conclusion

Archival materials supplemented with oral interviews with key players make it possible to construct a fuller narrative than has been available hitherto, bringing out the significance of the involvement of Joan Cooper and Geoffrey Otton. We have examined the drafting of the speech within the DHSS; the content of the speech itself; the evidence that Joseph cited in support of his cycle hypothesis; and Joseph's interest in the cycle in the years after 1972. The argument has been that the speech was a curious mixture, and can be read in several different ways. It appeared novel, but had elements of underclass stereotypes familiar from the previous 100 years. It conceded that low incomes were important, but the solutions that it offered were based on home helps and health visitors. And while it claimed to be based on evidence, it noted that much was not known. The speech was primarily an individual obsession of Joseph himself, but the civil servants transferred from the Home Office played a key part in its drafting. Moreover, while the speech located the problems of families within the broader context of poverty and disadvantage, the primary focus was on individual behaviour and parenting. Although he acknowledged longitudinal studies such as the NCDS, Joseph's sources were mainly drawn from psychiatric and criminological literature. Finally, there is much evidence that Joseph continued to be troubled by the cycle in the years after 1972. This chapter has explored the cycle of deprivation speech, its background, and its timing and content. The following chapter explores its longer-term antecedents, in terms of Joseph's own personality and family background, the policy context of the early 1970s, and the broader influence of the US literature.

Notes

[1] Harriett Wilson papers, Newcastle upon Tyne, 'Extract from *Woman's hour*: of current concern', broadcast 27 September 1972. These papers are currently in the possession of John Veit-Wilson to whom I am extremely grateful for his generosity in making his mother's papers available to me.

[2] Interview between the author and Robin Wendt, Chester, 22 May 2006.

[3] National Archives, Kew, London (hereafter NA) BN 13/163: K. Joseph to Secretary, 21 January 1971.

[4] NA BN 13/179: J. E. Pater to N. Jordan-Moss, 12 July 1971.

[5] Interview between the author and Geoffrey Otton, Bromley, Kent, 4 May 2006.

[6] Interview between the author and Geoffrey Otton, Bromley, Kent, 4 May 2006.

[7] Interview between the author and Geoffrey Otton, Bromley, Kent, 4 May 2006. See also NA MH 152/72: E. Bishop to R. R. G. Watts, 16 November 1972; NA MH 152/84: J. Cooper to P. Benner, 12 March 1976.

[8] NA BN 13/189: memo by K. Joseph (nd); NA BN 13/189: R. Wendt to M. Riddelsdell, 22 June 1971.

[9] NA MH 152/72: R. G. Wendt, 'Social deprivation', 14 July 1971.

[10] Adrian Sinfield papers, J. Cooper, 'The cycle of deprivation' (nd).

[11] Adrian Sinfield papers, G. Otton, 'The cycle' (nd).

[12] NA MH 152/72: J. D. Cooper, 'The cycle of deprivation', WPTD (Working Party on Transmitted Deprivation), 3 January 1972.

[13] Interview between the author and Alan Clarke, London, 24 May 2006.

[14] Interview between the author and Robin Wendt, Chester, 22 May 2006.

[15] Interview between the author and Adrian Sinfield, Edinburgh, 26–27 May 2006.

[16] NA MH 152/72: J. D. Cooper to J. B. Cornish, 1 February 1972.

[17] NA MH 152/89: M. Bannister to K. Joseph, 6 April 1972.

[18] NA MH 152/89: M. Bannister to K. Joseph, 27 June 1972.

[19] NA MH 152/89: A. M. Lamb to J. Cooper, 5 September 1972.

[20] NA MH 152/89: M. Douglas, 'Note on a possible contribution from anthropology to the study of industrial poverty: casualties of the system and the family response to failure' (nd).

[21] NA MH 152/72: 'Notes of a meeting on 15 May 1972 between Secretary of State and Professors Mary Douglas, Eric Miller, and Clyde Mitchell' (nd).

[22] Interview between the author and Geoffrey Otton, Bromley, Kent, 4 May 2006.

[23] Adrian Sinfield papers, 'The cycle of deprivation', 29 June 1972, p 3, para 9. Here the references are to the original typescript as distributed by the DHSS. The speech was subsequently published as Joseph, K. (1972) 'The cycle of family deprivation', in Joseph, K. *Caring for people*, London: Conservative Political Centre, pp 29-46, and an abridged version as Joseph, K. (1975, Fontana edn) 'The cycle of deprivation', in

Buttersworth, E. and Holman, R. (eds), *Social welfare in modern Britain*, Glasgow: Collins, pp 387-93.

[24] Adrian Sinfield papers, 'The cycle of deprivation', 29 June 1972, p 4, para 15.

[25] Adrian Sinfield papers, 'The cycle of deprivation', 29 June 1972, p 4, para 16.

[26] Adrian Sinfield papers, 'The cycle of deprivation', 29 June 1972, p 5, para 16.

[27] Adrian Sinfield papers, 'The cycle of deprivation', 29 June 1972, p 5, para 16.

[28] Adrian Sinfield papers, 'The cycle of deprivation', 29 June 1972, p 6, para 17.

[29] Adrian Sinfield papers, 'The cycle of deprivation', 29 June 1972, p 6, para 20.

[30] Adrian Sinfield papers, 'The cycle of deprivation', 29 June 1972, p 9, para 27.

[31] Adrian Sinfield papers, 'The cycle of deprivation', 29 June 1972, p 10, para 32.

[32] Adrian Sinfield papers, 'The cycle of deprivation', 29 June 1972, p 13, para 41.

[33] Adrian Sinfield papers, 'The cycle of deprivation', 29 June 1972, p 15, para 46.

[34] Adrian Sinfield papers, 'The cycle of deprivation', 29 June 1972, p 20, para 66.

[35] Interview between the author and Geoffrey Otton, Bromley, Kent, 4 May 2006.

[36] Interview between the author and Geoffrey Otton, Bromley, Kent, 4 May 2006.

[37] Adrian Sinfield papers, 'The cycle of deprivation', 29 June 1972, pp 6-9, paras 21-6.

[38] NA MH 152/76: K. Joseph to R. C. O. Matthews, 10 August 1973.

[39] Keith Joseph papers, Conservative Party Archive, Bodleian Library, Oxford, KJ 8/1: K. Joseph to J. Street, 1 July 1975.

[40] Joseph papers, KJ 11/3: N. Bessell, 'Social policy commission on children', 21 April 1975.

[41] Joseph papers, KJ 11/3: K. Joseph to P. Chitnis, 6 May 1975; Joseph papers, KJ 11/3: K. Joseph to C. C. Butler, 25 June 1975.

[42] Nicola Madge papers, London: K. Joseph to N. Madge, 27 July 1982.

TWO

From problem families to the cycle of deprivation

Introduction

Whereas the previous chapter focused on the drafting and content of the cycle speech, this chapter attempts to explain its longer-term and more immediate origins. Earlier work has focused on the cycle of deprivation as a stepping stone in the longer-term history of the underclass. Among the most notable of these antecedents were the Charles Booth survey of London in the 1880s; studies of families such as the Jukes and the Kallikaks; the emphasis in the Wood Report (Board of Education and Board of Control, 1929) on a 'social problem group'; the investigations of E. J. Lidbetter in the East End of London (Lidbetter, 1933); Eugenics Society-sponsored surveys of problem families in the late 1940s; and the culture of poverty theory elaborated by Oscar Lewis in the US in the 1960s (Wootton, 1959, pp 51-62; Rutter and Madge, 1976, pp 246-8; Coffield, 1983, pp 11-36; Macnicol, 1987; Welshman, 2006a). Overall, the cycle hypothesis illustrates important continuities in late 19th- and 20th-century thought on poverty. Joseph's language of this period, emphasising the rescue of mothers in inner-city areas, is reminiscent of that of 19th-century evangelical reformers.

Other work has focused on Joseph's own background, and life with his family (Denham and Garnett, 2001a, 2002), or on contemporary policy developments in Britain and the US (Macnicol, 1987). Martin Loney (1983), for example, in his study of the Community Development Programme, has argued of the late 1960s that social work was attractive to the then Labour government because it could ameliorate social problems in a non-punitive fashion, it was cheap, and it involved limited social change. The same climate that facilitated the Seebohm Report (Committee on Local Authority and Allied Personal Social Services, 1968) helped the Community Development Projects (CDPs), along with interest in community work funded by the Gulbenkian Foundation. Moreover, Loney has written that:

> the original assumptions of the CDPs were strongly focused
> on individual rather than social structural failings. The

societal failings which were recognised had to do with
the failure of the social services to direct relevant and
appropriate attention to the deprived. (Loney, 1983, pp
55-6)

The creation of the CDPs further reflected the emergence of Labour
attitudes to delinquency, with the centrality of the family and the idea
that there was an identifiable core of problem families that were both
materially deprived and socially inadequate. These families required
skilled social work intervention. Thus while the establishment of the
CDPs (1969) preceded the cycle speech, the views that underlay them
were similar to those of Joseph, indicative of a Conservative paradigm
of social problems, and of an official consensus on poverty.

This chapter attempts to explain the background to and timing of
the cycle speech by tracing these longer-term continuities. It looks
in particular at, first, Joseph's own family background and approach
to poverty; second, his interest in problem families; third, the broader
policy context of the late 1960s and early 1970s, including debates about
poverty, abortion, and family planning; fourth, the DHSS Preparation
for Parenthood initiative, including a seminar at All Souls College,
Oxford, in April 1973; and, fifth, the influence of debates in the US, that
focused on debates about IQ, the culture of poverty, and the benefits
of early intervention (such as the Head Start programme) as a means
of countering the effects of poverty on human development. Overall,
the cycle speech can be seen to have had more complex origins than
is usually acknowledged.

A cycle of enrichment

As the biography by Andrew Denham and Mark Garnett (2001a) makes
clear, Keith Joseph (1918-94) is a fascinating political figure. As MP
for Leeds North-East (1956-87), Joseph displayed a strong interest in
questions of healthcare and social policy from the 1950s onwards. He
first entered the Cabinet in 1962 under Harold Macmillan, as Minister
of Housing and Local Government, but had been a junior minister
from 1959. As Secretary of State for Social Services, 1970-74, Joseph
played a central role in the background to the 1974 health service
reorganisation. He was a key advocate of monetarism in the mid-1970s,
as well as founding the think tank, the Centre for Policy Studies. In
the 1980s, he served in the Thatcher governments as Secretary of State,
first for Industry, and then Education and Science. Geoffrey Howe,

who knew Joseph from 1965 as a junior spokesperson in the Shadow Cabinet, later recalled:

> Keith was a fascinating man to work with; hugely intelligent (a fellow of All Souls) yet immensely unsure of himself; eager to question everything, including not least his own premises; always thinking aloud, even the unthinkable. To make a long journey with him was like travelling with a foraging squirrel: he was constantly tearing articles out of newspapers, writing notes to himself and stowing them about his person. Problems sometimes arose for him from the need to make order from this whirlwind of ideas, and so to arrive at sustainable executive decisions. (Howe, 1994, p 39)

Joseph's own background, his genuine concern with poverty, the concept of the problem family, and the policy context of the early 1970s all played a part in explaining the timing and content of the speech. In an interview given in November 1973, for example, Joseph admitted his sense of guilt over his privileged upbringing and affluent family background. An only child from a close Jewish family, Joseph was successively a pupil at Harrow School, student at Magdalen College, Oxford, a baronet and alderman of the City of London, a Prize Fellow of All Souls College, Oxford, and a Director of the family Bovis construction firm. As the journalist Terry Coleman observed, it had indeed been a good example of the 'cycle of enrichment, enrichment not only in money, but in all sorts of good things' (Coleman, T., 'Captain of the Second XI', *The Guardian*, 12 November 1973, p 13). Joseph conceded that his concern with poverty, housing, and deprivation had a lot to do with his own life, not only his own childhood, but his family life with his wife and four children. Robin Wendt later recalled:

> I think that Joseph's Jewish background had quite an effect on all this. I believe he came from that element of Judaism which was synonymous with social concern and believing that you ought to be doing good in the world.[1]

Joseph himself later recalled of his early years as an MP that:

> My main motivation was then, as it has been since, the escape of a society and of individuals from poverty ... I had arrived anxious to eliminate poverty ... I simply arrived in

> Parliament full of good-will, with passionate concern about
> poverty. (Denham and Garnett, 2001a, p 55)

Joseph's account is corroborated by evidence from the biography by
Denham and Garnett. As a young boy at school in London, for example,
he had sneaked food out of his house to feed a beggar in Sloane Square,
and during a vacation as a student at Oxford he had stayed with a
miner's family near Rotherham (Denham and Garnett, 2001a, pp 22,
32). His biographers provide numerous examples of Joseph's charity
work and genuine concern with poverty and homeless people, which
included the founding of the Mulberry Housing Trust, membership
of the National Council of Social Service, and support for the CPAG.
They note that Joseph was often motivated by the personal financial
plights of friends and colleagues, and there were numerous unpublicised
acts of charity, both in London and in his constituency, such as when
he bought a musical instrument for a man he had encountered at a
hostel for homeless people (Denham and Garnett, 2001a, p 225). Robin
Wendt recalled Joseph's social concern, arranging on one occasion to go
anonymously to the St Mungo charity on the Embankment (Timmins,
1995, 2001 edn, p 290). Joseph was always aware of the less fortunate,
and the importance of family background (ODNB, 2004).

When it came to the family, a further factor was Joseph's traditional
views over the respective roles of the parents, with the father as the
main breadwinner, and the mother nurturing the children. Denham
and Garnett provide some support for this argument, highlighting his
assumption that children would suffer deprivation unless they were
brought up by a married couple in a committed and stable relationship.
As MP for Leeds North-East, Joseph was keenly interested in the
future of the family, as in all aspects of social policy. In the 1950s, in his
policy work on arts and amenities, for example, Joseph had noted that
young people lacked 'a sense of purpose and of personal responsibility'
(Denham and Garnett, 2001a, p 221). In 1959, he suggested that
work camps, or youth clubs in church halls, might provide a means of
channelling the energies of adolescents. There is no doubt that Joseph
was fond of children. Denham and Garnett record an anecdote of a
friend being surprised when they found him reading *The tale of Peter
Rabbit* to the family's two young children. It was this that led him to
be interested in child development, and its relationship with such
activities as reading, watching television, play, and music (Denham
and Garnett, 2001a, p 142). This was accentuated by Joseph's concern
that his political career might leave him with little time to spend with
his own children. If anything, these concerns were highlighted by the

failure of his own first marriage, from the mid-1960s, although he and his first wife Hellen only finally separated in 1978. On another occasion, Joseph told an interviewer: 'nobody's asking people to be ideal parents, just good enough parents. What terrifies one is the home in which parents don't talk to each other and this occurs across the class barriers' (Cunningham, J., 'The family way', *The Guardian*, 4 June 1973, p 9). Denham and Garnett hint that with his emphasis on parenting, Joseph may himself have been compensating for falling below the standards that he had laid down (Denham and Garnett, 2001a, pp 222-3).

Home-made casualties

While there is no doubt that Joseph's concern with poverty was genuine, Denham and Garnett also record how he tended to distinguish between the deserving and undeserving poor, focused on malingering and benefit fraud, and concentrated on unemployability rather than unemployment. While he was sympathetic to the genteel poor, especially older people and those with disabilities, he regarded the low paid and the unemployed – the non-disabled poor – as problems (Denham and Garnett, 2001a, pp 81, 134, 153, 178, 188, 191, 256, 309). In March 1968, for example, Joseph had argued that the Victorian distinction between the 'worthy' and 'feckless' poor had some relevance to current conditions, and in a speech he referred to the 'undeserving poor' (Denham and Garnett, 2001a, pp 178, 191). Moreover, Joseph's concern with low-income families was of a particular kind, and closely bound up with the concept of the problem family.

John Macnicol (1999) has traced continuities between the problem family concept of the 1950s and the underclass notion of the 1980s, concluding that the emergence of the culture of poverty in the 1960s and the cycle of deprivation in the 1970s suggests a linear development between 1945 and 1995. Macnicol suggests that the debate over the problem family provided a kind of rehearsal for the underclass debates of the 1980s, particularly in respect of the methodological difficulties faced by researchers. However, he also notes that by the 1990s much had changed, most obviously in relation to the labour market, demography, and family formation (Macnicol, 1999). Bob Holman argued earlier that the cycle of deprivation view of poverty was similar to the problem family explanation, in that faulty parenting was perceived as the vehicle that failed to equip the new generation for a competitive society. However, while the problem family concept stressed individual pathology, the cultural deprivation thesis identified a common pattern among a certain group of families (Holman, 1978, p 97).

Either way, the problem family loomed large. In an article in the *Daily Telegraph*, for example, published in March 1966, Joseph, at that time Chief Opposition Spokesperson for Labour, had laid out plans to provide help 'for the really needy'. He argued that not all the poor were old, and not all the old were poor; there were also those whose problems were 'self-inflicted'. Some mothers on low incomes managed admirably, but others, because of the number of children, poor health, or unstable temperament, could not cope, and these became problem families. Joseph wrote that many social problems stemmed from 'low-income families with several children, and from households with self-inflicted wounds' (Joseph, K., 'Help for the really needy', *Daily Telegraph*, 22 March 1966). Some of these homes were close-knit and loving, but where they were not, the children often formed the same kind of household from which they had come, and a cycle repeated itself. He argued that:

> As part of a social policy seeking to reduce misery and to narrow the breeding-grounds of delinquency and crime we would provide more help for those small areas where the evils of bad environment, low earnings and broken or fatherless families in need tend to be concentrated – a policy of positive discrimination. (Joseph, K., 'Help for the really needy', *Daily Telegraph*, 22 March 1966)

These ideas were developed in a pamphlet on new priorities for social security published in October 1966 by Conservative Political Centre. Joseph argued that a competitive society could and should be a compassionate society; indeed unless society was efficient, there would not be the resources for effective compassion. Nevertheless, he included among categories of need problem families, whose poverty was not caused primarily by lack of income, but by difficulties in managing money and in using welfare services. Joseph claimed that problem families had various interrelated difficulties – of temperament, intelligence, money, and health – and while the numbers were small, the difficulties tended to be chronic, to recur in the next generation, and to blight the lives of the children (Joseph, 1966a, p 16). He located problem families within a larger set of groups – deprived children, 'deserted wives', families of alcoholics and prisoners, and those who had experienced broken marriages and homes. What these groups had in common, Joseph suggested, was that their misfortunes were 'to a greater or lesser extent inflicted from within'; they were 'the home-made casualties' (Joseph, 1966a, p 16; Denham and Garnett, 2002, p 195).

These problem groups were characterised by families of low income and low intelligence, with more than the average number of children. A cycle was created and repeated, whereby broken homes and bad parents were reproduced. Joseph argued that broken homes produced juvenile delinquents, writing that 'the children of such households are at risk – and society is at risk because of the damage they may do and because they may create similar feckless households of their own' (Joseph, 1966a, p 17). However, his solutions were more modest. More social workers and home helps should be recruited to provide care in the home, and while money was important, effective social services were also crucial (Joseph, 1966a, p 27). He wrote that:

> If the community can intervene effectively in what is often in itself misery and may also be an incubator of future misery and delinquency, then we would be narrowing the breeding-grounds of crime and unhappiness. (Joseph, 1966a, p 33)

The 1966 pamphlet is recognisably the 1972 cycle speech in embryonic form. Moreover, in response to press criticism of his Edgbaston speech, in October 1974, Joseph inadvertently provided further evidence of the link with the problem family debate. He admitted that from the beginning of 1971 he had been very interested in, and concerned about, problem families. He said: 'I suppose I had regarded myself as a person long associated with concern for problem families, and it seems to me grotesque for people to suggest that my motives in making this speech were improper or sinister' (*The Times*, 21 October 1974, p 1). Joseph said that 'children who do not get any guidance on how to behave from their parents suffer from emotional starvation which can continue from generation to generation' (*The Times*, 21 October 1974, p 3). In a separate letter to *The Times*, Joseph argued that this short section of his speech had been grossly misrepresented, and he had assumed that his concern for problem families and for the cycle of deprivation would have protected him from the sensationalism of his reference to what he regarded as a serious and worrying trend. Moreover, the theme on which he had touched, 'the deeply humane one of seeking ways to reduce the number of problem families, was one to which I had devoted years of thought and work' (*The Times*, 22 October 1974, p 15).

As Denham and Garnett have noted, the cycle speech was not so much a call for open debate as an invitation to researchers to find empirical support for ideas that Joseph held already (Denham and Garnett, 2001a, p 224). In this respect, Joseph's cycle speech can be seen as part of a search for intellectual solutions to moral dilemmas. He was influenced by the problem family literature, such as the Sheffield studies cited in the cycle speech, but was apparently unaware of the important critiques that had been published as early as the mid-1950s (Philp and Timms, 1957). By the late 1960s and early 1970s, the concept had fallen out of favour even with those professional groups that had gained most from endorsing it. This supports Denham and Garnett's point that Joseph was a man of academic enthusiasms, but showed little sign of the scepticism normally associated with the term 'intellectual'. Robin Matthews, who knew Joseph well as a member of the same college, later recalled that:

> In All Souls he was regarded by some as one of the least intelligent Research Fellows, Prize Fellows ever elected. He was not highly regarded intellectually in All Souls, although he was generally well liked.[2]

Overall there seems much evidence to support Denham and Garnett's point that Joseph was still 'a mixture of enthusiasm, compassion, and ignorance on the subject of poverty' (Denham and Garnett, 2001a, p 225).

The broader policy context, 1968-74

If Joseph was influenced by the problem family concept, the broader policy context of 1968-74 was also significant. Although the problem family concept was a key component, other work has suggested that Joseph's thinking on social deprivation, children, and family planning were all interconnected. The compromises inherent in the 1967 legislation concerning abortion and family planning were not accepted as a permanent settlement, and there were demands that the NHS should provide a comprehensive and free family planning service, including facilities for abortion on demand. The birth control campaign was established in 1971 to promote planned parenthood, and soon after his appointment, Joseph was confronted with representations on this issue. In January 1971, the Lane Committee was established to review the 1967 Abortion Act. It has been suggested that Joseph's proposals about abortion and family planning were developed in the context of his thinking about social deprivation. The first office meetings devoted exclusively to family planning were held in the autumn of 1970. A free comprehensive service was ruled out. Instead, Joseph instructed officials to concentrate on a comprehensive domiciliary service for 'problem' groups, with encouragement for sterilisation in the case of 'really bad problem families' (Webster, 1996, pp 425-6).

The CDPs had provided a means of funding these extended family planning services, and, in February 1971, Joseph announced that he was making funds available for the expansion of family planning services in areas of social deprivation, and undertaking a review of family planning services. The departmental review of family planning policy was completed in May 1972, and experiments were conducted in Coalville in Leicestershire, and in Runcorn in Cheshire. Again a free and comprehensive service was ruled out in favour of a limited service designed 'to reduce the number of pregnancies likely to result in children at risk in the sense that their lives would be blighted by poor social conditions which might be passed on to future generations' (Leathard, 1980; Webster, 1996, p 426). The new arrangements for family planning (to require area health authorities to provide free family planning advice, but to apply prescription charges to supplies, except in certain cases that included 'special social need') passed into law as part of the 1973 National Health Service Reorganisation Act.

Correspondence between Joseph and Sir Philip Rogers (1914-90), then Permanent Secretary at the DHSS, confirms the overlaps between developing policies on family planning and the thinking on the cycle of deprivation. In September 1971, for example, Joseph argued that family planning represented a preventive policy for the cycle, and the aim was to reach 'the least accessible elements in the population', since normal departmental policy would not achieve the significant fall in the birth of 'probably-doomed children' that was sought.[3] What he termed the potential benefits to the nation justified a sustained effort. Joseph hoped that, from April 1974, the NHS would extend and reinforce family planning services to reach 'the inadequates, the non-copers'.[4] He was very much in favour of universal and effective domiciliary family planning services, expressing the hope that 'we can choose our path so as to prepare for the ultimate while serving first the households connected with the cycle and the twilight sector between them and the competent of all classes'.[5] He was not concerned about 'regretted pregnancies' as such; these children only became a health or personal social service problem when they were born to families 'so incompetent, indifferent or overwhelmed that they are from birth virtually doomed'.[6] It was this group that was his target. The question was what proportion of births was in that group, and how could the majority of mothers be most effectively reached. However 'irresponsible', people would not be made more responsible with the free supply of contraceptives. He claimed that he was not concerned with population as such, but with 'casual breeding and with unwanted pregnancies', and it was in social classes IV and V that most needed to be done.[7]

The archival sources reveal the continuities in Joseph's thinking with the better-known Edgbaston speech, indicating how his emphasis on 'human stock' was much more than an unfortunate phrase. This eugenic perspective was given full vent in the speech, which was entitled 'The Family and Civilised Values' and given on 20 October 1974. In drafting this, Joseph, then shadow Home Secretary, was influenced by an article in the journal *Poverty*, a CPAG publication (Denham and Garnett, 2001a, pp 268-9). In this article, the social researchers Arthur and Margaret Wynn had examined the question of whether family planning could do more to reduce child poverty. The Wynns had pointed out that the number of children with parents on Supplementary Benefit had doubled since 1959, to a total of 936,000 by 1972. Falls in the birth rate meant that the proportion of children born into poorer families had increased, compared to the numbers born into social classes I, II, and III. Poverty seemed to be both a cause and a consequence of illegitimacy, but so far family planning had not been very effective among women in social classes IV and V. The Wynns concluded by pointing out that there were no cheap solutions to the problems of child poverty. Allowances for one-parent families, increases in family allowances, cheap milk, and free school meals were all essential (Wynn and Wynn, 1974, pp 17-20). But there is also evidence that the speech had been drafted by the political writer and thinker Alfred Sherman (1919-2006), who was associated with the recently established Centre for Policy Studies. Joseph inserted into the speech the sentence 'the balance of our population, our human stock, is threatened'. Sherman deleted it, but Joseph reinstated it (Blake, R., 'Joseph Justified', *Times Literary Supplement*, 22 June 2001, p 29). Similarly, Joseph ignored other warnings about the resonances attached to the phrase 'stock', and the mention of classes IV and V (Martin, D., 'Keith Joseph's speech', *Times Literary Supplement*, 29 June 2001, p 17).

Towards the end of the Edgbaston speech, Joseph focused on the Wynns' parting shot that mothers under the age of 20 might, in future, be the mothers of possibly 35% of all British children. The article in *Poverty* had shown that a high and rising proportion of children were being born to mothers 'least fitted to bring children into the world and to bring them up' (*The Guardian*, 21 October 1974, p 7). They were born to teenage mothers in social classes IV and V, many of whom were unmarried, and some of whom had low intelligence or low educational attainment. Joseph argued that they were producing 'problem children, the future unmarried mothers, delinquents, denizens of our borstals, subnormal educational establishments, prisons, hostels for drifters' (*The Guardian*, 21 October 1974, p 7; *The Times*, 21 October 1974, p 3). These mothers were producing a third of all births, a high proportion of which were a tragedy for the mother, the child, and society. Proposals to extend birth control to these 'classes of people' provoked moral opposition, but if nothing was done, the nation moved 'towards degeneration' (*The Guardian*, 21 October 1974, p 7). Moreover, Joseph claimed that the *Poverty* article had shown that social classes IV and V made far less use of birth control than people in other social classes. In general, research showed that children of fatherless families with adolescent mothers had little chance of satisfying lives.

The effect was immediate – in the words of *The Times*, the speech provoked a 'tinderbox of reaction, most of it hostile'; Joseph's 'brief excursus into eugenics was bound to raise the roof since he introduced into it distinctions of social class' (*The Times*, 21 October 1974, pp 1, 13). *The Guardian* commented that the relationship between the number of births and social class was a 'statisticians' labyrinth', arguing: 'that many poor women would have been helped by a free contraceptive service is undeniable; this makes Sir Keith's refusal, as a Minister, to remove prescription charges for contraceptives all the more inexcusable' (*The Guardian*, 21 October 1974, p 10). The CPAG and Bill Jordan accused Joseph of making scapegoats of low-income families, and of juxtaposing emotive terms to create an atmosphere of moral panic (*The Guardian*, 21 October 1974, pp 8, 11; *The Times*, 21 October 1974, p 3). Even the famous Insight team from *The Sunday Times* set about disproving the figures, arguing that the birth rate was declining so fast, particularly among the working classes, that the prospect was of too few families, rather than too many (*The Sunday Times*, 27 October 1974, p 4).

In response, Joseph argued that it was not an issue of social class:

> It is because the children to whom I was referring are born to unmarried or single-parent teenage households, NOT, NOT, NOT because they are in socio-economic classes 4 and 5, that the children are at such risk of becoming tragedies in themselves and to society. (*The Times*, 22 October 1974, p 15)

As Secretary of State, he had given great encouragement to domiciliary family planning services, the aspect of provision he thought most likely to be helpful to vulnerable households. Overall it seems clear that this strand had always been present in Joseph's thinking, but had been kept in check by his civil servants at the DHSS. Geoffrey Otton has suggested that:

> I think his colours were probably increasingly showing on his eugenic approach to this, which eventually came out ... we had been aware that he had inclinations in that direction but had steered him off. But once he was out on his own as a politician, he went over the top in the Edgbaston speech and really discredited himself, I think, in the eyes of everybody who didn't like this subject anyway.[8]

The damage had been done. Given to promote Joseph's leadership claims, the Edgbaston speech effectively ended his chances of succeeding Edward Heath as leader of the Conservative Party (Denham and Garnett, 2001a, pp 265-71). The issue of family planning was to spill over into the Research Programme. Some of the studies that Joseph cited in the speech, such as the Sheffield problem family studies and the Oliver research in Wiltshire, had discussed the potential of family planning. Thus the debates over family planning had longer-term ramifications, as we shall see in the following chapter.

Preparation for Parenthood

Suzanne MacGregor (1981) has located the cycle of deprivation in terms of two paradigms of poverty. There were commentators who saw poverty as caused either by individual failure or by the special features of geographical areas, regions, or the inner city. Those MacGregor deemed 'selectivists' considered what factors predisposed an individual to behave in ways likely to lead to poverty, and emphasised the values, customs, and attitudes associated with being poor, and the way in which they prevented the children of the poor from moving out of the vicious cycle of deprivation. 'Universalists', on the other hand, rejected the emphasis on individual factors, seeing structural patterns of inequality and justice as basic to deprivation, fostering the conditions, social, economic, and psychological, in which the poor were trapped. MacGregor noted of Joseph that 'his philosophy is one of individual responsibility and he has stressed the need to help individuals to function more adequately within society by better educational and social services for deprived families and better preparation for parenthood' (MacGregor, 1981, p 94).

As Joseph noted in the speech, his emphasis on the cycle was in the more general context of the DHSS initiative 'Preparation for Parenthood'. Joseph had discussed this with Margaret Thatcher, then

Secretary of State for Education and Science, in March 1972. Thatcher herself had been planning a large increase in day nurseries, and Joseph suggested that she should expand playgroups as well; together these might make a significant difference in the worst areas. On her own initiative, Thatcher expressed an interest in making progress on the cycle, through playgroups and by opening up school facilities. The questions were what settings and methods might be most effective, and which professionals might provide services. It was proposed that the process should be started while children were still at school, but that the task should not be left to the schools alone.[9] More broadly, in the autumn of 1972, the DHSS was involved in informal meetings with voluntary and professional organisations to discuss Preparation for Parenthood in the context of the cycle. By March 1973, 14 informal meetings had been held with professional, voluntary, and other organisations.

Following the cycle speech, Geoffrey Otton wrote to other departments, stating that 'the broad problem as we see it is that there appears to be a pattern of transmitted deprivation from parents to children through which problems continue to recur within families despite the improvement of community services'.[10] The aim was to gain a better understanding of the problem, the mechanisms of intergenerational transmission, the numbers caught up in the cycle and at risk of becoming so, and to find ways of developing preventive strategies and of influencing change for the better. In the months following the speech, Joseph made numerous visits to inner-city areas looking for pilot projects for Preparation for Parenthood. In some, he focused on the potential role of institutions. Reflecting on a visit to York, for example, he noted that 'they say the Elizabeth Fry Home for neglectful mothers has been closed. Is not this just the sort of place we need open for "cycle" work?'[11] Other visits, such as one to Handsworth, Birmingham, suggested the usefulness of area initiatives where a range of schemes – playgroups, adventure playgrounds, childminders, family planning, and the involvement of mothers – might enable families to escape the cycle.[12] Nevertheless, there were also signs that on this, as on much else, Joseph was out of step with his civil servants. Joan Cooper commented of the Elizabeth Fry Home proposal that 'we do not want to revive facilities of this kind … in general training problem mothers away from fathers did not work out well'.[13]

On 27 March 1973, in Brighton, Joseph spoke again about the cycle of deprivation, at the Spring Study Seminar of the Association of Directors of Social Services. Here Joseph noted that the statutory and voluntary services worked with children and families at risk, and with 'the problem families, the vagrants, alcoholics and drug addicts, the disturbed, the delinquent and the criminal', observing that 'a deprived childhood lies behind many of these conditions'.[14] A research programme was in the process of being set up but in the meantime people could also be helped through Preparation for Parenthood. The consultations had raised questions about how broadly based the programme should be; at what times in a person's life knowledge should be made available; what methods could be used; and whether existing professionals or a new group should be responsible. Programmes had to be aimed at the 'difficult to reach', and might be through contacts with doctors, midwives, and health visitors. Experimental projects might also be used to test the most promising ways of promoting Preparation for Parenthood. Joseph gave a further account of what was being done in his speech on 27 June 1973, at the annual conference of the Pre-School Playgroups Association, now called the National Association for Maternal and Child Welfare.[15]

One of the main outcomes of the Preparation for Parenthood initiative was a seminar on 'Dimensions of parenthood', held at All Souls College, Oxford, on 10-13 April 1973. Chaired by Joan Cooper, the speakers included Professor Michael Rutter, from the Institute of Psychiatry, University of London; Dr Esther Goody, Lecturer in Social Anthropology at Cambridge University; and Urie Bronfenbrenner, from the US. Other participants included Margaret Edwards and Geoffrey Otton, from the DHSS; Mary Douglas; and Olive Stevenson, then Reader in Applied Social Studies at Oxford University. Professor Robin Matthews, then Drummond Professor of Political Economy at Oxford, whose post was attached to All Souls, was there as Chair of the SSRC. Joseph later wrote that the aim of the seminar had been 'to expose to the rigour of searching academic scrutiny ideas which we had been assembling about the role of parents, the quality of parenting, and the scope for helping people in their parental role' (DHSS, 1974b, p 7). What was interesting was that the All Souls seminar was organised by the DHSS; in the same week, the SSRC organised a conference for researchers interested in transmitted deprivation at the London School of Economics (LSE). The former was thus very much the initiative of Joseph and the DHSS, and was seen as such by most social scientists.

Many of the papers delivered at the seminar were of poor quality, and of limited usefulness. But one in particular stood out. In his paper, Michael Rutter stressed that little was known about the extent of intergenerational cycles of deprivation, and even less about the mechanisms and processes that underlay transmitted deprivation. He said that 'the Secretary of State's speech pointed to the problem, which is real enough, but its extent has yet to be determined by research'

(DHSS, 1974b, p 17). Research into these issues was urgently needed. Moreover, Rutter drew attention to what he regarded as seven myths or misconceptions about child development. These were: that development was largely fixed; that heredity led to familial cycles of deprivation; that the first five years were critical; that bad parenting was due to ignorance; that society knew how to bring up children; that parenting meant mothering; and that intergenerational transmission was familial. Rutter wrote, for example, that while parenting should be one focus in any programme designed to remedy the problems inherent in the concept of a cycle of deprivation, it was necessary to know how far the defects in parenting stemmed from constraints imposed by society, rather than from inadequacies of the parents themselves. He argued that 'in planning for parenthood we must not overlook the very important extrafamilial influences on personal growth and development' (DHSS, 1974b, p 22). As we will see in the next chapter, this was an early summary of the literature review that had been commissioned by the Joint Working Party. In identifying the central issue as being to determine the relative importance of individual characteristics and broader structural factors, Rutter provided an early hint of the debates that were to engulf the Research Programme.

As the rapporteur whose task was to sum up the seminar, Olive Stevenson stressed that participants had found it difficult to establish clear dialogue and mutual confidence, and to disentangle views based on firm empirical evidence from those that reflected unproven personal convictions. She observed that the comments of participants indicated considerable differences of emphasis in the interlocking factors involved in topics as complex as 'cycles of deprivation' and 'dimensions of parenthood'. This was particularly obvious 'in relation to the weight placed on social and economic factors, such as class structure with its effect on material conditions and educational opportunity and psychological factors such as inadequate performance of the maternal role' (DHSS, 1974b, p 106). She had three main concerns. First, that the concentration on Preparation for Parenthood should not divert attention away from the underlying social and economic difficulties of families. There was a fear that the notion of transmitted deprivation, along with plans to improve parenting, could perpetuate a view of parental failure that laid insufficient emphasis on the economic or social stresses that might have had a part in the origin of family difficulties, and which reinforced or exacerbated them. Second, the status of knowledge in terms of what constituted 'bad' or 'good' in family life. Third, anxiety that interventions should take into account the individuality of the people concerned, and their situations. The seminar thus ended with a plea that Preparation for Parenthood should start by asking the parents themselves what they wanted. The wide focus on 'dimensions of parenthood' was both a strength and a weakness (DHSS, 1974b, pp 105-13).

Stevenson's acknowledged difficulties as rapporteur were borne out in her subsequent recollections of the seminar. What she remembered was that Professor A. H. Halsey, then Director of the Department of Social and Administrative Studies at Oxford, and heavily involved in the evaluation of the Educational Priority Areas (EPAs), made no secret of his antipathy to the proceedings of the seminar. Stevenson recalled:

> I was aware of intense discomfort at that seminar [Halsey] not saying anything. Very handsome man, he had a face like a thundercloud and I can't remember anything about what I did about being a rapporteur, except that I was uncomfortable writing it up, I had great difficulty.[16]

Stevenson claimed that those on the Left were furious that a seminar on parenting was held at All Souls, a perceived bastion of privilege, while the determinist focus of the cycle hypothesis was seen as the ultimate condescension to those who had come from a working-class background.

At this stage, the DHSS was still optimistic about the potential usefulness of research, and the Preparation for Parenthood initiative did lead to some research commissioned by the department. In particular, Mia Kellmer Pringle (1920-83), the psychologist who was the first Director of the National Children's Bureau, was asked to summarise what was known about the needs of children. The National Children's Bureau had sponsored the NCDS, and its Director was well known to Joan Cooper at the DHSS, and to the national network of Children's Officers.[17] Moreover, Kellmer Pringle was in some ways a natural choice: Barbara Tizard later wrote that 'although a considerable scholar, with an almost obsessive concern for detail, Mia Pringle was only interested in research that had a direct bearing on a practical problem. She was not only, or perhaps essentially, an academic' (ODNB, 2004). In the event, Kellmer Pringle argued that children had four basic emotional needs that had to be met: the need for love and security; new experiences; praise and recognition; and responsibility. If one of these remained unmet or was inadequately met, development became stunted or distorted, and the cost in the long term was high. What was needed, she argued, was a different attitude to parenthood and childrearing, and the provision of more adequate services for families and children (Kellmer Pringle, 1974, 1980 edn, pp 13-14, 148-61).

The book was influential in certain circles and best-selling, being translated into German, Swedish, and French. Similar work was commissioned by the DHSS from Rhona and Robert Rapoport, then at the Institute of Family and Environmental Studies, London, who noted that Preparation for Parenthood dealt more with what they termed parentcraft than with parenting, and argued that the heavy emphasis on children's developmental needs as the reference point narrowed the broader perspective adopted in the consultations (Rapoport et al, 1977, p 145). The Kellmer Pringle book in particular was very much in the social work mould of the DHSS; it was a world away from some of the publications that would come out of the Research Programme.

What was interesting in some of the subsequent speeches was that Joseph showed signs of some rethinking. In the second cycle speech, for example, in March 1973, Joseph stressed that 'in drawing attention to the intergenerational transmission of deprivation and to Preparation for Parenthood I am in no way suggesting that dealing with these matters is an alternative to tackling the more visible aspects of deprivation: it is additional, not alternative, to what we are doing elsewhere'.[18] The government hoped that research would help to devise additional weapons to use in the attack on deprivation and maladjustment. In the report on Preparation for Parenthood, Joseph again stressed that the debate about the cycle had not distracted the government from its priorities in the areas of low income, unemployment, poor health, and poor housing. He conceded that the term 'cycle' was 'a shorthand one and, as such, imprecise and open to much conceptual questioning' (DHSS, 1974a, pp 5-8). Better knowledge and greater sensitivity to the needs of her children could not on their own help a mother to fulfil her role if she was hindered by isolation, poor housing, and unsympathetic public agencies and staff. He conceded of the All Souls seminar that the exploration of territory which, for the government at least, was unfamiliar 'has been to alert us to the complex issues involved and to warn us against over-simple and under-sensitive reactions to the problems we perceive in families struggling to cope with multiple deprivations' (DHSS, 1974b, p 8). One of the most important points to emerge in the course of the discussions was that 'damage was not irreversible' (DHSS, 1974b, p 8). Joseph wrote in the foreword to the Kellmer Pringle book that:

I know there are some who see the problem simply in terms of alleviating material deprivations – poverty and poor housing. I applaud and share their urgent desire to do this. But I am not shaken from my view that there is another dimension to the problem and that one of the ways of tackling it is likely to be by promoting wider understanding of the emotional needs of children and of the importance from the earliest years of the quality of the relationships between a child and those who are responsible for his care. The two approaches are not mutually exclusive. (Joseph, 1974)

The influence of the US on the cycle of deprivation

So far the cycle speech has been located solely within the domestic policy context. However, earlier writing has also tended to link the cycle with the parallel culture of poverty debates in the US. In any case, this is of broader interest given recent debates about policy transfer (Dolowitz, 2000). Joan Higgins (1978), for example, argued that the poverty programmes of the 1960s and 1970s in the US and Britain were based on various assumptions about the nature of poverty, the characteristics of the poor, and the most effective ways of eradicating social problems. She suggested that those responsible for the EPAs and CDPs adopted the concepts of a culture of poverty and a cycle of deprivation. The notion of a culture of poverty became accepted in Britain as it had in the US, influencing the style of poverty programmes in the 1960s and 1970s, and being eagerly promoted by Conservative politicians, particularly Joseph (Higgins, 1978, p 105). Martin Loney (1983) argued of the CDPs that the premise that problem families were found in particular areas was both a cause and an effect of the individual pathology of the poor, and a neutered culture of poverty theory came to complement traditional casework strategies. Loney wrote that 'the community development objectives of the CDPs followed logically from the basic project assumptions. Community development could act as a catalyst to break up social pathology by revitalising the poor and involving them in constructive plans for improvement' (Loney, 1983, pp 60-8). Similarly, John Macnicol (1987) has related the timing of the cycle speech to the rediscovery of poverty in both Britain and the US, situating it within a combination of reformist social engineering (evident in debates about educational disadvantage) and a more conservative 'social pathology' interpretation that emphasised cultural deprivation. Macnicol claimed that the cycle speech was part of a broader government agenda to push the balance more towards the latter (Macnicol, 1987, p 296).

The culture of poverty theory and cycle of deprivation notion have often been bracketed together. The timing was similar, with Oscar Lewis's theory being most influential only a few years earlier. Higgins (1978) located both within what she termed 'individualistic and culturally determinist theories of poverty'. It was the problem family approach writ large; the analysis accepted uncritically that the causes of poverty came from within the individual, family, or community and not from without. These assumptions led to what she termed a 'doors' rather than a 'floors' approach to solutions, addressed to the victims of poverty rather than to its causes (Higgins, 1978, p 110). In his book *Poverty* (1978), Bob Holman provided a fuller treatment of what he regarded as cultural explanations of poverty. Holman argued that there were strong similarities between the culture of poverty and cycle of deprivation theories, particularly in identifying family behaviour as the vehicle which transmitted poverty. Overall, Holman argued that cultural explanations had been much criticised; the poor had motivations and aspirations common to the rest of society, and there was little evidence of a separate culture; there was much evidence of families breaking out of poverty; and there was little evidence that the solutions proposed by advocates of the cultural approach were effective. Holman concluded that behaviour stemmed not from transmitted family patterns, but from external forces: 'given the capacity of adverse external forces to affect human behaviour, it is hardly surprising if attempts to solve poverty by persuading parents to improve their methods of socialisation or by compensating children for their home experiences have had little effect' (Holman, 1978, p 140).

In the US, the Head Start programme was an important legacy of the 'War on Poverty' in the Kennedy and Johnson administrations. The 1950s and 1960s had witnessed major changes in experts' perceptions of children's intellectual development. Previously they had believed that IQ was fixed at birth and there was little that could be done to alter it; increasingly they argued that a child's IQ was not solely determined biologically, and environment played a part, especially during childhood. Urie Bronfenbrenner, for instance, later located the emergence of early experimental programmes of pre-school education, such as Head Start, in the context of theory and research in the 1950s, which pointed to the beneficial effects of early stimulation in animals and humans (Bronfenbrenner, 1975). An emphasis on the effects of an impoverished childhood spurred efforts to develop pre-school programmes for disadvantaged Americans.

Head Start was established in 1965, under the Office of Economic Opportunity's Community Action Program, with eight-week summer programmes serving around 560,000 children. However, many of these children were taught by parents or neighbours rather than professionally trained teachers, and there were concerns that summer programmes did not provide children with lasting benefits. Subsequently, Head Start was moved from the Office of Economic Opportunity into the new Office of Child Development in the Department of Health, Education, and Welfare. More emphasis was placed on how to improve its effectiveness, and it was increasingly complemented with Follow Through and other experimental demonstration programmes. A related programme was Home Start (1972), which combined home-based and centre-based activities (Silver and Silver, 1991, pp 84-92, 260-9). Overall, its historian concludes that Head Start was a low-cost but low-quality programme, 'rather than saving money, taxpayers paid more in the long run because disadvantaged children were not given a real opportunity to become equal and productive citizens' (Vinovskis, 2005, p 155).

Certainly it was the US that generated the most systematic evidence on the effectiveness of early intervention as a means of countering the effects of poverty on human development. In an important paper, published in 1975 but available to researchers since at least 1972, Bronfenbrenner summarised the evidence. He argued that research studies indicated that children showed substantial gains in IQ and cognitive functioning in the first year of intervention, but that they then began to show a progressive decline, and it was the children from the most deprived economic and social backgrounds that profited least. Families willing to become involved in parent intervention programmes tended to come from the upper levels of the disadvantaged population. Moreover, Bronfenbrenner argued that what was needed was intervention at the 'ecological level', since 'the critical forces of destruction lie neither within the child nor within his family, but in the desperate circumstances in which the family is forced to live' (Bronfenbrenner, 1975, p 594). Thus he argued that intervention programmes should be reoriented, so that approaches were family centred, cut across contexts, had continuity through time, and drew on the child's own parents, family members, adults, school personnel, and other children.

British researchers were certainly interested in what was going on in the US. Both Alan Clarke and his wife Ann were at this time international experts on what was then termed 'mental subnormality'. While their earlier work had been concerned with IQ, later work explored training and work (Clarke and Clarke, 1953; Clarke and

Hermelin, 1955; Clarke and Clarke, 1958, 3rd edn 1974). They engaged with some of the research from the US. Arthur Jensen (1969), at the University of California, Berkeley, for example, had argued that educational interventions had failed to produce lasting effects on children's IQ, indicating that environmental factors were not nearly as important in determining IQ as heredity and genetic factors. He drew on evidence from the US Commission on Civil Rights (1967), that compensatory education programmes had not significantly raised the achievement of participating pupils (Jensen, 1969, pp 2-3). The Clarkes, on the other hand, argued that while Head Start programmes did lead to accelerated development among children, other children subsequently caught up within three or four years, indicating that the programmes were not long enough; there needed to be some reinforcing situation, for example changes in parental attitudes.

Subsequently, they explored 'mild subcultural subnormality', arguing that 40% of this group suffered from a combination of below-average heredity and below-average environment. They again argued of the literature on Head Start that apparently uniform environments did not operate in exactly the same way on individuals; there were strong individual differences. Nevertheless, significant shifts in developmental paths could be achieved, and the means existed for 'upgrading' those sections of the population that were 'under-functioning' for social reasons (Clarke, 1973). In turn, this research was of obvious interest to the civil servants who were grappling with Joseph's insistence on the cycle of deprivation. In November 1971, for example, John Pater had suggested to Geoffrey Otton that papers by Clarke might be relevant to Otton's 'cycle of deprivation activities', in that they appeared to show a possible way of improving the standards of children of inadequate parents, by giving children intensive nursery schooling from the age of four months, and mothers special training in homemaking.[19] One paper by the Clarkes that remains in the DHSS files had asked whether it was possible to distinguish between mental subnormality arising from, first, pathological and constitutional factors; and, second, social factors. However, the removal of the children from inadequate parents or institutions was also paralleled by a shift in intellectual and educational attainments. Thus the Clarkes questioned whether the total removal of children from inadequate parents was possible or desirable.[20]

Apart from this interest in the research literature, discussions between Joseph and the President of the Ford Foundation had led to the latter sponsoring a visit to the US by 13 British specialists, concerned with various aspects of the education and care of young children. The hope was that the British team would be able to benefit from US experience in operating social policies devised to break the cycle of deprivation. The team included Geoffrey Otton, Joan Cooper, and Tessa Blackstone (then a Lecturer at the LSE and Fellow of the Centre for Studies in Social Policy), and the visit took place in October and November 1972. In turn, a visit to Britain was made by a US team in the summer of 1973, to study the workings of the reorganised local authority Social Services Departments. The British team focused on early intervention in the education and care of young children from poor families, visiting Head Start programmes and other initiatives in Atlanta, Chicago, Houston, New York, Portland, San Francisco, and Washington. Nevertheless, influenced in part by Bronfenbrenner's summary of the evaluation literature, Blackstone's report was hesitant about the possible role of pre-school education and care in breaking the cycle of deprivation. In fact the report expressed doubts about giving the concept of the cycle too prominent a place in explanations of the persistence of poverty and disadvantage, or in remedial or preventive policies. Poverty was seen as deriving more from the circumstances in which individuals found themselves, than from individual traits or behavioural deficiencies. Blackstone wrote that 'the concept of the cycle of deprivation tends to emphasise behavioural pathology, the nature of poor people, rather than economic and social factors, or the nature of poverty itself' (Blackstone, 1973, pp 62-3).

In many ways it was not Oscar Lewis but Urie Bronfenbrenner who supplied the most direct link between developments in the US and the cycle speech. Bronfenbrenner had been involved in the setting up of Head Start, having testified before the House of Representatives Education and Labor Committee's Ad Hoc Subcommittee on the Poverty War Program in 1964, and having been a member of the Head Start Planning Committee and Early Childhood Development Task Force (Zigler and Valentine, 1979, pp 77-86; Vinovskis, 2005, pp 45, 75, 105, 110). His research comparing parental involvement in England and the US had been mentioned in the cycle speech, and he spoke at the All Souls seminar. Summarising his earlier paper (Bronfenbrenner, 1975) on evaluations of Head Start, he suggested that it was the extent and seriousness of impairment of intellectual function, especially among children from low-income families, that had led to early intervention programmes in the US. He claimed that the success of intervention efforts was positively correlated with the degree to which parents were accorded high status and actively involved in the programme. When primary responsibility for the child's development was assumed by professionals, and the parent relegated to a secondary role, the intervention was less effective, particularly in terms of its long-term effects. Nevertheless, Bronfenbrenner again argued that the powerful forces that inhibited and warped the development of children lay neither within children nor their families but 'in the larger social context in which the family lives' (DHSS, 1974b, p 99).

Earlier work has often pointed to the similarities between the culture of poverty and cycle of deprivation formulations. These links are if anything strengthened when the Head Start programme is examined more closely. Even so, the US debates focused more on IQ, and Head Start had a limited effect on social policy in Britain in the early 1970s. In this respect it points not to the success but to the failure of policy transfer (Dolowitz, 2000). Several explanations can be offered. First, many British social scientists were naturally sceptical about US models, and particularly wary of the influence of the 'culture of poverty' on the 'War on Poverty'.[21] Second, as Bronfenbrenner's work demonstrated, early evaluations of Head Start were critical; the greatest gains were in the first year, and the children from the most disadvantaged backgrounds benefited least. Third, while they saw the benefits of Head Start as a programme for the poor, British observers were sceptical of the coverage and structure of provision, and of the quality of the programmes, arguing that any programmes had to be comprehensive and involve parents, and include provision for monitoring and evaluation. Fourth, and perhaps most importantly, there was not the political will in this period to make substantial investment in programmes for pre-school children. This area had traditionally been the responsibility of the voluntary sector, and up to March 1974 the Conservative government was happy to continue to delegate responsibility. The Labour government elected in March 1974 was more interested in structural solutions to poverty, but its focus was on inequalities among adults, rather than the welfare of children under five. It would only be with the election of the New Labour government in May 1997, and the influence of longitudinal data, that a sustained effort would be made to focus on pre-school children.

Conclusion

It is important to locate the cycle speech in the context of a pathological emphasis on individuals and the family that had been a theme in debates about poverty over at least the previous 100 years. Among these connections are the emphasis on intergenerational continuities; anxiety about the burden placed on welfare agencies; the eugenic concern with the quality of the population, and with family planning; the preference for limited remedies such as better parenting and social workers; and with the mention of poverty, the way that behavioural interpretations were blended with an acknowledgement of the significance of structural factors. The clearly eugenic tone to Joseph's views on problem families shows how his foray can be placed in the larger context of thought about poverty. Research into the cycle of deprivation hypothesis thus opens up bigger questions about the idea of poverty in the late 19th and 20th centuries.

Nevertheless, aside from these longer-term antecedents, the cycle speech had more immediate policy origins. First, because of his awareness of his relatively privileged upbringing, Joseph had a genuine interest in and concern with family background, homelessness, and poverty. Second, through the 1950s and 1960s, he was increasingly influenced by the concept of the problem family, particularly since it tended to emphasise behavioural rather than structural factors in the causation of poverty and deprivation, and underscored his focus on parenthood. Third, the wider context was provided by the policy context of the early 1970s, with debates about deprivation in inner-city areas, and the potential contribution of family planning, where Joseph's eugenic concern with population and births in social classes IV and V was self-evident. Fourth, there was the Preparation for Parenthood initiative at the DHSS, which illustrated how its concern was primarily with parenting, rather than poverty. Fifth, there was the influence of the US, partly through the culture of poverty theory, but also more specifically through the interest shown in Head Start, and the direct personal link supplied by Bronfenbrenner. As has been noted, the DHSS had commissioned research from Mia Kellmer Pringle, and some of the issues raised in seminars and elsewhere provided early hints of the debates that would engulf the Research Programme. It is to the establishment of the DHSS–SSRC Joint Working Party, and to the Transmitted Deprivation Research Programme, that we now turn.

Notes

[1] Interview between the author and Robin Wendt, Chester, 22 May 2006.

[2] Interview between the author and Robin Matthews, Cambridge, 25 May 2006.

[3] NA BN 13/163: K. Joseph to P. Rogers, 16 September 1971.

[4] NA BN 13/229: K. Joseph to P. Rogers, 13 January 1972.

[5] NA BN 13/229: memo by K. Joseph, 21 March 1972.

[6] NA BN 13/229: memo by K. Joseph, 27 April 1972.

[7] NA BN 13/230: memo by K. Joseph, 17 February 1973.

[8] Interview between the author and Geoffrey Otton, Bromley, Kent, 4 May 2006.

[9] NA BN 13/188: R. G. Wendt to N. Jordan-Moss, 22 March 1972. See also the correspondence in NA ED 207/100, October 1971 to August 1972.

[10] NA MH 152/72: G. J. Otton to P. Grant, 13 July 1972.

[11] NA MH 152/89: minute by K. Joseph, 5 September 1972.

[12] NA MH 152/89: K. Joseph to G. Otton, 11 September 1972.

[13] NA MH 152/89: J. Cooper to R. R. G. Watts, 14 September 1972.

[14] Harriett Wilson papers, 'Secretary of State's speech at the Spring Study Seminar on the Cycle of Deprivation of the Association of Directors of Social Services, Brighton, 27 March 1973', p 2. This was published as Joseph, K. (1973) 'The cycle of deprivation', *Community Schools Gazette*, vol 67, no 2, pp 61-72.

[15] Harriett Wilson papers, 'Cycle of deprivation and the importance of parenthood: Sir Keith Joseph speaks to the National Association for Maternal and Child Welfare', 27 June 1973.

[16] Interview between the author and Olive Stevenson, Middleton Cheney, Oxfordshire, 20 July 2006.

[17] Interview between the author and Geoffrey Otton, Bromley, Kent, 4 May 2006.

[18] Harriett Wilson papers, 'Secretary of State's speech at the Spring Study Seminar on the Cycle of Deprivation of the Association of Directors of Social Services, Brighton, 27 March 1973', p 15.

[19] NA MH 152/72: J. D. Cooper to G. Otton, 22 November 1971.

[20] NA MH 152/72: A. M. Clarke and A. D. B. Clarke, 'What are the problems? An evaluation of recent research relating to theory and practice' (nd), pp 1-24; interview between the author and Alan Clarke, London, 24 May 2006.

[21] Interview between the author and Tessa Blackstone, London, 6 July 2006.

Part Two
The Transmitted Deprivation
Research Programme

Part Two of the book explores the DHSS–SSRC Transmitted Deprivation Research Programme. Chapter Three traces the early discussions between the DHSS and the SSRC; the conceptual difficulties faced by the Joint Working Party; the seminar 'Approaches to research on transmitted deprivation'; the Rutter and Madge literature review; the background to the launch of the Programme; and the attitude of the Labour government. Chapter Four turns to early attempts to commission research; the stance of the DHSS; the applications that were received; research projects in progress; and the perspective offered by the Royal Commission on the Distribution of Income and Wealth (RCDIW). Chapter Five looks at the final years of the Programme; attempts at evaluation; the attitude of the DHSS; efforts to compare projects and the drafting of the final report; and the way that the results of the Research Programme were received. Chapter Six then turns to the broader outlook of social scientists on the Research Programme, exploring this through the work of Harriett Wilson, Adrian Sinfield, and Peter Townsend.

THREE

Conceptual difficulties: setting up the Research Programme

Introduction

Whereas Part One of the book was concerned with Joseph and the cycle speech, Part Two explores the origins and direction of the Transmitted Deprivation Research Programme. One of the problems with the existing secondary literature is that very little is known about the period between the cycle speech (June 1972) and the launch of the Research Programme (May 1974). In his useful (1983a) article, Richard Berthoud, for example, moves quickly from the content of the speech itself, to the setting up of the Joint Working Party. He acknowledges the importance and impact of the literature review by Michael Rutter and Nicola Madge (1976). Nevertheless, his focus is on the Joint Working Party's First Report (August 1974). Berthoud argues, for instance, that this failed to mention what the issue was; the focus was on 'intergenerational continuities', but while the Report acknowledged that the term 'deprivation' was ambiguous and controversial, it assumed that everybody knew what it meant. Thus while the Report placed less emphasis on personal inadequacy, it allowed economic disadvantage, 'social handicap' n, moral deviance, and psychiatric difficulties to be covered by the same term, implying that they were various symptoms of a common condition. While the aim of the Research Programme was to answer a question of detail (intergenerational continuities), it failed to identify the fundamental question of the relationship between individual behaviour and the power of social institutions. Berthoud writes that 'by failing to define deprivation, the Working Party allowed researchers working on the Programme to interpret it as they liked, but also permitted a strong assumption in favour of the equation of poverty with personal inadequacy' (Berthoud, 1983a, p 156).

How the Joint Working Party arrived at this point is the subject of this chapter. It surveys the setting up of the Research Programme, from the first discussions between the DHSS and SSRC in the summer of 1971, to the publication of the First Report by the Joint Working Party in August 1974. It explores the informal discussions between the DHSS and SSRC that took place in advance of the cycle speech, the first formal meetings of the Joint Working Party, and the composition of its membership. The chapter traces the conceptual difficulties encountered by the members of the Joint Working Party, in attempting to define 'deprivation', reflected in an important early paper 'Approaches to research on transmitted deprivation', and a conference held at the LSE on 15 April 1973. It looks at the commissioning of the literature review, from Michael Rutter and Nicola Madge, and at its impact, and at the formal launch of the Research Programme in May 1974. The final section of the chapter examines the difference that the election of the Labour government, in March 1974, made to the Research Programme, and to discussions between its social policy advisor, Brian Abel-Smith, and Barbara Castle, as Secretary of State for Social Services. The argument of the chapter is that there were discussions between the DHSS and SSRC about research on transmitted deprivation prior to the cycle speech, and that these, along with the conceptual difficulties indicated in the 'Approaches' paper, help to explain how the Joint Working Party arrived at the stance that it adopted in its First Report. More generally, these debates were to have an extremely important bearing on the direction subsequently taken by the Research Programme, as were changes in the broader political context, where the evaporation of ministerial support from 1974 explained the approach subsequently adopted by the DHSS.

Early discussions

As we saw in Part One, very soon after his arrival at the DHSS in June 1970, Joseph had become messianic about the family and deprivation, and spurred on by him, a small team of civil servants began to produce working papers. Recognising that the issues were complex and the research likely to be long term in nature, advice was also taken from the SSRC as to whether the problem of the cycle of deprivation could in fact be researched. For instance, Joseph approached the political economist Andrew Shonfield (1917-81), Chair since 1969 of the SSRC, and Director of the Royal Institute of International Affairs. Son of Rabbi Victor Schonfeld, Shonfield had been a student with Joseph at Magdalen College, Oxford, in the 1930s. In July 1971, for example, Shonfield thanked Joseph for the opportunity to discuss the problems of children from 'blighted and deprived backgrounds'.[1] He agreed that the SSRC ought to be able to help the thinking of those who were engaged in the task of providing some practical policy solutions. But while Joseph knew Shonfield personally, and his approach to social scientists was in line with his academic response to policy issues, his involvement with the SSRC was in some ways surprising (Denham and Garnett, 2002, p 196). In 1975, Shonfield acknowledged that Joseph had been 'personally very sympathetic to the social science approach to the welfare problems that have always exercised him deeply' (Shonfield, 1975, p7) and, as Secretary of State for Social Services, an ally and supporter of the SSRC. However, Shonfield also revealed that as a shadow minister, Joseph had been suspicious about the membership of the SSRC, complaining that its Council and committees 'were packed with people committed to the Left in British politics' (Shonfield, 1975, p 7; *The Times*, 19 November 1975, p 15; 21 November 1975, p 6).

If Joseph's approach to the SSRC was complex, temporarily suspending his instinctive suspicion of social scientists in the interests of the cycle, the involvement of the SSRC in the Research Programme also seems surprising. The SSRC itself had been formed in 1965 following the report of the Heyworth Committee (DES, 1965), to fill the buffer role between politicians and social investigators. One reason why it may have been more compliant than normally was due to *A framework for government research and development* (1971) produced by the public servant and zoologist Lord Rothschild (1910-90), then Director-General of the Central Policy Review Staff. Although the SSRC was explicitly excluded from the Rothschild Report, this recommended that applied research and development commissioned by the government should be controlled in accordance with a 'customer–contractor' principle (*A framework for government research and development*, 1971, pp 1, 9, paras 4, 22, table 3). In 1971-72, social science accounted for only £2.2 million of net research council expenditure, of a total of some £109 million. But it has been suggested that it was because of the Rothschild Report that the SSRC 'leapt in where lesser angels might have feared to tread' (*Times Educational Supplement*, 10 May 1974; SSRC, 1972, pp 2-6).[2] The SSRC was well aware that the social sciences were expected to produce useful results, and it took on the Research Programme partly for reasons connected with the politics of the research council system (Robinson, 1975, p 11; Shonfield, 1975, p 6; Young, 1975, p 5).

Nevertheless, what is clear is that the cycle of deprivation was very much Joseph's idea, and the SSRC would not have taken it on without him. The concept came from the Secretary of State, in the Rothschild parlance he was the 'customer'. Moreover, the SSRC remained uneasy about its involvement – the Research Programme was not central in the policy discussions of its Council, and it effectively hived off the project to a committee, the Joint Working Party. Raymond Illsley, then Professor of Sociology at the University of Aberdeen and Director of its Medical Research Council (MRC) Medical Sociology Unit, later recalled that since members of Council or of Council committees were not involved in the earlier discussions:

> it was news to us, people like me, when it was announced that we were going to have a Programme on Transmitted Deprivation, it came as a blow ... I didn't even know there was a Joint Working Party. It was one of those things which were kept unnecessarily secret.[3]

Certainly most of the key players in the Joint Working Party (such as Peter Willmott and Michael Rutter) were not members of Council. Moreover, as we shall see shortly, those who were more central to the SSRC – such as Illsley – were to be very critical of the Joint Working Party's early papers. The committee structure that had been established under its first Chair, Michael Young, meant that the SSRC was tied more strongly than the other research councils to disciplinary divisions (Matthews, 1975, p 9; Young, 1975, pp 4-5). It thought that major projects should originate from subject disciplines or subdisciplines, and it was not keen on taking on projects that had different origins. Finally, it is important to note that the SSRC was not a research institute; it did not have a scientific staff, except for administrative purposes. The most significant point is that the project did not originate with the SSRC, and most of its members were not very interested in it.[4]

These discussions between the DHSS and SSRC continued in the summer and autumn of 1971, revealing that the former was primarily interested in practical issues such as the causes of deprivation, and intergenerational patterns. Joseph proposed setting up a discussion group of academics that might advise on the potential of long-term research, and Shonfield met again with the DHSS in October. Within the DHSS, it was agreed that the SSRC would register the department's research needs in relation to social welfare, and this would help it to look more strategically at long-term problems.[5] Alice Sheridan, Deputy Director of the Social Work Services Division, argued, for example, that Shonfield might bring together a group of social scientists to help with problems in the personal social services. Her suggestion was that the DHSS would state the problems, the group would refine them, and would offer them to appropriate researchers for short-term testing or preparatory work. In terms of the DHSS preoccupation with deprivation at that time, there was a perceived need to define and measure those factors that placed individuals or families at long-term risk extending beyond one generation. There was concern about the nature and scale of interrelated financial, social, emotional, and genetic

—

factors, and the extent to which the methods and services needed to counteract them could in fact be identified.[6] However, DHSS civil servants were sceptical. Sheridan herself suggested that closer relationships were of limited usefulness, and the experience of the US had been one of prolonged tensions between academics and policy makers. She noted that 'no matter what we do we will be left with the need for people to take decisions and to take them in the light of imperfect knowledge'.[7]

By early 1972, therefore, the SSRC and DHSS had had preliminary discussions about research into 'the cycle of transmitted social deprivation', and the latter had drafted the papers by Joan Cooper and Geoffrey Otton that were discussed in Chapter One. The SSRC had told the DHSS that it would like to bring together, on an informal basis, a small group of social scientists to discuss the question, since there was a possibility that the DHSS might be willing to place a contract with the SSRC to undertake research in this field. In February 1972, therefore, the SSRC wrote to those who might take part in a meeting with the DHSS: Michael Rutter, who had spoken at the All Souls seminar; the sociologist Professor Peter Willmott (1923-2000), of the Institute of Community Studies; Tony Atkinson, then Professor of Economics at the University of Essex; and Professor David Donnison, then Director of the Centre for Environmental Studies.[8]

Apart from Donnison, who was later to become Chair of the Supplementary Benefits Commission (1975-80), the other three were to play a major part in what became the Joint Working Party. Rutter would some months later publish his *Maternal deprivation reassessed*, even though this first edition did not discuss possible intergenerational cycles of disadvantage (Rutter, 1972, 2nd edn 1981). Willmott was perhaps best known as co-author of the classic *Family and kinship in East London* (Young and Willmott, 1957). Atkinson's first book had been concerned with the adequacy of social security provision for low-income families, and possible reforms to the social security system. By the early 1970s, he had become particularly interested in wealth, its advantages, accumulation, and distribution (Atkinson, 1969, 1972). Thus Rutter, Willmott, and Atkinson represented the main disciplines seen as relevant to the cycle of deprivation – psychiatry, sociology, and economics.

The first formal meeting of the SSRC and DHSS representatives was on 29 March 1972. The SSRC was represented by Robin Matthews, who had recently taken over from Andrew Shonfield as Chair of the SSRC, David Donnison, Michael Rutter, Jeremy Mitchell, and Sy Yasin. The DHSS was represented by Norman Jordan-Moss, Joan Cooper, and

Alice Sheridan. Jordan-Moss said that the DHSS had been trying to frame an approach towards deprivation and identifying 'at-risk' groups. Joseph had taken the view that deprivation appeared to be cyclically transmitted across generations, and wondered whether government and local authorities might be in a position to intervene. The DHSS was now approaching the SSRC to see whether this was a researchable problem, seeing the SSRC as its guide for longer-term research. Initial questions and topics included whether there was a transmission process and how it operated among the deprived; whether the various types of malfunctioning could be considered manifestations of the same phenomenon; what transmission mechanisms might be at work, and when these occurred; the role of the school and peer group; and the possible critical points for intervention. When Matthews commented that what was needed was a strategy rather than a list of proposals, the DHSS replied that it was talking about a programme of research that might develop into a strategy. It was agreed that the next stage was to set up a joint committee 'to explore the possibility of designing a research programme into the cycle of transmitted deprivation and to advise the DHSS and SSRC how such a programme could be implemented'.[9]

It was around this point that Alan and Ann Clarke were approached for their advice on whether this was a researchable idea. As we saw in the previous chapter, they were obvious contacts given their interest in IQ and the influence of the Head Start programme in the US on the development of pre-school children. Alan Clarke responded with a rather bad-tempered paper to the effect that it was a foolish question, much was known already, it was researchable, but the interesting question was whether one could determine the escape rate, and enumerate the factors that led to individual or group escapes from the cycle.[10] At this stage, then, Clarke had no doubt that the cycle hypothesis was researchable, and this was communicated to the DHSS and SSRC.

At its next meeting, therefore, the SSRC welcomed the approach from the DHSS and agreed that they should work together to set up a Joint Working Party on the cycle of deprivation with the terms of reference agreed at the March meeting. The SSRC members were Tony Atkinson, Michael Rutter, and Peter Willmott, along with Maurice Freedman from the Institute of Social Anthropology at the University of Oxford, and Roy Parker from the Department of Social Administration at the University of Bristol. Robin Matthews later recalled: 'I think Mike Rutter, he was a very important figure in all this, he was the expert whereas the rest of us were amateurs'.[11] The DHSS members were Joan Cooper and Geoffrey Otton, along with

John Cornish from the Central Planning Research Division. The Co-Secretaries of the Joint Working Party were R. R. G. Watts (who had helped to draft the cycle speech) for the DHSS, and Sy Yasin for the SSRC. Ann Stevenson from the SSRC was to take the minutes. It was agreed that Robin Matthews, Jeremy Mitchell (SSRC), and Norman Jordan-Moss (DHSS) would attend the first meeting of the Working Party, and thereafter as required.[12] In fact, Matthews had relatively little to do with the Research Programme once it had been established. He later recalled it as being a relatively small part of his work as Chair of the SSRC: 'I was interested in the early stages and once it got under way I felt right, well I can think about something else now'.[13]

Conceptual difficulties

By May 1972, therefore, the SSRC had agreed to help the DHSS research the cycle of deprivation, and the SSRC had also commented on a draft of the cycle speech.[14] Following the speech, the Joint Working Party was convened and held its first meeting on 19 July, the same day as the official publication of the Rothschild Report on R&D. The terms of reference of the Joint Working Party had been amended slightly to read: 'to explore the possibility of designing a research programme into the cycle of transmitted deprivation and to advise the DHSS and the SSRC how such a programme could be implemented'.[15] The SSRC representatives were confirmed as comprising Tony Atkinson, Maurice Freedman, Roy Parker, Michael Rutter, and Peter Willmott. The Joint Working Party was chaired by Robin Matthews as Chair of the SSRC. The SSRC members thus comprised specialists in anthropology, economics, psychiatry, social administration, and sociology. There were seven DHSS representatives on the Joint Working Party, including two each from the Local Authorities Social Services Division, the Social Work Services Division, and the Research Management Division. Key members included Joan Cooper and Geoffrey Otton. Cooper was to play an active role on the Joint Working Party until her retirement in 1976. Other prominent DHSS members were Alice Sheridan (serving on the Working Party 1972-82); and Margaret Edwards, Principal in the Local Authorities Social Services Division. Richard Berthoud has argued that the membership of the Joint Working Party was important – it demonstrated that whereas the SSRC regarded the 'problem' as one taking in all the social sciences, the DHSS assumed it was one of individuals, the responsibility of the personal social services (Berthoud, 1983a, p 155). What was most noticeable was that there were no representatives from the other divisions of the DHSS, including those concerned with income maintenance and social security.

The main items for discussion at the first meeting of the Joint Working Party were the terms of reference, clarifying its task, initial decisions on the direction of work, and commissioning a literature review. Differences between the members were apparent in the early working papers. One, by Sy Yasin, of the SSRC, defined the population of interest as being 'those individuals, families or groups who for long periods of time constitute a problem to Society in that they require support and attention from the State'.[16] This was very much an administrative definition, familiar from earlier research into the social problem group, and little more than a statistical artefact. Yasin claimed it was easier to identify those who were the recipients of government aid and concern because they were in extremely dire circumstances, than those who were vulnerable to becoming grossly deprived. He argued that the justification for offering a definition along these lines was its applicability to government policy. He wrote that 'Government's concern with the cycle of transmitted deprivation stems from the hypothesis that the cycle produces a population who ultimately become a financial burden to the State'.[17] However, in discussion it was suggested that this should also include those who came to be a problem, and it was amended to read 'attention or support from the State'.[18] Moreover, the government's definition of 'problem persons' changed through time, and 'transmitted deprivation' might or might not explain this population. The focus of interest lay in the intergenerational transmission of 'problem' individuals and groups; it was not possible to investigate all types of deprivation. Even this was a multiple problem with interacting and overlapping elements. Thus other research sponsored by the DHSS might be relevant, especially on the dynamics of family poverty.

Discussion papers prepared by Joint Working Party members (Atkinson, Freedman, Parker, Rutter, and Willmott) for the second meeting held in October 1972 both reflected their disciplinary backgrounds and indicated important problems. The anthropologist Maurice Freedman, for example, suggested that the research should deal with the communities or groups within which problem families were found; they were not independent of the social environment. Anthropologists took kinship as the chief mechanism for the transmission of culture across generations. But the social anthropologist was unlikely to make any progress in studying a problem of this sort unless he, first, adjusted the concepts in which the problem was phrased to those of the people who were to be studied, and, second, looked at ideas and behaviour within the broader context. Freedman therefore warned that the Research Programme would need to be funded for years, rather than months.[19]

As a sociologist, Peter Willmott conceded that biological and psychological processes were obviously important to transmitted deprivation, but his working paper was concerned with social factors, the institutional and the cultural. Willmott wrote: 'the focus is on poverty and the poor, that is, upon the kinds of deprivation associated with low incomes rather than, for example, behavioural problems that are reproduced generation after generation among people whose lives are otherwise comfortable'.[20] Inequality tended to be cumulative, since families were often disadvantaged in several respects, and the correlation between different types of deprivation was high. There was a process of multiple or reinforcing deprivation affecting some low-skill, low-income families, and this gave rise to a family and community setting in which the children started life with considerable handicaps and limited life chances. Thus multiple deprivation and transmission were so strongly interconnected that it would be sensible to study both at the same time. In other words, it would be useful to study both the dynamics of poverty, and the processes of transmitted deprivation, through small-scale research with families. Willmott suggested that the culture of poverty theory was useful although flawed, since it suggested that cumulative inequality was culturally reinforced over the generations. Small-scale studies of families might tease out the relative influence of institutional constraints, subcultural patterns of adaptation, and personal characteristics such as intelligence.

Michael Rutter, on the other hand, whose background was psychiatry, wrote that the concept of the cycle implied that the process was due to some environmental loss, which led to a failure in development or in functioning, which in turn tended to produce a deficient environment for the next generation. However, this implication was too restrictive since not enough was known about the process. The failure in functioning could be due to the loss of some crucial environmental influence, but, equally, it could be due to a lack rather than a loss, a distortion rather than a deficiency, or even an excess rather than a deficit. In short, it should be recognised that it was premature to restrict the possible environmental influences to only one type. Rutter wrote that the cycle concept implied an environmental effect, but this hypothesis should be tested rather than assumed. The question of cause was not the sterile one of the extent to which problems were genetically or environmentally determined, but the extent to which transmission across generations (rather than the variance within a generation) was genetically or environmentally determined, with different sorts of environmental and genetic circumstances. The focus should be on family problems, but the research should also look at school and community influences, and at subcultures. Thus he argued that the problem of the cycle of deprivation 'constitutes not one, but many research questions', and he agreed with Freedman that it would be necessary to think in terms of programmes of research, some extending over several years.[21]

Tony Atkinson wrote that there was still uncertainty about the direction of the Research Programme and, as an economist, he noted that economic factors did not appear to be central to it. In terms of causal links, there was a desire to distinguish between factors internal to the family and those external; in reality the truth was somewhere between these extremes. Nevertheless, it was crucial for policy purposes to form some idea of the relative importance of the two factors, to guide attempts at intervention. The economic factors were likely to fall mainly into the category of 'external', and one possible area of research was the extent to which economic factors were correlated with degrees of risk. This could help indicate the intergenerational factors that could be analysed, and define the subgroup of the population potentially at risk. Overall, research was needed into the transmission of poverty across the generations, the role of economic factors, and the family's relationship to the external environment.[22]

With his background in social administration, Roy Parker argued that the issue was complex and vulnerable to the subconscious infiltration of value assumptions; it was important that the questions were clear and precise. Psychological terminology was mixed up with economic and sociological formulations, and while the varieties of deprivation often overlapped, unless the relevant conceptual frameworks were kept reasonably distinct, there was a danger of confusion. For example, people might be led to assume that if problems of emotional or educational deprivation were overcome for children in one generation, the problems of low wages or poor housing would be solved in the next. Above all, Parker felt that the central concepts of cycle, transmission, and deprivation were all too vague. He was concerned about what might be done as a result of research on transmitted deprivation, and it was because of this that he was particularly anxious about the planning stage. Parker noted that 'much of what we take out at the end, will, inevitably, reflect what we put in at the beginning'.[23] With hindsight, this turns out to have been a particularly perceptive comment on the Research Programme as a whole.

These initial meetings of the Joint Working Party were fairly informal, and were held in a small *pied-à-terre* that Robin Matthews then owned in London, in Tavistock Square. Participants recalled them as friendly and constructive, and the Joint Working Party as a harmonious group.[24] Tony Atkinson, for example, later recalled that:

> I think there was quite a lot of sense that this was intellectually interesting and the cross-disciplinary aspect was both challenging and again something I think people engaged with … I don't think there was any great sense that this was an urgent issue that we had to report on quickly, so it wasn't like a Royal Commission or a Committee of Enquiry or anything of that sort.[25]

Although the Research Programme was later to fragment, as academics from different disciplines interpreted its central themes in their own way, at this stage the members of the Joint Working Party viewed it as a genuine attempt to make sense of the questions, and to see what research might be conducted.

This required ongoing discussion about how best to define the population to be researched. Originally defined as 'those individuals, families, or groups who for long periods of time constitute a problem or who may come to be a problem to society in that they require attention or support from the State', the SSRC suggested instead 'members of families or groups who display problems of deprivation: economic, social, physical or mental, through succeeding generations and who, because of these problems require attention or support from the State for long periods of time'.[26] Again it was clear that the main interest of the DHSS was in practical policy issues. It noted that 'the interest of the Department must lie and concentrate on the practical aspects and its concern with the more esoteric aspects of the social sciences must at present be limited'.[27]

In trying to summarise these early working papers, Robin Matthews noted of the debate about definitions that 'our aim is to study the extent, mode, and remedies for inter-generational transmission of certain attributes regarded as socially pathological, and this is probably a sufficient guide-line at the present stage'.[28] The use of the terms 'deprived' and 'deprivation' were both descriptive and a hypothesis. Moreover, Matthews observed that whereas Willmott regarded poverty as the key area for research, Atkinson saw it as something that might be correlated with the attributes that were to be investigated. There was a separate DHSS research programme on poverty, but clearly it could not be regarded as outside the remit of the Working Party altogether. At the second meeting of the Working Party, in October 1972, it was noted that there were very different approaches to the problem arising from the different disciplinary backgrounds of its members; the use of the term 'deprivation' could have been more precise; the study of deprivation should not be confined to intergenerational transmission; and research on poverty was not its primary objective. Depending on the viewpoint of the observer, the conceptual issues could be seen variously as clear–cut, complicated, or deep–seated. It was important to recognise that some of the research that would be recommended for support would be essentially speculative.[29]

Attributes versus burdens

These conceptual difficulties were reflected in an important early paper 'Approaches to research on transmitted deprivation' (1972). This noted the complexity of the concept of the cycle of deprivation, but argued that what were termed 'attributes' had to be identified in terms of individuals; then the mechanisms leading to the transmission of the attributes in individuals over succeeding generations had to be determined. Attributes included low economic status, low occupational skill, job instability, educational backwardness, emotional or behavioural characteristics, and defects in interpersonal relationships. The paper argued that any administrative category involved the presence of two features – the attribute, and the attribute coming to official notice. It also tried to classify possible areas in which mechanisms might operate. The tone was optimistic. While the issues were complex and poorly understood, it should be possible to carry out research to provide partial answers to some of the questions that underlay the concept. These answers could have direct policy implications, and indicate which kinds of interventions were likely to be effective.[30]

Thus the third meeting of the Working Party, in December 1972, noted the difficulties in conceptualising the problem in research terms in the absence of any agreed underlying theory; it recommended that the word 'deprivation' should be avoided; and it warned that it was important not to predetermine which set of variables was causal. Four types of 'deprivation' or trouble were identified: deviance from norms, impairment, nuisance to society, and burdens to the individual or the family. The DHSS felt that the core of the research should be on the types of 'trouble' that led to expenditure by statutory and voluntary bodies, and where there was a possibility of intervention. It was more concerned with the impairment, nuisance, and burden aspects of deprivation rather than deviance from norms. Nevertheless, the Working Party agreed for the time being to incorporate all four aspects. It noted that all the proposed strategies for research took individuals as the focus for study, while ignoring the social context and societal relationships. While agreeing that the primary source of data was individuals, it argued that the societal context was crucial, and should be included in any research.[31]

The 'Approaches' paper was the subject of a conference held at the LSE on 15 April 1973. Whereas the All Souls seminar a few days earlier had been organised by the DHSS, this was very much a conference for researchers organised by the SSRC. Moreover, this also illustrated tensions between the two. Norman Jordan-Moss had written earlier in the month that the conference was partly an important step in the Research Programme, and partly 'an exercise in research diplomacy'. This was not only a major new research initiative in a much under-researched field, but a 'well publicised and widely observed experiment in post-Rothschild co-operation between a major Department and a still-young Research Council'.[32] It would involve compromises on both sides. The SSRC had to be ready to ensure the DHSS did not have to wait indefinitely for some results to help shape policies and action; the DHSS had to accept that some aspects of the problem might call for ongoing research over a long period. In drafting the 'Approaches' paper, R. R. G. Watts had argued that whereas the SSRC had a 'disdain' for action research projects, the DHSS had a more open mind, and had certainly not ruled them out.[33] These tensions between the SSRC and DHSS would become more apparent as the Research Programme got under way.

By the time of the conference, the revised version of the paper stated that the research task was to 'determine the extent to which an inter-generational cycle exists with respect to different "problems", to elucidate the underlying mechanisms of transmission, and then to consider policy implications in the light of the research findings'.[34] In exploring 'problems', it differentiated between 'attributes' (personal characteristics or qualities) and 'burdens' (inadequacies in the physical or social environment as they impinged on individuals). Attributes could be measured across different axes, such as in statistical terms, as an administrative category, in terms of impairment, through a person's self-perception, and in terms of values. The 'Approaches' paper argued that attributes would first have to be identified in terms of individuals. These included economic status, occupational skill, job stability or instability, educational skills, emotional or behavioural characteristics, and defects in interpersonal relationships. Attributes applied to individuals but did not imply any kind of personal inadequacy.

Burdens, on the other hand, were seen as the possible mechanisms that might influence transmission. A United Nations report on socially deprived families had included genetic influences, individual (non-genetic) influences, family influences, the communal environment, services and institutions, and the societal setting. The 'Approaches' paper made the point that the mechanisms underlying transmission might lie outside the family, and because of the general uncertainty about mechanisms it was best to avoid the word 'transmission'. It preferred the phrase 'intergenerational continuities (or discontinuities)'.[35] Moreover, tighter operational definitions would be required for particular studies. Research into intergenerational continuities would involve two issues – the extent to which attributes were transmitted, and the mechanisms by which transmission occurred – and these would have to be considered separately. It would be important to know what was different about those individuals who failed to show continuity, and the mechanisms that underlay the breaking of the cycle. The paper expressed some pessimism about a research programme. Research could provide answers to some of the questions that underlay the concept of the cycle of deprivation. These could lead to knowledge that could form the basis for effective intervention. Nevertheless, the paper stated that:

> The fact that knowledge is still at this relatively primitive state means that it is not now possible to design any set of studies or even programmes of studies, which could provide hard tests of alternative explanations to arrive at a definitive solution (on completion of the investigations) to the problem of the 'cycle of deprivation'.[36]

Apart from simply bringing researchers together, the LSE conference, which was chaired by Robin Matthews, was designed specifically to explore the twin perspectives of sociology and psychology. The 'Approaches' paper was introduced by Michael Rutter and discussed by Raymond Illsley and Professor Mike Miller, from the Centre for Environmental Studies. After lunch, there was a further paper by Professor Lee Robins, from the Department of Psychiatry at the Washington School of Medicine in Missouri in the US, and this was discussed by Mia Kellmer Pringle and Professor Jack Tizard (1919-79), from the Department of Child Development at the Institute of Education. Other participants included Keith Joseph himself, Tony

Atkinson, Tessa Blackstone, Joan Cooper, Nicola Madge, Geoffrey Otton, Roy Parker, Peter Townsend, Donald West, Peter Willmott, and Harriett Wilson. But what was particularly interesting was the way the conference illustrated the strong suspicions on the part of the social science community that the Research Programme was politically motivated. Raymond Illsley, in particular, argued that while the original cycle speech applied as much to social structures as to individuals, the 'Approaches' paper smacked of the nature–nurture debate. It was not clear what percentage of the population was implicated in transmitted deprivation, and the attributes were a 'ragbag'. Whereas mental illness was clearly an attribute, skin colour became a problem because of the way some white people use it as a marker for race, and delinquency was a legal status that changed from time to time. Illegitimacy, on the other hand, was a status, not an attribute; it only became one through stereotyping and other social processes. The notion of attributes detracted from the situational context and the process of social interaction. In reality there was a massive overlap of different types of deprivation, occurring in combination, and rather than focusing on attributes, the focus should be on social policies. Illsley argued that 'the focus therefore of that research I think should not be individual attributes but social policies and how social policies may or may not produce perpetuation'.[37] The key issue was to break the cycle of deprivation, where the mechanisms were understood.

It was his earlier work in Aberdeen on infant death, social class, and maternal background that led Illsley to stress the significance of social environment and experience, rather than psychological attributes or inborn characteristics. He believed that the emphasis on individual achievement was inimical to the importance of improving the lot of children and mothers. Moreover, Illsley resented particular aspects of Conservative policy, such as the regulation that had forced Aberdeen City Council's Health Committee to charge women attending the local birth control clinic for a service supplied free since the late 1940s. Aberdeen had deployed an exceptionally large team of health visitors to provide health education, and the MOH had written earlier that 'there are safe and simple methods of birth control – including ten different oral contraceptives – and planned parenthood can greatly reduce unwanted children, neglected children, physically and mentally crippled children, and worn-out mothers' (MacQueen, 1969, p 301). It was particularly the refusal of the Conservative government and Joseph as the relevant Secretary of State to provide free contraceptives that fuelled the anger of some social scientists. Illsley had observed the Aberdeen experiment at first hand, and in his criticism of the

'Approaches' paper, noted that local programmes were beginning to break the cycle of deprivation, and it was Joseph who had stopped the contraceptive pill being provided free.[38] More generally, he was suspicious of the genetic connotations of the phrase 'transmitted', and it was this that led him to stress the significance of 'situational factors', and 'made one emphasise, or even overemphasise, other approaches to what was being proposed'.[39]

Illsley's stance can best be summed up as a suspicion of political motives, rather than (like Peter Townsend) one of outright hostility. Mike Miller was similarly suspicious of the 'Approaches' paper and its political origins; critical of the lack of boundaries in the proposed research and use of attributes and burdens; and anxious about the term 'mechanism'. From the floor, the sociologist Harriett Wilson (1916-2002), well known for her work on parenting and poverty (see Chapter Six), argued that research problems were often formulated in a way that reflected political motivations.[40] This was an early sign of the later antagonism that the Research Programme was to engender among some groups of social scientists. Sir Keith Joseph was sitting in the front row with his civil servants. As a reaction to Miller's questioning of government funding and motives, he got up and walked out (Donovan, 2001, p 185).

The Rutter and Madge literature review

One of the first steps taken by the Joint Working Party was to commission a literature review from Michael Rutter. This was carried out jointly with Nicola Madge, who had recently completed an MSc in Child Development at London University, and who had been recommended to Rutter by Jack Tizard. Niece of the sociologist and poet Charles Madge (1912-96), Madge's parents were friends with Peter and Phyllis Willmott. Thus while much younger than the members of the Joint Working Party, and one of the few women, Madge's entrée was eased by these personal connections. The review started off as a summary of current research perceived as relevant, based on information from contacts with funding bodies, government departments, other individuals and organisations, and follow-up visits. Thus this initial review covered the Birmingham Child Development Study; the Cambridge Study on Delinquent Development; research by Elizabeth and John Newson at the Child Development Research Unit at Nottingham; the London Child Health Survey; the NCDS; a delinquency study in Tower Hamlets; the Sheffield studies of problem families; work by Rutter and colleagues at the Family Study Unit; the

Douglas national longitudinal study; and work at the MRC Medical Sociology Unit in Aberdeen.

Some of this research, such as that on intergenerational criminality and longitudinal studies, was seen as relevant, offering the prospect of revealing more about transmission mechanisms. Other studies, which had paid attention to extra-familial influences, were seen as less so. Overall, although many of these studies had generated information that was relevant to the cycle, few had been designed to investigate this precise research question. The review concluded that 'the value of many projects may be more in their unfulfilled potential than in their analysis, findings and interpretations to date'.[41] In the event, some researchers were approached immediately to see if their material could be adapted for the purposes of the Joint Working Party: the Cambridge Delinquency Study; the authors of the Sheffield problem family studies; and the Douglas national longitudinal project. Others were to be contacted for an exchange of ideas: the Newsoms; the NCDS; Rutter and colleagues; and the MRC Medical Sociology Unit.[42]

Although the full literature review was not finally published until 1976, a large part was ready remarkably quickly, by June 1973. Rutter and Madge called this a 'rough first draft only', but it was extremely thorough, covering overlaps between variables, delinquent and criminal behaviour, ability and attainment, psychiatric status, poverty, social status, and job stability.[43] By any standards, it was a comprehensive and open-minded piece of work, completed very quickly. The literature review had an important bearing on the Research Programme as a whole, and its main thrust can be seen in the final published version. The purpose of the review was to examine what evidence existed that might support the 'cycle of transmitted deprivation', and to consider what it was that created these alleged continuities between generations. Rutter and Madge admitted, however, that it had quickly become clear, when they had begun work, that there were some serious problems with their brief, and that changes had been necessary. Most importantly, Rutter and Madge decided that they preferred the term 'disadvantage' to the original 'deprivation', they substituted the plural 'cycles' for the singular 'cycle', and they dropped the phrase 'transmitted' (Rutter and Madge, 1976, pp 3-6).

In trying to summarise the current state of knowledge, Rutter and Madge made several other important provisos. They emphasised that they did not equate poverty with maladjustment, the suggested focus on the family was too narrow, and they would discuss environmental and constitutional factors bearing on deprivation and disadvantage. Rutter and Madge pointed out, for instance, that there were as many discontinuities as continuities in the experiences of these families. They argued further that intergenerational continuities in disadvantage were only part of the broader question of disadvantage. Many children brought up in conditions of severe disadvantage developed normally and went on to produce perfectly happy families of their own. Although intergenerational cycles of disadvantage did exist, 'the exceptions are many and a surprisingly large proportion of people reared in conditions of privation and suffering do *not* reproduce that pattern in the next generation' (Rutter and Madge, 1976, pp 5-6 [emphasis in original]). Rutter and Madge remained sceptical about Oscar Lewis's culture of poverty, claiming that 'neither a wholly subcultural nor a wholly situational interpretation of the behaviour and attributes of poor communities is tenable' (Rutter and Madge, 1976, p 30). Each had its own limitations and both failed to take account of individual differences. It was also unlikely that the concept was relevant to Britain – Lewis had said it was most likely to develop in 'rapidly changing societies', which Britain plainly was not. Overall, Rutter and Madge concluded that 'the culture of poverty concept is inadequate for an analysis of British society' (Rutter and Madge, 1976, p 30).

The literature review included historical studies, emphasising the longer-term antecedents of the cycle hypothesis. In the case of problem families, for instance, Rutter and Madge traced the work of Charles Booth, E. J. Lidbetter, the Wood Committee (1929), and the Eugenics Society, and a shifting emphasis from social conditions to personal problems. They argued that studies of problem families were essentially studies of particular characteristics, the analysis was tautological, and therefore the concept of a distinct problem family lifestyle was open to 'serious objection' (Rutter and Madge, 1976, pp 246-8). In many ways, the findings of the different studies, and the differences between investigators, were simply a function of how groups had been defined, and merited little serious attention. It was not justifiable to discuss problem families as a homogeneous group separate from the rest of the population. Nonetheless, Rutter and Madge argued that it was important to consider families who suffered from a combination of severe disadvantages or problems. There was a marked overlap between different forms of social disadvantage, and for problem families an improvement in social circumstances might be as important as help with personal problems and relationships. Problem families did not constitute a group that was qualitatively different from other members of the population. Rutter and Madge concluded that 'just as stereotypes of "*the* problem family" are to be distrusted, so are package remedies based on notions of a homogeneous group' (Rutter and Madge, 1976, pp 255-6 [emphasis in original]). Yet families with multiple social disadvantages and/or personal problems did give cause for concern, both in terms of the present and with regard to problems that might persist into the next generation. While the concept of the problem family was too vague, the evidence apparently showed that there was a substantial number of families with multiple problems, some of which involved extended dependency on the social services.

In terms of Joseph's original thesis, the authors of the literature review argued that there was no single problem of a cycle of transmitted deprivation. Rather there were many forms of disadvantage that arose in various ways, and which showed varying degrees and types of continuities between generations. There certainly were continuities over time. However, only some were familial – there were marked regional continuities, for example, in disadvantage. There were also numerous discontinuities. Many children born into disadvantaged homes did not repeat the pattern of disadvantage in the next generation. Even where continuities were strongest, many individuals broke out of the cycle. Equally, many people became disadvantaged without having had disadvantaged parents. Rutter and Madge summed this up by stating that 'familial cycles are a most important element in the perpetuation of disadvantage but they account for only a part of the overall picture' (Rutter and Madge, 1976, pp 303-4). For instance, the continuities were weaker over three generations than two, and the extent of continuity varied according to the type and level of disadvantage.

Despite these arguments, Rutter and Madge did echo Joseph in arguing that behavioural and educational factors might be as significant as the socioeconomic in causing deprivation. They claimed, for example, that it might be possible to influence cycles of disadvantage without necessarily embarking on wholesale social change. First, cycles of disadvantage were found at all levels of society. Second, correlations with inadequate living conditions provided a poor guide to levels of disadvantage. Although overcrowding, for example, was worse in Scotland than in England, evidence from schools indicated that Scottish children were better readers, on average, than their English counterparts. The reasons for this remained unclear. Thus research was needed into why children might be disadvantaged in one respect, but were often not disadvantaged in another. Rutter and Madge concluded that:

> If research into such cycles merely reconfirms that children disadvantaged in one respect are often also disadvantaged in other respects it will have failed. What are needed are investigations to determine why this is often *not* the case

and how we can bring about discontinuities in cycles of
disadvantage. This is the challenge for the future. (Rutter
and Madge, 1976, p 327 [emphasis in original])

When it was finally published in 1976, the literature review was
generally reviewed favourably, as we shall see in Chapter Five. It did
much to draw in social scientists who otherwise would have been
hostile to the whole notion of transmitted deprivation.

The end of the beginning

Even by the summer of 1973, the Rutter and Madge literature review
had had an impact, and there was evidence of some rethinking. The
Joint Working Party felt that there was so much material in the review
that it would be sensible to digest its findings properly before fully
detailed plans for new research were put forward and a final report
presented. One working paper, for example, noted that while the
hypothesis of transmitted deprivation could be accepted in general
terms, the mechanisms were very complex and would require
modifying hypotheses, which would involve a broadening of the area of
study.[44] The draft interim report of the Joint Working Party (July 1973)
proposed that the SSRC should manage the Research Programme,
acting as a contractor, putting out work to subcontractors. The funding
would come from the DHSS. The DHSS was inclined to go along with
this, since it would secure a broad costed plan for the Programme, it
would put the SSRC on the same footing as the MRC, and in light
of cuts it seemed only sensible to delegate in this way.[45]

Nevertheless, it is clear that the DHSS went along with this with
some reluctance; it was aware, for example, that this would mean that
the Programme would not be carried out in the way the department
would have chosen. More generally, the experience of drafting the
interim report further exposed tensions between the DHSS and
SSRC. One of the civil servants on the Joint Working Party, Bryan
Rayner, wrote of the SSRC that 'it is depressing that they seem so
reluctant to accept suggestions from here. I think it may be necessary
to put it across to them that this really is a Joint Working Party and
not simply an exercise for the SSRC to get the Department to accept
their views'.[46] Margaret Edwards described the draft interim report as
'disappointing and tentative' and viewed the Research Programme as
'rather untidy', while Alice Sheridan argued that 'the academic world
is very suspicious of the SSRC and has very little regard for it'.[47] The
draft interim report, which became the First Report of the Joint

Working Party, is worth exploring further, since it offered a summary of the earlier debates, suitably distilled and rationalised for public consumption. This was considered by Joseph as Secretary of State and by the SSRC in October 1973, but published only in August 1974. In the meantime, the DHSS and the SSRC signed a contract whereby the former would finance and the latter administer a programme of research into transmitted deprivation.

The impact of the literature review by Rutter and Madge can be seen in the First Report of the Working Party, which outlined why research would be worthwhile, and gave some examples of the kinds of research that might be conducted. As Berthoud has noted, the Working Party in its First Report acknowledged that both 'deprivation' and 'transmitted' were ambiguous terms; it admitted that 'the theoretical framework for the understanding of the whole phenomenon cannot be said to be firmly constructed' (SSRC–DHSS, 1974, para 13). However, it still argued that the literature review by Rutter and Madge, along with discussions at the LSE conference and with individual researchers, had led the Working Party to the view that 'there is convincing evidence that inter-generational continuity is an important feature of deprivation, but that the causal mechanisms are not well understood, and that there is a good prospect that more research will contribute to improvements in social policy' (SSRC–DHSS, 1974, para 6). What were suggested were parallel and sequential studies, along with additional work grafted on to relevant studies already under way.

Statistical data relating to samples of individuals or families was seen as a key resource, as were longitudinal studies, but these were to be supplemented by intensive studies of samples in particular regions. Attention was also to be directed to the personal or environmental characteristics that enabled individuals to break out of the cycle. Thus there was room for anthropological studies of families in their social context that would produce hypotheses rather than test them. Topics and proposals for research were divided into, first, background and concepts; second, the extent of intergenerational continuities; third, causal mechanisms; and, fourth, intervention. The first included the components of deprivation (attributes and their overlap), intragenerational continuities, and concepts of deprivation. The second included income and poverty, reliance on social services, 'colour', and housing. The third embraced familial influences, social stratification, the culture of poverty, the educational system, areas and neighbourhoods, and stigma. The fourth focused on provision for the under-fives, housing policies, and social security. It was recognised that identifying causal mechanisms would be the most difficult part of the research. Overall, the Working Party recommended that the DHSS and SSRC should begin to put in place the preliminary work necessary to enable studies to be mounted on these topics (SSRC–DHSS, 1974, paras 15-21). In terms of costs, the programme of research could take seven years, with a budget rising to £150,000 per year – an extremely large research programme at that time.

Labour and transmitted deprivation

It seems probable that one reason for the hiatus between the completion of the interim report by the Working Party (July 1973), and its publication as the First Report (August 1974), was the election of the Labour government in March 1974, along with wider Labour uncertainty about the Research Programme. Following the election, Barbara Castle (1910-2002) had been appointed Secretary of State for Social Services, and she was careful to stress in an early speech that study of a cycle of deprivation should be in parallel with a broader anti-poverty strategy, arguing that the previous stress on Preparation for Parenthood was meaningless for families living under disadvantage. At a conference organised by the British Association of Social Workers (BASW), at Manchester University, on 29 March 1974, Castle said she had always feared that the research might be used as an excuse for not redistributing income and wealth. Castle stated that 'I simply do not believe, for instance, that there can be any meaningful preparation for parenthood for families whose children are condemned to grow up in crowded homes, crowded schools, crowded streets, on meagre budgets under the shadow of endless nagging insecurity' (Castle, 1974, p 2). She was careful to locate the research into transmitted deprivation within a broader anti-poverty strategy.

This was the new Secretary of State's first major ministerial speech. In *The Times* the following morning, this was reported as: 'she [Castle] told the conference she had a suspicion that the research studies ordered by the previous government into how deprivation is transmitted between generations might be an alibi for not redistributing wealth', and what she hoped to mount was an anti-poverty strategy (*The Times*, 30 March 1974, p 2). The SSRC rang Geoffrey Otton at the DHSS, expressing concern that Castle's speech indicated a loss of commitment to the Research Programme. Otton wrote to assure the SSRC that this was not the case, and Castle subsequently reluctantly endorsed it.[48] Castle regarded Brian Abel-Smith (1926-96), Professor of Social Administration at the LSE, as her most outstanding expert adviser (Castle, 1993, p 461). In some respects, he echoed her view, arguing in May 1974 that while the

All Souls seminar had been valuable, the Preparation for Parenthood consultation exercise had been disappointing. Abel–Smith confided to Geoffrey Otton that the 'Secretary of State asked me again about the £0.5 million to be spent on the research and I told her what I thought it might find out which would be useful. Am I right in saying that she could not reduce the expenditure from *her* budget now even if she wanted to do so?'[49] Civil servants shared Abel-Smith's feelings regarding Preparation for Parenthood and the All Souls seminar, but they confirmed that there was a formal commitment to the SSRC to provide the funding for the research.[50]

The concept of transmitted deprivation was unacceptable to Labour politicians for ideological reasons, and regarded as patronising and misguided by Castle and her advisors. Geoffrey Otton later recalled that Castle had an entirely different set of priorities. Whereas Joan Cooper had spent half an hour a day talking to Joseph, her successor as Chief Social Work Officer, Bill Utting, a former Director of Social Services for Kensington and Chelsea, saw Castle much less frequently. Overall, Otton's analysis was that 'she [Castle] clearly did not believe in it but was quite happy to let us mess around, and the subject, as what had been actually a very high profile element in DHSS business, just petered out in the way that these things do'.[51] Instead, Castle's time at the DHSS was marked by the battle with NHS consultants over private practice, and the issue of pension reform.

Thus because of the election of the Labour government in March 1974, along with wider Labour uncertainty about transmitted deprivation, the Research Programme was only publicly launched in May 1974, when the DHSS and SSRC announced that the former would finance and the latter would administer a programme of research into transmitted deprivation, costing £500,000 to £750,000 over seven years. The terms of agreement between the DHSS and SSRC had already been discussed and agreed informally. They envisaged seven years, but the agreement initially was for four; after three years there would be a review, and the arrangements for the remaining three years would be determined. The work was seen as falling into two parts: first, identifying appropriate research projects, placing contracts with investigators, and administering research funds; second, ensuring proper scientific appraisal of the Research Programme, and adequate monitoring and management of the Programme once the research was under way. The start date was regarded as being 1 January 1974. An Organising Group of three would develop proposals within the Programme as defined by the Joint Working Party, seek out researchers, and evaluate proposals with the help of consultants who would make recommendations. The management of the Research Programme was thus the responsibility of the SSRC – how the work was to be carried out, where, by whom, and by which type of employee. The DHSS would need to be satisfied that funds were being used satisfactorily, and would reimburse the SSRC for administering and managing the Research Programme.[52]

Press reaction to the launch was interesting, since this was the first public acknowledgement of the existence of the Joint Working Party. *The Times* noted that the Working Party had refined the concept beyond the level of blaming problem families; the research would examine how some people managed to break out of the cycle; and the emphasis would be on practical research aimed at influencing social policy (*The Times*, 9 May 1974, p 3). Some reactions were fairly predictable. The *Times Educational Supplement* was generally critical of what it regarded as the neglect of education, noting 'a strong emphasis, in the personnel, on economists and sociologists, and in the aims of the project, on reducing the numbers of people dependent on the social services, and hence their cost' (*Times Educational Supplement*, 10 May 1974, p 6). Similarly, a leader article in the journal *New Society* stressed the tendency to focus on the poor and 'deprived', in the social work sense of the phrase (Anonymous, 1974, p 368). But others were more interesting. In its leader article, the *Times Higher Education Supplement* argued that the involvement of academics, in what had been a highly political interpretation of the causes of poverty, risked confusing the issue. Peter Townsend had been one of the most prominent critics of the Programme; in his view, the SSRC should protect social scientists and not get mixed up with government contracts (*Times Higher Education Supplement*, 17 May 1974, p 12). Much later, in February 1979, Tom Luce, Assistant Secretary at the DHSS, was to write that:

> Dissatisfaction with the arrangement has occasionally surfaced on the SSRC side, and is thought to continue below the surface. I am not sure of the reasons, but suspect that the Council feels itself compromised vis a vis the scientific community generally, and its own notions of scientific independence, through being the agent of a Government Department in the management of a programme with an explicitly political origin.[53]

Controversy would continue to dog the Research Programme as it had the cycle speech.

Conclusion

As was acknowledged at the start of this chapter, one of the problems with existing secondary work is that very little is known about the period between the cycle speech and the launch of the Research Programme. It is that gap in knowledge that this chapter has attempted to fill. Thus it has surveyed the setting up of the Research Programme, from the first discussions between the DHSS and SSRC, to the publication of the First Report by the Joint Working Party in August 1974. It has explored the informal discussions between the DHSS and SSRC that took place in advance of the cycle speech, the first formal meetings of the Joint Working Party, and its composition. The chapter has traced the conceptual difficulties that the members of the Joint Working Party struggled with, in attempting to define 'deprivation', and the way that these led to the important early 'Approaches' paper, and the LSE conference. It has looked at the commissioning of the literature review, from Michael Rutter and Nicola Madge, and at its impact, and at the formal launch of the Research Programme, in May 1974. A final section of the chapter has examined the difference that the election of the Labour government, in March 1974, made to the Research Programme, and at discussions between Barbara Castle, as Secretary of State for Social Services, and her advisor, Brian Abel-Smith.

It is clear that the Research Programme departed dramatically from Joseph's original thesis. A cycle of deprivation that was essentially a behavioural interpretation of poverty, which stressed the importance of intergenerational continuities, became instead a cycles of disadvantage concept that was concerned more with structural factors and emphasised the discontinuities in the experiences of families. While Berthoud's analysis is helpful, it is clear that there were other factors at work here. First, part of the answer lies with the conceptual problems that the Joint Working Party grappled with, and that were revealed in the 'Approaches' paper; these were reflected in the First Report of the Joint Working Party, which failed to define both 'deprivation' and 'transmitted' adequately. Second, there were differences within the SSRC itself from the outset, most obviously between those members whose original disciplines were psychiatry (Rutter) and sociology (Willmott). Third, there was the influence of the Rutter and Madge literature review, which changed the scope of the Research Programme dramatically. Fourth, the election of the Labour government in March 1974, and the very different approach of Barbara Castle to questions of deprivation and disadvantage, meant that ministerial support for the Research Programme evaporated, with a consequent effect on the view taken by civil servants, who were in any case sceptical of the possible contribution of social science. In the next chapter we explore the subsequent direction of the Research Programme, from its formal launch in May 1974, to the publication of the Third Report by the Joint Working Party, in November 1977.

Notes

[1] NA MH 152/72: A. Shonfield to K. Joseph, 23 July 1971.

[2] On the history of the SSRC see Young (1975), Matthews (1975), and Robinson (1975).

[3] Interview between the author and Raymond Illsley, Box Hill, Wiltshire, 13 September 2006.

[4] Letter from Robin Matthews to the author, 3 June 2006.

[5] NA MH 152/72: A. Shonfield to N. Jordan-Moss, 15 October 1971.

[6] NA MH 152/72: A. M. Sheridan to N. Jordan-Moss, 1 November 1971.

[7] NA MH 152/72: A. M. Sheridan to N. Jordan-Moss, 11 August 1971.

[8] Adrian Sinfield papers, J. Mitchell to A. B. Atkinson, 25 February 1972; interview between the author and Michael Rutter, London, 4 July 2006.

[9] Adrian Sinfield papers, 'The deprivation cycle' (nd); NA MH 152/72: R. R. G. Watts to G. Otton, 'Cycle of deprivation research', 30 March 1972.

[10] Interview between the author and Alan Clarke, London, 24 May 2006.

[11] Interview between the author and Robin Matthews, Cambridge, 25 May 2006.

[12] Adrian Sinfield papers, 'The deprivation cycle' (nd).

[13] Interview between the author and Robin Matthews, Cambridge, 25 May 2006.

[14] NA MH 152/72: N. Jordan-Moss to R. C. O. Matthews, 30 May 1972; NA MH 152/72: J. Mitchell to N. Jordan-Moss, 26 June 1972.

[15] NA MH 152/72: minutes of the 1st meeting of the Working Party, 19 July 1972.

[16] NA MH 152/72: S. Yasin, 'WPTD 5', 19 July 1972.

[17] NA MH 152/72: S. Yasin, 'WPTD 5', 19 July 1972

[18] NA MH 152/72: minutes of the 1st meeting of the Working Party, 19 July 1972.

[19] NA MH 152/72: M. Freedman, 'WPTD 9', 30 August 1972.

[20] NA MH 152/72: P. Willmott, 'WPTD 10', September 1972.

[21] NA MH 152/72: M. Rutter, 'WPTD 11', September 1972.

[22] NA MH 152/72: A. B. Atkinson, 'WPTD 12', September 1972.

[23] NA MH 152/72: R. A. Parker, 'WPTD 13', 26 September 1972.

[24] Interview between the author and Robin Matthews, Cambridge, 25 May 2006; interview between the author and Nicola Madge, London, 3 May 2006; interview between the author and Michael Rutter, London, 4 July 2006.

[25] Interview between the author and Tony Atkinson, Paris, 18 April 2006.

[26] NA MH 152/72: C. M. Cunningham to R. R. G. Watts, 3 October 1972.

[27] NA MH 152/72: 'Note by the Department of Health and Social Security', 'WPTD 14', October 1972, p 3.

[28] NA MH 152/72: R. Matthews, 'WPTD 16', 19 October 1972.

[29] NA MH 152/72: minutes of the 2nd meeting of the Working Party, 19 October 1972.

[30] NA MH 152/72: SSRC, 'Approaches to research on transmitted deprivation', 'WPTD 21', 12 December 1972, pp 3-14.

[31] NA MH 152/72: minutes of the 3rd meeting of the Working Party, 21 December 1972.

[32] NA MH 152/72: N. Jordan-Moss to D. M. Woolley, 9 April 1973.

[33] NA MH 152/72: memo by R. R. G. Watts, 6 April 1973.

[34] Harriett Wilson papers, SSRC, 'Approaches to research on transmitted deprivation', 'WPTD 21 (revised)' (nd).

[35] Harriett Wilson papers, SSRC, 'Approaches to research on transmitted deprivation', 'WPTD 21 (revised)' (nd) p 6.

[36] Harriett Wilson papers, SSRC, 'Approaches to research on transmitted deprivation', 'WPTD 21 (revised)' (nd) p 17.

[37] Harriett Wilson papers, H. Wilson, 'SSRC–DHSS conference, LSE, 16 April 1973'; NA MH 152/74: Conference 'Approaches to research on transmitted deprivation', 15 April 1973, transcript, pp 1.10-1.19; interview between the author and Raymond Illsley, Box Hill, Wiltshire, 13 September 2006.

[38] Harriett Wilson papers, H. Wilson, 'SSRC–DHSS conference, LSE', 16 April 1973.

[39] Interview between the author and Raymond Illsley, Box Hill, Wiltshire, 13 September 2006.

[40] NA MH 152/74: Conference 'Approaches to research on transmitted deprivation', 15 April 1973, transcript, p 2.10.

[41] Nicola Madge papers, 'Review of current research, WPTD 28' (nd), p 27.

[42] NA MH 152/74: minutes of the 4th meeting of the Working Party, 26 March 1973.

[43] Adrian Sinfield papers, M. Rutter and N. Madge, 'WPTD 31', 21 June 1973.

[44] Adrian Sinfield papers, M. Rutter and N. Madge, 'WPTD 32', 21 June 1973.

[45] NA MH 152/77: B. R. Rayner to A. M. Sheridan, 25 July 1973.

[46] NA MH 152/76: B. R. Rayner to M. Edwards, 16 July 1973.

[47] NA MH 152/76: memo by M. R. Edwards, 18 July 1973; NA MH 152/76: A. M. Sheridan to B. Rayner, 30 July 1973.

[48] NA MH 152/81: P. J. Lewis to R. S. King, 1 August 1975.

[49] NA MH 152/78: B. Abel-Smith to G. Otton, 28 May 1974.

[50] NA MH 152/78: R. S. King to B. Abel-Smith, 29 May 1974.

[51] Interview between the author and Geoffrey Otton, Bromley, Kent, 4 May 2006.

[52] NA MH 166/1515: J. Locke to M. James, 16 May 1974.

[53] NA MH 166/1518: memo by T. R. H. Luce, 15 February 1979.

FOUR

From a cycle of deprivation to cycles of disadvantage

Introduction

The existing secondary accounts of the Research Programme, by Richard Berthoud (1983a) and Alan Deacon (2003), are based on the three published progress reports by the Working Party and on studies from the Programme itself, notably the final report by Muriel Brown and Nicola Madge (1982a). Berthoud has argued, for instance, that at the time of the cycle speech, the SSRC operated entirely in 'responsive' mode. It publicised its presence to the research community, and waited for social scientists to come up with projects. The SSRC had little experience of commissioning research, demand for funding was weak, and the nature of the Programme was relatively unclear. This meant that promoting a pre-planned multidisciplinary research programme was something of an uphill struggle. He alleges that the SSRC in 1972 had 'never been asked an important question by an outsider' (Berthoud, 1983a, pp 156-7, 162). In their overview of the Research Programme, Muriel Brown and Nicola Madge give a brief and arguably misleading summary of its general direction (Brown and Madge, 1982a). If there is a gap in knowledge between the cycle speech and the First Report of the Joint Working Party (SSRC–DHSS, 1974), even less is known about the Research Programme and the applications that were received, not least those that were unsuccessful, or projects that went ahead but did not lead to publications.

This chapter traces early attempts to commission research, some of the applications that were received, and reports by referees. While it is not possible to give a flavour of all the projects that were funded, it looks at one in particular, that by the team led by Frank Coffield at Keele University. The chapter looks in particular at the efforts that were made to correct the perceived imbalance of the Research Programme, away from the emphasis on familial processes, to take more account of socioeconomic factors. Here the appointment of new members to the Joint Working Party, along with the approach of Brian Abel-Smith and David Owen as Minister for Health, seemed to be critical. One section offers a different perspective on the Research Programme, by exploring those involved with the RCDIW, and in particular its report on low incomes (RCDIW, 1978). The final section of the chapter traces the attitude of the DHSS civil servants towards the Research Programme, and their growing exasperation with it. This period is concerned for the most part with applications rather than outcomes. Nevertheless, it is a key aspect of the story. The chapter argues that a full understanding of the direction taken by the Research Programme, and in particular the shift from the behavioural focus of the cycle hypothesis to the structural emphasis favoured by many researchers, is only possible through analysis of the available archival sources, supplemented by oral interviews. These shed new light on tensions between the social scientists and the DHSS civil servants, between the social scientists, particularly the psychologists and sociologists, and within individual research teams.

An uphill struggle: early attempts to commission research

While Barbara Castle was clearly less committed to the concept of transmitted deprivation than Keith Joseph, Labour had endorsed the Research Programme, and the Joint Working Party had to get on with the task of commissioning research. In terms of administering the Research Programme, the Joint Working Party remained in existence, but appointed a smaller Organising Group to consider applications, to discuss the areas that required investigation, and to encourage applications in those areas (SSRC–DHSS, 1974, foreword). Initially this Organising Group was chaired by Peter Willmott, and comprised Alan Clarke and Kit Jones, then Secretary of the National Institute for Economic and Social Research (NIESR).

Flyers produced by the SSRC outlined the background to the Research Programme, and described the application process. The first stage for applicants was to send in a four- to five-page outline of the proposed research. This was meant to include some reference to completed research; a brief statement of objectives and proposed methods; a paragraph showing how the research would contribute to the Research Programme; and a curriculum vitae. These outlines were considered by the Organising Group, which met monthly; if its members liked the proposal, applicants were invited to submit full research subcontract applications, on SSRC forms. These full applications were sent to external referees for comment before they were considered again by the Organising Group, and applicants were interviewed. In contrast, the Joint Working Party met much less frequently, to consider the recommendations from the Organising Group, only three times a year. Nevertheless, if a quick decision was necessary – to keep staff or data sets together or if the amount requested was under £10,000 – the Chair of the Joint Working Party could endorse a recommendation by the Organising Group without the application going to a full meeting (*Times Educational Supplement*, 10 May 1974, p 6).[1]

As Berthoud has noted, the key point about the way the research was commissioned was that it was set up in responsive mode, rather than as a large-scale, pre-planned, directed programme. Alan Clarke, for instance, later recalled that:

> It [the Research Programme] took the direction it did because this was entirely determined by the people who applied; put it this way, an absurd example, if no one had applied, or they were all rubbish, the Programme would not have gone on. As it was, most of them were good and some were rubbish and that determined the direction, so it wasn't a question, although I suppose it could have been, of a group being brought together to say I want to commission Rutter to do this and his colleague Quinton to do that and someone else to do that and we will direct the Programme; it wasn't that, we were a reflective group.[2]

The unsuccessful applications were as revealing as the successful, and there were many of the former in this period, including from Harriett Wilson at Birmingham University, and Michael Richards at Cambridge University.[3] One, on the intragenerational aspects of policy, was viewed as too general and all embracing, and lacking intellectual coherence. It was seen as of doubtful relevance to transmitted deprivation, and being more an evaluation of attitudes to social policies and the development and influence of pressure groups. Although relevant to deprivation, it was seen as not contributing much to the study of transmission.[4] Another unsuccessful application came from Margaret Stacey (1922-2004), then Professor of Sociology at the University of Warwick. Around the same time, members of the Organising Group met Bill Jordan, who amplified the points made in his book *Poor parents* (1974).[5]

Michael Rutter later conceded that the early applications were not very impressive, and the Joint Working Party had faced a dilemma: should it set high standards, and say it would only support the best, or should it set lower standards in order to encourage applications, with the intention of attracting better ones?[6] In the event it settled for the latter strategy, and the net outcome of this initial period was that by December 1974 nine projects had been funded:

- a computer simulation of intergenerational family processes led by Dr H. Greenwood and Bill Bytheway, at Keele University;
- a conceptual and empirical study of transmitted deprivation, led by Frank Coffield, at Keele University;
- a study of the transmission of 'maladaptive coping patterns', by the Rapoports, at the Institute of Family and Environmental Studies, London;
- a longitudinal study of child development in single-parent families, led by Stephen Wolkind, at the London Hospital;
- a study of the intergenerational inheritance of social advantage and disadvantage, directed by Keith Hope, at Nuffield College, Oxford;
- a follow-up of ex-Borstal boys, by Professor F. H. McClintock, at the University of Edinburgh;
- a pilot study of an intergenerational cycle of deprivation, by Ada Paterson, at the University of Edinburgh;
- an exploration of intergenerational continuities in low incomes, using Rowntree's 1950 York study, led by Tony Atkinson, at the University of Essex; and
- a study of married children in problem families, by W. L. Tonge and John Lunn, following up the earlier Sheffield studies (SSRC–DHSS, 1975, appendix 1), Sheffield.

By any measure, it was an odd list, very different in terms of theme and experience of applicant, and appearing to lack any coherence. A summary of the position reached in June 1975 is given in the Second Report of the Joint Working Party (SSRC–DHSS, 1975). This was extremely brief, the main body of the report consisting of only six pages, and it was the brevity of this report that led to concern expressed by David Owen and Brian Abel-Smith, as we will see later in the chapter. By June 1975, the Organising Group had:

- considered 51 outlines;
- met 22 potential applicants;
- received 17 formal applications;
- recommended 12 to the Joint Working Party;
- of which 11 had been funded (SSRC–DHSS, 1975, p 1).

In addition to the original nine studies noted above, a further two had been funded: a study of the processes of the transmission of deprivation in families of pre-school children, by Philip Graham and Jim Stevenson, at the Institute of Child Health, London, and a feasibility study of mother–child interaction and 'development failure', by Alex McGlaughlin, at the University of Hull (SSRC–DHSS, 1975, appendix 1). Richard Berthoud later recalled that it was the SSRC's methods that struck him at the time as odd:

> Partly being in entirely responsive mode, secondly having a pretty low threshold of acceptability. I suppose they had to if they wanted to commission anything. It did seem to me an awful lot of the projects would not pass rigorous scrutiny from the start, and in particular the proportion of projects which were not only not proposing to do anything very rigorous, but also starting off with a position which was almost as political as Keith Joseph's but with less excuse.[7]

What was not apparent from the Joint Working Party's Reports was that some of these early projects had quickly run into serious problems. One was the computer simulation of intergenerational family processes, by Greenwood and Bytheway at Keele University. The main problem was that the Research Unit at Keele had closed shortly after the project began, and Bytheway had departed for the University of Swansea, leaving the project in the hands of Richard Dajda, the Research Assistant.[8] Bytheway had been in charge of the project, and Dajda's responsibility was originally only the computer simulation. An independent assessor appointed by the Joint Working Party met with Dajda in August 1975. He suggested that the original proposal did not indicate how the main objectives were to be achieved, and only one, the modelling of family processes, could be operationalised. Dajda had given a seminar paper in March 1975, but this demonstrated limited progress, and the most recent report indicated that the group were less than halfway into their modelling. He wrote that 'my initial reaction is that Mr Dajda, however technically competent he may be, is in some difficulty when it comes to the more substantive problems of hypothesis generation and testing'.[9] It was not Dajda's fault. He had been left in a position that he would not have chosen for himself, his interest was mainly in operationalising and testing the ideas and theories of others, and his priorities were computer simulation as a social science technique, and only secondly transmitted deprivation.

One of the researchers, Keith Hope, was also asked to make an assessment of Dajda's work. Hope was more positive, arguing that Dajda had a good grasp of what could be done with available techniques and data. If aspects of the work assigned to other researchers had not come to fruition, this could not be laid at Dajda's door, but were to do with the closing of the Keele Unit.[10] While the SSRC members of the Joint Working Party were not experts in computing, they nonetheless had serious misgivings about the progress of this study. While the original application had four objectives, only the attempt to model family processes had received attention. The SSRC concluded that 'it seemed that the contract was funding nothing more than the kind of actuarial exercise conducted by insurance companies and that work was not likely to progress beyond the basic model stage'.[11] Taking all of this into account, the Organising Group concluded in November 1975 that the reports pointed to Dajda's technical competence, but also to the limitations of his models in the context of research into transmitted deprivation. The only option was to let the research run its course and 'look forward to the completion of an interesting, if perhaps doomed, project'.[12] In the event, the referee of the final report noted somewhat charitably that 'the author is to be congratulated for his perseverance against what for others might have proved insuperable odds'.[13] Even so, he or she concluded that while it might be painful to cut off a simulation study before simulation had been attempted, on balance this decision should be taken.

The difficulties that the Organising Group and Joint Working Party faced can be illustrated through some of the other applications they received in this period. In October 1975, for instance, the Joint Working Party considered an application from a Ms Barker on the control and distribution of income within families. However, it was seen as being not relevant enough to the Joint Working Party's brief, there were weaknesses in the methods, and it failed to link to broader theoretical concerns.[14] Interestingly, the Organising Group considered an outline from Alan Walker, then at the University of Essex, who proposed to investigate, through a cohort originally interviewed in 1968-69, the extent of continuity of deprivation within a single generation. This is intriguing, given Walker's opposition, in the 1990s, to cycle of deprivation and underclass concepts (Walker, 1996). Other applications that were ultimately successful, nevertheless received a critical reception from referees. The Home Office, for instance, was critical of an application from Donald West, stating that:

We do not find Dr West's portrayal of the present proposal as an investigation of 'transmitted deprivation' entirely convincing. Dr West does not attempt to define what he means by 'transmission' or 'deprivation' (although several assumptions are implicit in the text). Moreover the research was not originally designed for the purpose Dr West now thinks it will fulfil.[15]

Another application, on family attitudes to health and health services, came from Raymond Illsley and Mildred Blaxter, both then based in the MRC Medical Sociology Unit at the University of Aberdeen. Blaxter has vividly recalled the occasion of her interview:

I remember very clearly sitting on the grass on the Embankment in London, in the 1970s, whence I had been summoned by SSRC to defend my research proposal, which they were very doubtful about supporting. We were sitting on the grass in the Embankment because there had been a bomb scare in the old SSRC building, and there I was with a circle of very eminent social scientists around me, some of whom … were asking me, 'But where is your control group?' And round in an outer circle were a group of interested by-passers [sic] and bystanders, listening to this free entertainment, who, in fact, were rather enthusiastic, and kept on saying things like, 'That's interesting. Give her the money'. And at one point they actually applauded! After that, of course, they *had* to give me the money, so that project owes everything to a bomb scare. (Blaxter, 2004, p 55 [emphasis in original])

Blaxter was quite right that the Joint Working Party was doubtful about the proposed research. The application was refereed by Margot Jefferys (1916-99), then Professor of Medical Sociology at the University of London, who argued that there were problems in the evidence for the hypothesis that healthcare deprivation was repeated through the generations. She thought Illsley and Blaxter could only demonstrate at a very general level that healthcare behaviour was comparable between grandmothers and mothers. Moreover, Jefferys was sceptical about studying the mechanisms involved. She concluded that while the study should be supported, 'there is a need for a good deal of tightening up and greater clarity about the objectives of the study'.[16] The Organising Group wrote to Illsley asking, 'do you expect simply to demonstrate correlations and, then, to explore their implications or do you intend that your findings will provide evidence of causal mechanisms at work in the health attitudes/behaviour relationship?'[17] Jefferys subsequently argued that a rejoinder from Blaxter did not allay her original doubts about the project. She wrote that rather it added to them 'and to my feeling that far too little thought has been devoted to defining the conceptual terms such as "cycle of health deprivation" which are used so loosely'. While continuities in health deprivation might exist, the concept of health deprivation had not been properly defined and empirically studied. Jefferys argued that 'it is this sociological clarification of a loose term that is lacking in previous work and unfortunately in Mrs Blaxter's proposal'.[18]

Given these problems, it was hardly surprising that anxieties about the direction of the Research Programme and the quality of applications came to a head in February 1976, in a letter from Alan Clarke. Clarke noted that 'much of the material which we looked at in our last meeting seemed to me to hit a new low', since there had been common errors, or the potential for errors, seen in the applications, particularly in methodology.[19] He argued that, in considering preliminary or final applications, the Joint Working Party needed to spell out more clearly what it needed to know. Nevertheless, Clarke went further than this, arguing that social science research was generally held in low esteem, partly because of prejudice, and partly because it was methodologically weak. He advocated the principles of communicability, replicability, and refutability, and suggested that if social problems were seen as not amenable to this sort of analysis, social science ceased to exist. Clarke argued that applicants should demonstrate proficiency in effective research methods; they should show a familiarity with the literature and an awareness of pitfalls; a hypothesis should be clearly stated and not be so vague or wide as to be irrefutable, and samples should permit generalisations; the methods of data collection and evaluation should be clearly spelt out and provide indications of the type of controls used; researchers should allow for the possibility of mistaking correlates for causes; and the reliability of the evaluation or assessment should be satisfactorily checked, and established in relation to an external criterion. Overall, Clarke suggested that 'these precautions have a general applicability which we will ignore at our peril, and at the expense of our credibility as a Working Group'.[20]

What this demonstrated was Clarke's background as a psychologist and lack of sympathy for qualitative research. Unsurprisingly, his proposals were opposed by Peter Willmott and Vic George, of the University of Kent, the other members of the Organising Group.

The Group as a whole felt that 'truly scientific' social science would not cover many of the proposed studies that came before it. A strict application of Clarke's criteria would imply a narrow conception of research regarded as legitimate, and exclude historical, anthropological, and psychoanalytic studies. It was agreed, therefore, that Clarke's criteria might be applied to explanatory studies, but that allowance should be made for descriptive and speculative research.[21] In any case, unsuccessful applicants had also on occasions written to the SSRC, criticising what in their view was the excessive caution of the Joint Working Party. When an application from his department was turned down, Professor F. M. Martin, of the University of Glasgow, wrote that:

> I had understood that the Group was concerned by the small amount of work being carried out on the sociological side. If there is a serious wish to encourage such studies it is counterproductive to insist on very rigorous methodological criteria ... there has to be a certain amount of risk-taking with exploratory and often tentative approaches otherwise the problems that we are concerned with will simply not be investigated at all.[22]

Cycle or web of deprivation? Research in progress

What this book does not attempt to do is to examine each of the research projects in detail; a synthesis was attempted in Muriel Brown and Nicola Madge's (1982a) final report on the Research Programme as a whole, and in any case this would be an impossible exercise. Nevertheless, it is necessary to say something more about the individual projects, and about what lessons, if any, they have for current initiatives on child poverty and social exclusion. Choosing any one project from the many that were funded is invidious. Nevertheless, the Coffield project at Keele University was one of the first projects to be funded, and in many ways was one of the most interesting. Moreover, combining archival research, oral interviews, and published documents illustrates interesting differences, not only between research projects, but within research teams. Richard Berthoud has argued that while the Coffield team identified the key issues, it adopted a research method that was unlikely to yield answers. The project was extremely small scale, and was only able to illustrate the characteristics of 'deprived' individuals and families. In this it replicated the earlier problem family studies, although it was critical of them. Berthoud argues that the Coffield project was more useful in 'advancing the question, than in providing an answer' (Berthoud, 1983a, p 160). In this section an attempt is made to fill this gap by looking in more detail at the project.

One of the most interesting applications came from Frank Coffield, then at Keele University, whose original discipline at Glasgow had been psychology, but who was pursuing research on juvenile delinquency. He had also followed debates about the culture of poverty, notably the critique by Charles Valentine. Coffield had noted the Joseph cycle speech, had been in the audience at the BASW conference at Manchester in March 1974 at which Barbara Castle had spoken, and was interested in deprived areas (Coffield, 1975). With Philip Robinson, a colleague at Keele who was a sociologist, and Jacquie Sarsby, who had previously carried out anthropological fieldwork in India, Coffield drafted an application. They were not very experienced researchers. Together they felt that the very static, immobile type of society found in the Potteries area of Staffordshire would be ideal for an intergenerational study – a method complementary in ways to that subsequently adopted by Atkinson's team based on the 1950 Rowntree survey of York.[23]

In their application (in 1974), Coffield, Robinson, and Sarsby stated that their project was interdisciplinary in scope, and aimed to combine the approaches of psychology, sociology, and anthropology to look at both individual and socioeconomic factors. The empirical research was to be conducted on a housing estate in North Staffordshire, which had been identified by local officials and professionals as an area where deprivation was transmitted from generation to generation within the same families. The team proposed to test the adequacy of the cycle thesis in three ways: first, by a conceptual analysis of the cycle and transmitted deprivation; second, by a demographic study of the local area; and, third, by an anthropological study of families deemed to be 'successful' and 'unsuccessful'. They noted that 'in all three sections we shall pay particular attention to the debate between individual and structural explanations of failure'.[24] Coffield, Robinson, and Sarsby noted that in exploring the life experiences of members of the same family, they would be asking to what extent deprivation was transmitted within the family; how far the lifestyle of the problem family was an adaptation to the structural problems they faced; and to what extent their problems were family created or socially created. This reflected the influence of the writers in the US whom Coffield admired, such as Oscar Lewis, Elliot Liebow, and William Foote Whyte. The main conceptual problems were perceived as being the concept of transmission, and the interrelationship between individual and structural explanations of deprivation.

Coffield and Robinson were interviewed by Alan Clarke and Peter Willmott. Coffield later recalled: 'we were certainly interviewed in a very formal way and we were in for two hours, we really got quite a roasting, well we felt like that'.[25] He felt that it was Willmott who was more amenable to qualitative research, while Clarke was the psychologist interested in hard data; in fact Coffield perceived the qualitative method as being a problem throughout the project, unacceptable to Clarke and Michael Rutter, but defended by Willmott given his community studies background. Moreover, Coffield got the impression that the Organising Group was under pressure to get some quick results, and it was this that led to their using the lists of problem families compiled by social workers. Thus while the Group was aware that this was an administrative category, it was worried about lengthy anthropological fieldwork, and so used these lists as a short cut.

The team rewrote the proposal and resubmitted it, and it was accepted. As part of the first round of successful applicants, Coffield also attended a seminar at Sunningdale, the Civil Service Training College, attended by Joseph, the sociologist Basil Bernstein, and various civil servants. Bernstein (1924-2000) was then Professor at the Institute of Education, London, famous for his work on the relationship between language and culture, his 'elaborated' and 'restricted' codes, charted in his four-volume series *Class, Codes and Control* (1971-90). The seminar proved to be eventful for the relatively junior Coffield:

> To my horror Sir Keith Joseph spoke first and then Basil Bernstein and then myself and God I was 33, and I was flying in very high company … a lucky thing that happened at the top, it was unbelievably icy at the beginning, senior civil servants were there and about three ministers from Education, Social Services – Department of Health and Social Security, DHSS in those days – and the Home Office was there and they seemed frightened to speak in front of Sir Keith. Basil Bernstein began speaking and he talked about the hierarchy of knowledge being an important issue and he turned round and wrote 'heirarchy' on the board and Sir Keith Joseph leapt up and said 'I'm sorry to interrupt Professor Bernstein but you've spelt hierarchy wrongly'. And Bernstein never even as much as looked at the board, he threw the piece of chalk up and caught it in his hand and said 'For a hundred measly pounds you expect spelling as well Sir Keith?' and the place collapsed with laughter and

it was easy to speak after that, the ice had been broken and everyone just piled in, it was a very useful occasion.[26]

The Coffield study was published in 1980, the first of the early projects to appear in book form. But as with Rutter and Madge's literature review, its findings tended to challenge, rather than confirm, the theory of the cycle of deprivation. Four families had been selected – the Barkers, representing a large family; Ada Paterson, an 'inadequate' mother; the Martins, a long-term unemployed family; and the Fieldings, a family regarded as 'coming out' of deprivation. Vince Barker, head of the Barker family, in many ways fitted the culture of poverty stereotype. He certainly lived for the present and did not defer gratification, perhaps because he anticipated a time when he might be less physically robust and incapable of earning an adequate wage packet. Nonetheless, there were other features that contradicted the traditional stereotype. For one thing, the Barkers possessed insurance following a fire at their home. Similarly, Elsie Barker saved for Christmas, and managed her finances as carefully as she could. The case of the other families was similarly complex. In the Martin household, for example, there was evidence that possessions were not neglected, but in fact were looked after carefully. The garden was cultivated, at least for a time, and ornaments were carefully arranged in the front room. Sally Martin spent a lot of her time washing and ironing, while Peter Martin was constantly repairing or improving household objects (Coffield et al, 1980, p 161). He, too, was interested in gardening, and had managed to keep his first job at a garage for over a year.

What the published book does not demonstrate are the problems faced by the research team. The Coffield study had sought to examine the cycle of deprivation through intensive case studies. It was based on participant observation of a small number of 'multi-problem' families. The team entered the social world of these families for two years, joining family celebrations such as wedding anniversaries, birthday parties, and christenings, as well as more general family activities. Nevertheless, this proved onerous, as Coffield recalled:

> One of the problems we [the research team] had was being ill so often, we used to go and stay for as long as we could at weekends and so on because we were lecturers with full teaching loads and we would try and stay as much of the full day as we could, eating with them and so on and we were really surprised. They didn't have fridges in the summer of '76, which was the hottest summer I think we've had

in 30, 40 years. I had a family at the time and they were about five miles away without me and I was inside these incredibly hot houses, the heating would be on all the time, the temperatures 70 and 80 degrees, the milk was off, the kids were streaming with colds and so on. All these problems were there, we were there regularly.[27]

The team did not find a commissioned paper on the concept of deprivation very helpful, nor did they have much contact with the researchers on other projects.

Reviewing the problem family literature, including the Sheffield studies, Coffield and his colleagues argued that the term 'problem family', along with the term 'transmitted deprivation', should be abandoned (Coffield et al, 1980, pp 201-2). Overall, Coffield and his colleagues argued that the cycle of deprivation was too simple an idea to explain the complex lives of the four families that they had spent so long studying in such minute detail. Employing a different metaphor, they concluded that 'the *web* of deprivation, rather than the *cycle* of deprivation, depicts more accurately the dense network of psychological, social, historical and economic factors which have either created or perpetuated problems for these families' (Coffield et al, 1980, pp 163-4 [emphasis in original]). The complexity lay in the interacting and cumulative nature of the deprivations – no single hypothesis could explain the complex mesh of factors. They argued that it was only the dynamic interplay between structural factors and their effects on the personality of individuals that could 'do justice to the complexity of the lives we are struggling to understand' (Coffield et al, 1980, p 159). Their conclusions cast doubt on explanations that either sought to lay the blame for deprivation on the inadequate personalities of the poor, or only on the economic structure of society. Unfortunately the debate had been polarised into these competing, extreme positions. Although the cycle of deprivation had an appealing simplicity, the reality was that families moved in and out of established categories of deprivation. In general, Coffield and his colleagues argued that the term 'cycle of deprivation' tended to simplify complex issues. While there were factors that might increase the probability of a family being labelled as a problem, 'the causal processes are many, complex and interrelated, the exceptions numerous, and the critical precipitating events different in each case' (Coffield et al, 1980, pp 169-70).

But again this understates the problems the research team faced. While the study aimed to test the cycle of deprivation thesis in three ways, in the event it was the anthropological arm of the study, rather than the conceptual and the demographic, which absorbed the bulk of the time of the researchers.[28] Looking back, Coffield felt that they should have had sharper, more clearly defined research questions that they could have homed in on. The other problem was that the team was overwhelmed by the amount of data that it had collected on so many different issues. It could barely get it all transcribed. Coffield and Robinson had full teaching loads, and it was in the vacations that they tried to make sense of it. When it came to analysing the data, there were no easy explanations. Identifying causal mechanisms was particularly difficult. Coffield as the psychologist stressed the role of behavioural factors, Sarsby the socioeconomic context. In the end, the team agreed to record Sarsby's minority view in the book. Coffield recalled:

> There were no easy explanations, the sheer complexity of the issues that these families threw up and the difficulty in suggesting what policies should come from it, I mean it was a baptism of fire as far as I was concerned. There was no simple approach, we had no easy remedies and it was extremely difficult to discover why certain people had succeeded and others failed. There were so many factors involved.[29]

Reflecting on the project two years after the publication of the book, Coffield came to the same conclusions. The idea of a cycle or circle created the wrong mental image, because it implied a simple linear progression, whereas the data that his team had collected showed how the different variables were complex, interacting with, and contaminating, each other. The 'transmission' of deprivation could not be attributed to any one single factor. Importantly, Coffield argued that the data indicated that it was a mistake to focus exclusively on either behaviour or structure:

> Our families were caught in a dense web of economic, medical, social and psychological problems which overlapped and interacted; their problems needed amelioration, no matter what their parents or grandparents were like. Moreover, our families moved in and out of the official categories of deprivation even during the two years of fieldwork. (Coffield, 1982, pp 10-12)

Coffield subsequently attempted to draw more definite conclusions about the causal mechanisms. However, he argued that distinctions between structural and individual factors more accurately reflected traditional academic divisions between sociology and psychology, than real differences in the factors that impinged on the lives of the families (Coffield, 1983, p 24).

In the event, the book was not well received by the SSRC, which was influenced by commentators critical of the way that the Coffield team had dealt with child abuse. The social work community was sensitive to criticism in the wake of the Maria Colwell inquiry (1978). More generally, the book was not widely or well reviewed. Ann Shearer, for instance, was uncertain how far the descriptions of the families advanced understanding of their situation, and argued that it was not clear what biases the researchers brought to their participant observation. They were aware of their concentration on personal factors and family patterns, rather than wider social and environmental realities, but had done little to correct this. There was little in the book about the providers of services, or the concept of transmitted deprivation, and the final conclusions were tentative. Shearer wrote that 'people aren't problems to be solved, however much tidier the world would be if they were' (Shearer, 1981, p 559). Moreover, she argued that the book ducked the policy implications of the research, focusing again on the individual family, and ignoring poverty and economic structures. Arguably most revealing was the way the book was lambasted for an anachronistic focus on problem families and for ignoring 'situational effects'; it blamed neither the victims nor the system, and failed to opt 'for a radical redirection of social policy based on a recognition of the structural causes of poverty' (Raban, 1982, p 120). In part this reflected broader changes between 1974 and 1981. These themes are taken up again in Chapters Five and Six.

Towards a more structural emphasis

The Coffield study had attempted to look at both behavioural and structural factors. In this it was unusual, particularly since it was one of the first applications to be funded. In fact, the feeling on the part of the SSRC towards the end of 1974 had been that there was a strong sociological or psychological bias in the subcontracts awarded, and a dearth of proposals on more economic aspects. The SSRC suggested that perhaps work should concentrate on encouraging the latter, by writing to economists, publishing short articles in relevant journals, and by inviting some to speak at meetings. It was hoped that Kit Jones, with her contacts at the NIESR, might know relevant researchers.[30]

Similarly, when the SSRC took stock of the Research Programme, it found that in terms of the discipline of study:

- 43% of the funding (£27,617) had been awarded to psychiatry and psychology;
- 16% (£10,238) to anthropology;
- 16% (£10,045) to statistics;
- 12% (£7,706) to sociology;
- 10% (£6,620) to criminology;
- and only 3% (£1,886) to social administration.

Four projects were focusing on the intergenerational extent of deprivation (Atkinson, Hope, Paterson, and Tonge and Lunn); two on familial processes (Rapaport and Wolkind); one on community influences (Coffield); one on the intragenerational extent of deprivation (McClintock); and one was the computer simulation (Greenwood, Bytheway, and Dajda). Overall, eight projects were looking at broadly individual factors, and only one at structural factors. The SSRC therefore concluded that these imbalances should be corrected in future research.[31]

Some of this was due to the personalities involved. Suzanne Reeve, then DHSS Secretary of the Joint Working Party, for instance, later argued that the original membership had been reasonably balanced, with Tony Atkinson and Roy Parker representing the disciplines of economics and social administration. However, they quickly became disenchanted and, giving different reasons, dropped out, leaving the field clear for domination by the psychological-psychiatric interests. Reeve wrote that:

> Both Professors Clarke and Rutter are powerful personalities as well as being academic heavyweights, and none of their fellow academics has been prepared to mildly disagree with them, let alone take issue with them on imbalance within the Research Programme. Professor Willmott, while being a nice man is painfully conscious that he is only a Professor once a week and has no confidence in his abilities to win an argument. So more often than not, he does not argue. As a result, the research commissioned so far is heavily biased towards the psychological aspects of deprivation, and little attention has been paid or resources allocated to projects more concerned with economic and social aspects.[32]

Reeve argued that the Research Programme was still dominated by psychiatry; when Michael Rutter asked for a £75,000 grant, the Organising Group made a decision in 30 seconds, while the DHSS and Central Statistical Office had serious doubts about the value of the research.[33] Following some 'stealthy activity' by her, the Organising Group discussed the imbalance. It made three suggestions. First, it felt that the term 'transmitted deprivation' was discouraging applicants outside psychology and psychiatry, and even proposed a return to the 'cycle of deprivation' terminology. Second, an academic from social administration might be recruited, possibly Vic George from the University of Kent, or Michael Hill from the University of Oxford. Third, that Geoffrey Hawthorn, from Churchill College, Cambridge, might look at concepts of deprivation. The Joint Working Party agreed that the areas being supported showed a strong bias towards psychological and psychiatric approaches, and the Organising Group should now actively encourage research on the interaction between families and the social structure, with the aim of enhancing policies aimed at intervening in the cycle. The title of the Research Programme could not be changed at that stage, but the aims might be explained more clearly.[34]

In fact this central question, of the relative importance of individual characteristics and broader structural factors, had already come into the assessment of individual applications. Reviewing an application on children in violent families, for example, Dennis Marsden, from the University of Essex, had written that:

> On the question of theory, I would suggest that they might learn a great deal from Dr Harriett Wilson's work with deprived families. She seems to me to have made a good start towards the problems of relating life style to economic deprivation, and has a strenuous (too strenuous?) theoretical approach.[35]

Marsden's main feeling was that the proposed project would benefit from the close oversight of a rather sceptical, policy-oriented theoretician with a mistrust of social workers. Vic George suggested similarly that an application from Michael Rutter concentrated on the social services, and might have looked at the contribution of taxation policy and occupational welfare benefits, drawing on Titmuss's work on the social division of welfare.[36]

By the summer of 1975, interesting critiques had begun to surface by social scientists who were critical of the Research Programme.

Tom Burns (1913-2001), for example, Professor of Sociology at the University of Edinburgh, queried the terms 'cyclical', 'transmission', and 'deprivation'. He noted that the 11 projects that had been funded situated the area of study in the developmental and learning patterns, behaviour, and coping mechanisms of deprived individuals and families. To his mind, there was an old-fashioned and outmoded 'psychologism' running through the projects, reminiscent of studies of problem families, a reliance on clinical methods of sampling, and of the kind of work that had made the psychiatrist John Bowlby (1907-90) famous. Burns was also alarmed by the reappearance of the culture of poverty. He argued that 'it does look as though what resources are at the disposal of the Working Party could easily be frittered away in a large number of small research projects which do not, on the face of it, seem to follow any recognisable plan, or to be likely to yield any cumulative results'.[37] Burns suggested that deprivation was created and maintained by social organisations and institutions. The research should focus on the structures of services, the ideologies and practices of health professionals, and interactions between professionals and clients. The concern should be with how services failed certain types of clients.

These debates were embodied in the Second Report of the Joint Working Party (SSRC–DHSS, 1975). It noted that the subcontracts awarded had emphasised psychology and psychiatry, and processes within the family had received more attention than the interrelationships between the family and outside institutions. There was a particular interest in the people who broke out of potential cycles, and neither 'deprivation' nor 'transmission' was unambiguous; it was this that Geoffrey Hawthorn had been appointed to investigate. Moreover, the Joint Working Party again emphasised that the word 'transmission' should not be taken to imply that the Research Programme was only concerned with the role of the family in problems such as poverty, limited economic opportunity, bad housing, psychiatric difficulty, and educational handicap. Overall, the Joint Working Party stressed that it was eager to correct the imbalance in the research supported; the research was not intended to be confined to the study of individual and family influences. Its meaning was wider and was intended to encompass the influence of social policies and socioeconomic factors (SSRC–DHSS, 1975, pp 4-6).

The debates were also reflected in new appointments to the Organising Group and Joint Working Party. For example, as we have seen, Kit Jones had been replaced on the Organising Group by Vic George, then Professor of Social Administration at the University of Kent. Born in Cyprus, George had trained as a youth leader and taken a degree in social administration at the University of Nottingham, later working as a social worker for migrants, and as a Child Care Officer for the London County Council. He subsequently became a Lecturer in Applied Social Science at the University of Nottingham. A flavour of his interests at this time is given in his history of the development of social security in Britain since the Beveridge Report (George, 1968). As a relatively new recruit, George brought a fresh perspective to the Organising Group. He argued that it should spend time considering the gaps in funding, and on how to encourage work in areas such as education and social values. In his view, the absence of an agreed intellectual framework was holding the Organising Group back. The First Report had broadly defined a set of concerns and emphases, but members needed something more specific.[38] Nevertheless, the new appointments in some cases exacerbated personal tensions. George had not been the preferred choice of either Michael Rutter or Alan Clarke, who had wanted another candidate.[39] Clarke regarded George as a Marxist sociologist, and he later recalled more generally that:

> A number of sociologists were very uptight about the whole concept of transmitted deprivation because they didn't like the determinist ethos of that concept and there were some very critical comments by some way-out Marxist sociologists about the uselessness of this Programme. They didn't affect me in any way at all but I think probably they annoyed Peter Willmott because he was a distinguished sociologist himself. There was a sociology attack on the whole business.[40]

Research extravaganzas

A further factor in the question of whether the Research Programme had a sufficiently structural emphasis was Labour's political uncertainty about it, originally apparent in the Barbara Castle BASW paper (Castle, 1974), and subsequent comments by Brian Abel-Smith (see pp 100-1, this volume). This debate had rumbled on in the background. Suzanne Reeve noted in June 1975, for example, that the SSRC was aware that the political enthusiasm had gone from the work. Current ministers did not take an interest, and Norman Jordan-Moss and Joan Cooper no longer attended meetings. Reeve wrote that the 'SSRC is aware that the project is now of less significance and I think the quality of their contribution is suffering accordingly'.[41] Certainly there was ongoing discomfort on the part of David Owen, as Minister for Health. At the committee stage of the Children Bill, in July 1975, for example, Owen had expressed concern at 'research extravaganzas' and about some of the research being funded on the cycle of deprivation. He thought that some of the research projects should be evaluated, observing 'that [the Research Programme] is a relic of a time when we had a lot more money, and I am not convinced of the effect on long-term policy of some of that research'.[42] Owen had asked to discuss the Research Programme with Abel-Smith, and DHSS civil servants were concerned that Owen's statement in the House of Commons would attract the attention of the SSRC. They suggested that their response should not be that he was critical of the Programme as a whole, but that he shared the concern of the Joint Working Party about the overemphasis on psychology and psychiatry in the contracts awarded.[43]

It is clear that Owen was disappointed with the scope of the Research Programme, and thought that it should include some long-term cohort studies. He proposed a meeting with Derek Robinson, the Oxford economist who had succeeded Robin Matthews as Chair of the SSRC.[44] In October 1975, Abel-Smith queried why the Research Programme had not made more use of the two major national longitudinal studies, the NCDS and the Douglas study, since this seemed the most promising approach. He noted that Owen would want to see more stress on environmental factors such as poverty and bad housing, observing that the Atkinson project seemed a step in the right direction. Furthermore, Abel-Smith echoed Tom Burns in arguing that the Joint Working Party's Second Report (SSRC–DHSS, 1975) gave the impression that the money was going to be dissipated in a series of relatively minor projects with a common theme, but without an integrated strategy that would answer the key questions.[45] In the event, civil servants pointed out that the Second Report, which had seemed so 'scrappy', did not comprise the full activities of the Research Programme. When Owen was given an updated list of projects, he noted the three major new studies by Atkinson, Rutter, and Donald West, recognised the possibility of longitudinal studies, and dropped his original plan to see Derek Robinson.[46] What this episode illustrates is the influence of the Labour government on the direction of the Research Programme, along with the role of specialist advisors such as Abel-Smith. At the DHSS, the civil servant Tom Luce later alleged that ministers had never considered the Programme properly, apart from David Owen who was both interested and showed a disposition to criticise.[47]

The Joint Working Party was fully aware that there had been criticisms from sociologists like Tom Burns. It stated that it did not take such a narrow view, and had sought applications from sociologists, economists, and social administrators. It was because it had received so few that the imbalance had occurred; it funded the best research that came before it, and no one was in favour of artificially preserving a balance. It saw two kinds of criticisms. First, a less radical genuine anxiety about the balance in the Research Programme. Second, a more radical one that suggested that individual attributes were unimportant in the transmission of deprivation, and deprivation would disappear with a more equitable distribution of wealth and income.[48] The Organising Group publicised its desire to include more socioeconomic studies, and had some success in commissioning them. A contemporary SSRC flyer conceded that while applications had been invited from anyone who might be interested, the response from social administration had not been enthusiastic, perhaps because the Joint Working Party's areas of interest had been misunderstood.[49]

Attempts were made to correct the perceived imbalance in the research, and gradually competition for funds increased. Nevertheless, referees were no less critical of some of the more structural applications. In a report on an application on housing, for instance, Clare Ungerson, then at the University of Kent, wrote that, while the content was fascinating, 'what worries me is their [the applicants'] apparent narrowing down of causation to the allocation policies of local authorities ... what other factors are they going to take into account?'[50] It was revealing of the difficulties faced by the Organising Group that this study was in the end funded, and the same was true of an application from Richard Brown and Jim Cousins.[51] Commenting on this application, Kit Jones suggested that she had grave doubts about the proposal. The applicants were primarily interested in the labour market rather than in transmitted deprivation; the potential connections between the two were not made clear in the proposal, and no hypothesis was offered on the mechanisms that linked them. The benefit of studying employer recruitment policies was not clear, and the literature review on labour market studies was not well organised. Overall, Jones argued that the study needed to be given more careful thought and to be focused more narrowly.[52]

Part of this stage of the Research Programme was concerned with the organisation of seminars and workshops, designed to bring researchers together, and these also reflected the attempt to give it a more structural flavour. There had been a seminar on multiple deprivation (March 1975), and one on structural aspects of deprivation had first been suggested after Illsley's commentary on the 'Approaches' paper at the LSE conference in April 1973. The SSRC suggested that socioeconomic factors might include the influence of unemployment, social areas, and capitalism on the continuity of deprivation, evaluations of policies, and action research at the local level.[53] The Organising Group began to plan a third seminar, on socio-structural explanations for transmitted deprivation, and on evaluating the effects of social policies. Suggested speakers included some of those who had earlier been critical, or who were associated with a more 'structural' viewpoint: Tom Burns, David Donnison, Bob Holman, Raymond Illsley, and Adrian Sinfield.[54]

The Research Programme and money

The feeling that the Research Programme was insufficiently 'structural' was reflected in the workings of the RCDIW. Chaired by Lord Diamond, one of its members was Tony Atkinson, and one of its reports focused on lower incomes. Cyril Smith, Secretary to the SSRC, in August 1976 told Fred Bayliss, Secretary to the RCDIW, that there were only two transmitted deprivation projects that were directly related to lower incomes – those by Atkinson. He noted of the other projects that 'I think it is unlikely that in most cases the research workers will be giving any special attention to matters of income'.[55] Smith proposed a meeting with Frank Field, then of the Low Pay Unit, and Richard Layard, from the LSE. Dorothy Wedderburn, then Director of the Industrial Sociology Unit at Imperial College, London, subsequently wrote that she found it difficult to imagine how some of the projects were being conducted if they were not giving any special attention to matters of income.[56] Bayliss then confirmed that Smith had said that the dominant influence in the Joint Working Party was exercised by psychologists, and apart from Atkinson there was very little in the Programme that would interest the RCDIW.[57]

Personnel involved in the RCDIW acknowledged that the Rutter and Madge literature review (1976), which had just been published, was a very important contribution to the debate, and despite the authors' main research interests being in psychiatry and child psychology, did offer a thorough review of the literature in other fields, including the social sciences.[58] But those who acted as observers at some of the Research Programme's conferences produced critical reports. The fourth conference, for example, held at the LSE in September 1976 was chaired by Peter Willmott and Vic George, and featured papers by Clare Ungerson on housing; Michael Power on social work services; Adrian Sinfield on income maintenance; and Richard Layard on earnings. However, overall the observer's report concluded that 'there were four presentations and the conference spent most of its time criticising the methodologies used in them rather than in identifying useful research objectives'.[59] A meeting was held between members of the Joint Working Party and the RCDIW, at the Institute of Community Studies, in December 1976. The RCDIW's Secretary concluded shortly afterwards that 'it is quite clear that we shall get little detailed help from the DHSS–SSRC Programme'.[60] He observed of some of the interim project reports that 'none of these authors make the mistake of over-simplification or of reaching practical conclusions, that might be challenged, or any conclusions other than those pointing to further research'.[61]

In the event, the RCDIW's report on low incomes (RCDIW, 1978) did look at life-cycle effects and intergenerational continuities, drawing on the Atkinson study of incomes in York, and taking evidence from Michael Rutter and Nicola Madge. It confirmed the importance of life-cycle effects, in that children, parents with younger children, and older people were more likely to experience low incomes. Many of those who had a lower income in one year had moved out of the lower income group in the next, but there was less upward mobility among pensioner households and one-parent families than among households of married couples with children. Fathers and sons tended to have similar occupational levels and earnings, and to be in households of similar income levels, but this was against a background of considerable intergenerational mobility (RCDIW, 1978, pp 126-35). The report concluded that research on the relative importance to incomes of genetic and environmental factors had been 'inconclusive'. It was not known why some individuals and families had lower incomes than others – heredity, family background, early environment, and education all played a part. Nevertheless, the report ventured that the greater the role played by genetic endowment or inherited social and economic disadvantages, the greater was the justification for maintaining safety nets (RCDIW, 1978, pp 148-53).

In an addendum, George Doughty, David Lea, and Dorothy Wedderburn went further than this, arguing that the genetic argument contributed nothing to an understanding of lower incomes. It ignored the decisive importance of factors bound up with the structure and functioning of the economy, and those affecting access to education and training (RCDIW, 1978, p 157). In many respects, the RCDIW anticipated more recent work on poverty dynamics. Overall, the latter phase of the Research Programme did seem to have a more marked structural emphasis. Frank Field had applied for funding for a project looking at poverty and low pay in three towns, and at changes over time. However, he subsequently withdrew his application because of 'the casual and unhelpful way the SSRC was considering the project'.[62] In fact the view of the SSRC was that the Low Pay Unit lacked the skills and experience to conduct a sample survey. Valid comparisons over time on such a topic were very difficult to establish, and there was no evidence in the application to show that these had been fully considered, let alone overcome.[63]

Muriel Brown, from the Department of Social Science and Administration at the LSE, had been appointed to the Joint Working Party, and was also, by November 1977, a member of the Organising Group. In December 1977, for example, Brown noted of a proposal for research on the significance of money that 'money is extremely important, both to the impact of deprivation on individuals and families and to the transmission of deprivation intergenerationally'.[64] In part, she was responding to Dorothy Wedderburn's earlier point about the extent to which the researchers were looking at income. The proposed Steering Group included key figures from social policy (Sally Baldwin, Kay Carmichael, Hilary Land, David Piachaud, and Barbara Rodgers). Areas for enquiry included a survey of the literature; the handling of money; money problems among the clients of Social Service Departments; the significance of debt; evaluations of existing interventions; and action research on the impact of money advice centres. Subsequently, this did become a Low Incomes Research Steering Group, chaired by Brown.[65] However, while it ultimately led to the literature review on the money problems of the poor (Ashley, 1983) it was striking how limited and belated this was. These broader questions, of the attitude of social scientists to the cycle speech and Research Programme, are explored more fully in Chapter Six.

Transmitted deprivation: the stance of the DHSS

Differences between the SSRC and DHSS had been apparent from the outset, particularly over the relevance of the Research Programme to policy. The concern of the DHSS was with research of interest to public policy, especially the personal social services. The problem as it saw it was that there was a pattern of transmitted deprivation from parents to children through which problems continued to recur within families despite the improvement of community services; its concern was to achieve a better understanding of the problem, and to find ways of developing a preventive strategy.[66] Agreeing the terms of agreement for the Research Programme, the policy relevance of the research was again uppermost, since the objectives were seen as being to:

> commission research into aspects of the cycle of transmitted deprivation within the programme as defined by the Joint Working Party. The research should be aimed as far as possible at producing results which will give guidance for policy and action for intervention in the cycle.[67]

Much of the growing unhappiness of the DHSS was due to the election of the Labour government in March 1974, as has already been noted. The DHSS had always seen the emphasis on the cycle of deprivation as a personal crusade on the part of Joseph, and as ministerial interest in the Research Programme evaporated, civil servants no longer attended Joint Working Party meetings. By the autumn of 1975, DHSS officials were blaming the SSRC for the difficulty in achieving a balanced Research Programme. Joan Cooper complained to Brian Abel-Smith, for example, that the response had been better from the 'soft sciences' than the 'hard sciences', and there had been few applications to match that by the Atkinson team of economists.[68] As the research got under way, there is no doubt that day-to-day relationships between the DHSS and SSRC were difficult. The DHSS was concerned that the role of the Organising Group, and the procedures of the Chair, meant that some research had been funded that had not been subject to close scrutiny.[69]

  Briefing Patrick Benner, Deputy Secretary at the DHSS, on the history of the Research Programme, Joan Cooper noted 'I can fill you in with some of the inevitable difficulties which have since occurred'.[70] Having read the background papers, Benner argued that the concept of the cycle of deprivation was an interesting one, but 'of uncertain relevance from the practical point of view'.[71] Everyone would agree that harmful effects were produced by poverty, bad housing, the unsatisfactory upbringing of children, the absence of local social cohesion, and all the other factors that were thought to play a part in the cycle of deprivation. He could see that research might be needed into each of these in order to define more precisely what their harmful effects were, the means by which they were produced, and the most effective corrective steps that might be taken. This was an area where action was needed, whether or not the cycle of deprivation proved to be a reality. However, Benner thought that the action taken would be the same regardless of whether harmful effects were transmitted from one generation to the next, and from that point of view the cycle of deprivation could almost be regarded as a 'non-issue'. Demonstration of the existence of the cycle might increase the urgency of measures to grapple with 'known social evils', but limited resources precluded significantly greater effort being made. Indeed it was arguable that the diversion of research effort to the cycle merely reduced that which could be put into the investigation of known problems. Benner was cautiously supportive of attempts to give the Research Programme greater intellectual coherence. He noted of Geoffrey Hawthorn and Harold Carter's paper on the concept of deprivation that 'I have read the circulated paper with much interest. It is very much the sort of thing – though a good deal longer – which I might have written as a weekly essay at Oxford on moral or political philosophy'.[72] However, he was neither particularly interested in intergenerational continuities, nor very supportive of more abstract research.

By the spring of 1976, the DHSS was more concerned than ever that the Research Programme should produce results that would guide policy and intervention strategies. Geoff Hulme, for example, noted that the review of the Research Programme was not due to be carried out until the end of the third year. He stressed that:

> In present circumstances we are naturally more than ever concerned that the programme should as far as possible produce results which will give guidance for policy and action. We should maintain our interest in securing a balance between work of long-term value and work which might be helpful in the reasonably near future.[73]

In March 1976, Benner, Cooper, and Hulme discussed Benner's misgivings about the value of the Research Programme with Sir Douglas Black (1913-2002), Chief Scientist to the DHSS.

One area where DHSS civil servants did take an interest was in appointments to the Joint Working Party. In May 1976, for example, Alice Sheridan noted of Professor Peter Leonard at Warwick University that he had allegedly swung to Left-wing views in recent years, and this might lead him to be opposed to the theory of transmitted deprivation.[74] Similarly, Michael Rodda, Senior Research Officer at the DHSS, argued that the Joint Working Party needed a methodological counterweight to Michael Rutter, and neither the suggested replacements of Adrian Webb, Professor of Social Policy at Loughborough University, nor Dennis Marsden would provide this. His preference was for either Jennifer Platt or Hilary Land.[75] For her part, Alice Sheridan argued more generally that there was no need for anyone else from the DHSS to be involved in the Joint Working Party; it was just going to be a struggle to keep 'some sort of order and discipline' in what it did, and to see how it related to DHSS priorities.[76]

There were more direct criticisms of the Organising Group. Civil servants argued that although it was responsible for guiding the SSRC's initiatives to promote interest in the Research Programme among researchers, it did not have a clear idea about the amount of money available. It found it difficult to establish priorities, and to know what sorts of initiatives were necessary to maintain a reasonable balance in the research.[77] Not surprisingly, civil servants were concerned mainly with research of interest to the DHSS, especially the personal social services and intervention.[78] For example, Geoff Hulme checked how far the literature review by Rutter and Madge (1976) and the Research Programme covered the link between 'unwanted pregnancies' and cycles of deprivation. He wrote that 'on the face of it forms of intervention designed to prevent such pregnancies, including family planning and sex education strategies, should be among the potential topics for research under the intervention part of this Programme'.[79] Other civil servants proposed reducing or terminating the commitment to the Research Programme, and transferring the funds released to other projects.[80] By early 1977, it was felt that the DHSS should play a smaller part in the Joint Working Party, and only send a couple of people to its meetings. Patrick Benner advised that it did not want to give the impression that the DHSS was withdrawing, and if it was going to reduce its representation, it would be best to do so 'by stealth'.[81] In a subsequent note, Benner again stressed that 'I feel that there are a number of things where it might be better not to get too closely involved, bearing in mind that we may not want to have the final report pinned on us more than we can help'.[82] These anxieties intensified over the final report, as we shall see in the next chapter.

Conclusion

This chapter has traced the early years of the Research Programme, from its formal launch in May 1974. It has explored early attempts to commission research, and some of the applications that were received, such as that from Mildred Blaxter and Raymond Illsley at the University of Aberdeen. Drawing on a combination of archival research, oral interviews, and published documents, it has looked in some detail at the project led by Frank Coffield at Keele University. The chapter has sought particularly to explain the increasingly structural focus of the Research Programme, looking at the efforts that were made to correct the perceived imbalance, away from the emphasis on familial processes, to take more account of socioeconomic factors, and at the way this issue coloured relationships with the RCDIW. Here the appointment of new members to the Joint Working Party, and the attitude of David Owen and Brian Abel-Smith, seemed to be critical. The chapter has also traced the attitude of the DHSS civil servants towards the Research Programme, and at their growing exasperation with it.

The chapter has argued that Berthoud is correct in suggesting that in this period the SSRC was not accustomed to running a pre-planned, multidisciplinary programme of this kind, and found it difficult to commission the type of studies that were thought to be required. Yet while Berthoud stresses the problems faced by the Joint Working Party, he underplays the significance of the broader political context in dictating the shift from the original behavioural emphasis of the cycle to the more structural focus of the Research Programme. The overall argument of the chapter has been that the move towards socioeconomic factors was less a takeover of the Programme, than an attempt to balance the original bias towards psychology. The archival sources reveal the problems that the Joint Working Party struggled with, the poor quality of the applications that it received, and the critical response of referees to applications. If anything, disciplinary differences between members were accentuated from the mid-1970s with the increasing influence of psychology (Clarke) combined with the structural focus of new members (George). I have already discussed the reaction to one study: that by the team led by Coffield. In the next chapter I explore how these different debates played out in the remainder of the Research Programme, and the response to some of the other studies, when they began to be published in the early 1980s.

Notes

[1] Adrian Sinfield papers, A. Edmond and M. Brennan, 'DHSS–SSRC contract on research into transmitted deprivation' (nd).

[2] Interview between the author and Alan Clarke, London, 24 May 2006.

[3] NA MH 152/78: minutes of the 8th meeting of the Joint Working Party, 16 May 1974.

[4] NA MH 152/79: minutes of the 8th meeting of the Organising Group, 2 October 1974.

[5] NA MH 152/79: minutes of the 8th meeting of the Organising Group, 2 October 1974.

[6] Interview between the author and Michael Rutter, London, 4 July 2006.

[7] Interview between the author and Richard Berthoud, University of Essex, 2 May 2006.

[8] Private correspondence between Bill Bytheway and the author, 24 June 2005.

[9] NA MH 152/82: 'Comments by Ian Cullen on his meeting with Richard Dajda', 22 August 1975.

[10] NA MH 152/83: K. Hope, 'Report to DHSS–SSRC Committee on Deprivation re Mr R Dajda', 30 September 1975.

[11] NA MH 152/82: SSRC, 'Progress report from Dr Greenwood and Mr Dajda', 3 October 1975.

[12] NA MH 152/83: minutes of the 19th meeting of the Organising Group, 21 November 1975.

[13] NA MH 166/1516: 'Referee C' (nd).

[14] NA MH 152/83: minutes of the 11th meeting of the Joint Working Party, 3 October 1975.

[15] NA MH 152/80: I. J. Craft to A. Edmond, 1 April 1975.

[16] NA MH 152/83: application from R. Illsley and M. Blaxter, 'Family attitudes to health and health services' (nd).

[17] NA MH 152/83: M. Brennan to R. Illsley, 30 December 1975.

[18] NA MH 152/85: M. Jefferys to C. Blackler, 25 March 1976.

[19] NA MH 152/84: A. D. B. Clarke to M. Brennan, 2 February 1976.

[20] NA MH 152/84: A. D. B. Clarke to M. Brennan, 2 February 1976.

[21] NA MH 152/84: minutes of the 22nd meeting of the Organising Group, 13 February 1976.

[22] NA MH 152/80: F. M. Martin to A. Edmond, 18 June 1975.

[23] Interview between the author and Frank Coffield, Newcastle upon Tyne, 8 April 2003.

[24] NA MH 152/85: application from F. Coffield, P. Robinson, and J. Sarsby, 'A conceptual and empirical study of the transmitted deprivation thesis' (nd).

[25] Interview between the author and Frank Coffield, Newcastle upon Tyne, 8 April 2003.

[26] Interview between the author and Frank Coffield, Newcastle upon Tyne, 8 April 2003.

[27] Interview between the author and Frank Coffield, Newcastle upon Tyne, 8 April 2003.

[28] NA MH 152/85: F. Coffield to C. Blackler, 16 March 1976.

[29] Interview between the author and Frank Coffield, Newcastle upon Tyne, 8 April 2003.

[30] NA MH 152/79: 'SSRC', 1 November 1974.

[31] NA MH 152/79: SSRC, 'Balance of research', 5 December 1974.

[32] NA MH 152/80: S. E. Reeve to G. Hulme, 12 June 1975.

[33] NA MH 152/80: S. E. Reeve to G. Hulme, 12 June 1975.

[34] NA MH 152/80: minutes of the 9th meeting of the Working Party, 26 February 1975, papers for the 10th meeting of the Working Party, 1 July 1975.

[35] NA MH 152/83: application from Mr J. D. H. Chaney and Mrs C. E. Stubbs, 'Children in violent families: deprivation and intergenerational continuities'.

[36] NA MH 152/83: V. George to M. Brennan, 19 December 1975.

[37] NA MH 152/80: T. Burns, 'Memorandum on research into transmitted deprivation', 16 June 1975.

[38] NA MH 152/82: minutes of the 17th meeting of the Organising Group, 9 September 1975, p 10.

[39] NA MH 152/80: S. Reeve to G. Hulme, 12 June 1975.

[40] Interview between the author and Alan Clarke, London, 24 May 2006.

[41] NA MH 152/80: S. Reeve to G. Hulme, 12 June 1975.

[42] NA MH 152/81: House of Commons Standing Committee A, 22 July 1975, p 470.

[43] NA MH 152/81: P. J. Lewis to R. S. King, 1 August 1975.

[44] NA MH 152/82: M. G. Lillywhite to G. Hulme, 22 September 1975.

[45] NA MH 152/82: B. Abel-Smith to G. Hulme, 2 October 1975.

[46] NA MH 152/82: B. Abel-Smith to D. Owen, 9 October 1975; NA MH 152/82: D. Owen to K. Joseph, 16 October 1975; NA MH 152/82: B. Abel-Smith to J. Cooper, 17 October 1975.

[47] NA MH 166/1517: T. R. H. Luce to E. Shaw, 16 August 1977.

[48] NA MH 152/82: minutes of the 10th meeting of the Joint Working Party, 1 July 1975.

[49] Adrian Sinfield papers, A. Edmond and M. Brennan, 'DHSS–SSRC contract on research into transmitted deprivation' (nd).

[50] NA MH 152/82: application from G. L. Millerson and B. Ineichen, 'Housing factors in transmitted deprivation' (nd).

[51] NA MH 152/83: minutes of the 20th meeting of the Organising Group, 12 December 1975.

[52] NA MH 152/84: minutes of the 21st meeting of the Organising Group, 16 January 1976.

[53] NA MH 152/82: SSRC, 'Third seminar', 3 October 1975.

[54] NA MH 152/82: minutes of the 17th meeting of the Organising Group, 9 September 1975, p 10.

[55] NA BS 7/656: C. Smith to F. Bayliss, 18 August 1976.

[56] NA BS 7/656: D. Wedderburn to F. Bayliss, 17 September 1976.

[57] NA BS 7/656: F. Bayliss to D. Wedderburn, 21 September 1976.

[58] NA MH 152/73: J. F. Gilhooly to F. Bayliss, 9 December 1976.

[59] NA BS 7/656: J. F. Gilhooly, 'Note of SSRC–DHSS fourth conference on transmitted deprivation: LSE, Tuesday 28 September 1976', 30 September 1976.

[60] NA BS 7/656: A. Johnson, 'Note of a meeting held at the Institute of Community Studies, Bethnal Green, on 10 December 1976', 13 December 1976; NA BS 7/656: note by F. Bayliss, 6 January 1977.

[61] NA BS 7/657: note by F. Bayliss, 11 February 1977.

[62] NA MH 152/73: F. Field to C. Blackler, 7 April 1977.

[63] NA MH 152/73: W. G. Runciman to F. Field, 22 April 1977.

[64] NA MH 152/73: M. Brown, 'Proposals for research on the significance of money in the transmission of deprivation', 21 December 1977.

[65] NA MH 152/73: P. Cawson to E. Shaw, 3 July 1978; private correspondence between the author and Muriel Brown, 11 February 2007.

[66] NA MH 152/72: N. Jordan-Moss to R. C. O. Matthews, 10 April 1972.

[67] NA MH 166/1515: J. Locke to M. James, 16 May 1974.

[68] NA MH 152/82: J. Cooper to B. Abel-Smith, 16 October 1975.

[69] NA MH 152/84: memo by S. Reeve, 9 March 1976.

[70] NA MH 152/84: J. Cooper to P. Benner, 12 March 1976.

[71] NA MH 152/84: P. Benner to J. Cooper, 18 March 1976.

[72] NA MH 152/85: P. Benner to S. Reeve, 3 May 1976.

[73] NA MH 152/84: G. Hulme to S. Reeve, 29 March 1976.

[74] NA MH 152/86: A. M. Sheridan to S. Reeve, 12 May 1976.

[75] NA MH 152/86: M. Rodda to P. Lewis, 27 May 1976.

[76] NA MH 152/86: A. M. Sheridan to J. Cooper, 21 June 1976.

[77] NA MH 152/86: memo from P. Lewis, 9 July 1976; NA MH 152/86: S. E. Reeve, 'Note of an informal meeting at SSRC on 23 June 1976', 12 July 1976.

[78] NA MH 152/88: G. Hulme to C. H. Wilson, 14 December 1976.

[79] NA MH 152/88: G. G. Hulme to C. H. Wilson, 16 December 1976.

[80] NA MH 152/88: R. Toulmin to G. G. Hulme, 20 December 1976.

[81] NA MH 152/87: P. Benner to G. Hulme, 18 February 1977.

[82] NA MH 152/87: P. Benner to M. Rodda, 24 February 1977.

FIVE

The final years of the Research Programme

Introduction

This chapter surveys the final years of the Research Programme, from the publication of the Third Report of the Joint Working Party, to the appearance of the first books in the Heinemann series in the early 1980s. The changing responsibilities of the Organising Group can be seen through its periodic progress reports to the Joint Working Party. In the spring and summer of 1977, for example, it was meeting fairly frequently, considering outline applications, looking at progress reports, and thinking about commissioning papers on subjects including race relations, education, housing, occupational status, the extent of deprivation, and the transmission of wealth. By the summer and autumn of 1978, it was meeting less frequently, looking at fewer research outlines and applications, and at more progress reports and final reports. The chapter explores attempts by the Joint Working Party to respond to referees' reports on the projects that had been funded, and evaluate the Research Programme as a whole. It traces efforts to compare projects across the two main themes of familial processes and socioeconomic factors, and the commissioning of the final report from Muriel Brown and Nicola Madge. It further explores the attitude of the DHSS to the Research Programme, and the broader reaction to it through reviews of the early Heinemann books in academic journals, newspapers, and other periodicals.

An overview of the direction and achievements of the Research Programme is provided by the Joint Working Party's Third Report (SSRC–DHSS, 1977), which was slightly more substantial than the sketchy Second Report (SSRC–DHSS, 1975). By then, some 21 projects had been funded, six papers commissioned, and four seminars held. Particularly large-scale projects, measured by the size of grant awarded, were those on childhood experiences and parenting behaviour, by Michael Rutter and David Quinton (£80,431); adult delinquency and social deprivation, by Donald West (£47,619); intergenerational continuities in low income, by Tony Atkinson and colleagues (£44,381); and adoption and special needs, by John Triseliotis (£30,075). Thus the Joint Working Party claimed that it was covering the four original domains of concepts and definitions, intergenerational continuities, causal mechanisms, and intervention (SSRC–DHSS, 1977, pp 1-10, appendix ii). The Third Report again stressed that although the main initial emphasis in studying causal mechanisms had been on familial processes, researchers were examining the interrelationships between familial and social factors, such as occupational status and housing conditions. It also stressed the policy relevance of the research. In terms of future strategy, the Report stated that in the next phase of the Programme two different approaches would be used – new empirical projects and literature reviews. Proposed reviews would cover regional inequalities, intergenerational continuities, education, ethnic origin, policy interventions, and the distribution of income within the family (SSRC–DHSS, 1977, pp 1, 4-5, 9, 11-12).

However, the overall argument of the chapter is that, the merits of individual projects notwithstanding, the Joint Working Party struggled to keep control over the Research Programme. There was no real ministerial interest in the research, and consequently less involvement from the DHSS side. Reports by referees on some of the early projects were extremely critical; the twin focus on familial processes and socioeconomic factors remained separate from one another; and limited attempts were made to evaluate the Research Programme, to see what lessons might be learnt from it. The chaotic nature of the commissioning process presented Muriel Brown and Nicola Madge with a nightmarish task in attempting to summarise the research and draw some conclusions. Moreover, by the early 1980s, with growing inequality, rising unemployment, and the election of the first Thatcher government, opinions were much more polarised. Whereas the literature review by Michael Rutter and Nicola Madge had been extensively reviewed on its publication in 1976, and favourably received, most of the books generated by the substantive projects were not reviewed widely, and where they were, received a critical reception. This was particularly true of the final report. The result was that the cycle hypothesis and Research Programme were effectively forgotten about for the next 20 years, until the election of New Labour in May 1997, along with new policies on child poverty and social exclusion, led both politicians and researchers back to the relationship between policy, poverty, and parenting.

'Less than worthwhile': early projects

From the inside, the final years of the Research Programme were characterised by progress reports on the projects that were currently under way, referees' comments on the final reports from some of the early projects, and drafts of some of the later reports, such as the literature reviews. Applications continued to come in, and some of these were funded, including the team led by Israel Kolvin (1929-2002), Professor of Child Psychiatry at the University of Newcastle upon Tyne. This project had come about entirely by chance, through a meeting between Alan Clarke and F. J. W. Miller, which had led Clarke to suggest a follow-up to the Newcastle 1,000 families study.[1] Nevertheless, in general what was striking about this period was the critical tone of many of the referees' reports. Peter Willmott, for example, admitted that many of the final reports were weak. They had a common origin in the early days of the Programme, when funds were plentiful and a number of risks had been taken. Most of them were too long, and required further work. In several cases, reports on pilot or feasibility studies had led to a firm decision that a more major study should not be funded. Willmott reflected philosophically that the cost had not been high and, although disappointing, they had not been entirely fruitless.[2]

There is much evidence that some of the early projects were less than impressive. One of the first to be funded was a pilot study of an intergenerational cycle of deprivation, led by Ada Paterson, at Edinburgh University. Paterson had linked the records of a selected sample of people receiving assistance from a local authority Social Work Department. She and a colleague had drawn up pedigrees for 24 families in one area in Scotland, recording evidence of mental illness, psychiatric difficulties, large families, alcoholism, and crime. They argued that an intergenerational cycle of applying for assistance did exist in families, but not all family members used the available assistance to the same effect. The pattern was not as extensive or regular as was commonly believed, and was unpredictable.[3] Although a short account of this project was later published (Paterson and Inglis, 1976), referees invited to comment on Paterson's final report were extremely critical. One noted that 'concentrating on "problem families" is not very helpful for the elucidation of the transmission of deprivation', while another concluded that 'the study was not particularly worthwhile and little has been learned from it'.[4] This was not so much the fault of the investigators, as of the Joint Working Party, which had funded it in the first place. A third referee thought its most striking characteristic was its naivity, writing of Paterson and Inglis that:

> Their findings merely retrace ground covered by earlier
> investigators working from about 1900 to the middle
> 'thirties. The same difficulties were encountered: of definition,
> of sampling, of incomplete records, of interpreting reported
> tittle-tattle, of finding ways to analyse and make sense of
> badly compiled, unstandardised and incomplete records
> filled in or not by untrained social workers who were given
> no guidelines.[5]

This referee said that they dreaded the publication of the report. The
research had been carried out as planned, but the funders of the research
were no wiser at the end. Drawing on these reports, the Joint Working
Party noted that:

> The final report from Dr Paterson was poor, failing to
> reach the standards of Lidbet's [sic] work of forty years ago.
> There was no basis for useful generalisation from a sample
> so dangerously unrepresentative.[6]

This was a damning indictment. The Lidbetter research into the 'social
problem group' sponsored by the Eugenics Society in the 1920s had
been bedevilled by methodological problems, and only one volume
had been published (Lidbetter, 1933; Welshman, 2006a, pp 47, 53-5).
   FSU clients were thought to epitomise the kind of families Joseph
had in mind when he popularised the concept of the cycle – those
with multiple problems whom the social services felt required long-
term casework. A similar project to the Paterson one was a paper
commissioned from a researcher working on FSU case files in East
London. Sylvia Gilpin had earlier worked with Peter Willmott at the
Institute of Community Studies, and she proposed a follow-up study
to look in more detail at family relationships.[7] However, referees were
critical of the use of the FSU files as if they were medical records;
they thought that it was impossible to draw out causal processes and
intergenerational patterns; and they argued that the report revealed
some important dilemmas about the assumptions and approaches that
historically had characterised FSU work.[8] The Organising Group
agreed that this was neither a productive line of enquiry, nor very
useful to the Joint Working Party. It noted that 'what interesting points
it [Gilpin's report] did contain were obscured by unnecessary detail.
One view in the Group was that little would be achieved by pursuing
her report further'.[9] This was effectively the end of this project; four

or five days' funding was approved to enable Sylvia Gilpin to write a shorter, more reflective, report.

Another project that dated from this early period was a feasibility study by David Donald and colleagues at the Glasgow College of Technology, on a sample of families who were 'situationally' deprived (Donald et al, 1978). Here referees were critical of the use of valuation rolls as the source of the area-based sample; they said that the final composition of the sample limited analysis; they questioned the appropriateness of the measures of deprivation, since poverty was not included; and argued that there was a failure to link attitudinal responses to situational variables. Overall, the referees doubted the value of a major study, and the Joint Working Party agreed, noting that 'the researchers were proposing to tackle large and complex problems without clearly stating their objectives, or their methods of data collection'.[10] Subsequently, the Organising Group produced an even more damning assessment. In its view, Donald and his colleagues were unable to distinguish between personal and structural factors; they were incapable of analysing their own data; they had presented a series of indecipherable tables and a report that was not particularly readable; and the project had limited generalisability. Overall the study had proved to be 'less than worthwhile'.[11]

The other early project was that by the Rapoports on the transmission of 'maladaptive' coping patterns. One referee thought that the results did not go much beyond case studies known to social workers, new light had not been shed on the transmission of deprivation, and the work was not worth supporting further. A second argued that the report lacked conceptual clarity, and the general lessons to be learnt were that 'it is easier to formulate a project than to carry it out well'.[12] Another referee (possibly Dennis Marsden) suggested that the paradigm on which the research was based offered too individualistic a framework, and the key themes needed to be understood in relation to collective experience rather than individual or intrinsic capacities. Pathologies needed to be related to working-class culture, that culture needed to be related to economic and employment conditions, and the families should be located within a larger context. While the study provided useful information, it needed to be situated within 'a more social collective understanding of working class experience'.[13] A fourth referee found that the Rapoports ignored external circumstances, basing their approach on the assumption that 'there is perfect equality of opportunity and that families who are in a mess have only themselves to blame'.[14]

In fairness, many of the larger projects had proceeded smoothly; this was true, for instance, of those by Atkinson and colleagues, Coffield and colleagues, Rutter and Quinton, and Illsley and Blaxter. But similar criticisms were made of some of the other projects. G. L. Millerson and Bernard Ineichen at the University of Bristol had carried out a research project into the role of housing factors in transmitted deprivation; as noted earlier (page 127), this had been limited in December 1975 to a feasibility study. Clare Ungerson had been critical of the original application, and referees were similarly critical of the draft report. They argued that hypotheses had not been clearly formulated and the research design could not adequately focus on the research problem; the study had been split into two parts and there was little possibility of linking them; the authors did not outline the economic and social context of the local authorities, thereby preventing generalisation; and the methodology precluded a useful study of the actual operation of the allocation system.[15] More generally, the place of housing in the Research Programme provided a good example of the dichotomy drawn between structural factors and personal characteristics (Welshman, 2007c).

Referees were equally critical of some of the later reports. One was the literature review on the impact of social policy on transmitted deprivation by Olive Stevenson, Professor of Social Policy and Social Work at the University of Keele, and Roger Fuller, a sociologist also then at Keele (Fuller and Stevenson, 1983). Stevenson was an interested observer of the debate over transmitted deprivation. In the 1960s, for instance, she had deeply resented the attacks by people such as Barbara Wootton on social casework (Stevenson, 1963). Moreover, in the following decade, she was aware that the Left-wing councils of the major cities were hostile to social workers, seeing them as unnecessary. If anything, it was 'One Nation' Tories such as Joseph who were more appreciative of social work. As with the attack on social casework, Stevenson resented the Leftist critique of social work, later recalling of Child Care Officers that 'they were anything but mini-psychoanalysts, they were very practical women running about in cars with potties and cots'.[16] Indeed Stevenson had some sympathy for Joseph as a politician with sincerely held ideas who had become caught in intense ideological crossfire, and it was her involvement in social work that had led her to see the debate as unnecessarily polarised.

It was perhaps Stevenson's background that explains why the review was not better received by the referees, both of whom had a background in sociology and social policy, and who saw social work encroaching on the terrain of social policy. Stevenson herself had few illusions about the degree of her involvement in the Research Programme, later recalling of the review that 'it was commissioned at the tail-end of the enthusiasm'.[17] One of the referees was David Donnison, shortly to become Professor of Town and Regional Planning at the University of Glasgow. A busy person, he had read only the first and last chapters, and those on social security and community development. However, Donnison wrote that:

> I thought the whole review failed to clarify the purpose of all this reading. Lacking any clearly defined point to the exercise, the authors were unable to draw the kind of conclusion one would expect from a literature review – or indeed any clear conclusions.... In short: despite the vast amount of literature touched on, this is a pretty unreadable job which will not help anyone much.[18]

Another referee, Phyllis Willmott, wrote that:

> The title of the review does not reflect the contents. It is hardly at all about the impact of social policy on transmitted deprivation, but is mainly a review of research on some selected social policies and some fairly broad social policy issues ... I am afraid that if I had to sum up in a sentence what this review tells me about the impact of social policies on deprivation I would have to say practically nothing.[19]

Perhaps the most telling indictment of the early commissioning process was that one of the researchers secured funding for one project, but submitted a report on an entirely different one. This was accepted by the SSRC.

Assessment: towards the end of the Research Programme

New SSRC members, at the time of the Third Report by the Joint Working Party, included Dennis Marsden from the Department of Sociology at Essex University; Muriel Brown from the LSE; and Adrian Webb from Loughborough University. After the publication of the literature review by Rutter and Madge (1976), the original Joseph emphasis on the cycle and on individual families was perceived to have widened to encompass structural issues such as poverty, inequality, poor housing, and lack of educational opportunity (Rutter and Madge, 1976). For someone like Brown, that made the Research Programme more interesting, but also raised questions about its policy implications – the area that was of greatest interest to her.[20] Dennis Marsden similarly offers an interesting case study. Born in Huddersfield, he had been educated at a grammar school and Cambridge University, later working at the Institute of Community Studies and teaching at a secondary modern school. In 1965, he moved to Essex University to take part in a national survey of poverty, and his book *Mothers alone* (Marsden, 1969) had grown out of this work. By the mid-1970s, he was a Senior Lecturer at Essex, and had recently published *Workless* (Marsden and Duff, 1975), a study of unemployed men and their families. As we shall see later in the chapter, Marsden had reviewed the Rutter and Madge literature review favourably, and can be seen as the type of social scientist that it drew in to the Research Programme. If anything these changes of personnel accentuated the differences between the members; Alan Clarke later bracketed Marsden with Vic George, recalling of the former: 'he was another hostile case I think, he struck me as an out and out environmentalist and he argued as such and he was a rather disruptive influence on the Joint Working Party actually. Querying what was going on'.[21]

Differences between members notwithstanding, in this final period, the Organising Group, the Joint Working Party, and indeed the SSRC itself began to look forwards, to the remainder of the Research Programme, but also backwards, in considering what might be learnt from the experience of commissioning research. One of the main issues was the Strategic Review envisaged at the end of the first three years. This was discussed by the Organising Group as early as October 1976. The level of funds for new research offered only limited scope for influencing the final shape of the Research Programme, and there was a need to think carefully about how the money should be spent. One view was that the Organising Group should be more directive, since existing projects had reflected the interests of the researchers as much as the needs of the Programme. Another was that the Organising Group could concentrate the remaining funds in one programme. A third view was that the funds were not adequate, and some of the proposed themes were specialist topics that were adequately covered by other centres or departments.[22] In the event, the Organising Group proposed to put a substantial part of the remaining funds into studies of intervention strategies.

In connection with the Joint Working Party's wish to look at the problem of intervention without mounting large-scale action research projects, the DHSS agreed to identify those policies most relevant to the transmission of disadvantage. This was difficult for the DHSS, since connections could be made between almost any aspect of DHSS activity, and preventing inter- or intragenerational continuities in deprivation. There were some obvious documents, such as *Prevention and health: Everybody's business* (DHSS, 1976) and *Priorities in the health and social services* (DHSS, 1977), but the literature was almost limitless. The DHSS noted that 'we have not felt able to provide a simple list of policies because of the complexity of the task and the wealth of relevant material'.[23] Most interesting was the DHSS view of its policy objectives in relation to transmitted deprivation. It included such areas as genetics, maternity services, 'marital violence', alcoholism and addiction, and physical disability. Some of the aims were to get local authorities to establish genetic screening services, to screen women with a high risk of Down's syndrome and spina bifida, to prevent the suffering of individuals and the burden on the family, and to get women most at risk to doctors early in pregnancy. Most tellingly, in the case of children the aim was to pursue the philosophy of the 1969 Children and Young Persons Act, 'to prevent the deprived and delinquent children of today becoming the deprived, inadequate unstable and criminal citizens of tomorrow'.[24]

For its part, the SSRC noted that by December 1976, for example, 21 projects had been funded at a cost of £280,000. However, it thought that the draft structure for the final report was rather descriptive, and it identified three broader problems. First, there was the issue of how to finance the remainder of the Programme. Second, there had been methodological problems; the fourth conference on socioeconomic factors, for instance, was not viewed as having been very productive. Third, there were gaps in the Programme that needed to be filled. The Organising Group realised that it could no longer operate in an entirely responsive mode, and would need to take a more proactive role. The SSRC therefore suggested that it should explore alternative ways of commissioning the research that was needed, such as approaching one or two teams to undertake much of it.[25]

In the event, the Organising Group attempted to make the Research Programme more coherent, by encouraging the publication of research studies, and by filling in perceived gaps by commissioning reviews. It suggested more generally that with limited resources it was best to focus on a limited number of areas. Considering the Programme within the framework offered by the First Report, it suggested that literature reviews of housing, education, and 'colour' would cover areas that were not going to be tackled in depth. Other work might focus on intervention studies, the extent of deprivation in Britain as a whole, income and poverty, and the culture of poverty. Nevertheless, it was recognised that at the end of the Programme there would be a lot of unanswered questions, and so the final report would have to include suggestions for future research. In terms of evaluating the Programme, there was to be an interim review in 1978, which would be revised and finalised in 1981. The overall emphasis, then, was on strategies of reviewing, evaluating, and commissioning.[26]

When the Organising Group's 'Future strategy' paper was considered by the Joint Working Party in February 1977, Michael Rutter was invited to comment on his anxieties about the Research Programme. Rutter was extremely critical. He argued that there had been a plethora of pilot and feasibility studies that had not been followed through and which had produced very little that was useful; an artificial dichotomy had been drawn between social structure and familial processes, and studies had neglected the interaction between them; some of the research supported had been of poor quality, and refereeing had been inadequate; the role of the DHSS had aggravated the problem; and in some cases applicants had been treated badly. Peter Willmott, on the other hand, looking forwards rather than backwards, was slightly more conciliatory, arguing that with limited resources, a more selective approach should be taken to funding in future, focusing on the extent of continuities in deprivation; continuities in low income; and intervention, with the DHSS identifying relevant policies. This approach was broadly agreed by the Joint Working Party.[27] With hindsight, Rutter's comments can be seen as remarkably open and objective of a project in which he had been centrally involved; they bear out the later arguments of Berthoud about the commissioning process (Berthoud, 1983a).

If there was a concern to look ahead to what remained of the Research Programme, Rutter's paper highlighted the need to look backwards, to see what might be learnt from the earlier work. The SSRC had recently created a Research Initiatives Board, to operate in a more flexible way, and to promote research in previously neglected areas. It was the Board that suggested that it would be helpful to pass on the lessons learnt in the Programme, in terms of drawing up contracts and commissioning research. Prompted by the SSRC, Peter Willmott and Alan Clarke began to reflect more rigorously on the decision-making machinery and processes of the Organising Group, and the management and content of the Research Programme. They felt that a larger group than the Organising Group was desirable, because of the large sums of money involved, admitting that 'we have found it difficult to keep a clear enough view of the funding over the life of the Programme as a whole. We seemed to move rapidly from a feeling of affluence to a realisation that we could not be as comprehensive as we had hoped'.[28]

They admitted that they had not anticipated the implications of the feasibility studies adequately. Moreover, the initial strategy, to issue a general invitation to researchers to submit proposals within the context of the First Report, had resulted in an imbalance, with most of the proposed work emphasising familial processes and child development. While they had tried to correct that bias, it had been difficult to find good researchers interested in socioeconomic or social policy studies, and able to put forward strong proposals.

Willmott and Clarke drew a series of further lessons. In any future research programme, reviews should be commissioned from the start and used strategically; the financial commitments and funds available monitored; feasibility studies treated with caution; and the balance of the programme kept in mind throughout. Workshops should be used to maintain continuity in the debate and to encourage comparability between projects; conferences to inform outsiders and stimulate proposals; and discussions and consultations held with researchers and referees at different points in time as appropriate. The lessons to be learnt in the management of a research programme were that research commissioning should be restricted to a limited number of themes; reviews should be commissioned; and researchers should be warned that funding a feasibility study did not imply any obligation to fund a larger study.[29] This report on the experience of commissioning research went to the Research Initiatives Board of the SSRC. Not surprisingly, there were doubts about whether this should be published. It was seen as too negative, of little interest to the public, and it would show the SSRC as rather naive and unable to 'see round corners'.[30] In the event, a toned-down version did emerge (SSRC, 1978).

Chickens coming home to roost and pigs in pokes: the DHSS

In Chapter Four, it was noted that the DHSS became less interested in the research following the election of the Labour government in March 1974 and as it came to have increasing doubts over the usefulness of the Research Programme. Barbara Castle was sacked by James Callaghan in April 1976, and there is little evidence that her successor as Secretary of State for Social Services, David Ennals (1922-95), showed much interest in the Research Programme. The earlier DHSS concerns about the value of the Research Programme were to come to a head over arrangements for the final report.

By the autumn of 1977, civil servants were seeking the agreement of the relevant Minister of State to complete the second half of the planned seven-year Research Programme. The initial period had been 1 January 1974 to 31 December 1977; the revised agreement was to cover the period 1 January 1978 to 31 December 1980. The DHSS was minded to tell the SSRC that it was willing to agree a contract for the remaining three years to allow the completion of the Programme. Nevertheless, civil servants noted that drafts of the Strategic Review had been generally critical, highlighting flaws in the way in which the Programme had been established. One draft conceded that:

> it has become increasingly clear that the original conception was too broadly based for a coherent programme of research to be planned and undertaken within the available resources which would have confirmed or refuted the hypothesis of a cycle of deprivation.[31]

Another stated that:

> The work so far suggests that it is impracticable to develop or test any general theory of deprivation: there are many ways in which disadvantage continues between and within generations and the pattern of causation is complex.[32]

But on balance it was best to continue. Expenditure on the Research Programme had peaked; it represented a modest proportion of the total DHSS investment in research; the bulk of the work had already been commissioned; and a refusal to renew the Programme would impair relations with the SSRC and damage its reputation within the research community.

Muriel Brown later recalled that when she joined the Joint Working Party in 1977, the DHSS members were not very prominent, and the only one with whom she had much contact was Alice Sheridan. Because of the original focus on the Local Authority Social Services Division, the effect was that, within the DHSS, there was no involvement from those concerned with the income maintenance services, or about educational opportunity in its widest sense.[33] Certainly Alice Sheridan remained as forthright as ever, noting of one application, for example, that 'I have never thought much of this application but I do not see how we can possibly turn it down unless anyone puts forward the view that technically it is now so weak as to be useless'.[34] Moreover, in a period when there was increasing pressure on resources, there were renewed doubts about the relevance of the cycle to policy. Michael Partridge, then Under-Secretary at the DHSS, and later a Permanent

Secretary, expressed doubts about continuing research 'on such a nebulous subject' at a time when cuts were having to be made in services for older people.[35] He argued that transmitted deprivation was a 'portmanteau term', and suggested limiting research to subjects of central importance, rather than searching for new ideas that might interest the SSRC, but which were of only marginal significance for the DHSS. Its main concerns were in Child Benefit, disincentives to work, longitudinal studies of poverty, and reliance on social security benefits. One of the greatest gaps in statistics about social security benefits, for example, was how long people or families remained on benefit, and what effects this had on the lifestyle of the family and its future development.

Discussions about the extent of DHSS involvement in the Joint Working Party revealed wider tensions about the responsibilities of the Joint Working Party and its relationship with the Organising Group. One of the grumbles of the DHSS was over the way that the Joint Working Party and Organising Group operated. Civil servants claimed that they had detected obvious dissatisfaction on this point from Jack Tizard and Michael Rutter. Peter Willmott had indicated that he would be willing to review relationships between the Joint Working Party and the Organising Group.[36] Moreover, around the same time, Sheridan noted that in the Strategic Review, the Organising Group had assumed a very definite tailing-off process. She noted: 'that they have done so is our good fortune given the changed financial circumstances and the queries that there have always been about the wisdom of undertaking this Programme'.[37] Sheridan alleged that the Joint Working Party was not an easy group, some of its members having very strong views about arrangements between government and a research council for carrying out programmes. Writing of DHSS representation on the Joint Working Party, Tom Luce reflected that 'we shall never find the elusive happy medium between neglect and interference so far as this body is concerned'.[38]

A second source of unhappiness was over the personalities involved. Geoff Hulme noted that it was David Ennals who had suggested that the DHSS should take the lead in proposing changes to the Organising Group and its Chairpersonship. He wrote that 'there is some dissatisfaction with Professor Willmott but it is a thankless task and I am very doubtful whether we should fare better if we make a change at this late stage'.[39] In June 1977, Alice Sheridan noted of the Organising Group that most people were likely to be wary of joining it at this late stage. The three people who had turned down the invitation (Kit Jones, Vic George, and Robin Matthews) 'know of some of the very difficult times the Group has had and some of the criticism made of it'.[40] When Jack Tizard resigned from the Joint Working Party in January 1978, Sheridan suggested that he should not be replaced, for purely defensive reasons. She wrote that:

> I think there is a slight chance that at some stage when this programme is wrapped up someone in the political or academic field will move in with major criticisms of the Department having either spent the money or launched a programme in this subject area. The reasons why this programme seems to be more at risk than most of our work in the 'social field' are first because of its political history and secondly because of the emotive nature of the subject. If this should occur most of the heat will have to be taken by the SSRC.[41]

When Tom Luce considered who might succeed Peter Willmott as Chair of the Organising Group, he wrote that 'it is not on the face of it a very attractive proposition. The Programme does not enjoy a very high reputation in academic circles generally'. The new Chair would have some difficult tasks at the end of the Programme, without having any real influence on the research as a whole.[42]

A final area of concern was over the costs of the Research Programme, which of course was the responsibility of the DHSS. The original contract had provided for an increase in annual expenditure from a modest start to £150,000 halfway through. In fact, expenditure peaked in 1977 and 1978 at £135,000, and an allowance of £150,000 per annum was made until 1981, on the assumption that this was unlikely to be required. Nevertheless, while the total cost over seven years was estimated in September 1977 as being £537,000, this was at 1976 prices. Moreover, there was evidence that budget estimates for the years 1976-77, 1977-78, and 1978-79 had been turned into expenditure ceilings. Thus it was in an atmosphere of mounting panic that the DHSS realised that all the figures they had been working on had been at 1976 prices.[43] Civil servants from the Office of the Chief Scientist quickly had to revalue the total budget for the seven years at 1978 prices.

Briefing notes by the DHSS on the history of the Research Programme charted its progress and costs, and conceded that the original bias towards familial processes had never been properly redressed.[44] The Office of the Chief Scientist had had a limited role on the Joint Working Party, but even that of the DHSS Local Authority Social Services Division had been 'more akin to the Greek Chorus than to the main actors in the drama'.[45] Nevertheless, the DHSS did believe that while scientific breakthroughs could not be expected, the Programme did have to be evaluated. One suggestion was that Maurice Kogan, then Professor of Government and Social Administration at Brunel University, should with colleagues do a study of the SSRC–DHSS machinery for managing the Programme. Indeed civil servants alleged that it was Michael Posner, the then Chair of the SSRC, who thought that 'research into research' was usually a waste of time.[46]

By the summer of 1980, DHSS civil servants had virtually given up on the Programme, seizing on criticisms by referees of original applications and progress reports.[47] David Benham concluded that the Research Programme would not provide many new ideas or unexpected insights, and some of the studies were 'distressingly trite'. While the research would add to knowledge about the nature and extent of particular aspects of deprivation – health, housing, and so on – it would not 'take us much further on such questions as the interaction of various kinds of deprivation and the cumulative effect of such interaction on need for services'.[48] Most researchers had found some evidence of intergenerational continuities in deprivation, but while transmission appeared to be a significant factor, it was far from being all-important in the way envisaged when the Programme was set up. Tom Luce agreed that the Programme 'does not seem to have proved anything in relation to its (rather ambitious) set of hypotheses'.[49] Most strident was Alice Sheridan who argued that there had never been much chance of the Programme being 'successful' in the sense of demonstrating the relationships and interactions of deprivation. Overall, she concluded that 'with this background we are fortunate to have got what we have, but we are likely to be open to criticism for having spent so much to get so little'.[50]

Increasingly the focus of the civil servants moved to their tactics for dealing with the final report. Alice Sheridan alleged that if Muriel Brown was co-author, the DHSS would not get the sort of report it needed. She expressed surprise that the SSRC wanted to distance itself from the Programme; it had agreed to take on the responsibility, even if it did not realise it was buying 'a pig in a poke'.[51] Sheridan suggested that, in setting up the Research Programme, the DHSS had postponed or avoided decisions on awkward matters, and some of these chickens were likely to come home to roost via the final report. The SSRC was likely to be criticised by academics, and this would affect what Brown and Madge would say about the policy implications of the Research Programme. Overall, Sheridan warned that the DHSS needed to be well placed to anticipate what was coming. She noted: 'we have been involved in the Programme, for better, or probably for worse, via the Working Group so we had better be in a position to make as useful a job as circumstances permit of the outcome'.[52] Sheridan did not see why the authors should write on an explicitly personal basis. Rather it was because the SSRC was vulnerable, and likely to be criticised by academics, that explained the distancing, and the emphasis on authors writing in a personal capacity. Certainly whereas the SSRC saw the final report as the pinnacle of the Research Programme, the DHSS advocated a strategy where it regarded the monographs and individual publications as the main outputs, and sought to use its influence to draw attention to them, and away from the final report.[53] The less the DHSS had to do with the final report, the easier it would be to dissociate government from it, if that turned out to be necessary or desirable.[54]

A study of collaboration between the DHSS and SSRC, by Maurice Kogan of Brunel University, had initially been put aside in view of SSRC sensitivities. When it was subsequently published, it focused more generally on the DHSS implementation of Rothschild, and the process of promoting research, and made no reference to the Research Programme (Kogan et al, 1980). But the experience did prompt more general reflection on working with the SSRC, since the only significant experience of close cooperation had been on transmitted deprivation. The DHSS felt that useful lessons had been learnt, in that the breadth of the Programme had made it difficult to control, as had the SSRC way of working. It had been almost too easy to find researchers to do some of the work, that which interested them, and more difficult to get some of the less attractive jobs done, such as the final report. Moreover, once money had been committed, the DHSS had little control over how it was spent, and had found it virtually impossible to withdraw from the commitment. It suggested that in future the onus should be put on the SSRC and funds granted only in response to specific proposals.[55]

Frank Coffield reflected subsequently that problem families and civil servants had one thing in common – they did not understand long-term anthropological or ethnographic fieldwork – and the only image both groups had of social research was the statistical survey. He claimed this caused ethical problems with the families and 'intellectual rejection' among the civil servants (Coffield, 1983, p 11). In explaining the stance of the DHSS members on the Research Programme, Berthoud is correct that the DHSS saw 'the problem' as one of individuals and the personal social services, whereas the SSRC saw it as one suitable for broader social scientific analysis. But archival evidence reveals more deep-seated

DHSS scepticism about the Research Programme as a whole. This led to personality clashes, particularly with the social scientist who typified the qualitative approach: Peter Willmott. Perhaps most importantly, the DHSS members were essentially concerned throughout with the policy implications of the research, and saw the conclusions drawn by Brown and Madge as being impractically broad and unrealistic. What were the long-term implications for DHSS involvement in research projects? As Chief Scientist to the DHSS, Sir Douglas Black was involved in discussions regarding misgivings about the value of the Research Programme. It seems highly probable that the experience of the DHSS with transmitted deprivation affected its involvement in the Black Report (DHSS, 1980) on inequalities in health. Certainly on the part of the ESRC there was a perception that the question of transmitted deprivation had been settled by the Research Programme, and the focus moved instead to health inequalities.[56]

As many definitions of deprivation as studies

Many of the research projects had been concerned mainly with the psychological and familial processes involved in transmission, while others focused on socioeconomic or sociological or structural factors. But while the imbalance in the Research Programme was recognised as a weakness, the two main themes were constantly separated from one another. For example, two separate workshops had been established to discuss projects in each of these two broad groups. In 1977, the Organising Group decided to start the evaluation of the Research Programme as a whole. Nicola Madge, then of the Thomas Coram Research Institute, was asked to look at the subcontracts that dealt with family processes, and Richard Silburn, from the Department of Social Administration and Social Work at the University of Nottingham, at those that dealt with 'socioeconomic' issues. Silburn, for example, was given the brief 'to compare and contrast the subcontracts on their operational definitions of deprivation, their selections of their samples, questions asked, tests used etc., and to examine comparability across them' (Silburn, 1978, p 1).

These reports were completed in the summer of 1978. Nicola Madge offered summaries of 12 projects, including those by Coffield, Illsley and Blaxter, Rutter and Quinton, and West. She noted that comparison was difficult because of the varying quantity and quality of information available in the different projects; the contrast in the size and scope of the studies; and the different stages reached by researchers. Not all studies had been designed to answer questions relating to the cycle of deprivation, but instead had 'involved a re-analysis or re-orientation of part of a broader project' (Madge, 1978, p 2). Her emphasis was on method, and the approach was more descriptive than evaluative. Perhaps the most important difference between the projects resulted from their sampling techniques, illustrating the fact that more than one question was being asked. Some projects used controls while others did not, some projects had large samples, some very small ones. Sources of data included interviews, psychological examinations, official records, and direct observation. Finally, researchers had used a variety of research techniques to look at intergenerational comparisons. Overall, Madge found that the projects differed enormously in their aims and hypotheses, and that 'there are about as many definitions of deprivation employed by researchers as there are studies' (Madge, 1978, p 6).

Richard Silburn attempted to summarise eight projects, including those by Atkinson, Coffield, and Illsley and Blaxter, working from the original applications, progress reports, and draft or final manuscripts. However, Silburn had also quickly realised that the projects were at very different stages of their development and execution. He noted that:

> It would be very difficult to compare and contrast so disparate a group of studies; moreover when one considers how the assumptions, the methods and even the goals of a research project are modified in the course of the research activity, too close a comparison would be futile. (Silburn, 1978, p 2)

Indeed Silburn went further, arguing that the projects were so varied, so different from one another in their thinking, their theoretical justifications, and their proposed research methodologies, even in their basic definitions of the problem, that they defied easy comparison (Silburn, 1978, p 3). The result was that his report was much less ambitious than originally intended, offering merely a descriptive summary of each project. In some cases, Silburn was critical of individual projects. He noted of the intergenerational comparisons in the Coffield project, for example, that 'the data is of a character which is rich in highly specific and informative detail, but from which it is impossible to generalise with any confidence' (Silburn, 1978, p 22). What was apparent was the variety of the criteria adopted as measures or indicators of deprivation; fundamental differences in assumptions and preconceptions about deprivation, and in research design; and differences in sampling and in the way that researchers had approached the question of intergenerational transmission.

It was Chris Trinder, then in the Department of Political Economy at University College London, who had worked with Tony Atkinson on the Rowntree follow-up study, who was given the task of organising the workshops. He wrote that their purpose was 'to help evaluate the overall Programme of research and to facilitate the cross change of ideas both between subcontract holders and with outsiders'.[57] However, while two workshops had been held in 1977, the next was not until October 1978. The groups exploring socioeconomic factors and familial processes remained separate from one another. The first attempt at a joint meeting, at Sheffield University to discuss the reports by Silburn and Madge, was not until January 1979. This was to make the task of Brown and Madge all the more difficult.

Making bricks with very little straw: the writing of the final report

Richard Berthoud has suggested that, at the start of the Research Programme, little thought was given to the final report, and this seems correct. But by the summer of 1977 the Organising Group had begun to turn to this, arguing that adequate time would have to be allowed for the writing of it. In terms of possible content, the literature review by Rutter and Madge offered an obvious model, but there seemed little point in simply revising that in light of later research. The Organising Group argued that:

> All this suggested that the final report should not try to be exhaustive in presenting research findings, but should be a reflective document, taking a more conceptual approach to the subject of Transmitted Deprivation and drawing on a wide range of material arising from inside and outside the Programme.[58]

It gradually sketched out possible contents, suggesting that it should cover the background to and content of the Research Programme; the components of disadvantage and evidence for its transmission; causal mechanisms; and interventions.[59] The final report should therefore be a substantial yet readable book.

At one stage, the Organising Group was thinking of a series of chapters written by independent researchers. Richard Berthoud, for example, had been asked by the Organising Group to consider writing a chapter on the extent of deprivation, lifetime opportunity, and intergenerational continuity. But the amount of information available on these topics was variable, and other problems were the constraints of a single chapter, and the earlier review by Rutter and Madge (1976). Berthoud thought it would be possible to compare different aspects of deprivation (housing, employment, resources, health, education, family, and crime) across a range of variables (sex, age or stage in the life cycle, social class, geographical location, and ethnic group). The General Household Survey and the Douglas cohort study provided evidence on these. However, other questions were more difficult to define. In particular, tracing intergenerational continuities and analysing lifetime opportunities raised complex issues of what should be studied (Berthoud, 1983b).[60]

Berthoud was also to turn down the invitation to help to write the final report, regarding the task as too difficult (Berthoud, 1983a, pp 163-4). Indeed finding authors willing to take on this daunting task was to prove problematic. The original plan was for a tripartite authorship of Peter Willmott, Alan Clarke, and Muriel Brown, whose interests in community issues, psychological needs, and policy perspectives were seen to be complementary. But Willmott's resignation as Chair of the Organising Group meant he obviously would have a very limited involvement, while Clarke asked for Nicola Madge as his Research Assistant, and ultimately dropped out altogether.[61] The SSRC was not happy at the prospect of the work being left entirely to Brown and Madge, and had approached more established academics – mostly economists – to provide leadership and intellectual weight to the writing team, but without success.[62] This may in part have been because the SSRC itself was anxious to keep its distance from the Research Programme, as Alice Sheridan had earlier alleged. But this was one point on which the DHSS and SSRC were agreed; the former concurred that it was necessary to have someone 'of higher fire power and status'.[63]

By the summer of 1979, contracts for the final report had been signed with Muriel Brown and Nicola Madge, both then at the LSE. The DHSS continued to seek a third author, who would complement Brown and Madge, and become the 'guiding intelligence' of the writing team. In the view of David Benham, this point needed to be made forcefully to the SSRC; he noted that 'they are not good, it seems, at standing up to Muriel Brown'.[64] Brown and Madge had different but complementary perspectives that should have been helpful in looking at the interaction of the structural and the personal. Madge had been trained in psychology, and of course had worked with Michael Rutter on the earlier literature review. She had specialised in the accumulation and analysis of data, was interested in the psychological aspects of the research, and subsequently edited the collection *Families at risk*

(Madge, 1983). Brown, on the other hand, had worked originally on homelessness, and had earlier been a Lecturer in Social Policy at Manchester University. She was more interested in the wider field of social welfare, including income maintenance, health, education, and social work, and her research experience had been with policy issues. She later edited *The structure of disadvantage* (Brown, 1983a, 1983b).

Brown was concerned with the overall structure of the report, with the concepts and setting up of the Programme, and with the implications for policy and practice. Madge took charge of the lengthy section on the extent, distribution, and form of deprivation, where her work on the earlier literature review was clearly relevant, and also of the section on explanations for deprivation. However, a third author could not be found, and Brown and Madge therefore faced the task of making sense of the Research Programme on their own. Whereas Brown had started out with the expectation that she would be a contributor to the final report, she felt she had been landed with it, and abandoned by the Organising Group.[65] It is also arguable that Nicola Madge was extremely well qualified to carry out a literature review, but not to answer the larger questions that underlay the Research Programme, and that Brown and Madge had set themselves as authors of the final report.

In their capacity as the authors of the final report, Brown and Madge organised several seminars: 'Mechanisms of Transmission' in November 1980, and 'Implications for Policy and Practice' in January 1981. They were very much aware of the political difficulties surrounding the Research Programme, and knew that the final report would not be the only output from it. However, Brown later conceded that by then the Research Programme had become incredibly cumbersome, not at all an easy thing to pull together into a report. Doing justice to all the work that had been funded, or in part funded, by the Programme, and making sense of it had become an unwieldy and very demanding task. The main difficulty was the sheer number and incredible variety of projects that had been funded; as we have seen, the Joint Working Party had commissioned research on the basis of applications received, and many existing projects had turned to the Research Programme in order to get funding. This was clear from the summaries by Madge and Silburn. Muriel Brown later recalled:

> as a research programme it was a nightmare, it's not the way one would set up a research programme or do anything particularly. Doing a literature survey is one thing, you look at all sorts of things and note as you go through that this

is piecemeal and uneven. If you set up a research project, then you might try to do something about that unevenness and say right, we need to know more about this and more about that. We specifically need to know more about the interaction of things.[66]

Moreover, Brown and Madge were aware that, apart from the difficulty of making sense of the material, they had to make the final report different from the earlier literature review by Rutter and Madge, which was regarded as an important publication, and had caught the imagination of a wide readership.[67] Their focus on explanations and interventions meant that it was always going to be different, but the amount of evidence risked making it tedious and unreadable.

Although Brown and Madge were committed to looking at the interaction of personal and structural factors, most of the research fell into one camp or another. Brown recalled:

It was hugely disappointing that there was so little focused research that could give us clear answers: this is what we could do for this particular problem. Instead we had just more and more data showing us how very complex and interlocking and depressingly difficult it was.[68]

Although the report arguably did not need to accumulate more evidence of the extent of deprivation it included a lengthy section on this, and Brown felt the whole point of the exercise was to focus on the policy implications of the research. There was a long debate over the title, *Despite the welfare state* (1982a), but the aim was to focus on the failures of the welfare state, and its agencies, to tackle transmitted deprivation, and on the role of social provision to mediate effectively between the personal and the structural, rather than on the failures of problem families. In their concern for policy, Brown and Madge emphasised the failures of institutions.[69]

Despite the welfare state

In the final report itself, Brown and Madge noted that the focus of the Research Programme had shifted, from a cycle of deprivation to cycles of disadvantage, and with it the tenor of explanation and the scope of policy implications. Whereas the initial focus on problem families had led to explanations of their problems 'in terms of individual pathology, deviant patterns of parenting and maladaptive subcultures', the wider concern with mapping deprivation in society had led to explanations 'in terms of the class structure and the interplay of broad social and economic structures' (Brown and Madge, 1982a, p 3). They wrote that the thrust of explanation 'must be structural rather than personal and the scope of the policy implications must relate to the range of interlocking inequalities in life chances that characterise our society' (Brown and Madge, 1982a, p 3). At the same time, the development of the Research Programme had been constrained by its starting point, and it had retained its primary preoccupation with transmitted deprivation and the family. The evolution of the Research Programme from a narrowly defined problem to a whole range of social processes had broadened the scope of policy implications; 'much of the research concerned with very broad definitions of deprivation has inevitably concluded that disadvantage is deeply rooted in the structure of our society' (Brown and Madge, 1982a, p 5).

Brown and Madge did admit that the Research Programme's output was uneven; some topics were covered in detail, others barely touched upon. The research 'has not been guided by a single and consistent viewpoint' (Brown and Madge, 1982a, p 26). The Research Programme had never had 'a specific theoretical base nor a single precise framework', and issues such as the nature of deprivation, what transmission entailed, and the relative importance of psychological or familial, and socioeconomic or structural, causes of deprivation, had never been resolved (Brown and Madge, 1982a, p 28). The focus of the research had tended to be on personal and family circumstances, the studies had stemmed from the proposals of researchers, and these had been guided rather than directed by the DHSS and SSRC. Brown and Madge therefore echoed the earlier report by Madge on the number of definitions of deprivation (Brown and Madge, 1982a, p 29). They conceded that 'it is strikingly evident that very different things were being studied by different investigators' (Brown and Madge, 1982a, p 31). Overall, Brown and Madge wrote that examination of the ways in which researchers had interpreted the concept of deprivation revealed 'an extraordinary diversity of approach', and while attempts had been made to discuss the concepts involved, 'no real consensus was reached on the subject' (Brown and Madge, 1982a, p 35).

Although it had originally been anticipated that the final report would have a chapter on 'causal mechanisms', this was ditched in favour of one on 'explanations of deprivation', exploring genetic factors, personal characteristics, family composition, life experiences, cultural patterns, socioeconomic status, the physical environment, and institutions, administration, and policies. Indeed Brown and Madge were cautious about matching causes and effects, writing that the causes of deprivation could not straightforwardly be dichotomised into the structural and the familial, and that 'most aspects of deprivation have multiple causes of which the respective effects are all but impossible to disentangle' (Brown and Madge, 1982a, p 183). On the other hand, the chapter on implications for policy and practice was lengthy, covering such areas as low incomes, labour market opportunities, housing problems, education, the health services, and the personal social services. The essence of their approach was that 'much deprivation is deeply rooted in the structure of our society and affected by the network of unequal opportunities and life chances that the structure maintains' (Brown and Madge, 1982a, p 269). But they also conceded that the compromises on theory and failure to agree on the manifestations and explanations of deprivation during the Research Programme had precluded clear-cut implications and led to the 'rather incoherent pragmatism' that characterised their discussion of policy (Brown and Madge, 1982a, p 295).

The desire to focus on the interaction of the personal and the structural came through strongly in an article in *New Society* published just before the final report. Brown and Madge argued that explanations of deprivation had become stereotyped. A Right-wing approach argued for a reduction in the scope of social services and a concentration of help on the most needy; the causes of poverty and poor housing were attributed mainly to the individual. A Left-wing approach saw social services as irrelevant, since the causes of deprivation lay within the socioeconomic structure. Brown and Madge regarded these extremes, and the crude explanations of deprivation on which they were based, as 'unnecessary and unacceptable' (Brown and Madge, 1982b, p 53). Nevertheless, they also argued that the Research Programme had underlined that lack of income was the 'common denominator' of deprivation, and the welfare state did not do enough for those most in need (Brown and Madge, 1982b, p 54). Brown and Madge attempted to avoid the wholly familial or wholly structural explanation of deprivation by focusing on institutional interventions and shortcomings, in the Fabian belief that even if structural divisions within society could not be changed, their impact could be modified by improvements in the delivery of welfare.[70]

The authors of *Despite the welfare state* had argued that as the Research Programme had broadened, so had the scope of the policy implications. In *New Society*, they referred to the extent of deprivation and intergenerational transmission, but located these firmly in the context of social policies designed to eradicate poverty and child neglect. However, the focus on policy was controversial, since there were some members of the Joint Working Party who felt that policy implications were beyond the authors' remit. The DHSS clearly was looking for recommendations, but only in narrow areas of policy. Brown felt that the DHSS would have been happiest if she and Madge had given it some clear instructions on how a few specific interventions within its remit would have made a big difference. Civil servants were aware that they could not do anything about the main structural factors, and instead wanted ideas on how to improve services for children, or the delivery of care for single mothers.[71] This was encapsulated in a meeting that Joseph, then Secretary of State for Education and Science, had with Brown and Madge following the publication of the final report. The meeting was a disappointing one for the authors, since Joseph returned to the concerns of the cycle speech, focusing, for instance, on small-scale interventions, such as the potential role of health visitors.[72]

Overall, the attempt by Brown and Madge to relate familial processes to structural forces failed to appeal to either end of the policy spectrum. It was the cost implications of their wide-ranging recommendations around improvements to the delivery of welfare that influenced the dismissive response to the final report. Their attempt to link their detailed suggestions to the finding of the Research Programme, and not just to advocate what they thought was needed, proved to be a serious weakness. One of their final contacts with the DHSS came in June 1983, in a letter from Alice Sheridan to Muriel Brown about a meeting that the two had had in February of that year with Bill Utting, then Chief Social Work Officer at the DHSS. In her characteristic style, Sheridan wrote that the discussions had been:

> helpful in the rather tedious process that we have to go through to try to see how to take forward those matters on which we agreed were important. We are running various proposals inside the Department, but I think it will be a little time yet before we know how successful we are likely to be, but we travel hopefully.[73]

Brown tried to follow through individual policies in meetings with DHSS civil servants, but disillusioned with both academic research and the Civil Service, she soon afterwards left academic life, working in the voluntary sector for a time, and subsequently retraining as a psychoanalytic psychotherapist. Her departure from academic work was a sad, but in some ways oddly fitting, conclusion to her involvement in the Research Programme.

'Moral fibre: the forgotten factor': book reviews

In assessing the broader response to the Research Programme, it is helpful to compare the reviews of the *Cycles of disadvantage* book by Rutter and Madge (1976), which were generally favourable, with those of the other studies, including the final report (Brown and Madge, 1982a), which were much more critical. *Cycles of disadvantage* had been widely reviewed, including in *The Sunday Times*, where a journalist noted that many conventional wisdoms would have to be discarded because of this 'extremely useful' survey (Potter, E., 'The broken home: not all to blame', *The Sunday Times*, 5 December 1976, p 10). The literature review was generally seen as systematic and comprehensive, even if the interactions between the variables, and their relative influences, remained hypotheses, and the authors failed to take up the policy implications of their work (Empson, 1977). In the journal *New Society*, Jeremy Seabrook (1977) was more critical. He argued that the review was 'deeply comforting for those who fear that their professional interest in disadvantage may be damaged by its sudden and inconvenient elimination' (p 29), since its only conclusion was that so little was known about causes that the only remedy was more research. Seabrook lambasted the review as an 'avalanche of ponderous and myopic truisms' that took no account of how people actually felt about themselves and their lives (Seabrook, 1977, p 29). In turn, the psychologist Hans Eysenck (1916-97), from the Institute of Psychiatry, London, responded that the book was so important for discussions of social policy that *New Society* should have it reviewed for a second time by someone competent to understand it and interested in its conclusions (Eysenck, 1977).

Indeed the book was reviewed favourably by many of those hostile to the cycle of deprivation hypothesis. Dennis Marsden, for example, wrote that the literature review was a 'monumental achievement'. Rutter and Madge had approached their task with determination, industry, and open–mindedness, covering fields as disparate as income and housing distribution and policies, intellectual attainment, social mobility, delinquency, subnormality, psychiatric disorder, parenting behaviour, and ethnicity. Indeed their comprehensiveness, rigour, and clarity of expression meant that 'the shoddy thinking of the original notion of transmitted deprivation is shot to ribbons, and paradoxically the very thoroughness of this review calls into question the whole enterprise of the Working Party' (Marsden, D., 'Exploring deprivation', *Times Higher Education Supplement*, 25 March 1977, p 17). Marsden argued that any weaknesses stemmed from their sources; the lack of discussion of research on policy making; and neglect of the limitations of research methodology. In particular, factorial analysis indicated that not enough was known about the social processes at work; it was not clear what kind of research would bring about significant advances in understanding; and the whole notion of the separation of causal factors (such as genes and environment) was suspect.

Some of the early books in the Heinemann series were reviewed favourably. Mildred Blaxter, in particular, was praised for her craftsmanship in bringing together a huge range of research reports and in producing a useful and readable book – *The health of the children* (Blaxter, 1981). Similarly, one reviewer of *Mothers and daughters* (Blaxter and Paterson, 1982) concluded that Blaxter had shown that there was little evidence to demonstrate transmission of attitudes between generations, and simple models of illness behaviour, or of the culture of poverty, were out of date and required rethinking (Scrivens, 1983a, 1983b). A reviewer of Juliet Essen and Peter Wedge's *Continuities in childhood disadvantage* (Essen and Wedge, 1982) juxtaposed rival explanations, writing that they had provided further evidence 'that structural factors rather than personal pathology are at work blighting the lives of many children and their parents' (Holman, 1983, p 359). In *The Observer*, an article on Tony Atkinson's study of York (Atkinson et al, 1983) argued that it had shown that the Thatcherite belief that everyone could improve their lot if they really wanted to was misplaced (Davie, M., 'Why the poor stay poor', *The Observer*, 19 June 1983, p 16).

However, many of the other books were either not reviewed extensively, or where they were, received a critical reception. A review of the 1983 Madge collection *Families at risk* concluded that for practitioners it was disappointing; knowledge about which deprivations were transmitted in families was tentative at best; there were gaps about what constituted 'good parenting'; there was little reference to minority ethnic groups; and no sense of how families said they experienced the problems (Cook, 1983). In reviewing Donald West's (1982) study of delinquency, Laurie Taylor, then Professor of Sociology at the University of York, noted that there was only partial correlation between such factors as low income, large families, criminal parents, and the likelihood of a court conviction. Overall, while there was much interesting material, it was a 'clumsy conceptual model'. Taylor wrote that West was relatively unconcerned about much delinquency, eclectic about causes, against institutional sentences, optimistic about treatment, and uncertain about the application of his findings to current economic and social conditions. Using a railway metaphor, and noting that the Cambridge delinquency project had begun 21 years earlier,

Taylor wrote that 'a journey which got under way with some rather extravagant huffing and puffing is now most appropriately concluded by this modest toot' (Taylor, 1982, p 271).

The response to *Despite the welfare state* was perhaps most interesting of all. By 1982, the broader political climate was very different to 1972, when the cycle speech had been made. The combined effect of increasing inequality, rising unemployment, and the election of the first Thatcher government in 1979 had served to polarise opinions (Deacon, 2002a). Writing in the *Financial Times*, for instance, Ian Hargreaves noted that Brown and Madge claimed to have found 10 million people experiencing a 'poverty-stricken life'. Yet they steered a middle course in explaining deprivation, and suggested that the only way to deal with the problem was by a fragmentary and piecemeal improvement of benefits and opportunities (Hargreaves, I., 'Report claims up to 10m poverty-stricken', *Financial Times*, 9 July 1982, p 9). Bob Holman thought that Brown and Madge had produced a 'brilliant' review and evaluation, but were disappointing on explanations of deprivation; in his view, poverty had disappeared from political debate (Holman, 1982).

Ruth Lister regarded the book as rather tedious and repetitive, but nevertheless argued that the Research Programme had not borne out Joseph's focus on parental values and attitudes, stressing instead that poverty was the major problem (Lister, 1982). John Edwards wrote that while Brown and Madge said they were not totally wedded to personal pathology accounts, the emphasis remained on deprivation in the family, and no systematic structuralist account had emerged. Edwards suggested that, by token reference to social structural causes of deprivation, many of those involved in the Programme had sought to distance themselves from Joseph (Edwards, J., 'Running in families?', *Times Higher Education Supplement*, 26 November 1982, p 16). Similarly, Jan Pahl chose to stress Brown and Madge's point that 'cash may not compensate for all deprivations, but it goes a long way to prevent their turning into disadvantages' (Pahl, 1983, p 550).

Others were more critical. In his preface, Norman Fowler, then Secretary of State for Social Services (1981-87), observed that the projects formed merely 'a rich quarry for future study and research' (Brown and Madge, 1982a, p x). Moreover in *The Times*, David Walker concluded that social values mattered as much as economics in deciding people's fate. To explain the invulnerability of individuals and families to economic stress required unscientific notions such as character, values, and morality. The piece had the headline 'Moral fibre, the forgotten factor' (Walker, D., *The Times*, 12 July 1982, p 8). Maurice Kogan at

Brunel University noted that the concept of relative deprivation had turned the discussion into a 'veritable Dutch auction of misery', and that the lack of knowledge about causes and mechanisms was reflected in Brown and Madge's proposals (*The Times Educational Supplement*, 16 July 1982, p 2).

Other reviewers suggested that while the Research Programme offered a test of the customer–contractor principle a week before public debate of the Rothschild review of the SSRC, it had used complex research to reach what appeared to be common-sense conclusions (*The Times Higher Education Supplement*, 16 July 1982, p 5a). Rudolf Klein, then Professor of Social Policy at the University of Bath, suggested that the relationship between social scientists and policy makers was bound to end in a mutual sense of betrayal. From the perspective of Joseph, the programme of research had been subverted and used by the research community to pursue its own ideological preoccupation with mapping the extent of poverty in society. Klein suggested that the Research Programme had not shown the research community at its best. Researchers had climbed on a financial bandwagon intent on pursuing their own individual interests, rather than addressing themselves to their brief, or working out a coherent programme of research. The result had been 'a dialogue of the deaf' (*The Times Literary Supplement*, 17 December 1982, p 1401).

The SSRC seemed embarrassed. In his preface to *Despite the welfare state*, Michael Posner (1931-2006), an applied economist who was the then Chair, conceded that the Programme had deviated from its original conception, writing that 'it is their book and we neither own it nor disown it' (Brown and Madge, 1982a, pp vii). The cover of the *SSRC Newsletter* in March 1983 bore the caption 'The poverty of research?', situating the final report in the context of earlier work on poverty by Mayhew, Booth, Rowntree, Titmuss, Coates and Silburn, and Townsend. Noting that whatever one's views on the quality of the research, the quantity was impressive, a series of articles attempted to evaluate the research and the usefulness of the outputs. Contributors included Alan Clarke, Muriel Brown, Nicola Madge, and a range of researchers independent of the Research Programme. These last were the most interesting. Michael Harloe, then a Lecturer at the University of Essex, for example, wrote that the policy conclusions were disappointing. In his view they comprised a series of limited proposals without any explicit link to a coherent strategy, but accompanied by passing references to the need for more fundamental change. June Lait (1983, p 13), previously at Swansea University, wrote of the book's 'massive, dull repetitiveness, unleavened by any lightness of touch'. The social scientists had reached a conclusion that could have been drawn by the average layperson, while the recommendations sought to abolish a condition (deprivation) that could not be described or defined satisfactorily, and about which there was no consensus.

As previously noted, the most extensive review was that by Richard Berthoud, then a Senior Research Fellow at the Policy Studies Institute. Initially commissioned as a book review, this gave Berthoud an opportunity to crystallise thoughts he had had for some years, and grew into a more lengthy evaluation of the Research Programme as a whole.[74] Moreover, having studied modern history as an undergraduate at Oxford University, Berthoud had become a survey researcher, and was thus neither immersed in a particular academic discipline, nor aligned with any of the main groupings. He argued that the team led by Coffield was the only one to identify the fundamental issues in the deprivation debate and to confront them head on; the other projects ignored, avoided, or skirted around the central question of the Programme. Other projects looked at low incomes or childcare difficulties, but not at the relationship between them. In the words of Berthoud, Brown and Madge had had to 'make bricks with very little straw' (Berthoud, 1983a, p 164).

In his view, the final report was remarkably uncritical of the Research Programme; the concept of 'deprivation' had not been adequately defined; and whereas Rutter and Madge (1976) had asked questions, opened doors, and refused to reach conclusions, Brown and Madge had not felt that the evidence had permitted them to answer questions, close doors, and stick their necks out. In particular, the section on implications for policy and practice was too diffuse to be useful. Berthoud concluded that intergenerational continuities were not a central theme, and the correlation between parents and children was important, but far from crucial; equally it was not clear why the link existed, or what should be done about it (Berthoud, 1983a, pp 168-9). Berthoud suggested that the debate on transmitted deprivation contributed to Joseph's scorn for the social sciences. In fact, Joseph's appointment of Lord Rothschild (December 1981) preceded the publication of the final report (July 1982). Robin Matthews later recalled of the same period that:

> By that time the Conservatives had come back into power and I was afraid that they would think this is a caricature, saying that you can solve all social problems by throwing money at them, and I said to Keith Joseph, 'I'm sorry, the final volume's not very satisfactory, in my opinion'. He was

terribly polite about it, he said 'No, it's very interesting, very interesting', but it wasn't very good or very interesting.[75]

Overall it seems that the Research Programme fuelled an existing scepticism about social scientists into an active dislike, an experience intensified by the fact that it was Joseph's own cycle hypothesis that had been ignored and subverted.

Conclusion

This chapter has explored the final years of the Research Programme, from the publication of the Third Report by the Joint Working Party (1977), to the reaction to the early books in the Heinemann series in the early 1980s. Many projects were funded that were innovative in their own right, and led to important publications. Among these were those on intergenerational continuities in low income by Tony Atkinson and colleagues; on childhood experiences and parenting behaviour by Michael Rutter and David Quinton; on adoption and special needs by John Triseliotis; and on adult delinquency and social deprivation by Donald West. The Organising Group did attempt to make the Research Programme more coherent, by encouraging the publication of research studies and by commissioning the reviews. There were therefore genuine attempts to pull it all together. Nevertheless, the overall argument of the chapter has been that, from roughly 1977 onwards, the Joint Working Party struggled to keep control over the Research Programme, and there was much less interest in it from the DHSS side. Referees' reports on some of the early projects and some of the progress reports were critical, and unsuccessful attempts were made to compare projects. Although not made public at the time, many of these problems were admitted frankly by individual members, such as Alan Clarke, Michael Rutter, and Peter Willmott, and were summarised in the Organising Group's Strategic Review, and the report to the Research Initiatives Board of the SSRC.

The way that the Research Programme was organised, and the resulting chaotic nature of the research that was produced, therefore presented Brown and Madge with a nightmarish task in attempting to summarise the research and draw some conclusions from it. Moreover, by the early 1980s, with the election of the first Thatcher government, opinions were much more polarised. By then, and partly because of the Research Programme, the SSRC itself was in serious danger of abolition. Whereas the literature review by Michael Rutter and Nicola Madge had been extensively reviewed on its publication in 1976 and favourably received, many of the other books were not reviewed widely, and where they were, received a critical reception. This was particularly true of the final report on the Research Programme as a whole. While Brown and Madge were committed to looking at the interaction of personal and structural factors, most of the research had favoured one or the other, and they were unable to offer clear explanations of the relationship between them. The result was that the Research Programme was effectively forgotten about for the next 25 years. As Richard Berthoud later reflected of *Despite the welfare state*, 'up to a point, it buried the subject for a while didn't it, researchers had burnt their fingers studying deprivation and it didn't come back as a subject until before or after the '97 election'.[76] The reaction to the final report provides a guide to broader economic, political, and ideological changes between 1972 and 1982, and some insights into the attitudes of social scientists, especially those in social policy. This is the theme that is pursued further in the next chapter, looking at three social scientists in particular: Harriett Wilson, Adrian Sinfield, and Peter Townsend.

Notes

[1] NA MH 152/75: A. D. B. Clarke to D. Benham, September 1979; interview between the author and Alan Clarke, London, 24 May 2006.

[2] NA MH 166/1517: minutes of the 16th meeting of the Joint Working Party, 24 June 1977, p 6.

[3] NA MH 152/81: A. Paterson and J. Inglis, 'Intergenerational cycle of deprivation: report of a pilot study 1974-1975' (nd), p 25.

[4] NA MH 166/1516: 'Referees A and B' (nd).

[5] NA MH 166/1516: 'Referee C' (nd).

[6] NA MH 152/83: minutes of the 11th meeting of the Joint Working Party, 3 October 1975.

[7] NA MH 152/83: S. Gilpin, 'Final report of project examining East London Family Service Unit case files' (nd).

[8] NA MH 166/1516: 'Referees A and B' (nd).

[9] NA MH 152/87: minutes of the 29th meeting of the Organising Group, 8 October 1976.

[10] NA MH 152/75: D. Donald, A. Hutton, and P. D. Taylor, 'The temporal stability of deprivation in West Central Scotland: a feasibility study' (nd).

[11] Minutes of the 48th meeting of the Organising Group, 26 January 1979. In the possession of the author.

[12] NA MH 166/1526: 'Referee B' (nd).

[13] NA MH 166/1526: 'Referee C' (nd).

[14] NA MH 166/1526: 'Referee D' (nd).

[15] NA MH 152/75: B. Ineichen and G. Millerson, 'Housing factors in transmitted deprivation: a feasibility study' (nd).

[16] Interview between the author and Olive Stevenson, Middleton Cheney, Oxfordshire, 20 July 2006.

[17] Interview between the author and Olive Stevenson, Middleton Cheney, Oxfordshire, 20 July 2006.

[18] NA MH 152/75: D. Donnison to S. Duncan, 17 March 1980.

[19] NA MH 152/75: O. Stevenson and R. Fuller, 'The impact of social policy on transmitted deprivation' (nd).

[20] Interview between the author and Muriel Brown, Bristol, 7 July 2006.

[21] Interview between the author and Alan Clarke, London, 24 May 2006.

[22] NA MH 152/87: minutes of the 29th meeting of the Organising Group, 8 October 1976.

[23] NA MH 152/88: C. Blackler to P. Lewis, 16 November 1976; NA MH 152/88: 'DHSS–SSRC contract on research into transmitted deprivation: intervention and future strategy', 22 December 1976; NA MH 166/1515: E. Shaw to C. Blackler, 25 April 1977.

[24] NA MH 166/1515: 'Annex C: DHSS views of policy objectives in relation to transmitted deprivation' (nd).

[25] NA BS 7/656: SSRC, 'Contract with DHSS on transmitted deprivation: strategic review', December 1976, pp 1–27.

[26] NA MH 152/88: Organising Group, 'Future strategy', 3 February 1977.

[27] NA MH 166/1516: minutes of the 15th meeting of the Joint Working Party, 3 February 1977, pp 3-4.

[28] NA MH 166/1517: 'Transmitted deprivation: experience of commissioning research' (nd).

[29] NA MH 166/1517: 'Transmitted deprivation: experience of commissioning research' (nd).

[30] NA MH 152/73: A. R. Y. Turner to E. Shaw, 14 February 1978.

[31] NA MH 166/1517: memo from T. R. H. Luce, September 1977.

[32] NA MH 166/1517: G. G. Hulme to P. Benner, 27 September 1977; NA MH 166/1517: G. G. Hulme to B. Abel-Smith, September 1977.

[33] Interview between the author and Muriel Brown, Bristol, 7 July 2006.

[34] NA MH 152/87: A. M. Sheridan to C. H. Wilson, 17 August 1976.

[35] NA MH 152/88: M. J. A. Partridge to C. H. Wilson, 30 December 1976.

[36] NA MH 152/87: C. H. Wilson to G. G. Hulme, 16 February 1977.

[37] NA MH 166/1517: A. M. Sheridan to E. Shaw, 19 August 1977.

[38] NA MH 166/1517: T. R. H. Luce to E. Shaw, 16 September 1977.

[39] NA MH 152/87: G. G. Hulme to P. Benner, 17 February 1977.

[40] NA MH 166/1517: A. M. Sheridan to P. Benner, 17 June 1977.

[41] NA MH 166/1517: A. M. Sheridan to A. J. Davies, 30 January 1978.

[42] NA MH 166/1518: memo from T. R. H. Luce, 2 October 1978.

[43] NA MH 166/1517: A. J. Davies to G. G. Hulme, 5 October 1977.

[44] NA MH 166/1517: M. Cooper, 'Briefing note on history and programme of the Joint Working Party on transmitted deprivation', 1 March 1979, pp 2-3.

[45] NA MH 166/1517: minute by J. Barnes, 8 March 1979.

[46] NA MH 166/1517: T. R. H. Luce to P. V. Foster, 30 April 1979.

[47] NA MH 152/90: V. Keddie to D. Benham, 10 June 1980.

[48] NA MH 152/75: D. Benham to T. R. H. Luce, 20 June 1980.

[49] NA MH 152/75: T. R. H. Luce to D. Benham, 30 June 1980.

⁵⁰ NA MH 152/75: A. M. Sheridan to D. Benham, 2 July 1980.

⁵¹ NA MH 166/1518: A. M. Sheridan to T. R. H. Luce, 19 February 1979.

⁵² NA MH 166/1518: A. M. Sheridan to T. R. H. Luce, 19 February 1979.

⁵³ NA MH 152/75: T. R. H. Luce to J. Scott Whyte, 29 July 1980.

⁵⁴ NA MH 152/75: D. Benham to T. R. H. Luce, September 1980.

⁵⁵ NA MH 152/75: 'Note of a meeting held on 16 January 1980 to discuss relations between the department and the Social Science Research Council', January 1980.

⁵⁶ Interview between the author and Mildred Blaxter, Bristol, 12 September 2006.

⁵⁷ NA MH 166/1518: letter from C. G. Trinder, 29 September 1978.

⁵⁸ NA MH 166/1518: 'Paper from the Organising Group to the Joint Working Party on the Final Report' (nd).

⁵⁹ NA MH 166/1518: 'Possible contents'.

⁶⁰ NA MH 166/1518: R. Berthoud, 'Summarising the extent and continuity of deprivation', January 1978.

⁶¹ Interview between the author and Muriel Brown, Bristol, 7 July 2006; interview between the author and Alan Clarke, London, 24 May 2006.

⁶² NA MH 152/75: memo from D. Benham, 31 July 1979.

⁶³ NA MH 166/1518: memo by T. R. H. Luce, 15 February 1979.

⁶⁴ NA MH 152/75: memo from D. Benham, 9 October 1979.

⁶⁵ Interview between the author and Muriel Brown, Bristol, 7 July 2006.

⁶⁶ Interview between the author and Muriel Brown, Bristol, 7 July 2006.

⁶⁷ Interview between the author and Muriel Brown, Bristol, 7 July 2006.

⁶⁸ Interview between the author and Muriel Brown, Bristol, 7 July 2006.

[69] Private correspondence between the author and Muriel Brown, 13 February 2007, 20 April 2007.

[70] Private correspondence between the author and Muriel Brown, 13 February 2007, 20 April 2007.

[71] Interview between the author and Muriel Brown, Bristol, 7 July 2006.

[72] Interview between the author and Muriel Brown, Bristol, 7 July 2006.

[73] Muriel Brown papers, A. M. Sheridan to M. Brown, 30 June 1983.

[74] Interview between the author and Richard Berthoud, University of Essex, 2 May 2006.

[75] Interview between the author and Robin Matthews, Cambridge, 25 May 2006.

[76] Interview between the author and Richard Berthoud, University of Essex, 2 May 2006.

SIX

Poverty, structure, and behaviour: three social scientists

Introduction

The debate over transmitted deprivation offers intriguing insights into the perspectives of a generation of social scientists. Richard Berthoud has argued that the cycle hypothesis was a test of the ability of social scientists to contribute to a real debate. However, researchers who did not accept the myth that deviancy caused poverty were more concerned to argue that deviancy did not cause poverty than to 'examine what the relationship is between these two families of social problem' (Berthoud, 1983a, p 154). Alan Deacon has claimed similarly that, by the 1970s, the alleged rejection of individualist or behavioural accounts of poverty by theorists such as Richard Titmuss had hardened into an approach that precluded any discussion of such factors. It was this 'quasi-Titmuss paradigm or school' that, in its hostility to explaining poverty by reference to the behaviour of the poor, created the intellectual void that was filled by neo-conservative writers in the 1980s. Because it was increasingly preoccupied with the growth of material inequalities and paid less attention to altruism and the quality of social relationships, it also neglected how people's behaviours and activities represented some form of meaningful choice (Deacon, 2002a, p 14). Deacon argued that this hostility was exemplified in the debate about transmitted deprivation. The original challenge to see how discontinuities in cycles of disadvantage could be brought about was not taken up, and the whole scope of the Research Programme was altered. Explanations of poverty, child health, and even abuse emphasised the uneven distribution of income and wealth, the unequal structure of employment, and the class-related pattern of life chances (Deacon, 2002a, pp 24-6).

While there was a longer tradition of research into poverty, behaviour, and culture, social policy analysts seemed reluctant to enter this arena from the mid-1970s. Like Berthoud, Deacon argued that academics did not respond to the challenge of the Research Programme, regarding Joseph's research agenda as 'at best a red herring and at worst a distraction from the much more important issue of the generation and persistence of inequalities' (Deacon, 2002a, pp 23-6). This chapter uses the Research Programme to explore further the approach of social scientists to issues of poverty, deprivation, structure, and behaviour. In this it builds on the earlier work by Deacon, which took a collective biographical approach to explaining changing ideologies of welfare reform, focusing on Richard Titmuss, Charles Murray, and Lawrence Mead, along with Oscar Lewis, William Julius Wilson, and William Ryan (Deacon, 1996, 2002a, 2003). After exploring the broader changes identified by among others David Donnison and Howard Glennerster, this chapter looks particularly at the work of social scientists who were openly hostile, or at best marginal, to the Research Programme: Harriett Wilson, Adrian Sinfield, and Peter Townsend. They are chosen, not just as examples, but as illustrations of a particular viewpoint on the cycle and Research Programme.

An ideological red herring

Hints of the shifts to which Berthoud and Deacon refer are clear from contemporary documents. It is interesting, if not particularly surprising, for example, that the cycle speech is not mentioned in the *Year book of social policy for 1972*, and it is clear that even at this point, the interest of the social policy community was in the reduction of inequalities (Jones, 1973, pp vii-x; Townsend and Bosanquet, 1972b, pp 5-11). Frank Field, writing in 1974, had coined the phrase 'the cycle of inequality' (Field, 1974, p 62), and in the mid-1970s the reports of the CDPs began to appear, taking a more radical approach, and locating poverty programmes in the wider context of the needs of capitalism, economic restructuring, social control, and law and order (CDP, 1977). Similar debates were played out in social work, as illustrated by the radical journal *Case Con*. Roger Fuller and Olive Stevenson later pointed out that the debate had not always been polarised between those who favoured structural change and those who emphasised familial processes. They suggested that it was only by the mid-1970s, when the radical critiques of the CDPs had begun to appear, that it became difficult to make a contribution to the debate without nailing one's colours to an 'ideological mast' (Fuller and Stevenson, 1983, pp 2-4).

One of the first critiques of the cycle hypothesis was that by Bill Jordan. In *Poor parents* (1974), Jordan had argued that the cycle speech was part of an official trend of concentrating on the needs of the most deprived communities and inhabitants. Despite a lack of evidence linking poverty with maladjustment, the official stereotype of the bad parent persisted (Jordan, 1974, pp 3-8). He suggested that the question was not why deprivation and maladjustment persisted, but how they were reinforced by conditions of prosperity. It was fair to ask why some people remained poor, but this had nothing to do with maladjustment, and it was only poverty, not maladjustment, which was a distinguishing characteristic of the poorest sector. The cycle theory illustrated themes in official thinking that had a very long history; social policy had to be aimed at supporting the family and encouraging members to take responsibility for each other, but it also had to intervene in the lives of the poor to correct tendencies that were seen as potentially damaging (Jordan, 1974, p 16). Jordan argued that the cycle theory 'encapsulates a number of myths that are very prevalent in both the academic and the political spheres of social policy at the present time' (Jordan, 1974, p 173). The Joint Working Party focused on individual factors, and Joseph had modified his theory in face of the criticism it had received. Nevertheless, there was unlikely to be a concerted challenge to Joseph's ideas from academics attracted by research funds. In general, Jordan related Joseph's ideas to the persistence of the principles of the Poor Law in the development of the social services (Jordan, 1974, pp 8, 173-6, 189).

In some respects the stance of Bob Holman was similar to that of Jordan. Holman had taken the Diploma in Social Administration at the LSE in the early 1960s (the same year as Muriel Brown), and later became a Child Care Officer. In 1970, Holman was a Lecturer in the Department of Social Administration at Birmingham University; from 1967, he had been involved in the UN Working Group on Socially Deprived Families. Discussions between representatives had revealed differences over the term 'socially deprived families'; to some, it was confined to problem families; to others, it was sufficiently broad to include all women on the assumption that they suffered discrimination and deprivation, due to low wages and limited employment opportunities. This work was located within the wider context of the 'rediscovery of poverty' (Holman, 1970, pp 1-6). By 1973, Holman was a Senior Lecturer in Social Administration and Social Work at the University of Glasgow. He noted that Joseph linked the cycle with measures that reached children in their most formative years – playgroups, compensatory education, and Preparation for Parenthood schemes – and those that had a direct effect on the behaviour of adults, such as therapeutic relationships with social workers. Deprivation was seen as being due to inadequate childrearing practices, and it was families, rather than the rest of society, that were expected to change. In looking at the functions of poverty, Holman argued that those in poverty 'act as scapegoats, a vulnerable group on whom the blame for social problems can be placed, so diverting attention away from that minority which has some control over social affairs' (Holman, 1973, p 438). Holman argued that poverty and deprivation were preserved by social mechanisms such as the public schools and Oxford and Cambridge Universities; mass communication; and the social services themselves. Poverty remained, not because of problem families, but because 'certain social mechanisms require poverty to fulfil the function of maintaining inequalities' (Holman, 1973, p 442).

Reviewing the literature review by Rutter and Madge, A. H. Halsey also tended to emphasise the importance of structural factors. He wrote that Rutter and Madge had given 'an accurate and detailed map of the larger territories of disadvantage, deprivation and poverty in which the [cycle] theory always had a dubious place' (Halsey, A. H., 'Equals in society', *The Times Educational Supplement*, 17 December 1976, p 2). Yet while the review was up to date and authoritative in such areas as intellectual performance, educational attainment, and psychiatric disorder, it was less convincing in those of income, wealth, housing, and mobility. The literature review had gone to press before the publication of the first report of the RCDIW, and before the controversy over Cyril Burt's research. Halsey wrote therefore that 'in the end, we are left with a picture of many social circumstances and psychological variables with low correlations and ill-understood causative links to a formidably unequal outcome of material inequality' (Halsey, A. H., 'Equals in society', *The Times Educational Supplement*, 17 December 1976, p 2). He reviewed the literature review alongside Richard Berthoud's *The disadvantages of inequality* (1976), and drew from this what he regarded as the most valuable point: 'that deprivation is best thought of as a social structure of probabilities and not as a characteristic of definable and separate social groups' (Halsey, A. H., 'Equals in society', *The Times Educational Supplement*, 17 December 1976, p 2).

Reflecting on his Chairpersonship of the Supplementary Benefits Commission, David Donnison recalled that with hindsight the early 1970s stood out as the end of a period that had begun when he was a child in the 1930s. The debate about social security policies was for many years shaped by the assumptions of that time. People who worked in the 'Titmuss school' found that they had joined a much larger group of progressive social democrats who shared similar concerns and assumptions. They inherited the tradition of laborious social investigation that went back to the early Fabians, and worked inside a framework of assumptions within which most political debate took place. These were that the growth of the economy and the population would continue; the harsher effects of inequalities in incomes would gradually be softened by a 'social wage' and a growing burden of progressive taxes; and middle England would eventually support equalising social policies and programmes of this kind. Another set of assumptions were that government and its social services were the natural vehicles of progress; social policies dealt with the redistribution of the fruits of economic growth, the management of the human effects, and the compensation of those who suffered from them; and governments that allowed a return to the high unemployment, social conflicts, and means tests of the 1930s would not survive (Donnison, 1982, pp 19-21).

Donnison's recollections offer support for the idea of a Titmuss paradigm. By the early 1980s, the outlook was very different. In the introduction to her textbook on social administration, Muriel Brown noted that whereas the first edition (1969) had reflected a basic confidence in welfare, belief in economic growth, and enthusiasm for social reform, by the time of the sixth edition (1984) welfare was on the defensive, self-reliance emphasised, and the poor increasingly penalised (Brown and Payne, 1969, 1990 edn, pp vi-vii). There was a recognised need to take stock and rethink the basic economic, social, intellectual, and value assumptions on which social policy had been based (Glennerster, 1983b, pp 1-9). Nevertheless, questions need to be asked about the Titmuss paradigm; who was included within it; the timing of these shifts; and the reasons for them.

Poverty and parenting: Harriett Wilson

Understanding the stance taken by some social scientists in this period is possible through adopting a collective biography approach to three who were openly hostile, or at best marginal, to the main Research Programme: Harriett Wilson, Adrian Sinfield, and Peter Townsend. Harriett Wilson (1916-2002) is perhaps best known as the founder of the CPAG. Born in Berlin, her parents had suffered major financial loss in the catastrophic German inflation of 1923; as a result she experienced poverty and squalid conditions during her childhood, which profoundly affected her lifelong concern for those living in poverty. She had left Germany in 1935, later studying at the LSE and the University of Wales in Cardiff. A lifelong socialist, she was also a committed Christian, and for most of her adult life a Quaker. In the late 1950s, supported by Cardiff Quakers, she set up an experimental playgroup, the Ely Play Centre, on one of Cardiff's most deprived estates, where children's needs could be addressed, and their parents supported.

Wilson's early work was concerned with the relationship between juvenile delinquency and the home environment, specifically among problem families in Cardiff. Basing her evidence on referrals to the local Co-ordination Committee, Wilson argued that juvenile delinquency was home centred rather than area centred; problem families displayed both material deprivation and emotional insecurity; and it was this combination, along with the absence of a set of ideals to live up to, that conditioned the child from a problem family for a career as a delinquent (Wilson, 1958, pp 94-105). Subsequently, Wilson was more critical of the concept of the problem family, and the way it had been used by social workers. She wrote that while it might be seen as an advance in diagnostic thinking that problem families were no longer seen in terms of mental subnormality and temperamental instability, and immaturity was seen as the main cause, the literature was very impressionistic, and the importance of employment and health underplayed (Wilson, 1959, pp 115-18).

These arguments were brought together in her book *Delinquency and child neglect* (1962). Her aims here were to find out if problem families were a breeding-ground for delinquency, to compare families with delinquent children with those without, and to find out the connection between juvenile delinquency and parental criminality. She surveyed cases referred to the Co-ordinating Committee (Wilson, 1962, pp 31-2, 34-9, 62-3). Wilson noted that in the literature dealing with families suspected of child neglect, extreme stress situations were rarely discussed, and emphasis was placed instead on the inability of parents to make a success of their lives. Immature personalities were not the complete explanation, and the economic burden was also important. Families were assessed in terms of their living conditions, use of welfare services, family planning, attitudes to education, and spending patterns. But Wilson argued that these were not inherent or ineradicable characteristics of problem families; they were symptoms of living on a level below that generally acceptable to the community. The standards expected were too high, given that the material and personal resources necessary were not available (Wilson, 1962, pp 109-11). Wilson therefore concluded that none of the inadequacies found among problem families was unique to this group of people, and could be found in other social classes. Failure did not lie in the immaturity of the group, but in the inadequacies of social services (Wilson, 1962, p 159). Co-ordination Committees were concerned primarily with the prevention of neglect of a child's material needs, and the emotional needs of children could be overlooked. Families living in relative material comfort could be deprived of affection and suffer psychological ill-treatment.

Wilson's sociological work in the 1950s had been on children who came before juvenile courts; their families were poor, large, often with absent fathers, and lacked adequate social skills. They were seen as problem families with 'immature parents'. But Wilson questioned whether they were immature, and suggested that their lack of resources needed to be addressed first. It was thus in the context of there being a strong undercurrent of public opinion influenced by the Eugenics Society, along with the psychiatric orientation of the social work profession, that Wilson and others tried to bring about a new approach to the problem of poverty (Lowe and Nicholson, 1995, pp 613-14). In 1965, she organised a meeting at Toynbee Hall in London to discuss family poverty and the neglect of family allowances in the plans of the newly elected Labour government. Her proposals for a research and lobbying organisation led to the formation of the CPAG in the same year.[1] Subsequently, Wilson was concerned with the impact of poverty on parenting and childrearing practices.

In her later work on the socialisation of children, Wilson again argued that 'social deprivation' and its effect on children were largely a problem of families on marginal or inadequate incomes. She drew on evidence produced by Dennis Marsden and Adrian Sinfield among others, and argued that there was no convincing support for an intergenerational culture of poverty (Marsden, 1969, 1970; Sinfield, 1970). Wilson did concede that there were cultural aspects of deprivation, and that there was a role for parenting. Physical and mental ill-health occurred among all social classes, but it was only when they were combined with the absence of material resources that they became significant. The families whose incomes were at or beneath subsistence level were those where the fathers were in full-time work but earning low wages, chronically sick or disabled, unemployed, or where the families were fatherless. Nevertheless, Wilson argued that 'while these indices identify vulnerable groups they must not be taken to be sufficient as causes of social deprivation, for it is only in combination with lack of financial resources that they become handicapping' (Wilson, 1970, p 139). Not all children who were deprived showed signs of malfunctioning, and it was not clear what 'personality resources' were at work in those families that managed to bring up their children successfully despite financial and psychological stress.

In her later work at the University of Birmingham with Geoffrey Herbert, Wilson re-examined the concept of 'cultural deprivation', again arguing that issues such as the cleanliness of children and the home tended to be interpreted in terms of poor management, rather than low income and poverty. Wilson and Herbert argued that 'when such attitudes are not linked with detailed information on *per capita* income, housing, and other environmental conditions, it is no longer possible to interpret them correctly' (Wilson and Herbert, 1972, p 509 [emphasis in original]). In the Plowden Report (Central Advisory Council for Education, 1967), the problem of under-functioning at school had been presented as being largely dependent on parental attitudes, and home circumstances were seen as playing only a minor part. Overall, Wilson and Herbert argued that the concept of cultural deprivation needed revision, and that 'the boys are culturally deprived when seen at school; but they are conditioned to the tough world which is their home environment' (Wilson and Herbert, 1972, p 511).

It seems likely that Wilson and Joseph knew each other through their shared interest in the CPAG, but their paths had crossed again in the mid-1960s. Wilson had argued that it had become clear that children of large families were seriously disadvantaged, and she asked how they might be given an equal chance, including through family planning (Wilson, 1966). In response, Joseph had written that while he did not necessarily agree that wholesale increases in family allowances were the right answer, more cash was essential, along with free school meals, children's day centres, more social and health visitor support, suitable housing with rent rebates, and play facilities. Such a 'comprehensive approach' had been proposed by Edward Heath in a Birmingham speech, and in the Tory election manifesto. Joseph agreed with Wilson that the needs of existing large families should be separated from the question of whether the creation of large poor families could be discouraged (Joseph, 1966b). Interestingly the focus of both was the problem family, although they drew rather different conclusions from it.

Similarly, Wilson was clearly interested in the cycle speech. Her private papers contain annotated copies of both the full transcript, and of the Wright and Lunn Sheffield study. Wilson lent Adrian Sinfield copies of the articles by Wright and Lunn, and Oliver and Taylor, saying 'they make very good teaching material'.[2] In the case of the former, she was highly critical of the evidence on which the article was based, and sought to relate its arguments to wider data on unemployment and social class. In correspondence with Sinfield, in July 1972, for example, she agreed that the references to problem families in the speech were worrying, but also conceded:

> I admit I have some considerable difficulty in working out
> the implications of certain child-rearing practices which

we have observed … assuming one alters these people's environment, then there will be new opportunities for choices. People could then more easily adopt different behaviours, provided they see these as relevant to their situations.… In other words, for Heaven's sake let everybody go on pressing for material improvements, but let us not fool ourselves into imagining that that's all that's needed.… What is needed? I don't know the answer.[3]

Because of her work on poverty and parenting, Wilson was invited to the 'Approaches' conference held at the LSE on 15 April 1973. She was particularly critical of the use that the Joint Working Party made of the UN report on socially deprived families (1972); Wilson herself had been a member of that Group. More generally she was critical of the attempt to identify 'attributes' and 'burdens', noting that 'the attempt to establish a link between so-called causes and a phenomenon which one wishes to eradicate is logically fallacious and practically dysfunctional'.[4] She wrote to Mike Miller of the studies by Oliver and Taylor, and by Wright and Lunn, that 'they are worth reading as specimens of what we used to refer to as the "old eugenics approach to problem families" – I thought that had died out, but apparently it is being resuscitated'.[5] Miller himself replied that 'I too am unhappy about the Keith Joseph and SSRC formulations. I foresee the American experience – well-known and unhappy – being repeated here in its approach to poor people'.[6] At the conference itself, Wilson argued that research problems were often formulated in a way that reflected ideology – she noted of the Sheffield problem family studies that she was much more interested in the two thirds of children 'who've made it, who've become successful, pulled themselves up by their own boot straps out of the mud. How is it that they managed it? Why must we focus on the one-third of their offspring who have not allegedly made it?'[7]

On her copy of the DHSS report on the All Souls seminar, Wilson noted Tawney's comment, 'improve the character of individuals by all means, if you feel competent to do so, especially those whose excessive incomes expose them to peculiar temptations'.[8] But Wilson's most direct link with the cycle of deprivation was in an article written in the CPAG journal *Poverty*. Here she argued that in proposing Preparation for Parenthood, Joseph had conceptualised social deprivation as a generic term for a number of very different problems. She found it odd that in the 'Approaches' paper, 'genetic influences' headed a list of areas within which intergenerational influences were alleged to operate. People involved in fieldwork held very different views about deprivation. Some argued that improved home and school conditions would lead to more achievement-oriented children (a consensus model); some that middle-class education was irrelevant in the slums (a pluralism model); others that wholesale social change was necessary (a conflict model). Her own research on delinquency had indicated that an emphasis on better parenting made little sense in deprived areas, and the essential issue was the dynamics of the decaying city area (Wilson, 1974b). Improvements were necessary but not sufficient, and work should be much broader, drawing on the conflict model to emphasise powerlessness and unemployability.

In published articles, Wilson remained critical of the cycle hypothesis, arguing that there was no support for the theory that parental participation in children's activities, a warm and happy home atmosphere, and good marital relations were preconditions for the prevention of delinquency. Thus middle-class child-centred behaviour, as defined by John and Elizabeth Newson (Newson and Newson, 1968), was not operable in the milieu of poverty. Material shortages in the home and poor environmental conditions severely affected childrearing methods. Wilson suggested that the debate about Preparation for Parenthood should acknowledge the realities of life in slums, which forced parents to adopt imperfect methods of childrearing. Parents and children needed vast fiscal resources to improve their conditions before an attempt could be made to change their attitudes, they required urgent help, not retraining. They needed:

> large-scale fiscal measures to speed up slum-clearance and housing schemes, to improve local amenities, to boost family income by generous family allowances, to improve the job market in the inner city especially for the unskilled and the disabled, and to implement the proposed expansion of nursery provisions. (Wilson, 1974a, p 254)

In the same period, there was further correspondence between Wilson and Joseph over his Edgbaston speech. She conceded that with the cycle, Joseph had drawn attention to the intergenerational aspects of poverty, and introduced a new dimension to the poverty debate. Nevertheless, she also wrote that Joseph's interpretation of the relationship between family planning, abortion, and poverty diverted attention from the real issues. His appeal for a new morality would fail, and he belittled the consequences of living in poverty. She believed that the focus should not be on reviving Victorian sexual conventions, or stricter measures in dealing with delinquents, but a political concern with the problems of extreme inequality in a nation pledged to create equal opportunities for all children (*The Times*, 24 October 1974). Typically, Joseph wrote to thank Wilson for her letter to *The Times* following his 'clumsy reference to unwanted babies'.[9] He thought that while he and she would disagree on economics, and on the scope for further egalitarianism, they were equally concerned to reduce 'unwanted babies', especially in those groups least in a position to cope. Among the questions that troubled him were whether the climate of the time fostered casual parenthood, whether anything could be done about it, whether birth control awareness could reach the teenagers concerned, and whether domiciliary family planning was the most hopeful method. For her part, Wilson replied that free family planning services, along with domiciliary visits, worked with teenagers, but the real problem was elsewhere. People caught in the cycle of deprivation hung on to traditional beliefs about the role of women as wives and mothers; there was much resistance to open discussion of family planning; and only the eradication of poverty would solve the problem.[10]

Nevertheless, as with others critical of the cycle speech, Wilson was interested in applying for research funding under the Research Programme. One proposal was to test further hypotheses on her previous study of 56 families, exploring the association between 'social handicap' and delinquency with factors such as home literacy and parental interest, parental home background, size of family, mobility, stress, and equipment, space, and leisure.[11] This application was unsuccessful, probably because of the proposed methods. Dennis Marsden, for example, had written separately to Wilson that:

> Working out all your tests of significance on such small numbers are inappropriate even in a mathematical sense. You achieve truth and communicate it in spite of these kind of methods rather than through them.[12]

Wilson was encouraged by the publication of Rutter and Madge's (1976) literature review to make a second approach, in October 1977. The aim was to explore the relationship between a socially disadvantaged home and how boys functioned at school, and to relate the findings to delinquent behaviour, with a 10-year follow-up.[13] However, the Organising Group again found it difficult to judge from the outline whether a full application was likely to be successful. Tracing a small sample would be difficult, more detail on costs was needed, and the research might overlap with existing projects.[14]

Undeterred, Wilson returned to the themes of parenting and poverty in her work with Herbert, exploring families in a Midland city, and relating the development of children to the social and economic development of the home. They argued that the search for the causal factors of social deprivation were governed by basic sociological assumptions about the role of individuals in relation to the community; alternative explanations emphasised personal failure or the absence of political power. Wilson and Herbert argued, for instance, that 'the solution to educational failure of disadvantaged children may ultimately lie not in changes in educational methods, but in drastic fiscal measures to bring about a reduction of extreme inequality' (Wilson and Herbert, 1978, p 14). Their approach was to see the failure of the family to act in a protective capacity in situational terms; families subjected to long-term poverty had learnt adaptive patterns of living, which were seen by others as the result of failure to improve their circumstances. Behaviour was 'an adaptation to particular situations of deprivation which are passed on to the next generation in terms of commonly-held attitudes, beliefs and behaviour patterns' (Wilson and Herbert, 1978, p 184). If there was a cycle of deprivation, the explanation lay in the survival strategy adopted by parents, which overrode attention to the individual needs of their children; socialisation reflected and reinforced parental feelings of failure, and perpetuated inequalities within society. Wilson and Herbert wrote that:

> Poverty is not generated by 'inadequate' people who conglomerate in deprived areas; it arises in a social system in which low wages, inadequate welfare provisions, a chronic shortage of housing, and unemployment are allowed to exist. (Wilson and Herbert, 1978, p 198)

Wilson failed in her bid to become more directly involved in the Research Programme. Nevertheless, she was a very interested observer of the cycle hypothesis and the debate over transmitted deprivation. Like Joseph, her work had from the 1950s been concerned with parenting and poverty, initially based on problem families, later seeking to demonstrate that initiatives such as Preparation for Parenthood had to acknowledge structural factors and the realities of life in the slums. Through the CPAG Executive, she was in direct contact with others such as Adrian Sinfield and Peter Townsend following the cycle speech, acknowledging that it was not just material improvements that were required. Moreover, she played an important part in the 'Approaches' conference, in April 1973.

Unemployment and poverty: Adrian Sinfield

Wilson was in correspondence with Adrian Sinfield in this period, and his earlier career and work further illustrate how and why one social scientist approached questions of poverty and behaviour. After undergraduate work at Oxford, and a year working in a relief agency in Hong Kong, Sinfield had taken the Postgraduate Diploma in Social Administration at the LSE (1962-63), with Peter Townsend as his tutor, and a placement in the York FSU. Subsequently, as a Research Assistant at the LSE, Sinfield had conducted a survey of the unemployed and their families in North Shields for Townsend and Brian Abel-Smith. During a year in the US, as a Research Assistant at the New York State Mental Health Research Unit, in Syracuse, Sinfield replicated the Tyneside survey in a US setting. From 1965, until he moved to Edinburgh in 1979, Sinfield worked in Townsend's department at Essex, spending a subsequent year in the US in 1969-70.[15] Wilson was Deputy or Vice-Chair of the CPAG; although only on the Executive later, Sinfield was already lobbying her colleagues on unemployment.

Sinfield had earlier signalled his opposition to the culture of poverty theory, arguing that:

> The policies generally derived from such hypotheses centre on changing the individual in some way – by training or retraining, education, social casework or therapy. Essentially, the structure of society itself is accepted – the poor merely need help in adapting to it. (Sinfield, 1968a, p 206)

The theory could only explain why people remained poor when there were *opportunities* to escape; if the opportunities were not there, the motivation of the poor was not relevant, and if the poor were ill or retired and outside the labour force, neither motivation nor opportunity was relevant. In contrast, research into poverty had 'underlined the need to study poverty in its societal context as a relative lack of resources, intimately related to the issues of distribution and redistribution' (Sinfield, 1968a, p 206). The poverty of men and their families on Tyneside was still largely determined by the rewards they could command in the labour market, and those who were more dependent on society because they were outside the labour force were especially vulnerable to poverty and isolation (Sinfield, 1970).

In discussing unemployment, Sinfield had argued that while there were individual and personal factors, the extent to which people remained in employment depended mainly on the state of the labour market, through redundancy and recurrent unemployment. Sinfield was again critical of the terms 'culture of poverty' and 'underclass', noting that the suggestion in the latter that such groups were outside society 'in some way obscures the fact that their location at the very bottom of the social structure, which is one of their greatest handicaps, is to a great extent the result of the operation of social and economic forces' (Sinfield, 1968b, p 46). In this period Sinfield was an assessor for the Council for Training in Social Work, and the experiences of marking work by social work students were formative. He argued that social workers could become so engrossed in building relationships with their clients that they could lose sight of the bigger picture. They appeared to show little interest in command of resources, and the major discovery of the 1950s had been the problem family (Sinfield, 1969, pp 6-9, 12-13). Drawing on Clement Attlee's *The Social Worker* (1920), Sinfield argued that they needed to move beyond social casework to become social investigators interested in inequalities (Sinfield, 1969, pp 31-2, 35-6).

As with Harriett Wilson, it was inevitable, given his research interests, that Sinfield would take a close interest in transmitted deprivation. Following the cycle speech, Sinfield immediately distributed copies of the DHSS typescript to colleagues, mainly to point to what he regarded as disturbing aspects, such as the problem family terminology. Over the following year, Sinfield chased up the studies cited in the speech, with Donald West at Cambridge, Audrey Taylor in Swindon, and John Lunn in Sheffield.[16] For example, he asked Lunn about the employment records of problem families, sources of information on the types of job the men had, the length of time spent unemployed, the difference between reductions and disallowances, and information on benefits and earnings.[17] Sinfield's marginal comments show that he thought the study neglected overcrowding and unemployment, and he clearly felt there was little evidence for many of the statements made.[18] Lunn conceded that the data had come from health visitors, and his team had no information from the Department of Employment. He admitted that:

> We have no information on amounts earned and we didn't think the answers to questions about earnings would be sufficiently reliable, so we didn't prejudice our relationships with the families by making enquiries about money.[19]

But again, as had been the case with Wilson, Sinfield's concern about the speech did not mean that he was uninterested in becoming involved in the Research Programme. He acquired copies of the Joint Working

Party papers, and in July 1974 wrote for further information about the Programme, asking what sort of research would be accepted, and how and when applications for funds should be made.[20] Sinfield also noted that the original publicity had 'tended to leave the impression that this research was to be an alternative to the type of research into poverty and inequality carried out by many of us'.[21] By this, Sinfield meant people like Dennis Marsden, Peter Townsend, John Veit-Wilson, David Byrne, John Foster, and Hilary Land. The Joint Working Party wrote further to Sinfield in January 1975, in connection with the proposed seminar on multiple deprivation and its transmission.[22] One idea was to extend the 'misfortune' study being carried out by the SSRC Centre for Socio-Legal Studies at Oxford, but nothing came of this.[23]

Instead, Sinfield's main contribution to the Research Programme was through his commissioned paper on transmitted deprivation and the social division of welfare. As part of this, he gave a paper on income maintenance at the seminar on socioeconomic factors, held at the LSE on 28 September 1976. As was noted in Chapter Four, many of the proposals received in the first phase of funding had come from psychologists and psychiatrists who were primarily interested in individual and familial aspects of transmitted deprivation. Aware that research on the socioeconomic dimensions of intergenerational deprivation required special encouragement, the Joint Working Party in its Second Report (SSRC–DHSS, 1975) had addressed itself specifically to sociology, social administration, economics, and related disciplines. The response had been good, but 'also highlighted the difficulties of devising research in these disciplines which is both relevant and rigorous'.[24] The seminar was to explore this problem further, through four themes: housing, social work services, income maintenance, and employment.

In his paper, Sinfield argued that analysis of the transmission of any state or condition over time, and particularly from one generation to the next, needed to take into account the prevailing distribution of resources and power. In his view, the first conclusion to be drawn from past research and theoretical and policy debates was 'the importance of an adequate structural framework for research into the transmission of deprivation'.[25] Failure to establish this framework had led to what William Ryan in the US had termed 'blaming the victim', and looking at attitudes and behaviour in a social and economic vacuum had led to a partial understanding of problem families. Rather it was important to 'examine the mechanisms and processes in society by which power and advantage are maintained or enhanced as well as reduced' – what Sinfield termed 'income transfers' – across the social division of welfare.[26] Most debates about poverty and low income had focused on income per week, and assumptions about the long-term effect of such income had never been spelt out. Sinfield argued that in examining the experience of deprivation over time, the impacts of the initial cause of deprivation and of any policy response should be examined separately. Work on unemployment had revealed how little was known about the effects of reduced levels of income on people's attitudes and behaviour. Overall, the need was for comparative studies; the risk was of blaming the victim if 'only one group is put under the microscope'.[27] Sinfield's paper certainly struck a chord with some of those present. Frank Coffield, for example, congratulated him: 'I was delighted with your talk which (I hope you don't mind me saying) saved the conference for me'.[28]

Sinfield's commissioned paper on transmitted deprivation and the social division of welfare was completed in November 1976. He defined deprivation as the lack of four attributes of economic resources, social status, power, and security to the extent that participation or inclusion in society was significantly restricted. Thus he widened the definition of deprivation to include the absence of resources as well as the loss of them, and the term was not used in his paper 'as related to inadequacy in contrast to maturity, adequacy or personality balance'.[29] For him, transmission was concerned with the transfer of any resource, whether short term or long term, and, like Titmuss, Sinfield was concerned about stigma. He wrote that those excluded from occupational welfare and hidden public subsidies were more likely to be perceived and treated as in some way less adequate than as less privileged. But what was important was an adequate structural framework for research, since a failure in this respect would lead to blaming the victim. It was important to examine the mechanisms and processes by which power and privilege were maintained and enhanced, as well as reduced. The Organising Group felt that the most important message of the paper was that they should be looking at the rich as well as the poor, at the distribution of occupational and taxation benefits, and the effects of taxation policies. However, they were not convinced that at that stage of the Research Programme they could afford the time or the money to do this. Had Sinfield got his paper in on time, it might have had more impact.[30]

Sinfield made numerous attempts to put the case for more attention to external or structural factors, arguing that a relative and dynamic definition of poverty underlined the way that it was linked to issues of inequality, stratification, and the systems distributing resources throughout society. Harriett Wilson had offered one of the very few studies of social work clients that took poverty into account, while research by Townsend and others had shown 'that the basic causes of poverty are to be found in the social, economic and political institutions of society and in the systems which distribute and redistribute resources and opportunities amongst the members of a society' (Sinfield, 1974, p 61). Thus a focus on the personal characteristics, psychological attributes, or lifestyles of the poor as causes of their situation indicated a concern, not with the fact of poverty, but with the behaviour of the poor. Social workers had been taught, not to recognise poverty, but to discount or reinterpret it as a symptom of personal inadequacies (Sinfield, 1974, p 72). The reinforcement of existing inequalities deserved emphasis because it limited and distorted understanding of the causes of poverty and the extent of change needed to tackle them. Sinfield wrote that 'failure to recognise this has led to policies aimed more at changing the behaviour or attitudes of the poor than at removing the structural constraints which keep them poor' (Sinfield, 1975, p 18). Many programmes had contained a strong social control element, and much anti-poverty action had been concerned more with the behaviour of the poor, than with their being in poverty; the result was more control than welfare. The culture of poverty thesis had gained attention because it explained poverty by locating its causes within the poor. But Sinfield argued that access to the labour market was crucial, and provided an explanation for any cultural patterns that were found. Sinfield wrote:

> The poor have been treated as a separate isolated group with little recognition that the risk of poverty is spread much more widely throughout society, and so policies have tended to reinforce the gulf between the poor and those who are currently better-off. (Sinfield, 1975, p 21)

In his writing on unemployment, Sinfield continued to stress the role of labour market forces rather than individual characteristics. He argued that there should be better support for the long-term unemployed and for unemployed families; those out of work should be seen as equal citizens in a democratic society (Sinfield, 1976). He suggested that the social psychology theory of unemployment, for instance, had been 'illustrated and supported rather than tested and validated' (Sinfield, 1981a, p 37). Those without paid work tended to be found disproportionately among the young and the old, disabled people, and those in remote areas, and generally among the poorer and less powerful in society. Changes in the demand for, and supply of, labour influenced the social construction of definitions of the labour force in general and the unemployed in particular (Sinfield, 1981b, p 142). It was the state that designated certain states of dependency acceptable or reprehensible; unemployment was 'a social and economic tax with very unequal impact that works to reinforce and even shape the inequalities of our social structure' (Sinfield, 1981b, p 164). In this, Sinfield's work bears out Deacon's point about the way the upsurge in unemployment from the mid–1970s seemed to exemplify the futility of trying to solve social problems by changing people.

Sinfield was very concerned that the focus on the cycle threatened to shift attention from the growing poverty associated with rising unemployment. He was also very much influenced by his involvement with the culture of poverty debates, during his two stays in the US. In his correspondence with Harriett Wilson and other researchers, Sinfield saw the cycle hypothesis as a vehicle for problem family concepts, and being based on dubious evidence. Nevertheless, he was willing to become involved in the Research Programme. He saw this as an opportunity to warn of the dangers of blaming the victim; the need to avoid focusing on the poor alone; the significance of placing the study of deprivation within a broader context that took account of structural constraints; and the importance of taking account of the social division of welfare. Emboldened by the Charles Valentine critique of the culture of poverty, Sinfield's point of view was not that he regarded people in poverty as victims, whether passive or not, but that structural, or simply external, factors were the primary ones that explained their poverty, not their behaviour. Focusing on personal or behavioural characteristics could lead to policy closure, taking external issues off the agenda, and leading to a focus on work incentives and dependency, rather than the level of Unemployment Benefit, its adequacy, coverage, and take-up. Unemployment was rising through 1972 to peak in 1973, before falling again, and then rising again under Labour in the mid–1970s. Moreover, FIS had been introduced instead of the increase in family allowances that Sinfield and others had been arguing for. Thus the Joseph speech seemed to be an attempt to draw attention away from rising unemployment and its effects.

Relative deprivation: Peter Townsend

Peter Townsend was in this period Professor of Sociology at the University of Essex. Initially associated with the Institute of Community Studies, his earlier publications had been concerned with the family life of old people, residential homes for older people, learning difficulties, and poverty (Townsend, 1957, 1962a, 1962b). In fact, Townsend's original work, for Political and Economic Planning, had been concerned with poverty 10 years after the Beveridge Report, (Beveridge, 1942) and with unemployment and social security in Lancashire (Townsend, 1952a, 1952b). He later recalled how as a youngster during the Second World War he became aware of the lowering of social barriers and of the popular support for social reform. In Blackpool, some evacuees were lodged temporarily in a boarding house where Townsend and his mother were living:

> A poorly-dressed woman with leaden eyes climbed off the bus with a tearful baby and, without a thought for the landlady and two sharp-nosed women guests, undid her blouse and pulled out one of her breasts to comfort the child. I remember how shocked the three women were by her unselfconscious behaviour and, more important, how shocked they and many others were too by the poverty of the evacuees. (Townsend, 1958, p 93)

In the same piece, Townsend also wrote that:

> people often live differently and it is sometimes hard to understand what drives them to act as they do. To give them the benefit of the doubt, to assume they have good rather than bad motives when we know little or nothing about them, and to concern ourselves with their needs rather than their failings – these are generally regarded as being Christian virtues, and yet they are the essence of Socialism. (Townsend, 1958, p 118)

It was partly the experience of studying social anthropology at Cambridge University that led to Townsend being particularly interested in social conditions, relationships, systems, structure, and change.[31] In his early work on poverty, for example, Townsend had written approvingly of Harriett Wilson's emphasis on the economic stress experienced by problem families, arguing that individuals and families, whose resources fell seriously below those commanded by the average individual or family in the community in which they lived, were in poverty (Townsend, 1962b, pp 211-25). With Brian Abel-Smith, Townsend played a key role in the rediscovery of poverty (Abel-Smith and Townsend, 1965). Moreover, what Townsend argued was that systems of international social stratification interacted to produce poverty, and he rejected theories (such as the culture of poverty) that placed responsibility for poverty with the individual. The culture of poverty theory, for example, concentrated on the familial and local setting for behaviour and 'largely ignores the external and often unseen social forces which condition the distribution of different types of resources to the community, family and individual' (Townsend, 1970, p 41). The elimination of poverty required not the reform, education, or rehabilitation of the individual, or even the creation of more opportunities for upward mobility, but the reconstruction of the national and regional systems by which resources were distributed, or the introduction of additional systems that were universal and egalitarian (Townsend, 1970, pp 44-5).

Thus Townsend's reaction to the cycle thesis was in some ways predictable, that he would link it to the earlier history of the eugenics movement, locate it within wider debates about the value of IQ testing, and see it as 'a familiar attempt to account for poverty in terms of inheritance within families'.[32] Townsend had a few years earlier written a long introduction to Pauline Morris's sociological study of institutions for what were then termed the 'mentally retarded' (Morris, 1969). He later recalled:

> I remember going carefully into the whole emergence of the idea of the imbecile and the idiot and the fixed mental age, as Cyril Burt and others argued, and that this was almost a release from the Victorian and Edwardian corseting of social science in some respects, which was unfolding in the late '60s and early '70s and certainly allowed the Keith Joseph theory to be put into decent perspective. One was aware that he was operating too readily with the fixtures of mental endowment ... I was opposed to some of the orthodox assumptions of neo-liberal social philosophy which Keith Joseph epitomised.[33]

In this period Townsend was Chair of the CPAG, and working on what was to become *Poverty in the United Kingdom* (1979). More specifically, Townsend and the CPAG had clashed with Joseph in October 1970 over the Secretary of State's plans for the means-tested FIS (Denham and Garnett, 2001a, pp 202-5).

The BASW conference at Manchester University in March 1974 offered Townsend an opportunity to address a professional group who had traditionally been concerned with individual salvation. He set out a thorough critique of the cycle hypothesis, condemning it as being 'a mixture of popular stereotypes and ill-developed, mostly contentious, scientific notions. It is a conceptual bed into which diverse travellers have scrambled for security and comfort' (Townsend, 1974, p 8). Despite qualifications in the speech, Joseph had individualised or personalised forms of deprivation, or interpreted social forms in their personal or psychological outcomes. Townsend argued that the speech represented a process of selection: only certain types of deprivation; certain causal factors; certain interpretations of the term 'intergenerational transmission'; and particular solutions to the 'problem'. The thesis was a 'piece of ideological special pleading', it diverted attention from treating deprivation as a large-scale structural phenomenon to a residual personal or family phenomenon, it diverted attention away from potentially expensive policy measures, and it diverted blame from the government to the victim (Townsend, 1974, p 10).

Townsend located the cycle speech in the context of a concern about the values of the poor that in his view had dominated social policy for several hundred years, including more recently in the Wood Report (Board of Education and Board of Control, 1929), the Lidbetter research of the early 1930s, and the culture of poverty debates. In some ways, Britain had repeated the earlier mistakes of the US, in focusing on piecemeal, peripheral, and inexpensive policies on area deprivation, and in the more individualistic policies implied by the cycle theory. Deprivation in developing countries was a product, not of the weakness, backwardness, or inadequacy of a class or a people, but of the 'operating rules of access to resources shaped and applied by colonial powers, ruling elites, trading and marketing monopolies, defence facts [sic], those controlling communication networks, and leagues of nations' (Townsend, 1974, p 17). This called attention to the complex network of social, political, and economic systems of resource distribution that determined inequalities. Meanwhile his audience, social workers, continued to concern themselves with the emotional welfare of families, disregarding their economic and physical well-being (Townsend, 1974, p 22).

Denham and Garnett suggest that Townsend argued that the cycle speech was merely a new version of an old thesis, of 19th-century liberalism. Joseph had unwittingly exposed the double standards inseparable from his own creed, by concentrating on relatively cheap remedies for poverty (Denham and Garnett, 2001a, pp 222-3). Frank Coffield (who was at the BASW conference) later recalled:

> Peter Townsend did a speech in Manchester, gave a
> devastating critique of that and there was a huge number

of people in the audience, maybe two or three hundred people … it was the power of the speech as well, the power of delivery.[34]

Townsend was critical of the SSRC involvement with transmitted deprivation, and needless to say remained outside the Research Programme. The term 'relative deprivation' had been used as early as 1966, by W. G. Runciman, in the context of explaining individual and subjective perceptions of social position (Runciman, 1966). Townsend used the concept in a more objective and structural sense, that people might be relatively deprived even if not in an absolute sense, and all standards of comparison were relative to actual social contexts of meanings and observers. Thus Townsend used the term in a different conceptual sense from Runciman, writing in his monumental survey of poverty in the United Kingdom that:

> Individuals, families and groups in the population can be said to be in poverty when they lack the resources to obtain the types of diet, participate in the activities and have the living conditions and amenities which are customary, or are at least widely encouraged or approved, in the societies to which they belong. Their resources are so seriously below those commanded by the average individual or family that they are, in effect, excluded from ordinary living patterns, customs and activities. (Townsend, 1979, p 31)

In this, Townsend appeared to anticipate the later focus on social exclusion.

Earlier definitions of poverty, from Rowntree onwards, had tended to be based on some conception of 'absolute' deprivation or minimum needs. But the concept of relative deprivation also led to controversy, most notably between Townsend and Amartya Sen (Piachaud, 1981; Sen, 1983, 1985; Mack and Lansley, 1985; Townsend, 1985). Townsend, for example, wrote of Sen's approach that it was:

> a sophisticated adaptation of the individualism which is rooted in neo-classical economics. That theoretical approach will never provide a coherent explanation of the social construction of need, and hence of the real potentialities which do exist of planning to meet need. (Townsend, 1985, p 668)

Townsend himself later defined deprivation as 'a state of observable and demonstrable disadvantage relative to the local community or the wider society or nation to which an individual, family or group belongs' (Townsend, 1987, p 125). He drew on the Research Programme to demonstrate that deprivation took a variety of forms. Nevertheless, he conceded that the systematic study of deprivation was still in its infancy. Material deprivation was seen as the lack of goods, services, resources, amenities, and physical environment that were customary, or widely approved, in society. Thus indicators of material deprivation might include unemployment, car ownership, home ownership, and overcrowding. Social deprivation, on the other hand, embraced non-participation in the roles, relationships, customs, functions, rights, and responsibilities implied by membership of a society and its subgroups. The merits of his concept of deprivation were that it was non-monetary and multidimensional, whereas poverty was a one-dimensional monetary measure. Nevertheless, when it came to operationalising deprivation, the choice of indicators was crude and pragmatic (Jarman, 1983). Overall then, Townsend argued that deprivation was as important a concept as poverty for the analysis of social conditions, but that there were conceptual and practical difficulties. It was necessary to distinguish between deprivation and poverty; between material and social deprivation; between objective and subjective forms of deprivation; and between the measurement of deprivation in different areas and the kind of people experiencing that deprivation (Townsend, 1987, pp 125-41; Townsend et al, 1988, 1989 edn, pp 3-17, 30-40).

Along with his emphasis on relative deprivation, Townsend had always remained concerned to counter individual or cultural explanations of poverty. He had argued that Oscar Lewis's research method was interesting, but oriented towards individuals and uncontrolled; there was much bias and ambiguity; it was difficult to confirm the thesis; and the concept of a subculture of poverty was inconsistent. Lewis had not discouraged the prejudice that poverty was the fault of individuals, and he had diverted attention away from economic and social reconstruction towards social work and community psychiatry. In Townsend's view, the discussion about the cycle echoed much of the debate in the US. Joseph had placed greatest weight on assigning responsibility for deprivation to the individual and the family, and signalled a return to a mixture of social control and casework policies. Deprivation was 'treated as being a residual personal or family phenomenon rather than a large-scale structural phenomenon' (Townsend, 1979, p 71).

Townsend was concerned that exchanges about the nature, extent, and causes of poverty continued to be dominated by individualistic and structuralist perspectives. The former, especially in the US, stressed individual characteristics, subcultural phenomena, and free-market values, while the latter emphasised theories of dependency and development, stratification, neo-colonialism, and state policies. Recurring themes in the history of poverty were those of character deficiency or personal fault (although revealed through empirical studies to be misplaced or a minor factor in the causation of poverty), and analysis of the personal characteristics of the casualties of the economic and social system, such as through the underclass concept. An alternative structural approach had to be global, institutional, and class based, stressing the role of international institutions, and the feminisation of poverty (Townsend, 1993, pp 96-112).

Townsend's contribution is particularly important because his Manchester paper was the only major critique of the cycle of deprivation at that time. Frank Coffield later recalled:

> I was looking for someone who would take this on intellectually and Peter Townsend was the only one who seemed able to do so. So there was a sense I think on the Left that Joseph was having a field day on this issue.[35]

Moreover Townsend was critical of the SSRC involvement in the Research Programme. Unlike Wilson and Sinfield, he did not attempt to become involved in the Research Programme, instead very much standing aloof from it. As Deacon (2002a) has recognised, rising unemployment during the early 1980s served to provide support for this stance. Townsend argued that research had shown that the causes of the incidence and severity of unemployment were external to the person out of work. Moreover, unemployment was socially constructed; the economically active and inactive were differentiated according to social value (Townsend, 1981, pp xiv-xv).

Nevertheless, Townsend later admitted that when, in the 1970s, increasing attention began to be given to social exclusion as a criterion of poverty, he had failed to appreciate some of the positive arguments. Poverty had seemed to him to be the critical concept on which to build an analysis of structural change. Lack of income and resources more generally had clear effects, and external criteria had to be used to pinpoint the level of resources required. He noted that 'discrimination and exclusion seemed to be important ideas but secondary because they were effects rather than causes, or, at best, by-products of the engines of market-manufactured class' (Townsend, 1997, p 269). But he conceded that he had been wrong to believe that the attention given to social exclusion was a diversion from important issues. The term helped to pay more attention, not just to the denial of rights, but to the external creation and control of need. Social exclusion needed to be incorporated into policy, and absorbed into the definition, measurement, and analysis of poverty. In particular, the number of indicators needed to measure social deprivation needed to be enlarged (Townsend, 1997, pp 268-70).

Conclusion

Responses to the cycle speech and Research Programme provide intriguing insights into the approach that a generation of social scientists took to questions of poverty, behaviour, and culture. Dennis Marsden captures the issues well in a long letter to Muriel Brown and Nicola Madge, written in November 1981, when the typescript of *Despite the welfare state* must have been almost complete. Marsden wrote that there had been much discussion about the relationship between social structure and individual or family behaviour. The best exposition had been in Charles Valentine's *Culture and poverty* (1968), drawing in part on Elliot Liebow's *Tally's corner* (1967). Marsden argued that Brown and Madge's typescript seemed inconsistent in its treatment of culture, and they should have considered the hypothesis that all family or individual behaviour was in some ways structurally determined. The debate persisted because of its policy implications, and also because it reflected a lengthy argument within sociology and philosophy about the extent to which behaviour was determined by material, structural, or ideological factors. Overall, Marsden wrote that 'there is a strong theoretical debate about the impact of social structure upon individual attitudes and behaviour, which I do not feel has been adequately confronted in the Programme or report'.[36] In the absence of someone to expound the more complex arguments on structural influences and to make the case for a structural determinist hypothesis, Pauline Ashley (author of the literature review on money and the poor) was the only commentator left to raise these issues.

There is certainly evidence that many if not most social scientists favoured a structural explanation. The best-known examples are Bill Jordan and Bob Holman. However, adopting a collective biography approach to other social scientists who were hostile to the cycle hypothesis, or at best marginal to the Research Programme, reveals more about why they took the stance that they did. With Harriett

Wilson, Adrian Sinfield, and Peter Townsend, for example, there are marked similarities in the approach that they adopted. First, many including Sinfield had taken the Diploma in Social Administration at the LSE in the early 1960s, along with placements with FSUs. They had been greatly attracted to, and deeply influenced by, the Fabian outlook of their teachers – Richard Titmuss, Peter Townsend, and Brian Abel-Smith – and this led to a lifelong commitment. Second, Sinfield in particular had direct experience of the 'War on Poverty', the impact of the culture of poverty, and the US literature on blaming the victim. Third, there were direct personal links, including through the CPAG, which meant that they were united in their concern that the shift to the cycle hypothesis moved the debate away from the resources that people needed to escape poverty, and tended to personalise explanations of continuing poverty. Fourth, through their research, whether on the socialisation of children, long-term unemployment, or poverty itself, they were concerned with the question of the relationship between behaviour and wider structural constraints. Given the rise in unemployment in 1972, along with the introduction of FIS, these social scientists were concerned that the problem of poverty was once again being redefined.

This was not the whole story of course, and the work of others, such as Herbert Gans in the US and A. H. Halsey in the UK, had shown a willingness to engage with both structural and cultural explanations. Ethnographic and anthropological fieldwork in the US had come to view culture as an adaptive response to environmental factors; and the experience of the EPAs had thrown these debates into relief. Harriett Wilson's work had explored the links between parenting and poverty, even though she tended to favour a structural explanation. What appears to have happened is that this more subtle analysis became marginalised by the structural emphasis of much of the social policy community, especially after the famous Townsend (1974) paper. There was a difference, of course, between hostility to ideology on the one hand, and the attractions of research funding on the other, and the literature review by Rutter and Madge (1976) did help to draw social scientists in. However, although it has been argued that by then the die had largely been cast, and attitudes hardened in the late 1970s, with the publication of the early CDP reports, evidence of growing inequality, and rising unemployment, attitudes were pretty hard in 1972 itself, when unemployment had risen to one million. While many authors argue that the cycle hypothesis was tested in the Research Programme and found wanting, it would be more correct to say that it was ignored or subverted by many researchers, particularly those from social policy backgrounds. It was left to others to grapple with what they termed personal and economic factors, and it is only more recently that the debate about agency and structure has become a major theme in social policy.

In Part Three of the book, we move away from the cycle speech and Research Programme to look at the broader influences on New Labour since its election in May 1997. These include the concept of social exclusion, the indicators employed, the critiques mounted, and the emerging literature on poverty dynamics. We look too at policy developments, at New Labour's commitment to end child poverty, and at initiatives that have emphasised the role of parenting, such as Sure Start. The argument is that the perceived failure of policies on social exclusion, along with the emphasis on antisocial behaviour, has meant that the approach has narrowed, prompting a return to the concerns of Keith Joseph, and permitting a revival of the concept of transmitted deprivation. Social scientists were directly involved in the early stages of these debates, but as the focus has moved to the alleged benefits of early intervention, it is criminologists, psychologists, and educationalists who have moved centre stage.

Notes

[1] Harriett Wilson papers, H. C. Wilson, 'How the Child Poverty Action Group came into being' (1993).

[2] Harriett Wilson papers, H. Wilson to A. Sinfield, 22 June 1973.

[3] Adrian Sinfield papers, H. Wilson to A. Sinfield, 21 July 1972. Currently in the possession of the author.

[4] Harriett Wilson papers, 'Notes on WPTD 21' (nd).

[5] Harriett Wilson papers, H. Wilson to S. M. Miller, 22 March 1973.

[6] Harriett Wilson papers, S. M. Miller to H. Wilson, 5 April 1973.

[7] Harriett Wilson papers, 'SSRC–DHSS conference, LSE', 16 April 1973; NA MH 152/74: Conference 'Approaches to research on transmitted deprivation', 15 April 1973, transcript, pp 1.10-1.19.

[8] Harriett Wilson papers, 'The family in society' (nd).

[9] Harriett Wilson papers, K. Joseph to H. Wilson, 17 November 1974.

[10] Harriett Wilson papers, H. Wilson to K. Joseph, 19 November 1974.

[11] Harriett Wilson papers, H. Wilson, 'Research into transmitted deprivation: outline of a research proposal', February 1974.

[12] Harriett Wilson papers, D. Marsden to H. Wilson, 15 April 1975.

[13] Harriett Wilson papers, H. Wilson to M. Rutter, 7 July 1977.

[14] Harriett Wilson papers, C. Blackler to H. Wilson, 18 October 1977.

[15] Adrian Sinfield papers, A. Sinfield, 'Curriculum vitae' (nd).

[16] Adrian Sinfield papers, D. J. West to A. Sinfield, 29 August 1972; Adrian Sinfield papers, A. Sinfield to A. Taylor, 3 July 1973; interview between the author and Adrian Sinfield, Edinburgh, 26-27 May 2006.

[17] Adrian Sinfield papers, A. Sinfield to J. Lunn, 3 July 1973.

[18] Adrian Sinfield papers, Sinfield's annotated copy of C. H. Wright and J. E. Lunn, (1971) 'Sheffield problem families: a follow-up study of their sons and daughters', *Community Medicine*, vol 126, no 22, pp 301-7.

[19] Adrian Sinfield papers, J. Lunn to A. Sinfield, 20 July 1973.

[20] Adrian Sinfield papers, A. Sinfield to A. Stevenson, 12 July 1974.

[21] Adrian Sinfield papers, A. Sinfield to A. Stevenson, 13 September 1974.

[22] Adrian Sinfield papers, A. Edmond to A. Sinfield, 10 January 1975.

[23] Adrian Sinfield papers, C. Blackler to A. Sinfield, 4 August 1976; Adrian Sinfield papers, A. Walker to A. Sinfield (nd); Adrian Sinfield papers, A. Sinfield to C. Blackler, 11 March 1977.

[24] Adrian Sinfield papers, 'DHSS–SSRC contract on research into transmitted deprivation: fourth conference: socio-economic factors in transmitted deprivation: some approaches to research' (nd).

[25] Adrian Sinfield papers, A. Sinfield, 'Income transfers and transmitted deprivation: some preliminary comments for the fourth conference on socio-economic factors in transmitted deprivation, 28 September 1976' (nd), p 1.

[26] Adrian Sinfield papers, A. Sinfield, 'Income transfers and transmitted deprivation: some preliminary comments for the fourth conference on socio-economic factors in transmitted deprivation, 28 September 1976' (nd), p 2.

[27] Adrian Sinfield papers, A. Sinfield, 'Income transfers and transmitted deprivation: some preliminary comments for the fourth conference

on socio-economic factors in transmitted deprivation, 28 September 1976' (nd), p 7.

[28] Adrian Sinfield papers, F. Coffield to A. Sinfield, 21 October 1976; Adrian Sinfield papers, A. Sinfield to F. Coffield, 26 October 1976.

[29] NA BS 7/656: A. Sinfield, 'Transmitted deprivation and the social division of welfare', November 1976, pp 77-81, 96-110.

[30] Adrian Sinfield papers, C. Blackler to A. Sinfield, 15 November 1976; private correspondence between the author and Adrian Sinfield, 13 March 2007.

[31] Interview between the author and Peter Townsend, London, 3 July 2006.

[32] Interview between the author and Peter Townsend, London, 3 July 2006.

[33] Interview between the author and Peter Townsend, London, 3 July 2006.

[34] Interview between the author and Frank Coffield, Newcastle upon Tyne, 8 April 2003.

[35] Interview between the author and Frank Coffield, Newcastle upon Tyne, 8 April 2003.

[36] Nicola Madge papers, D. Marsden to M. Brown and N. Madge, 5 November 1981.

Part Three
New Labour and the cycle of deprivation

Chapter Six began to look at broader perspectives on the cycle speech and Research Programme, through the outlook of social scientists. This part of the book takes this further, moving beyond the narrow canvas of the 1972-82 period, to look at the emergence of new interest in these themes since the early 1980s. If debates in the US were marked by an intellectual void following the Moynihan Report (Moynihan, 1965), it is arguable that in Britain there was a similar void after the Research Programme. But gradually interest in policy, poverty, and parenting re-emerged to become a major plank of policy rhetoric. In Part Three, we link the cycle speech and Research Programme with New Labour policy since 1997. Chapter Seven traces the origins of the concept of social exclusion, attempts to operationalise it, some of the critiques that have been made, the literature on poverty dynamics, and the revival of agency. Chapter Eight explores policy developments including the approach of New Labour to child poverty and initiatives such as Sure Start, social exclusion, and antisocial behaviour, arguing that this has led to a revival of interest in transmitted deprivation.

SEVEN

The broader context: social exclusion, poverty dynamics, and the revival of agency

Introduction

At the end of Chapter Five, we noted the reaction to the Research Programme, when the Heinemann books began to appear in the early 1980s. Around the same time, and among academics and policy makers, the phrase 'transmitted deprivation' passed out of use, at least in Britain, and was replaced by that of 'underclass', later 'social exclusion', which is the term favoured by New Labour. The debates about the underclass, in both the US and Britain, cannot be dealt with here, and have in any case received much attention elsewhere (Welshman, 2006a, pp 127-82). Instead we jump forward 15 years or so, to the election of the Labour government in May 1997, and its emphasis on social exclusion. The origins of social exclusion have been related variously to the increasingly pejorative connotations of the term 'underclass'; debates about relative deprivation and an inability to participate in society; concepts of social capital and social isolation; and a growing emphasis on worklessness (Smith, 2005, p viii). Certainly the government's definition of social exclusion, with its emphasis on the structural causes of deprivation, its acknowledgement of the role of behavioural factors, and the stress on intergenerational transmission, immediately has echoes with the cycle speech and Research Programme.

This chapter explores continuities between the 1970s and the 1990s, and between the cycle hypothesis, the Research Programme, and social exclusion. We look first at how the idea of social exclusion evolved in France, and how it has been subsequently embraced by other European countries; in France, debates around the issue of deprivation have always been framed by discourses of exclusion and insertion. We look at how the language of social exclusion was imported into Britain, and became part of the vocabulary of New Labour. The chapter traces the relationship between the emphasis on social exclusion and the new literature on poverty dynamics, attempts to operationalise social exclusion, notably by CASE at the LSE, and the revival of agency among academics. But despite its appeal to academics and policy makers, the concept of social exclusion has been challenged, as being centred on paid work, and difficult to test empirically. The argument of the chapter is that it is these themes – the language of social exclusion, the influence of dynamic approaches to poverty, and an emphasis on behaviour and responsibility – that have at least in part provided the context for the revival of transmitted deprivation.

The origins of social exclusion

Hilary Silver has explored the origins of the concept of social exclusion. She points out that exclusion became the subject of discussion in France in the 1960s, and attributes the term 'social exclusion' to René Lenoir, then Secretary of State for Social Action in the Chirac government. In 1974, for example, Lenoir estimated that 'the excluded' made up one tenth of the French population. But it was only in the late 1970s that 'exclusion' was identified as the central problem of the 'new poverty'. Thus the term 'exclusion' referred to the rise in long-term and recurrent unemployment, and to important changes in social relations – family break-ups, single-member households, social isolation, and the decline of traditional class solidarity based on unions, workplaces, and networks. Exclusion was seen as the 'rupture of the social and symbolic bonds that should attach individuals to society' (Silver, 1994, pp 534-5). Conversely, the process of tackling exclusion, and of achieving goals of integration, cohesion, and solidarity, was called 'insertion'. In France, the guaranteed minimum income, the *Revenu Minimum d'Insertion* (RMI) provided one example of an insertion policy, designed to address exclusion. There was certainly a consensus on this issue, with presidential candidates of both the Right and Left in 1988 strongly supporting the RMI and wider policies against exclusion (Silver, 1994, pp 534-5).

That is not to say that the meaning of exclusion was not contested, by both the *Front National* and the far Left. Moreover, in the 1980s the meanings of exclusion and insertion were expanded to cover emerging new social groups and problems. One was the way in which insertion policies shifted from disability to 'youth in difficulty'. Another was the extent to which the twin themes of exclusion and insertion were increasingly concerned with the integration of minority ethnic groups. Silver describes how young *beurs*, second generation North African migrants from the housing projects of the *banlieues*, the suburbs or outskirts of the cities, argued through their cultural associations that since they lived in France they should have full citizenship rights. An official policy was adopted to integrate migrants, which managed to keep the key elements of Republican solidarity discourse, but also tried to marry these with multicultural meanings of integration. Following disturbances on the suburban housing estates, the exclusion discourse also encompassed the issue of the *banlieues*. Thus in terms of public policy in France, the many meanings of exclusion were expanded in the 1980s. These included wider questions to do with the perceived challenge of integrating migrants, problems faced by young people, and the exclusion that resulted from economic change (Silver, 1994, pp 534-5).

From France, the discourse of exclusion spread rapidly across Western Europe, and was adopted by the European Commission. Its White Paper *Growth, competitiveness, employment* (EC, 1993) had called for a resolution to fight social exclusion. Graham Room has noted of the history of research on poverty sponsored by the European Union (EU) that by the time the third programme was launched (1990-94), social exclusion had become the fashionable terminology. What was interesting was the way that social exclusion was part of a continental, and particularly French, model of social analysis that was very different from what might be called the 'Anglo-Saxon' tradition of Rowntree and Townsend. Room argued that whereas the notion of poverty tended to focus on distributional issues, and the lack of resources at the disposal of an individual or household, social exclusion was concerned with relational issues, such as inadequate social participation, lack of social integration, and lack of power. In the latter, society was seen as a status hierarchy or number of different collectivities, bound together by sets of mutual rights and obligations that were rooted in some broader moral order (Room, 1995b, pp 1-9). Thus social exclusion is 'the process of becoming detached from the organisations and communities of which the society is composed and from the rights and obligations that they embody' (Room, 1995c, p 243).

Around the same time, Serge Paugam (1996) sought to extend the conventional approach to poverty by taking account of non-economic indicators, and analysing it in terms of the accumulation of social disadvantage. Poverty was thus not a state, but a process of accumulation, and the concept of social disqualification was developed to explain the phases of this process. Indicators included precariousness on the labour market and the weakness of social links, material poverty, and other forms of 'social handicap'. Research on seven European countries (Britain, Denmark, France, Germany, Italy, the Netherlands, and Spain) had found that while the underlying structural causes were similar, the process manifested itself in different forms according to national economic development, the labour market, the strength of social links, and the degree of intervention by the state and public authorities in the lives of those who were marginalised. Overall, policies against poverty and social exclusion were a reflection of the economic and social development of the countries concerned, and the level of collective commitment to the plight of the less favoured members of the population. Paugam concluded that the degree to which those affected by poverty were integrated into the social system was 'a contributory factor in the social construction of poverty and of the status of poverty, and also the level of stigma attached to those labeled as poor' (Paugam, 1996, p 299).

Social exclusion was thus seen as a multifaceted, relational concept that described a complex set of social processes. It was 'a social process within a whole society rather than a way of categorizing individuals and groups within that society' (Allen et al, 1998, p 11). Moreover, it was suggested that, in the EU, the reason for combating social exclusion had shifted from one of achieving insertion, to one of promoting social and economic cohesion. First, social exclusion was seen in terms of a set of social processes that had their origin in structural changes that affected all groups within a given social structure and which changed the nature of the relationships among the groups. Second, these changes in social relations, which had been induced systematically, challenged the capacity of existing forms of urban governance. Third, the maintenance of social order depended on the existence of social boundaries among social groups. It was not that some groups excluded other groups, but that 'processes affecting the whole of society mean that some groups experience social boundaries as barriers preventing their full participation in the economic, political and cultural life of the society within which they live' (Allen et al, 1998, p 17).

Social exclusion rapidly became popularised. The International Labour Organization, for example, favoured social exclusion because it seemed to provide an integrated and dynamic perspective that revealed the processes, agency, and multidimensional nature of disadvantage. It provided a framework for analysing the relationship between livelihood, well-being, and rights, and also generated a collective moral responsibility for social integration. It argued: 'this way of describing disadvantage thus directs attention to the ability of persons to change their position within an income distribution and social hierarchy, as well as the form of the income distribution and hierarchy itself' (IILS, 1996, p 11). It encompassed both welfare and agency issues, and broadened traditional poverty analysis. Social exclusion was seen as relevant to anti-poverty strategies in countries at different stages of development, and with varying economic and social characteristics. Social exclusion appeared to occur within all economies, but manifested itself in different forms and intensities as a result of cultural and institutional specificities. Overall, social exclusion was viewed as a useful addition to traditional approaches to understanding and combating poverty, encompassing both distributional and relational aspects of disadvantage, and analysing causes as well as identifying outcomes.

But these differences meant that researchers struggled to decide how social exclusion might be distinguished from older concepts of poverty and deprivation, and how useful it ultimately was. Jos Berghman, for example, argued that the importance of social exclusion lay in the fact that it was a more comprehensive term than poverty, and referred to a dynamic process. Whereas poverty had to do with a lack of resources, social exclusion was more comprehensive, and was about 'much more than money' (Berghman, 1995, pp 10-28). Berghman tended to restrict the use of 'poverty' to the lack of disposable income, while social exclusion referred to the breakdown of the main social systems theoretically guaranteeing citizenship rights. He concluded that poverty might best be seen as part of, or a specific form of, social exclusion. Another way of distinguishing the two might be to view social exclusion as a process, and poverty as the outcome. Other researchers remained cautious, arguing that an emphasis on the 'multidimensional' nature of poverty could have the effect of obscuring the dynamic processes involved. Researchers should continue to draw on the insights offered by traditional research into the relationship between resources and deprivation, and the dynamics that lay behind patterns of disadvantage (Whelan and Whelan, 1995, p 29). Even Graham Room conceded that 'this notion of social exclusion has until now been used in a rather loose and incoherent manner, rendering it of little value as a guide for research or policy' (Room, 1995c, p 247).

Some European researchers attempted to operationalise the concept of social exclusion, using it to analyse long-term unemployment, and finding that the latter had a severe effect on people's standard of living, they became detached from key activities, and they were excluded from 'occupational milieux'. There were strong links between social exclusion, marginalisation, and long-term unemployment (Clasen et al, 1997). Nevertheless, it has also been noted that much work in other countries on aspects of multidimensional disadvantage has been single-country rather than comparative studies, and that there has been a distinct lack of comparative work on multidimensional disadvantage. This has partly been because there is a lack of comparable information on multidimensional disadvantage at a European level. It was only with the introduction of the European Community Household Panel

(ECHP) survey that multidimensional comparisons became possible. Some researchers have therefore sought to look at the implications of multidimensional disadvantage for potentially high-risk groups of individuals – young adults, lone parents, sick or disabled people, and retired people (Barnes, 2002, pp 1-23).

Social exclusion in the UK

Much of this debate was concerned with the language of paradigm and discourse. Silver (1994) has suggested that even when they are imported, poverty discourses change their meaning to fit dominant national paradigms. This is relevant and helpful in understanding how the concept of social exclusion has been imported into Britain, and how its meaning has been blended with other influences. Debates in France and other countries led Silver to distinguish between three paradigms of social exclusion, each based on a different conception of integration and citizenship. She claimed that, first, solidarity was evident in France, where exclusion was the 'breakdown of a social bond between the individual and society that is cultural and moral, rather than economically interested'. Second, specialisation could be found, where exclusion was really a reflection of social discrimination. Third, there was a monopoly, which described a process whereby powerful groups in society restricted the access of outsiders to resources through a process of 'social closure'. Silver claimed that the monopoly paradigm, in particular, drew on earlier discourses on the underclass and citizenship (Silver, 1994, pp 539-43, 549-72). What these shifts really meant in practice, and whether they could usefully be distinguished at all, remained uncertain. What is clear is that Silver was right in pointing out that, like 'underclass', the phrase 'social exclusion' had become a keyword, a term with its own history that could serve a variety of political purposes (Williams, 1976, 1983 edn).

A different way of approaching the same issue is to ask why poverty discourses seem to vary according to the country in which they have evolved. Kirk Mann had begun to do this in asking why there was no underclass discourse in Australia (Mann, 1994). Silver argued that poverty discourses tended to be nationally specific. For example, the exclusion rhetoric was dominant in France partly because the connotations it evoked came out of the dominant French Republican ideology of *solidarisme*. The term 'underclass', on the other hand, had more to do with liberal and conservative ideologies of citizenship, rejected by French Republicans, which had played a key role in many aspects of British and US social policies. Whereas in Britain and the

US, the underclass label had been the most common, in France it was the term 'exclusion' that tended to dominate. This could be because the 'new poverty' really was different in France compared to Britain and the US, although politics might also have a role to play. A second possibility was that in the 1980s the Socialists were in power in France, while it was the Republicans and Conservatives that governed in the US and Britain. Whatever the reason for these differences, Silver concluded that these variations in labelling the poor were best examined:

> in the context of conflicting paradigms of national identity, political ideology and social science…. Depending upon the paradigm in which they are embedded, poverty discourses attribute responsibility for the problem and shape the policy agenda. (Silver, 1996, p 113)

In some respects, social exclusion simply represented an updating of Peter Townsend's earlier formulation of poverty as relative deprivation, as noted in Chapter Six. Although Townsend focused on poverty, he stressed how the lack of resources that characterised the poor meant that they were unable to participate in normal activities. The task for academics was to construct social surveys that captured this sense of relative deprivation. This approach was subsequently applied in Britain in the early 1980s, in the 'Breadline Britain' survey, which similarly defined poverty in terms of 'an enforced lack of *socially perceived* necessities' (Mack and Lansley, 1985, p 45 [emphasis in original]).

In the 1990s, some British commentators thought that social divisions were widening and hardening (Hutton, 1995, pp 2-3). Groups such as the CPAG were equally aware of these widening inequalities, and by the mid-1990s had begun to move away from the concept of the underclass towards that of social exclusion. This reflected the influence of the earlier European debates, and also the increasing emphasis placed on citizenship. In part, too, social exclusión offered a means of describing poverty in less pejorative terms. For instance, the CPAG published *Britain divided: The growth of social exclusion in the 1980s and 1990s* (Walker and Walker, 1997). Individuals as well as pressure groups began to rethink the way that they had conventionally viewed poverty. Peter Townsend, for example, arguably the dominant figure in this field, now admitted that he had earlier been wrong in thinking that the term 'social exclusion' was a diversion from more important issues. Intellectuals close to New Labour helped to popularise the concept of social exclusion. In the context of the 'third way', Anthony Giddens, for example, argued that social exclusion could occur both at the bottom of society and at the top – in the former, when people were cut off from the opportunities that society had to offer, and, in the latter, when the more affluent groups withdrew from public institutions. Moreover, Giddens suggested that social exclusion might be both economic and cultural. In declining communities, housing fell into disrepair, and a lack of job opportunities produced educational disincentives, leading to social instability and disorganisation. His solutions included strategies that broke the poverty cycle, particularly education and training, but especially involvement in the labour force. Conventional poverty programmes should be replaced with community-focused approaches that emphasised support networks, self-help, and a culture of social capital (Giddens, 1998, pp 103-4, 109-10, 117).

How did New Labour come to adopt social exclusion as the label for its attempts to tackle poverty? While Townsend's theory of relative deprivation in some respects anticipated social exclusion, arguably more important was the way that New Labour was much more prepared to consider the influence of behaviour on poverty and deprivation than the Labour Party had been previously. It has been argued that in the US the publication of the Moynihan Report (Moynihan, 1965) had led to a void in which Liberals were unwilling to discuss issues of race and poverty. In Britain too, the postwar period (the Titmuss era) had been marked by a refusal to consider that poverty could have anything other than structural causes. But this was increasingly questioned by some thinkers and policy makers on the Left. In his important book *Making welfare work* (1995), Frank Field argued that welfare had to be based on a realistic view of human nature, since self-interest, not altruism, was the main driving force of mankind (Field, 1995, p 19). Influenced in part by his Christian beliefs, Field wrote that 'welfare influences behaviour by the simple device of bestowing rewards (benefits) and allotting punishments (loss of benefits) ... the nature of our character depends in part on the values which welfare fosters' (Field, 1995, p 9; 1996, pp 107-14). Thus Field advocated a system of stakeholder welfare, where welfare aimed to maximise self-improvement, reflected the significance of self-interest, and rewarded good behaviour.

Field was subsequently criticised for using the terms 'behaviour' and 'character' interchangeably, and for evoking the judgementalism of the 19th-century Charity Organisation Society. It was suggested that this was reminiscent of debates on the social residuum in the 1880s, and problem families in the 1950s (Field, 1996, pp 60-74). What is clear is that Field, and New Labour more generally, had been heavily influenced by US writers such as Charles Murray and Lawrence Mead. Alan Deacon (2000) claimed more generally that the Blair administration looked to the US for ideas for welfare reform, and that the language in which these policies were presented and justified drew heavily on that of American politicians and commentators. New Labour's debate on welfare marked its response to the challenge of Murray and Mead to pay more attention to issues of personal responsibility and moral obligation. Field was influenced by his Christian beliefs in coming to this conclusion, and other key members of the Blair government followed a type of Christian Socialism that made it possible to address inequalities while at the same time acknowledging the role of behaviour. It was suggested, therefore, that the approach of the Blair government to welfare reform was rooted in 'Anglicised communitarianism'. A welfare system was envisaged that was active rather than passive, which combined opportunity and responsibility, and which was based around paid work. Deacon concluded that the influence of American thinking had been crucial to the shift from the problem of inequality to the problem of dependency, and in increasing the attention New Labour paid to values and social morality (Deacon, 2000, pp 5-18).

The important differences between Britain and the US notwithstanding, with regard to welfare reform New Labour was more influenced by the experience of the US than France. As David Marquand noted, 'the Blair government looks across the Atlantic for inspiration, not across the channel' (Marquand, 1996, p 20). In particular, Blair and other intellectuals on the Left were influenced by the American emphasis on communitarianism. Its leading advocate, Amitai Etzioni, had written, for example, that 'we are a social movement aiming at shoring up the moral, social, and political environment. Part change of heart, part renewal of social bonds, part reform of public life' (Etzioni, 1993, 1995 edn, pp 247-8). Thus he had drawn attention to the roles of the family, schools, the 'social webs' that bound individuals together, and the overarching values that a national society embodies. Anthony Giddens, too, argued that civic decline was real and visible, and was seen in a weakening sense of solidarity in some local communities and urban neighbourhoods, high levels of crime, and the break-up of marriages and families (Giddens, 1998, pp 78-82). Civic involvement was least developed in areas and neighbourhoods marginalised by the sweep of economic and social change. One of the lessons of the 1960s' social engineering experiments, contended Giddens, was that external forces could best be mobilised to support local initiative. Social capital, with its emphasis on networks and reciprocity, became influential for similar reasons (Putnam, 2000).

Attempts to operationalise social exclusion

The initial policy emphasis on social exclusion by New Labour was accompanied by attempts to create appropriate indicators by which trends might be measured over the short and longer term. The JRF, for example, quickly established a battery of some 50 indicators, covering poverty and low income, children, young adults, older people, and communities. Indicators included low birth-weight babies, problem drug use (ages 15 to 24), suicide (ages 15 to 24), obesity, limiting long-standing illness or disability, and non-participation in civic organisations (Howarth et al, 1998, pp 8-10). Poverty was seen in terms of a lack of opportunities available to the average citizen, but social exclusion was useful because it widened the focus to include factors that could cause severe and chronic disadvantage. Thus indicators connected with long-term lack of paid work, or poor educational qualifications, were included alongside more conventional aspects of poverty (Howarth et al, 1999, pp 8-13). Subsequently, the number of indicators was cut. However, even this number and range was viewed by some as unmanageably large (Barnes, 2005, pp 1-32).

The term 'social exclusion' began to be adopted in research. It was seen as referring to 'persistent and systematic multiple deprivation and to indicate the dynamic processes through which individuals and communities come to be disadvantaged' (Lee and Murie, 1997, p 3). Social exclusion was concerned with more than distributional issues, relating also to citizenship and the role of the welfare state. The ESRC-funded CASE was established at the LSE in October 1997. Nevertheless, on an empirical level, researchers found it difficult to find evidence of social exclusion on the ground. Tania Burchardt, Julian Le Grand, and David Piachaud, for example, suggested that 'an individual is socially excluded if (a) he or she is geographically resident in a society and (b) he or she does not participate in the normal activities of citizens in that society' (Burchardt et al, 1999, p 229). They tried to operationalise a definition of social exclusion based around five types of activity: consumption, savings, production, political engagement, and social interaction. They perceived that there were five dimensions for 'normal activities' – to have a reasonable standard of living; to possess a degree of security; to be engaged in an activity that is valued by others; to have some decision-making power; and to be able to draw support from immediate family, friends, and a wider community. Using the British Household Panel Survey (BHPS), and interviews conducted in the years 1991-95, they found that for individuals there were strong associations between exclusion in different dimensions, and between exclusion in one year and subsequent years. However, very few people were excluded on all dimensions in any one year, and most were not excluded on any dimension. Burchardt, Le Grand, and Piachaud concluded that using these indicators there was no clear-cut category of socially excluded people. It seemed better to treat different dimensions of exclusion separately, than to think of the socially excluded as being one homogeneous group (Burchardt et al, 1999, p 241).

Burchardt has since conceded that these features of social exclusion – conceptual uncertainty and a lack of empirical work – are related. She has noted that those who have sought to operationalise the concept of social exclusion have tended to adopt one of two approaches. They have either concentrated on specific problems (the Social Exclusion Unit [SEU] approach) or they have characterised social exclusion as lack of participation in key aspects of society (Burchardt, 2000, pp 386-7). Moreover, she has argued that the BHPS data provide:

> no evidence of a group of individuals cut off from the principal activities of mainstream society over an extended period of time. Social exclusion in the sense of an underclass is not an empirically useful concept, at least in the context of the British household population. (Burchardt, 2000, p 400)

The picture that emerges is of a continuum from more to less excluded, with movements between excluded and non-excluded states, and each dimension of exclusion exhibiting different characteristics. Longitudinal data had revealed that it was not the same individuals who were excluded year on year.

Continuities with the cycle and Research Programme are evident in some of the reports produced by CASE. John Hobcraft has used data from the NCDS to look at what he terms the 'intergenerational and lifecourse transmission' of social exclusion, examining how experiences in childhood are linked to outcomes in adulthood. Hobcraft has explored the influences of childhood poverty, family disruption, and contact with the police, seeking to 'examine the extent to which social exclusion and disadvantage is transmitted across generations and across the lifecourse' (Hobcraft, 1998a, p iv). Preliminary analysis of 'focal variables' indicated powerful connections in experiences by age 16, and there seemed to be frequent life-course and intergenerational continuities in the transmission of social exclusion. Elsewhere, Hobcraft has argued that, for both men and women, early parenthood is strongly associated with lack of qualifications, extramarital births, and social housing. He has concluded that:

> There is overwhelming evidence from many domains that children 'inherit' from their parents; such inheritance includes their genes, the family environment, and childhood experiences during the life-course. (Hobcraft, 2002, p 71)

Nevertheless, Hobcraft concedes that the complexity of this research agenda means that not all problems can be solved, and many of the approaches and partial solutions he outlines are interim or partial steps along the way.

The impact of early poverty dynamics research

If Hobcraft explored intergenerational transmission, Giddens was influenced both by longitudinal studies and also by the revival of interest in questions of agency among social policy specialists, which had stressed the ability of individuals to influence their own circumstances. He noted, for example, that longitudinal research had shown how poverty was not a permanent condition, even though more people experienced it than was previously realised. But equally, Giddens argued that to be excluded was not the same as to be powerless to influence one's own circumstances, writing that 'the social and economic factors that can lead to exclusion are always filtered through the way individuals react to the problems that confront them' (Giddens, 2000, pp 105-6). Solutions should therefore have an enabling approach, building on the action strategies of the poor, with a stress on initiative and responsibility. Evidence from Germany, on coping strategies, had concluded that 'poverty has many faces'. Giddens conceded that specific help was needed for the long-term poor. It was neither necessary, nor desirable, however, that it should come only from government – more innovative policies would draw on a range of agencies (Giddens, 2000, pp 109-11, 114). Social exclusion directed attention to the social mechanisms that produced or sustained deprivation, and research could usefully focus on how people got out of poverty.

The antecedents of poverty dynamics research have been identified as including the Rowntree (1901) survey of York; those influenced by the labelling approach of interactionist sociology, who focused on processes of marginalisation and downward careers; and proponents of the cycle of deprivation, who described a process of cumulative psychosocial decay that was not necessarily linked to social institutions (Leisering and Walker, 1998b, pp 14-15). In his social survey of York, for example, Rowntree had described changes in the incidence of poverty over the life course. He seems to have been the first to recognise that 'the life of a labourer is marked by five alternating periods of want and comparative plenty', and that the periods of maximum risk were childhood, early middle age (when the labourer's own children were young) and old age (Rowntree, 1901, 1902 edn, p 136). Thus the 7,230 people shown by the survey to be in 'primary poverty' were only those who happened to be in one of these poverty periods at the time that the investigation was made. Many would pass on to relative prosperity as their children began to earn, and their places below the poverty line would be taken by those in the prosperous period before or shortly after marriage. Many classed as being above the poverty line were below it until the children began to earn. Thus Rowntree wrote that:

> The proportion of the community who at one period or other of their lives suffer from poverty to the point of physical privation is therefore much greater, and the injurious effects of such a condition are much more widespread than would appear from a consideration of the number who can be shown to be below the poverty line at any given moment. (Rowntree, 1901, 1902 edn, p 138)

However, Rowntree's successors assumed that poverty was long term; they were constrained by partial theories and by limited methods and data; they only sampled people in poverty; and they excluded those who had managed to escape (Leisering and Walker, 1998b, pp 14-15; Leisering and Leibfried, 1999, pp 15-16).

In the US, data taken from the Panel Study of Income Dynamics (PSID) survey played a central role in debates about the alleged existence of an underclass in the 1970s and 1980s. The PSID is a longitudinal survey on family economic status that is coordinated from the Survey Research Center at the University of Michigan. It is based on repeated annual interviews with a sample (or panel) of 5,000 American families. Some have claimed that the PSID data shows the dangers of using cross-sectional data to draw conclusions about the extent and causes of change. The early results showed that there was much turnover in the low-income population. While many people were forced to have recourse to welfare at some point in their lives, very few were dependent on it for extended periods of time. And evidence indicated that there was little association between people's attitudes and economic success (Duncan, 1984, pp 3-6). This evidence was used to cast doubt on the existence of an underclass (Welshman, 2006a, pp 147-50).

One of the key questions for the PSID team was whether it was environmental or behavioural patterns that led to improvements in economic status. Attempts were made to measure, over five years, people's attitude to time, whether they planned ahead, whether they avoided risks, the extent to which they drew on sources of information and help, whether they economised, and whether they increased their incomes by working at home. Yet the team found very little evidence that behavioural patterns like these had a consistent effect on people's income level. Similarly, on attitudes and personality, the team tried to measure people's aspirations and ambitions, whether they trusted or were hostile to others, and their confidence in their own abilities. Again, these had little effect on changes in economic status over time. What mattered most were people's demographic characteristics, including their age, gender, education, race, and family background. In an early report (1974), researchers conceded it was important to acknowledge that, in part, people were victims of their past, their environment, luck, and chance (Duncan and Hill, 1974, pp 61-100). But overall they concluded that:

> It is after all difficult to believe that there are not some situations where individual effort matters – in seizing opportunities for better jobs, moving to new areas or avoiding undue risks. But for public policy purposes and for arguments about the extent to which one could reduce dependency in our society by changing the behaviour and attitudes of dependent members, the findings certainly do not encourage expectations that such changes would make much difference. (Morgan et al, 1974, p 339)

Reviewing the PSID data in 1984, Greg Duncan, one of the Michigan researchers, summarised some of the main findings on the importance of people's attitudes. It seemed to be common sense that the most successful people were highly motivated, looked to the future, and were in control of their lives. However, Duncan pointed out that the association between attitudes and success at a single point in time did not prove that the attitudes caused the success. In fact it might well be the other way around. In further research, the team had examined the relative importance of attitudes, behaviour patterns, skills, demographic characteristics, and life events. Tests had been devised to explore people's motivation to achieve, their self-confidence, and if they looked to the future. Again, the PSID data showed that the most important cause of changes in income level were shifts in family composition, through births, deaths, children leaving home, and especially divorce and marriage. In contrast, there was little evidence that people with more positive attitudes were more likely to be successful (Duncan, 1984, pp 5-6, 14-28, 65).

The PSID data was much more wide-ranging than providing evidence solely on attitudes and behaviour. For one thing, it showed that there was considerable turnover in the low-income population. Only just over half the individuals living in poverty in one year were found to be poor in the next, and less than half those who experienced poverty remained persistently poor over 10 years. The PSID data also provided insights into the extent to which people relied on welfare. In the period 1969-78, for example, a quarter of the population derived income from some form of welfare on at least one occasion. But only 2% of the population was dependent on this income for extended periods of time. For the rest, many of these families were in the early stages of an economic crisis caused by the death, disability, or departure of a husband. When family members found full-time employment, or the mother remarried, they were no longer forced to rely on welfare.

The PSID data showed, then, that those people with persistently low incomes were not an underclass of young adults living in large cities. Instead, poor people were very likely to be black, older, and living in rural areas, especially in the South (Duncan, 1984, p 34). The picture that emerged was one of temporary need. There certainly was a small but not insignificant number of people who lived in households where poverty was the rule rather than the exception. The characteristics of the 'persistently poor' were different from the population as a whole, in that three fifths of this group were black. But one of the main findings of the PSID data was that apart from the persistently poor, the poor were not a homogeneous, stable group. One in four of the population was found to have lived in a poor family in at least one of the 10 years 1969-78, but for half this group, poverty years did not occur more than twice. Unlike the persistently poor, these people were no different from the population as a whole (Duncan, 1984, pp 60-1).

With the PSID data, it was possible to examine the argument that welfare programmes led to dependency in successive generations of families. The team examined parental families headed by a woman, that in 1968 had a family income just above the poverty line, but that did not receive income from welfare. In 1976, 7% of the white women from these families, and 25% of the black women, received welfare income. To an extent, then, it seemed that dependency was transmitted between generations. However, most people who received welfare were not dependent on it, and most of the rest only for short periods. Most adult children from families that had previously been on welfare were not on it themselves. And most of the adults that were on welfare did not come from families that previously had been. Was it more likely that parents who were on welfare would produce children who were also dependent on welfare? The evidence provided no clear answer. Even when some continuities between generations were found, the way these mechanisms operated remained unclear (Duncan, 1984, pp 82-3, 91). Greg Duncan argued that although case studies of families in poverty did provide a more vivid and complete picture of circumstances than statistical studies, they could not be considered to be representative of any larger group (Duncan, 1984, p 71).

In the early 1970s, preliminary analysis of the PSID data seemed to show that the bulk of those in poverty were poor for only a few years. The poor were a heterogeneous group, including a small minority who were persistently poor. This was important, because claims about dependency and a separate lifestyle among the poor rested on assumptions about the long-term nature of poverty. In the mid-1980s, other researchers used the PSID data to look at the length of 'spells' spent in poverty. Mary Jo Bane and David Ellwood, for example, used the data for the years 1970-82 to look more closely at what they called 'spell durations and exit probabilities' – 45% of spells ended within a year, and 70% of the spells were over within three years. Although many people had very short spells of poverty, the few with very long spells accounted for the bulk of all poverty, and represented the majority of the poor at any given time. In general, they agreed that those living in poverty were a very heterogeneous group (Bane and Ellwood, 1986, pp 1-23).

Recent dynamic analyses of poverty

The influential Bane and Ellwood article was published in 1986, and gradually British commentators began to use longitudinal data sets to look more closely at income dynamics among the low-income population. The term 'dynamic analysis' can have several meanings. It can refer to studies of income fluctuations from one year to the next, life-course perspectives, and studies of intergenerational continuities. The life-course perspective is of course not confined to poverty research; it has had, for example, a huge impact on research into health inequalities (Graham, 2001). Some of the early longitudinal studies in Britain included the NCDS (1958-); the British Cohort Study (BCS) (1970-); the BHPS (1991-); and the Millennium Cohort Study (2000-). Other studies have been based on dynamic micro-simulation models, using cross-sectional data, which have modelled household incomes over the lifetimes of a 'synthetic' population (Falkingham and Hills, 1995a).

As in the US, data from longitudinal studies have been recognised as playing a key role. It was argued that making time more explicit in the way that poverty and social exclusion were conceptualised, defined, and measured helped to clarify the differences between them (Falkingham and Hills, 1995b). Qualitative research, too, seemed to indicate that the different patterning of poverty over time, and the varying trajectories that people followed, meant that poverty had different social meanings and risks of social exclusion. What was most useful about the availability of better longitudinal data, suggested Robert Walker (1995), was that it helped to illuminate causes. Previous debates had adopted a view that was static, that individuals were poor because of their attitudes and behaviour, or because of structural factors such as low-paid jobs and processes in the labour market. But the triggers that precipitated poverty might embrace both personal and structural factors. This could help in understanding the relationship between poverty and social exclusion. Walker speculated that it was probable that poverty was neither a sufficient nor a necessary factor in social exclusion, although certain kinds of poverty might contribute to a risk of exclusion. In these cases, social exclusion could be a 'destination on a journey through poverty' (Walker, 1995, pp 102-28).

Lutz Leisering and Robert Walker argued as early as 1998 that dynamism was a distinctive feature of modernity, and that in order to understand modern society, a new, increasingly dynamic, science of society was needed. Policy making too needed to take account of the new realities that dynamic studies revealed and created. A dynamic approach to society and poverty was both a theory and a method. Leisering and Walker argued that such approaches were indispensable, since the concept of causality implied a temporal order that was fully unfolded only through longitudinal analysis. But narratives also provided a means to disentangle the processes by which structural changes of society impinged on individual lives and how individuals changed large structures. They claimed that understandings of the nature of poverty were reframed in four main ways. First, poverty was more differentiated and dynamic than was allowed for in traditional accounts or public debate. Second, poverty and the receipt of social assistance were not restricted to marginal groups. Third, one section of the population was less mobile and suffered long-term or recurrent spells of poverty. Fourth, although poor families risked being socially excluded, many of them retained some leverage over their circumstances. Dynamic research tended to provide little support for models of dependency, and provided evidence of both the determination of social processes, and a perspective that emphasised agency, change, and choice. It tended to point to policies that built on the agency of people in need, proactive policies that emphasised early intervention (Leisering and Walker, 1998c, pp 265-85; Jenkins, 2000, pp 529-67).

There have been three main approaches: studies of income dynamics from one year to the next; lifetime perspectives on the persistence of inequalities; and intergenerational studies. In terms of the first, the BHPS seemed to indicate that there was much movement in and out of poverty. Steven Webb argued from a preliminary analysis of the data that:

> There is not a single homogeneous group who are 'the poor' and whose lot is permanently to remain poor. Rather, fluctuations in personal circumstances lead to considerable variations in living standards even from one year to the next. (Webb, 1995, pp 17-18)

Others have used the first two waves of the BHPS to argue that most income changes from one year to the next are not very great. Sarah Jarvis and Stephen Jenkins distinguished between turnover and changes in real income. They compared income distribution to a tall apartment building with the numbers of residents on different floors corresponding to the concentration of people at different real income levels. Jarvis and Jenkins found that there was mobility in household net income from one year to the next in the poorest group. But most income changes from one year to the next were not very large, and there were substantial permanent income differentials. Jarvis and Jenkins remarked wryly that few of those living in the basement changed places with those in the penthouse (Jarvis and Jenkins, 1998a, pp 428-43; 1998b, pp 145-60).

Simon Burgess and Carol Propper have agreed that any snapshot picture hides the degree of mobility that does exist, and in general their analysis has confirmed that of Jarvis and Jenkins. People move out of poverty, but generally to an income level that is not much higher. Movements in and out of poverty are not random, and are associated with employment and family status. Burgess and Propper concluded that the key factors in determining household income were labour market factors such as labour supply, earnings generation, and household formation, and also 'dissolution processes' such as marriage, divorce, and fertility (Burgess and Propper, 1999, pp 269-72, 274). There is considerable movement in and out of the population in poverty, and this is determined by employment-related events, family structure-related events, and events associated with changes in income that fall into neither category. Overall, Burgess and Propper have concluded that a large minority of individuals experience poverty at least once in a number of years; for many this is a one-off event, but many who escape do not move far from poverty, and there is a group who experience repeated and persistent poverty (Burgess and Propper, 2002).

The second main approach has argued that an understanding of income and poverty dynamics benefits from taking a life-cycle perspective. This work explores the question of how life events, such as partnership formation and dissolution, having children, retirement, and the death of a spouse, affect the probability of moving up or down the income distribution. Robert Walker, for example, found from longitudinal data for the Netherlands and Germany that although most spells of poverty were short, much poverty was accounted for by a small number of people who were in the midst of very long spells of poverty. He suggested that there was 'not one kind of poverty but many', with different implications for social exclusion (Walker, 1995). More recent data from the first 10 waves of the BHPS (1991-2000) have suggested that particular life events are closely associated with either falling or rising trajectories, but that there is considerable heterogeneity in income trajectories following these different events. Overall, life-cycle factors do not explain as much of the variation in income trajectories as labour market factors, but they do have an important explanatory role in terms of rising trajectories (partnership formation and children becoming independent) and falling trajectories (having children and partnership breakdown). This work has demonstrated that the welfare state cushions people reasonably effectively against the potentially adverse impact of certain events (Rigg and Sefton, 2004).

The third approach has been in terms of intergenerational mobility – the question of to what extent there is a correlation between a parent's position in the earnings distribution and that of their children – and has the closest links with the themes of the Research Programme of the 1970s. Researchers had earlier used data on children and their parents to assess the extent of intergenerational mobility. This was the approach that the team led by Tony Atkinson had adopted in the Research Programme, looking at fathers and sons in York using the Rowntree survey (Atkinson et al, 1983). Thus intergenerational studies have clear links, both methodological and substantive, with the research done in the 1970s, and it is possible to compare the state of knowledge then and now. In the 1990s, researchers turned to longitudinal data from the NCDS. Lorraine Dearden, Stephen Machin, and Howard Reed, for example, argued that the extent of intergenerational mobility was limited in terms of both earnings and schooling. There was a clear intergenerational correlation between fathers, and both sons and daughters, in terms of labour market earnings and years of schooling (Dearden et al, 1997).

Elizabeth Such and Robert Walker have noted that the notion that parents, parenting, and culture contribute to the replication of social and economic disadvantage across the generations has become a signature of New Labour thinking. They have reviewed three bodies of evidence: intergenerational studies of mobility; life-course analyses; and research that unravels the possible processes that produce intergenerational transmission. Such and Walker have concluded that while intergenerational continuities exist, their apparent scale is magnified by the dynamics of social mobility. Evidence as to the mechanisms involved is fragile, but hints that family processes are only important in the context of low income, and that education both propels social advance and traps the disadvantaged (Such and Walker, 2002, p 185). They have acknowledged that the arrival of panel and cohort data means that understanding of the intergenerational replication of deprivation is much greater than in the early 1980s. Nevertheless, they have concluded that 'the inherent complexity of unravelling interactions between individual and structural processes and reticence in the face of ideological sensitivities mean that knowledge is still partial' (Such and Walker, 2002, p 190).

A further element of this research has been the relationship between childhood experiences and subsequent labour market performance as an adult. Paul Gregg and Stephen Machin (2001) have suggested that such studies of intergenerational mobility are important for looking empirically for transmission mechanisms; they shed light on which pre-labour market factors are connected to labour market success or failure; and they can inform future policy on child outcomes. Drawing on the NCDS and BCS, they have argued that childhood disadvantages are an important factor in maintaining and reinforcing patterns of immobility of economic status across generations. From their work, success in education emerged as a potentially important transmission mechanism underpinning links between childhood disadvantage and adult economic and social outcomes, and therefore of the extent of intergenerational mobility. Gregg and Machin have concluded that 'disadvantages faced during childhood display a persistent (negative) association with the subsequent economic success of individuals' (Gregg and Machin, 2001, p 146). They have since argued further from international comparisons that Britain is at the lower end of mobility scales, and that greater equality of educational opportunity is crucial (Blanden et al, 2005). This work has tended to suggest that initiatives to improve skills and employment opportunities are the most sensible way to tackle persistent poverty, and have highlighted the importance of the policy agenda to reduce child poverty and disadvantage (Blanden, 2006).

Overall, then, there has been much interest in income dynamics and social mobility. David Piachaud and Holly Sutherland have commented that 'poverty in childhood is important for social exclusion not only because of its immediate effect in constraining children's lives but also because it is a cause of social exclusion in later life' (Piachaud and Sutherland, 2002, p 141). John Hills (2004) has offered a useful summary. Lack of economic or social mobility has been seen as a marker for inequalities of opportunity, and understanding the links across people's lifetimes and between generations may shed light on the most effective ways of breaking continuities in disadvantage. There are relatively few people who are poor year after year, but most escapes from poverty are temporary, and particular groups suffer both from longer durations of poverty, and from greater chances of falling back into it if they do escape. There are intergenerational links in earnings position, and while they are not rigid, they appear to be getting stronger over time. Certainly there is no evidence that education has acted to reduce the links between people's socioeconomic position and that of their parents (Hills, 2004, pp 97–123). This work has influenced the Treasury, as we will see in the following chapter. Nevertheless, doubts over the causes of these trends remain unresolved. John Hobcraft, for instance, has noted that interpretation of these continuities depends on assumptions about causality, nature versus nurture, and about structural constraints and individual opportunity. It was hardly surprising that such 'thorny questions' had not been answered (Hobcraft, 1998b, p 119; Burgess and Propper, 2002, p 61).

Agency, structure, and public policy

A final strand in the trends that together have supported a return to the themes of the cycle hypothesis and the Research Programme of the 1970s has been the importance accorded to agency. It has long been recognised that the discipline of social administration was dominated by an empiricist tradition. As Peter Taylor-Gooby has pointed out, it was concerned with charting the shortcomings of state welfare, and ignored the place of welfare within a larger capitalist system (Taylor-

Gooby, 1981). Ramesh Mishra alleges that the dominant influence in social administration was Fabian socialism – it was pragmatic, centred on Britain, concentrated on the factual study of social problems, focused on statutory social services, and had no theoretical approach to its subject matter. In part this was due to the influence of Titmuss who furthered the study of social policy in many ways, but was not interested in theory (Mishra, 1989). This began to change in the 1980s. Eithne McLaughlin, for example, suggested that the relationship between social welfare and behaviour was central to understanding the outcomes of welfare provision, and essential for modelling future demand. The main problem was that social scientists tended to regard structure and agency as alternatives, whereas social welfare research should investigate the relationships between structures, values, and behaviour in the decision-making processes of individuals. It seemed likely that research into 'decision environments' would require new types of methodology and theory, and combine qualitative and quantitative techniques (McLaughlin, 1996).

McLaughlin's demand for a shift in the conceptual focus of research in poverty was echoed by Fiona Williams and Jane Pillinger. They argued that there should be a move from researching social groups as categories to:

> integrating an acknowledgement of people's, or groups' own agency, experience and understanding of their position, and seeing them as creative, reflexive agents both constrained by and enabled by, as well as creating, the social conditions in which they exist. (Williams and Pillinger, 1996, p 3)

Williams and Pillinger noted that research into poverty had become increasingly preoccupied with pathological approaches, whose concern with questions of motivation and behaviour was typified in the notion of the underclass. In response, research on poverty, unemployment, and lone motherhood had focused on meanings and discourses, including the social construction of the poor. But other changes in poverty research, including the concept of social exclusion, had also paved the way for a greater recognition of the heterogeneity of the poor. Overall, Williams and Pillinger argued that a new research paradigm could bridge the conceptual and methodological gaps that dichotomies in social science research had generated, and could create 'a more multidimensional view of what poverty means in relation to the quality of life' (Williams and Pillinger, 1996, p 3).

In a book that summarised research in an ESRC–Rowntree Foundation research programme, Fiona Williams, Jennie Popay, and Ann Oakley explored the potential for a new paradigm of welfare. In particular they were concerned to see how a new framework for research could incorporate new approaches that emphasised individual agency, without losing sight of the approach that stressed structural constraints. They suggested that the literature on stress, life events, coping, and social support failed to explain or illuminate the relationship between identity, agency, and structure. Williams, Popay, and Oakley agreed that, with the exception of Titmuss's work on altruism, research in the 1960s and 1970s focused on structural determinants, and inequalities were seen in terms of social class (Williams et al, 1999b). Williams and Popay concluded that earlier research had neglected individual experience and agency, so that the recipients of welfare were 'at best, shadowy, largely forgotten inhabitants of the research terrain' (Williams and Popay, 1999, p 157). The dichotomy had been represented in terms of an individualist (blame the victim) versus a structuralist (blame the system) approach. Williams and Popay concluded that there should be four levels of analysis: the welfare subject; the social topography of enablement and constraint; the policy context; and the dynamics of social and economic change. What was needed was that:

> we begin to investigate new ways of researching these issues, new ways of breaking down the separation of the individual from the social, new ways of understanding the relationship between human behaviour and social policy, and between social policy, social inequality and social change. (Williams and Popay, 1999, p 183)

Debates about stakeholder welfare evoked related debates about character, behaviour, and human nature (Deacon, 1996). Frank Field argued subsequently that agency had been neglected, writing that 'the welfare state has developed no room for such a discussion of behaviour, even though such a public debate is crucial for change to be successful and supported' (Field, 1998, p 53). He maintained that the state had to allow individuals the freedom to make their own choices, while retaining the responsibility for the framework within which those choices were made. Field was critical of Titmuss, and a resurgence in neo-liberal and individualistic ideas in the 1970s and 1980s also prompted Alan Deacon to go back to Titmuss's earlier writings. Deacon was struck by Titmuss's total opposition to 'judgementalism' – Titmuss seemed to reject personal responsibility in almost all circumstances, and was extremely optimistic about human behaviour. For Titmuss, social policies had to be universal, and non-judgemental. But Deacon argued that this neglect of behaviour had rendered Titmuss's analysis vulnerable to Thatcherism, to the concept of behavioural dependency, and to the arguments of Charles Murray and Lawrence Mead (Deacon, 1993, 1996).

Other commentators were increasingly interested in debates around questions of behaviour and motivation. A slightly different perspective on the same question was provided by Julian Le Grand, and his typology of people as being public spirited altruists (knights), passive recipients of welfare (pawns), or as self-interested (knaves). Le Grand argued that the development of quasi-markets in welfare provision, and the supplementation of 'fiscal' welfare by 'legal' welfare, were the result of changes in the way policy makers viewed human motivation and behaviour. Le Grand characterised the classic welfare state as 'one designed to be financed and operated by knights, for the benefit of pawns' (Le Grand, 1997, p 157). In contrast, more recent policies were based on a range of assumptions – that people were knaves; that knaves could be converted into knights; and that little was known about human motivation. However, Le Grand argued that neither set of policies had been based on evidence, and each was as likely to fail as the other. What was needed was a more complex view of human behaviour. There was some evidence, claimed Le Grand, that policies had begun to incorporate this (Le Grand, 1997, p 157).

Le Grand has subsequently argued that assumptions governing human motivation – the desires or preferences that incite action – and agency – the capacity to undertake that action – are key to the design and implementation of public policy. Policy makers fashion policies on the assumption that both those who implement the policies and those who benefit from them will behave in certain ways. He has argued, for example, that in the era of the classic welfare state (1945-79), public servants were seen as being motivated mainly by their professional ethic and were concerned with the interests of those they were serving. They worked in the public interest, and were seen as public spirited altruists (or knights). Taxpayers were similarly knightly in their willingness to pay taxes. Individuals in receipt of the benefits of the welfare state, on the other hand, were seen as essentially passive, or pawns, content with a universal but fairly basic standard of service. However, after 1979, claimed Le Grand, there were serious assaults on assumptions about motivation and behaviour. It was argued that the behaviour of public officials and professionals could be better understood if they were seen to be self-interested. The idea that knightly behaviour characterised those who paid for welfare was also challenged. Finally, it was seen as undesirable that the users of services were treated as passive recipients – rather the consumer should be king. The logic was that the most obvious mechanism of service delivery was the market (Le Grand, 1997, 2003). Nevertheless, Le Grand's metaphors have been subjected to remarkably little critical scrutiny so far (Welshman, 2007a).

Changing approaches to poverty are perhaps best illustrated by the work of Ruth Lister, who had reviewed Brown and Madge's final report in 1982, and in the 1990s had been extremely hostile to underclass formulations (Lister, 1996). She has noted that experiences and understandings of poverty are shaped by both socioeconomic and cultural contexts, and has argued that there should be less emphasis on the measurement of poverty, and more attention to its conceptual dimensions. Poverty has to be understood as social relations, since poverty has been constructed by the non-poor. Thus Lister has conceded that discourse (including underclass discourse) has been important, in constructing the poor as different or other. Furthermore she has devoted more attention to agency, acknowledging that agency was denied by postwar British social policy, and arguing that it is access to resources that mediates the link between agency and structure. Lister has suggested that the interplay between agency and structure is at the heart of contemporary efforts to theorise the dynamics of poverty, with researchers conceding that movements in and out of poverty are the result of individual actions, as well as wider economic and social processes along with government policies. Thus agency has to be understood within the context of structural, cultural, and policy constraints. People are actors within their own lives, but within the bounds of constraints. Thus Lister seems more prepared than previously to accept that poverty is a relational and symbolical as well as material phenomenon. She argues that the ways in which people conceptualise poverty affect their understanding and attitudes towards poverty, and hence their determination to do something about it (Lister, 2004, pp 3, 7, 99-157, 188-9).

Conclusion

The general thrust of the work of CASE can be seen in the collection *Understanding social exclusion* (Hills et al, 2002). This emphasised the need to distinguish social exclusion from earlier concepts such as the underclass; the concern with agency; the different empirical approaches to social exclusion that had been adopted; and the focus on dynamic analysis (Burchardt et al, 2002a, pp 1-12). Nevertheless, much of this has been a top-down phenomenon. One study has compared academic interpretations of the term 'social exclusion' with the understanding of people with direct experience of the phenomenon. Earlier definitions had focused on consumption, production, political engagement, and social interaction. In general, understandings of the term among residents of deprived neighbourhoods correlated well with more academic definitions, but in one or two areas there were significant differences. Residents placed more emphasis on the need for intervention to tackle social exclusion problems on the grounds of social justice and social solidarity, and they did not like the definition's heavy emphasis on the individual, preferring one that embraced the concept of the areas and neighbourhoods being excluded (Richardson and Le Grand, 2002, pp 496-515).

As we have seen, the concept of social exclusion emerged in France, and was associated with a relational view of poverty that was very different to the traditional British concern with individual and household resources. From the mid-1990s, New Labour adopted the language of social exclusion. In part, this reflected a determination to focus on the structural causes of deprivation, and to use the new evidence on poverty dynamics that resulted from the availability of longitudinal data sets. Nevertheless, part of the appeal of social exclusion to New Labour has been that it has made it possible to combine a commitment to tackle poverty with a cultural interpretation that reflects the importance it attaches to behaviour, and to people taking advantage of the opportunities that are offered to them. In this, as in the 'Americanisation' of debates on welfare, New Labour has arguably been much more influenced by experiences on the other side of the Atlantic than across the Channel. What is obvious is that these debates were played out against the backdrop of the 1970s' debates, along with limited direct reference to research on intergenerational continuities, as in the case of the Atkinson work. We will see this more clearly in the next chapter, where policy shifts since 1997 indicate a more focused return to the concerns of the cycle speech and Research Programme.

EIGHT

From transmitted deprivation to social exclusion

Introduction

Continuities between the cycle speech, the Research Programme, and current policy can be explored in relation to government initiatives on social exclusion and child poverty. How far do these illustrate links between the policies endorsed by New Labour, and the earlier cycle of deprivation hypothesis? Alan Deacon (2003) has suggested that New Labour has been concerned to strike a balance between responsibility and opportunity. Its policy on child poverty provides a good example of the 'third way' on welfare. Thus the ending of child poverty is often presented less as an objective in itself, and more as a means of reducing inequalities in opportunity. The emphasis that people should take up the opportunities that are offered has led New Labour to revisit earlier debates, including the Research Programme. Deacon concludes that New Labour's interpretation of the cycle of disadvantage does recognise the significance of structural factors, and in general its rhetoric is closer to an adaptive explanation. However, its emphasis that people should take full advantage of the opportunities that are created also reflects elements of the rational, permissive, and cultural explanations. Thus New Labour seeks both to 'level the playing field' and to 'activate the players' (Deacon, 2003, pp 123-37). Other work has explored policy developments against the historical backdrop of area initiatives in the US and the UK in the 1960s and 1970s, and looked at New Labour and Croslandite conceptions of equality in historical perspective (Alcock, 2005; Meredith, 2006).

In this chapter, we focus on the way that New Labour has chosen to tackle social exclusion and child poverty from its election in May 1997, relating this to CASE research and to work on poverty dynamics, and looking in particular at the Sure Start initiative. It is argued that these, along with the focus on transmission mechanisms and intergenerational continuities, point to marked continuities with the 1970s' debate over transmitted deprivation. Moreover, the chapter also looks at other pressures, most notably those around antisocial behaviour, and at Blair's JRF speech on social exclusion on 5 September 2006. The argument of the chapter is that New Labour started out with a focus on social exclusion; Blair's Beveridge Lecture on child poverty came out of the blue; the government has increasingly been drawn into debates about antisocial behaviour; and new initiatives on social exclusion mean that the continuities with transmitted deprivation are now much stronger than ever before. While the government initiated a wide-ranging attack on social exclusion, the perceived failure of those policies to meet the needs of the 'most socially excluded' means that the policy front has been narrowed. In particular, the key elements of Blair's York speech were all there in Joseph's cycle speech of 34 years earlier. Thus the wheel has come full circle.

The forgotten people

The different influences explored in Chapter Seven – the new emphasis on behaviour, debates about US welfare reform, and communitarianism – can be seen in Blair's first speech as Prime Minister in June 1997 at the Aylesbury estate in the London borough of Southwark. Blair stated that the government would deal with those living in poverty – what he called the 'forgotten people'. But he stressed that it needed to act in a new way because 'fatalism, and not just poverty, is the problem we face, the dead weight of low expectations, the crushing belief that things cannot get better'.[1] The next decade would be about 'how to recreate the bonds of civic society and community in a way compatible with the far more individualistic nature of modern, economic, social and cultural life'.[2] Blair continued: 'there is a case not just in moral terms but in enlightened self interest to act, to tackle what we all know exists – an underclass of people cut off from society's mainstream, without any sense of shared purpose'.[3] What was needed was a modern civic society based on an ethic of mutual responsibility and duty. Although problems were caused by changes in the nature of work, and long-term unemployment, there was also the danger that people were becoming detached, not just from work, but from citizenship in its widest sense. Welfare had to be reshaped to reward hard work, and a wider ethic of responsibility should be tapped. Solutions would be long term; would require greater coordination across government departments than previously; and would be based on policies that had been shown to work. Overall, the task was to 'reconnect that workless class – to bring jobs, skills, opportunities and ambition to all those people who have been left behind by the Conservative years, and to restore the will to win where it has been lost'.[4]

In a Fabian Society summer lecture, given in August 1997, Peter Mandelson, then Minister without Portfolio, had outlined what he regarded as the biggest challenge New Labour faced – 'the growing number of our fellow citizens who lack the means, material and otherwise, to participate in economic, social, cultural and political life in Britain today'. Moreover, he continued: 'this is about more than poverty and unemployment. It is about being cut off from what the rest of us regard as normal life. It is called social exclusion, what others call "the underclass"' (Mandelson, 1997, p 1). Mandelson argued that a permanently excluded underclass hindered flexibility, but flexibility on its own was not enough. The people that Labour was concerned about, those in danger of dropping off the end of the ladder of opportunity and becoming disengaged from society, would not have their long-term problems addressed by an extra pound a week on their benefits. Rather, personal skills and employment were, in the long run, the most effective anti-poverty strategy. Mandelson announced the creation of a new SEU, based in the Cabinet Office, which would 'harness the full power of government to take on the greatest social crisis of our times' (Mandelson, 1997, p 9).

In December 1997, in a speech given at Stockwell Park School, in the London borough of Lambeth, Tony Blair outlined government plans to tackle the problem of social exclusion. The speech marked the launch of the SEU, and the Prime Minister defined social exclusion in the following way:

> Social exclusion is about income but it is about more. It is about prospects and networks and life-chances. It's a very modern problem, and one that is more harmful to the individual, more damaging to self-esteem, more corrosive for society as a whole, more likely to be passed down from generation to generation, than material poverty.[5]

According to Blair, part of the answer lay in ensuring that those government departments concerned with the development of policy were coordinated more effectively. In a phrase that was to become a New Labour buzzword, 'joined-up problems' demanded 'joined-up solutions'. But Blair also argued that it was in people's own interests that social exclusion should be eliminated. The issue was as much about self-interest as compassion.[6]

Originally, the SEU reported directly to the Prime Minister, and was located within the Cabinet Office as part of the Economic and Domestic Affairs Secretariat. The SEU defined social exclusion as 'a shorthand term for what can happen when people or areas suffer from a combination of linked problems such as unemployment, poor skills, low incomes, poor housing, high crime environments, bad health, poverty and family breakdown'.[7] Its early reports covered truancy and school exclusion (SEU, 1998c); rough sleeping (SEU, 1998a); neighbourhood renewal (SEU, 1998b); and teenage pregnancy (SEU, 1999a). For instance, the report on rough sleeping argued that the sight of someone bedding down for the night in a shop doorway or on a park bench was one of the most potent symbols of social exclusion in Britain. Again it argued for a more integrated approach (SEU, 1998a). Similarly the report on neighbourhood renewal argued that there was no single definition of a poor neighbourhood; their characteristics included poverty, unemployment and worklessness, poor health, and crime, but other problems ranging from litter and vandalism to a lack of shops (SEU, 1998b).

The SEU claimed that the government was pragmatic, carrying little ideological baggage, and was therefore more open to academics' ideas than ever before. Apart from the SEU reports, it is equally important to examine government rhetoric. The use of the phrases 'cycle of disadvantage' and 'cycle of deprivation', and the emphasis on the transmission of poverty between generations is one of the most striking aspects of New Labour policy in the field of child health. This argument is strengthened by the existence of a more explicit attempt to revisit the earlier Research Programme, and to link academics and policy makers. In November 1997, a conference entitled 'New Cycles of Disadvantage' had been organised by CASE on behalf of the ESRC for the Treasury and other central government departments. The aim was to broaden Treasury links with sociologists and social policy specialists, and to revisit the idea of cycles of deprivation in light of new evidence. The Treasury was interested in cycles of disadvantage for three reasons. First, its core aim was to raise the sustainable growth rate and increase opportunities for everyone to share in its benefits. Second, Treasury policy cut across different government departments, and cycles of disadvantage were seen to result from multiple problems that required multiple solutions. Third, substantial amounts of public expenditure were devoted to mitigating the effects of cycles of disadvantage (Lee and Hills, 1998, p 26).

The conference indicated some new elements when compared to the earlier Research Programme. One was the availability of the new longitudinal studies explored in Chapter Seven, which meant that more importance was attached than previously to income mobility and poverty dynamics, with evidence indicating that the poor did not generally remain persistently poor. There was much reference to the role of place in poorer neighbourhoods, drugs and crime, and single parenthood (Lee and Hills, 1998, p 30). Despite these differences, the November 1997 conference illustrated interesting continuities with the earlier cycle of deprivation debates. The conference was introduced by Michael Rutter, then Professor of Child Psychiatry and Honorary Director of the MRC Child Psychiatry Unit (Rutter, 1998). Another was the emphasis placed on the evidence for genetic influences on individual differences in antisocial and other behaviour. And academics seemed no closer to deciding if a cycle of deprivation actually existed, or to detecting transmission risks and mechanisms.

A historic commitment

It has been argued that the Labour government elected in 1997 inherited unprecedented levels of poverty and inequality, and implemented a broad and ambitious social policy programme, taking on child poverty, worklessness, area and neighbourhood deprivation, and inequalities in health and educational attainment (Stewart and Hills, 2005, p 1). In his Beveridge Lecture (given at Toynbee Hall, London, in March 1999), Tony Blair made a historic commitment to end child poverty within 20 years. Blair said he would 'set out our historic aim that ours is the first generation to end child poverty forever, and it will take a generation. It is a 20-year mission, but I believe it can be done' (Blair, 1999, p 16). While the 1997 election manifesto had contained few references to reducing poverty, and none to social exclusion, Tony Blair's Beveridge Lecture marked a sea-change in the government's language and policy approach. Nevertheless, it is also true that this commitment came out of the blue.

In the Beveridge Lecture, the Prime Minister presented a blueprint for a new modern, popular welfare state. It would tackle the fundamental causes of child poverty, social exclusion, and the decay of communities, identified as embracing structural unemployment, poor education, poor housing, crime, and a 'drugs culture'. But people also had a responsibility to take the opportunities that were offered, and the welfare state should be an enabler, not a provider. Most help should go to those in most need, but fraud and abuse should also be rooted out. Public–private partnerships and voluntary organisations would have an increasingly important role in delivering welfare. And welfare was not just about benefits, but about services and community support (Blair, 1999, p 16). Focusing on what he termed 'child deprivation', Blair continued: 'we need to break the cycle of disadvantage so that children born into poverty are not condemned to social exclusion and deprivation. That is why it is so important that we invest in our children' (Blair, 1999, p 16).

The source of the cycles of disadvantage rhetoric in Blair's Beveridge Lecture was the ESRC–CASE seminar of November 1997. David Piachaud and Holly Sutherland have suggested that there have been three main components of the government's approach to child poverty. First, policies to alter income levels directly through the tax and benefit system. By April 2001, the main changes to the system of taxes and benefits for children were the Working Families' Tax Credit, Child Benefit, Children's Tax Credit, and Income Support. Second, policies to promote paid work. Third, measures to tackle long-term disadvantage, including the Sure Start strategy to offer help to families with children from birth up to the age of four in areas where children were most at risk from poverty and social exclusion. Piachaud and Sutherland concluded that poverty was only one of the many influences on child development, and the goal of equal opportunities for all children was more radical than was often realised (Piachaud and Sutherland, 2002, pp 146-54).

Other work has demonstrated the complexities involved in measuring child poverty (Piachaud, 2001; Toynbee and Walker, 2001, pp 10-43; Lowe, 2005, pp 406-9). Early analysis has indicated that the aim of ending child poverty within 20 years is unlikely to be achieved. Child poverty reductions have been achieved with 'work for those who can' strategies and real improvements in Child Benefit and Income Support. But to abolish child poverty would require more redistributive policies of raising Income Support faster than the rate of inflation and increases in earnings, and including increases for older children. Child Benefit would have to grow by the same amount, meaning increases in taxation on those who could afford to pay (Bradshaw, 2001, pp 9-27). Kitty Stewart has found that the number of children in poverty (households with less than 60% of equivalised median income) had fallen to 28% by 2002-03, from a peak of 34% in 1996-97, a drop of 700,000 out of 4.3 million poor children (Stewart, 2005, p 149).

In 2003-04, the number of children growing up in poverty stood at 3.5 million, or 28% of the total. To achieve its 25% target, the government needed to reduce the figure to 3.1 million for 2004-05. However, figures released in March 2006 indicated that it had fallen narrowly short. Child poverty fell by 700,000 to 3.4 million between 1998-99 and 2004-05. Poverty would have had to fall by a further 400,000 to achieve the government's own target (*The Independent*, 9 March 2006, p 20; *The Times*, 10 March 2006, p 18). Moreover, the number of children living in poverty rose by 100,000 in 2005-06, to 3.8 million (*The Financial Times*, 28 March 2007, p 3; *The Times*, 28 March 2007, p 2). Overall, while child poverty and child early development have been high on the agenda, there has been mixed success, and investment in tax credits and benefits, support for childcare, and wider health and education policies will have to continue for many years.

From Head Start to Sure Start

In some respects, this shift in the policy agenda has been paralleled by a move in the stance adopted by academic commentators. David Piachaud, for example, acknowledged that the government had tackled child poverty in three main ways, by promoting paid employment through the New Deal and other measures; by redistributing money to children with the Working Families' Tax Credit; and by tackling long-term causes of poverty, such as teenage births and exclusion from school. Yet Piachaud also argued that the quality of children's lives, and their opportunities in later life, depended on much more than their material circumstances. Tackling poverty was not enough, and there needed to be a broader radical vision of public policy for childhood. For instance, the nutrition of children was poor because many housing estates had only corner shops with no fresh food and high prices; families were bombarded with the advertising of junk foods; and many parents knew very little about nutrition, having learned little from their parents. Thus the influences on children's lives and opportunities were complex – improving education required not only good schools and teachers, but parental involvement and encouragement. Government, Piachaud argued, should focus on achieving childhoods that were 'happy, healthy and fulfilled and that nurture young people who are civilised and educated' (Piachaud, 2001, pp 446-53).

What, then, has been the impact of this research on policy making? Certainly research fostered by CASE has been concerned with early childhood interventions. Jane Waldfogel argued of the literature from the US, including the Head Start programme, that early childhood interventions could make a difference in improving outcomes for children. Children attending Head Start had higher test scores at the end of the programme than siblings who stayed at home or attended some other type of pre-school. Nevertheless, at that time (1999) not enough was known about the types of childcare children in Britain were using, nor about what types of early childhood interventions would achieve the best outcomes. Longitudinal research was essential (Waldfogel, 1999). This interest in Head Start was a striking continuity with the early 1970s, when Urie Bronfenbrenner had been involved in debates on both sides of the Atlantic; Alan Clarke had contributed to debates about efforts to boost IQ; and the Ford Foundation had sponsored the study tour in which Joan Cooper, Geoffrey Otton, and Tessa Blackstone had participated (Blackstone, 1973).

As we saw in Chapter Seven, Lutz Leisering and Robert Walker had argued that policy making should take account of the new realities that dynamic studies revealed and created. Alan Deacon has argued that Treasury conclusions about Sure Start were drawn from new analyses of panel data. Similar evidence had emerged in the 1980s, but what was new was New Labour's receptivity to such evidence. It could not be ignored by a government committed to promoting equality of opportunity and reducing social exclusion. In any case, New Labour was less resistant to conservative ideas about welfare dependency, and more willing to take tough measures to deal with parents perceived as inadequate or irresponsible (Becker and Bryman, 2004, p 32). Kitty Stewart has agreed that it was the evidence that pointed to the impact of poverty on outcomes in later life, along with evidence from the US on services for very young children, that pushed the Treasury, for the first time, to invest substantial funds in services for pre-school children (Stewart, 2005, p 145).

It was the new research using panel data sets that dominated a workshop on Persistent Poverty and Lifetime Inequality, organised by the Treasury in November 1998. It was claimed that looking at the dynamics of poverty and inequality of opportunity made it possible to pinpoint the processes and events that led people to be at greater risk of low income and poorer life chances. This data could provide evidence to underpin policy that would tackle these problems at source. Contributors to the workshop included Paul Gregg, John Hills, John Hobcraft, Stephen Jenkins, Stephen Machin, and Robert Walker. Jenkins looked at income changes from one year to the next; Walker at life-cycle trajectories; and Machin at intergenerational associations. Arguably most influential was the research on childhood disadvantage and intergenerational transmissions of economic status. Stephen Machin, for example, argued that 'pinning down the transmission mechanisms that underlie intergenerational transmissions is important, especially those associated with childhood disadvantage' (Machin, 1998, p 17). The NCDS data suggested a strong link between childhood disadvantage and poor economic or social outcomes at 23 or 33. Machin argued that:

> Disadvantage in the childhood years has effects long into
> adult life and there are often detrimental effects that spill
> over to the next generation. Having parents with low
> income or earnings during the years of growing up is a
> strong disadvantage in terms of labour market success and
> can contribute importantly to factors like adult joblessness
> and participation in crime. (Machin, 1998, p 21)

What was evident in the discussion was the importance attached to
childhood poverty, and to policies for early intervention to prevent
'downward cycles of deprivation and create upward cycles' (CASE and
HM Treasury, 1999, p 120).

Certainly the data on poverty dynamics had an important influence
on Treasury proposals to modernise the tax and benefit system,
published in March 1999, a few days after Blair's Beveridge Lecture. It
was suggested that by understanding the factors that influenced people's
trajectories through life, it was possible to develop strategies to counter
events that meant people were at greater risk of economic disadvantage.
Government could work to promote factors that helped people climb
a 'ladder of opportunity' (HM Treasury, 1999, p 5). In particular, the
evidence was interpreted as showing that the life chances of people
were determined by who their parents were, rather than by their own
talents and efforts. The Treasury argued that:

> Childhood disadvantage frequently leads to low educational
> attainment, low educational attainment leads to low pay and
> low employment, which in turns leads to low income and
> denial of opportunity for the next generation. There are
> strong links between people's own life chances and those
> of their parents and possibly even grand-parents. (HM
> Treasury, 1999, p 7)

Work was the route to opportunity, and educational attainment was
the most important transmission mechanism for cycles of disadvantage.
Children who grew up in disadvantaged families were more likely as
adults to be teenage mothers, live in social housing, be dependent on
benefit, and have a low income (HM Treasury, 1999, pp 26, 33).

Evidence from the Cross-Departmental Review of Young Children in
the Comprehensive Spending Review had convinced the government
that resources should be devoted to a new programme to pioneer a
coordinated approach to services for families with children under four.
It was claimed that there were risk factors (material, child, family, and

school) that could affect educational performance, which was a good indicator of later success in the labour market and more widely. Multiple risk factors greatly increased the chance of later social exclusion. Equally, there were protective factors that could counter risk, including strong early attachments to adults and parental interest. These helped explain how children from apparently similar backgrounds could differ in their achievements. Well targeted early interventions could enhance educational and social development for individual children, and could lead to long-term benefits for society. Effective interventions involved parents as well as children; were non-stigmatising (for example they avoiding labelling problem families); targeted a number of factors; lasted long enough to make a real difference; were based on the involvement of parents and local communities; and were sensitive to the needs of parents and children. At that stage, services for children aged seven and under cost around £10 billion a year, but were driven by vertically separated agencies, leading to fragmentation and a lack of coordination (HM Treasury, 1999, p 30). The Treasury therefore stated that, recognising the need for early intervention, the government was investing £540 million in the new Sure Start programme to target these patterns of childhood disadvantage. Sure Start aimed to 'promote the physical, intellectual, social and emotional development of children to make sure they are ready to thrive when they go to school' (HM Treasury, 1999, pp 31, 34).

The Sure Start initiative was launched in 2001. Its programmes work with parents and parents-to-be to improve children's life chances through better access to family support, advice on children's development, health services, and early learning. Its objectives include: to improve social and emotional development, health, children's ability to learn, and strengthen families and communities. While the design and content of Sure Start programmes has varied according to local needs, core services comprised outreach and home visiting; support for parents and families; support for good-quality play, learning, and childcare experiences for children; primary and community healthcare; and support for children and parents with special needs. It was claimed that Sure Start was founded on evidence that sustained support for children could help them succeed at school and help reduce crime, unemployment, teenage pregnancy, and other economic and social problems.[8]

Given the background to this initiative, it is not surprising that the rhetoric of Sure Start has contained echoes of the 1972 cycle speech and Research Programme. In April 2000, for example, Yvette Cooper, then Parliamentary Under-Secretary of State for Public Health, was reported as saying that higher state benefits for poor families were not sufficient to break the cycle of deprivation (*The Guardian*, 11 April 2000, p 4). In the introductory booklet to the fifth wave of Sure Start programmes, the declared aim was to 'break the cycle of disadvantage for the current generation of young children'.[9] Since then, the phrases 'cycle of deprivation' and 'cycle of disadvantage' have become a feature of the language of New Labour. As the *Opportunity for all* annual report stated in 1999:

> The key to tackling disadvantage in the future is the eradication of child poverty. Children who grow up in disadvantaged families generally do less well at school, and are more likely to suffer unemployment, low pay and poor health in adulthood. This poverty of opportunity is then more likely to be experienced by the next generation of children.... We need to break the cycle of deprivation, to stop it being transmitted through generations. (DSS, 1999, p 5)

The third annual report on poverty (2001) argued that 'for far too many children, disadvantage in early life leads to poor outcomes in adulthood that perpetuate the transmission of poverty across the generations' (DWP, 2001, p 40).

By 2004, Sure Start programmes were in place in 522 areas, reaching 400,000 children. There has been a reduction in re-registrations on the child protection register, but progress on other child health goals has been less impressive. By September 2005, Sure Start had cost some £3.1 billion since its launch in 2001, and was to be extended from its then total of 524 schemes, to 3,500 Sure Start Children's Centres, one in every neighbourhood, by 2010.[10] Nevertheless, the interim evaluation of Sure Start, based on a quasi-experimental, cross-sectional study, found that differences between Sure Start and comparison areas were limited, small, and varied by degree of social deprivation. It focused on mothers of children aged nine months, and children aged 36 months, in 150 Sure Start areas, and in 50 comparison communities. The outcome measures were mothers' reports of community services and the local area, family functioning and parenting skills, child health and development, and verbal ability at 36 months. Overall, it was found that Sure Start had beneficial results on non-teenage mothers (better parenting, better functioning in children) and adverse effects on children of teenage mothers (poorer social functioning) and children of single parents or parents who did not work (lower verbal ability). Sure Sure projects led by health services were slightly more effective than those led by other agencies, probably because of better access to children and established health visitor networks. Thus Sure Start seemed to have beneficial effects on the least socially deprived parents, and an adverse effect on the most disadvantaged families (Belsky et al, 2006). An earlier leaked version received wide publicity (*The Guardian*, 13 September 2005, pp 1, 29-30). Some commentators saw this as symbolising the increasing failure of the social democratic state (Ormerod, 2005).

New Labour, new language

Critiques of social exclusion have been relatively slow to appear. John Hills (2002) has argued that an implication of using the term 'social exclusion' is that one should not look simply at cash incomes, but at a much wider range of indicators of deprivation or inability to participate in contemporary society. The Blair government has talked about poverty as well as social exclusion, and there have been changes in tax and social security policy. Government action has not treated social exclusion as the deserved and inevitable fate of an underclass, so that pro-work policies – the New Deal, the National Minimum Wage, and the Working Families' Tax Credit – have been balanced with other policies, such as substantial increases in Income Support. Overall, Hills has suggested that the language of inclusion and exclusion since the late 1990s has not damaged more traditional concerns, and has led to a richer policy mix (Hills, 2002, p 243).

Nevertheless, Blair's use of the term 'underclass' in his Aylesbury estate speech was not accidental, and it is partly a recognition of these diverse influences that have led other observers to contest the meaning of social exclusion in Britain. Stephen Driver and Luke Martell were quick off the mark in commenting that the socially excluded are poor, but they are not simply the poor. The socially excluded lack the skills, capabilities, and even willingness to get and keep a job, and are cut off from the world of work and education. With rights came responsibilities; the government would fulfill its side of the bargain by helping the socially excluded find work; in return, the socially excluded must fulfill their responsibilities by doing something about their own condition (Driver and Martell, 1998, p 90).

Some of the early critiques saw social exclusion in terms of a Marxist 'reserve army of labour'. David Byrne, for example, argued that the general formulation of the idea focused on direct labour market participation and omitted the unwaged from consideration. His point was to emphasise the relationship between exclusion and the maintenance of a reserve army of labour (Byrne, 1997). Elsewhere, Byrne wrote that exclusion is 'a necessary and inherent characteristic of an unequal post-industrial capitalism founded around a flexible labour market and with a systematic constraining of the organisational powers of workers as collective actors' (Byrne, 1999, p 128). He argued that public policy in Europe and the US saw the socially excluded as marked by personal deficits; its remedy lay in the correction of these deficits through training. Moreover, Byrne argued that social exclusion derived from inequality and was 'a product of our post-industrial social order dominated by globalising capital and the superclass associated with that globalising capital' (Byrne, 1999, p 137).

Ruth Levitas is arguably the key writer in this area. She argued, for example, that social exclusion had become integrated into a new hegemonic discourse, where it was contrasted with integration into the labour market, and actually obscured inequalities. The discourse treated social divisions endemic to capitalism as resulting from an abnormal breakdown in the social cohesion that should be maintained by the division of labour. Although linked to Townsend's theory of relative deprivation, social exclusion 'actually obscures the questions of material inequality it was originally intended to illuminate' (Levitas, 1996, pp 5-20). The concept of social exclusion operated to devalue unpaid work, and to obscure the inequalities between paid workers, as well as to disguise the fundamental social division between the property-owning class and the rest of society. Social exclusion was embedded in three different discourses – a redistributionist discourse that was primarily concerned with poverty; a moral underclass discourse that focused on the moral and behavioural delinquency of the excluded; and a social integrationist discourse whose focus was on paid work. And one reason why social exclusion had been so powerful a concept was because it could have different meanings and move between these discourses. Levitas wrote that like the word 'underclass', the phrase 'social exclusion' could, almost unnoticed, 'mobilise a redistributive argument behind a cultural or integrationist one – or represent cultural or integrationist arguments as redistributive' (Levitas, 1998, p 27). Her claim was that New Labour had moved away from a concern with poverty towards an inconsistent combination of the moral underclass approach with an emphasis on social integration whose focus was on paid work.

Levitas subsequently extended her critique of social exclusion, suggesting that thinking in terms of social exclusion and inclusion could be a way of allowing a recognition of social deprivation to coexist with an uncritical acceptance of capitalism. The SEU concern with rough sleeping rather than homelessness (SEU, 1998a) suggested a concern with social order as much as deprivation, while the policy recommendations of the report on teenage pregnancy (SEU, 1999a) were mainly concerned with changing behaviour through better sex education (Levitas, 2000, p 361). The choice of indicators depended on views of the causation of social exclusion and their causal links with poverty. Moreover, Levitas suggested that the *Opportunity for all* annual reports (DSS, 1999; DWP, 2001) emphasised opportunities for individuals to escape from poverty rather than the abolition of poverty itself. The focus was on worklessness, and its supply-side failures, of the poor education, skills, and motivation of the workforce (Levitas, 2000, p 373). Indicators were chosen because they showed a reduction in exclusion without direct intervention, and were relatively easy to address. She concluded that 'it could be possible to claim "success" in reducing social exclusion without addressing the fundamental issues of poverty and inequality which afflict large parts of the population' (Levitas, 2000, p 381; Percy-Smith, 2000, pp 1-21).

Levitas has since argued that the distinctively social aspects of social exclusion have not been at the centre of debates about the development of definitions and indicators of social exclusion at national and EU levels. She writes that 'the normative judgements implicit in social indicators need to be explicit and interrogated, rather than taken for granted' (Levitas, 2006, p 128). The focus on worklessness, for example, ignores the socially necessary labour that takes place outside the labour market, and reflects the moral value placed on paid work, which stigmatises those outside it. Similar problems are apparent in the use of EU indicators, and in those used by Burchardt et al at CASE. The Poverty and Social Exclusion survey data suggest that it is poverty rather than joblessness that is the key problem. Levitas therefore concludes that indicators of social exclusion need to address the fabric of social life; there is a need for more qualitative research to explore the impact of poverty and worklessness on social relations; and the policy emphasis on paid work is a double-edged sword, reducing poverty but also creating problems of work–life balance (Levitas, 2006, p 155).

More recent work has indicated that the different ways in which social exclusion has been defined has continued to pose problems for researchers trying to operationalise the concept (Littlewood and Herkommer, 1999, pp 1-21). Matt Barnes, for instance, has pointed to the lack of clarity, suggesting that this can undermine policy making. He suggests that in the *Opportunity for all* reports (DSS, 1999; DWP, 2001) there is a lack of consideration of how to define and operationalise poverty and social exclusion, and little attempt to explain the multidimensional or longitudinal nature of disadvantage. Very few studies have concentrated on the measurement of social exclusion, and 'in general advances in the production of publicly disseminated social statistics of social exclusion have lagged behind theoretical innovations' (Barnes, 2005, p 21). There are no regular and publicly available statistics that illustrate both the multidimensional and longitudinal nature of social exclusion. The *Opportunity for all* indicators are unstructured and incomplete. A theoretical explanation for the selection of indicators is needed; some indicators do not appear to relate to poverty and social exclusion at all; the reports do not adequately differentiate between risk factors and output indicators of poverty and social exclusion; and the indicators are not designed to allow dynamic and multidimensional analysis. Overall, Barnes has argued that the notion of social exclusion has been used loosely and inconsistently, and attempts at conceptualisation are relatively underdeveloped; in particular there has been little attempt to measure its multidimensional and longitudinal nature (Barnes, 2005, pp 31-2).

Others have begun to analyse the discourse of SEU reports. Paul Watt and Keith Jacobs (2000), for example, analysed *Bringing Britain together* (SEU, 1998b) through discursive analysis, and using the threefold typology put forward by Levitas. They aimed to show how certain terms and key arguments legitimised activity and structured the parameters of policy intervention. The SEU report offered two views of poverty: the first recognised the extensive nature of poverty while the second focused on the behavioural peculiarities of those living in poor areas. In particular, the terms 'poor neighbourhoods' and 'housing problems' suggested that despite claims to novelty with regard to policies on urban regeneration, there were considerable areas of overlap with previous area-based approaches to tackling social exclusion. The problem of social housing in poor neighbourhoods was being redefined in terms of crime and antisocial behaviour, mainly for reasons of pragmatism and expediency. Watt and Jacobs argued that presenting policy prescriptions in this way was a means of endorsing a form of selective spatial targeting at the expense of structural intervention, increased public expenditure, and wealth and income redistribution (Watt and Jacobs, 2000, p 25).

Helen Colley and Phil Hodkinson (2001) argued that the report *Bridging the gap* (SEU, 1999b) had fundamental contradictions in its analysis of non-participation in learning and the solutions proposed. It located the causes of non-participation primarily within individuals and their personal deficits, and deep–seated structural inequalities were rendered invisible. Furthermore, a notion of the way in which the attitudes that reinforced social exclusion were handed down across generations also informed the report's focus on teenage and lone motherhood. The report presented an entirely positive view of labour market conditions, ignoring considerable evidence of large-scale structural unemployment and underemployment created in response to new technologies and globalisation. The report attempted to redress deep-seated structural problems through a strongly individualistic agency approach, while agency-enhancing activity was approached through a prescriptive structural framework. Colley and Hodkinson suggested that in its approach to social exclusion, the Labour government was both 'naïve and disingenuous' (Colley and Hodkinson, 2001, p 355).

In *New Labour, new language?* (2000), Norman Fairclough offered a more intensive study of New Labour speeches and policy documents. He made the point that whereas Labour used the word 'poverty' in an international context, it tended to reserve social exclusion for domestic policy. As in other areas, claimed Fairclough, New Labour tended to favour lists of achievements, rather than explanations of the relationship between causes and outcomes, and between different problems and agencies (Fairclough, 2000, pp 51-3). For New Labour, social exclusion was a condition people were in, not something that was done to them. Words such as 'exclusion' were used more than verbs such as 'exclude', and the focus was on outcome rather than process. Like Levitas, Fairclough believed that there was evidence that the behavioural and moral delinquency suggested by the term 'underclass' had been carried over into the construction of social exclusion. New Labour did not settle immediately on social exclusion – for a time it used both social exclusion and the underclass. Its approach to social exclusion was based in part on a social integrationist perspective that emphasised the importance of paid work (Fairclough, 2000, p 57). It was the perceived cultural deficiencies of socially excluded people that provided the justification for government interventions (Fairclough, 2000, p 61). Fairclough concluded that New Labour was committed to tackling social exclusion because of a combination of compassion and self-interest. Alleviation of social exclusion had replaced the longer-term Labour goal of equality, which was based on the belief that capitalist societies create inequalities and conflicting interests. He claimed that social exclusion shifted attention away from inequalities and conflicts of interests; New Labour assumed that there was nothing wrong with contemporary society as long as it was made more inclusive through government policy (Fairclough, 2000, pp 62-5).

More generally it has been argued that neither the terms 'underclass' nor 'social exclusion' have captured the complex mix of economic, social, and demographic forces that have together fashioned the new social problem of the replacement of traditional blue-collar work with low-paid work, and the growth of a socially and economically marginalised group at the bottom of society. Interviews on one south London estate revealed a picture of considerable creativity and resilience in dealing with the impact of this new industrial revolution (Smith and Macnicol, 2001). David M. Smith has argued that rebranding poverty as social exclusion mainly caused by worklessness thus legitimises the workfarist remedies of the New Deal. He has seen the SEU strategy in terms of prevention, human capital, poverty dynamics, and a focus on multidimensional disadvantage, and has suggested of indicators that 'there must now be a danger that the concept of social exclusion has become a vessel into which almost any social problem can be poured' (Smith, 2005, p viii). Smith viewed the emergence of social exclusion in terms of a remaining focus on the detrimental effects of welfare dependency in transmitting modes of behaviour that had a corrosive impact on the work ethic of the poor (Smith, 2005, p 58).

The reinvention of the problem family

Furthermore, despite New Labour's emphasis on child poverty, and on intergenerational continuities between childhood disadvantage and adult outcomes, there have continued to be countervailing pressures, of which one has been the focus on antisocial behaviour. In the late 1990s, commentators had recognised that the treatment of antisocial behaviour had become individualised, rather than acknowledging the wider difficulties faced by antisocial tenants, such as poor educational opportunities, unemployment, and substance abuse (Papps, 1998). Others suggested that policy initiatives were based around a perceived decline in moral responsibility. A communitarian outlook had led to their incorporating a strongly judgemental bias, and the adoption of punitive strategies. Tenants in council housing were seen as forming an underclass, and residualisation and exclusion facilitated increasingly interventionist and authoritarian policies (Haworth and Manzi, 1999; Burney, 2005).

As Home Secretary, David Blunkett had argued that children as young as three should be monitored for signs of behaviour that might identify them as disruptive teenagers (*The Times*, 19 April 2002, p 6). Moreover, it has been claimed that psychiatric research has suggested that antisocial behaviour in children could be the result of their genetic make-up. Researchers acknowledged the importance of environmental factors. Nevertheless, early interventions including family support and pre-school education were seen as potentially significant.[11] Furthermore, under the Respect initiative, outlined in January 2006, Tony Blair argued that there were intractable problems with the behaviour of some individuals and families, which could make life a misery for others, particularly in the most disadvantaged communities. The causes lay in families, in the classroom, and in communities. The Action Plan stated that 'poor behaviour and a lack of respect can be transmitted between generations and can result in children and young people getting involved in crime or antisocial behaviour' (Respect Task Force, 2006, p 6). Children who engaged in antisocial behaviour from an early age were more likely to face a lifetime of social exclusion and offending. Moreover, it was a small minority of problem families that were responsible for a high proportion of problems.

It was suggested that problem families could be required to go on compulsory rehabilitation courses covering anger control, money management, and parenting advice. Funding was made available for a National Parenting Academy and for parenting classes and other support groups for families. The police were to be given new powers to identify children under the age of 10 who were in problem families and at risk of becoming offenders, so that the authorities could intervene early. Moreover, Antisocial Behaviour Orders (ASBOs) were to be extended, to include the withdrawal of Housing Benefit and forced eviction of families who refused to improve their behaviour (Sennett, 2003, 2004 edn; Respect Task Force, 2006; *The Financial Times*, 11 January 2006, p 2; *The Guardian*, 10 January 2006, p 10). Subsequently, Housing Benefit was to be withdrawn where a person had been evicted for antisocial behaviour and refused to address the problem using the support and help offered. This reflected a feeling that the government's programmes were struggling to reach out to problem families resistant to state help, which also underlay the abolition of the SEU noted later (*The Guardian*, 6 June 2006, p 15).

At the time of writing, the latest development has been the selection of 40 'Respect Areas', which were seen as having a strong track record in tackling antisocial behaviour and its causes. These areas had signed up to family intervention projects; parenting classes; 'Face the People' sessions; action on antisocial behaviour; and using the Respect Housing Standard. By January 2007, £4 million in funding had been announced for 77 local authorities to employ parenting experts to help families whose children were seen as being involved in, or at risk of, antisocial behaviour. Local authorities were to be issued with a 'Respect Handbook'.[12] In Bolton, for example, it was reported that up to 16 hours a week intensive support was given to families at risk of losing their homes because of antisocial behaviour. The council does not offer 'tea and sympathy', but rather 'challenges parents to put their lives in order, making sure children go to school and that the family's finances, shopping and meals are under control' (*The Guardian*, 23 January 2007, p 5). A further 53 Family Intervention Projects (FIPs) were launched in April 2007. At the most intensive level, families deemed to require supervision and support 24 hours a day stay in a core residential unit. Overall, it was rather late in the day that the Respect Task Force turned to problems around parenting.

Deborah Ghate and Neal Hazel (2002) had earlier provided a helpful overview of research on parenting in poor environments, and on stress, support, and coping. The main question was identifying the correlates of parenting problems. Whereas earlier studies had focused on individual pathology or disease models, or on social inequality and social deprivation, more recent studies had shown that child maltreatment and parenting difficulties were associated with a complex web of interrelated factors in which socio-structural and socio-cultural factors interacted with and exacerbated psychological predispositions to poor parenting. Drawing on an ecological model of parenting, Ghate and Hazel suggested that this provided a framework for understanding how critical factors nested together at four levels: the socio-cultural level, the community level, the family level, and the level of the individual parent or child. Risk factors included living in an impoverished environment characterised by high concentrations of poor families and high levels of social and environmental problems; high levels of poverty and social and material disadvantage at the family and household level; and a diminished capacity to cope with stress at the level of individual characteristics of family members. Nevertheless, there had also been much interest in the concept of resilience, and in those protective factors that enabled some families to cope (Ghate and Hazel, 2002, pp 13-19).

Research studies notwithstanding, tackling antisocial behaviour has thus also become a key issue for the government, drawing on earlier underclass discourses, and in particular on the vocabulary of problem families (Such and Walker, 2005; Squires, 2006). It has been suggested that the withholding of Housing Benefit from people deemed to be antisocial, along with antisocial behaviour legislation, marks a subtle change in the role of the welfare state. Rodger has gone so far as to argue that 'the broad social policy agenda aimed at combating social exclusion is, increasingly, being re-framed in terms of the management of problem populations' (Rodger, 2006, p 124). The idea of segregating and re-educating dysfunctional families provides a good example of this approach. Similar revised constructions of the child and childhood, and new relationships between parents, children, and the state, are apparent in Scotland (Tisdall, 2006). Some of this work has drawn on research by psychiatrists and criminologists (Rutter, Farrington) originally fostered by the Research Programme. Moreover, it has gained prominence in the wider context of a moral panic about young people, with claims that there has been a serious rift between children and adults, one not witnessed in comparable European countries (*The Times*, 3 November 2006, p 4).

The revival of transmitted deprivation

As early as 2004, there were signs that the focus on social exclusion was perceived as misdirected. Yvette Cooper, then a minister in the Office of the Deputy Prime Minister (ODPM), suggested that the promotion of a communitarian notion of inclusion was not enough; long-term inherited inequalities had to be tackled too. Child poverty remained a significant problem, and the focus on the root causes of exclusion – unemployment, poverty, and early childhood opportunities – had to be sustained. Nevertheless, with hindsight more interesting was Cooper's image of inequalities cascading from one generation to the next, and what she variously termed 'inherited disadvantage' or 'inherited class injustices' (*The Guardian*, 22 March 2004). Moreover, the *Breaking the cycle* report (ODPM, 2004) that took stock of seven years of the work of the SEU focused much more than previously on the factors that allegedly transmitted poverty and disadvantage from one generation to the next. The main causes and consequences were:

> poverty and low income, unemployment, poor educational attainment, poor mental or physical health, family breakdown and poor parenting, poor housing and homelessness, discrimination, crime, and living in a disadvantaged area. (SEU, 2004, p 3)

The focus was much more on children, social capital, an alleged cycle of disadvantage, intergenerational transmission, and the most disadvantaged. This was interpreted as meaning that many of the people with the greatest and most complex needs had benefited least from efforts to tackle social exclusion (*The Guardian*, 14 September 2004).

Interestingly if not particularly surprisingly, the backing by the Conservative Party in April 2006 of the goal to end child poverty by 2020 was couched in similar language (*The Guardian*, 11 April 2006, p 26). Oliver Letwin, then the Conservative Party's Head of Policy, argued that the Party was committing itself to a programme of social justice.

The first step towards formulating policies was to recognise the true nature of the challenge. Although 700,000 children had been lifted out of poverty since 1997, there had been no substantial progress towards improving the plight of the worst-off. Moreover, he continued:

> This deep deprivation is all too often passed down the generations … successive governments have failed to end this cycle. This is the real challenge. If we don't empower people to break free from this trap, we will not end child poverty by 2020, or any other date. (*The Guardian*, 11 April 2006, pp 4, 26)

It was not a problem that could be solved by money alone; he praised the efforts of social entrepreneurs who were the heroes of the fight to liberate people from the 'cycle of multiple deprivation'. Letwin ended by stating that 'we have to begin the great debate that, as a country, we have been shy of having – the debate over the causes and cures of the cycle of deprivation' (*The Guardian*, 11 April 2006, pp 4, 26).

In February 2006, Blair argued that the government had to do more to tackle social exclusion, saying:

> We must be honest. For some, those who from generation to generation, are brought up in workless households in poor estates, often poorly educated and frankly sometimes poorly parented the rising tide has not helped lift them. (*The Financial Times*, 25-26 February 2006, p 2)

The interim evaluation of Sure Start was critical, appearing to lead to an acknowledgement by government that it had failed the socially excluded. Tony Blair was reported as saying that:

> When we started Sure Start – I was always a bit sceptical that in the end that we could do this – there was an idea it would lift all boats on a rising tide. It has not worked like that. Sure Start has been brilliant for those people who have in their own minds decided they want to participate. But the hard to reach families, the ones who are shut out of the system … they are not going to come to places like Sure Start. (*The Guardian*, 16 May 2006, p 13)

In June 2006, the work of the SEU was transferred from the Department of Communities and Local Government to a smaller Taskforce in the

Cabinet Office. It was regarded as having lost its influence since the first term, when it was based in the Cabinet Office and reported to Tony Blair directly. It now focused on preventive work among the most hard-to-reach children and families deemed to have been immune to much of the government's previous social exclusion drives. It was claimed that the *Breaking the cycle* stocktake had shown that some groups continued to face poor outcomes and multiple disadvantages. Hilary Armstrong, Cabinet Minister for Social Exclusion, was reported as acknowledging that the SEU programmes had failed to reach some of the poorest, most isolated, and vulnerable families. The work was to be trained on the 'high harm, high risk and high lifetime cost families', with the aim of intervening as soon as they appeared at risk of exclusion, breakdown, or criminal behaviour (*The Guardian*, 13 June 2006, p 14). Part of the work was to support the efforts of the Respect Unit, with improved programmes to help 'prevent the problem families of tomorrow'.[13]

A further push on social exclusion came in September 2006, in the JRF speech that followed a Chequers seminar. Four issues identified as challenges were: halving teenage pregnancies by 2010; supporting children in care; tackling chaotic parenting through the proposed National Parenting Academy, the extension of parenting orders, and a network of family support schemes; and helping benefit claimants with mental illnesses (*The Guardian*, 30 August 2006, p 8). In an interview with the BBC on 31 August, Blair defined those he was talking about variously as people with multiple problems, families where identification and intervention came too late, hard-to-reach families, or dysfunctional families. As in the social exclusion speeches in 1997, the problems that these families faced were perceived as being not simply about low income. But the key point was that there was now a belief that it was possible to predict, with reasonable accuracy, those families who were going to prove troublesome in the future. Action might even be taken pre-birth if necessary as families with alcohol and drug problems were being identified too late. Blair told the BBC interviewer:

> If we are not prepared to predict and intervene far more early then there are children that are going to grow up in families that we know perfectly well are completely dysfunctional and the kids a few years down the line are going to be a menace to society and actually a threat to themselves.[14]

He reiterated that more general forms of intervention, such as Sure Start, had not proved to be a rising tide that would lift all boats, and it was not just a problem of poverty (*The Guardian*, 1 September 2006, p 5).

In the JRF speech in York on 5 September Blair's thesis was that 'some aspects of social exclusion are deeply intractable. The most socially excluded are very hard to reach. Their problems are multiple, entrenched and often passed down the generations'.[15] Previously the debate had been divided into two camps – those who argued that the answer was to improve the material poverty of such families, and those who said that the families themselves were the problem – but while for some families material poverty was the root of their problems, for others it was the result of a multiplicity of lifestyle issues. Moreover, the success of measures to tackle child poverty, reduce unemployment, and improve public services meant that the persistent exclusion of a small minority stood out. Blair stated:

> About 2.5% of every generation seem to be stuck in a life-time of disadvantage and amongst them are the excluded of the excluded, the deeply excluded. Their poverty is, not just poverty of income, but poverty of aspiration, of opportunity, of prospects of advancement.[16]

Health visitors and midwives would seek to identify those most at risk, and for these children a two-year visiting programme would be put in place; on teenage pregnancy an expanded media campaign would be begun, and better access to contraceptives provided. Overall, where children were involved and in danger of harm, or where people were a risk to themselves or others, it was a duty not to stand aside: 'their fate is our business'.[17] Blair suggested that this was about coupling rights with responsibilities, acknowledging that both individual agency and structural causes were relevant (Welshman, 2006b).

Reporting of the speech the following day was limited because of speculation about Blair's departure date as Prime Minister (*The Guardian*, 6 September 2006, p 11; *Society Guardian*, 6 September 2006, p 3). But what were interesting were the six expert papers that were published to coincide with the speech. Three were papers that focused on the history of poverty and policy, and on conventional approaches to poverty (Howard Glennerster; Suzanne Fitzpatrick; and Donald Hirsch). Two explored childhood risk factors, risk-focused prevention, and identifying children at risk of high cost or harm adult outcomes (David Farrington; Leon Feinstein; and Ricardo Sabates). And one simply offered some first thoughts on exclusion and a broader agenda

(Peter Kenway).[18] In the content of the speech itself, the focus on those left behind by rising living standards and improved public services, and the selective use of evidence to support its arguments there were many similarities with the Joseph cycle speech. Indeed the involvement of David Farrington was a direct continuity, since he had worked with Donald West on some of the early Cambridge delinquency projects, as part of the Research Programme. Overall, the focus of government policies on social exclusion had moved to a more interventionist focus on those deemed hard to reach in earlier programmes, or what was perceived as a hard-core underclass.

In the government's Action Plan on Social Exclusion, published in September 2006 (HM Government, 2006), much more detail was given about why individuals and families allegedly remained socially excluded despite government policies on poverty and unemployment, and what should be done about it. In his preface, Tony Blair wrote that it examined:

> why, despite the huge progress we have made, there are still individuals and families who are cut off. About 2.5% of every generation seem to be stuck in a lifetime of disadvantage. Their problems are multiple, entrenched and often passed down through generations. (HM Government, 2006, p 3)

Many of the key points had been trailed in the York speech. Thus the Action Plan argued that because of increasing affluence and government efforts to reduce poverty, 'the persistent and deep-seated exclusion of a small minority has come to stand out ever more dramatically' (HM Government, 2006, p 13). International evidence had shown that around 2.7% of 15-year-olds could be described as having multiple problems. Nonetheless, understanding of risk and protective factors for outcomes perceived as negative had become more sophisticated and had the potential to identify warning signs early. It was the individuals and families who had failed to benefit from the improvements and opportunities available who tended to be caught 'in the deepest cycles of deprivation and disadvantage' (HM Government, 2006, p 19). The barriers were not only economic, but social and cultural. This meant focusing on 'deep exclusion as well as wide exclusion' (HM Government, 2006, p 20).

The report was underpinned by the belief that through early identification, support, and preventive action, problems could be tackled before they became entrenched and blighted the lives of both individuals and the wider society. Longitudinal research had revealed more about risk and protective factors. What was advocated was a lifetime approach. For example, it was suggested that international evidence indicated that intensive health-led home visiting during pregnancy and the first two years of life could radically improve outcomes for both mother and child, particularly in the most at-risk families (Olds, 2006). In childhood and the teenage years, the focus was on children in care and on teenage pregnancy. Finally, in the adult years, it was on people 'with chaotic lives and multiple needs', including those with severe mental health problems. These were people who 'become parents who are unable to parent effectively, therefore perpetuating the cycle of problems in their children' (HM Government, 2006, p 72). Overall, it was claimed that it was because of the success in tackling poverty and disadvantage that the most disadvantaged and persistently excluded groups had become more visible. It had become apparent that what worked for the vast majority of disadvantaged groups might not work for the most hard-to-reach individuals (HM Government, 2006, p 84). The report was peppered with the phrases 'cycle of deprivation', 'hard to reach', 'the intergenerational cycle of disadvantage', and 'chronic exclusion'.

At the time of writing, reviews of progress on social exclusion since *Reaching out* (Cabinet Office, Social Exclusion Taskforce, 2007) have been careful to stress the growth in household income, and improvements in employment, education, disadvantaged areas, health, and housing. This means that the perceived priorities are the poorest households, early intervention, and the life-cycle approach. Parenting has moved centre stage, since 'many of [the] adults suffering multiple problems are already parents (or may become parents), who are unable to parent properly and therefore perpetuate the cycle of problems in their children' (Cabinet Office, Social Exclusion Taskforce, 2007, p 7). The Social Exclusion Task Force was leading a cross-Whitehall review on excluded and at-risk families, exploring how intergenerational cycles of exclusion could end up resulting in problematic behaviour. This 'Families at Risk Review' was due to be completed in the summer of 2007. In the meantime, the Nurse–Family Partnership Programme was launched in May. First-time mothers would be assigned a health visitor 16-20 weeks into their pregnancy, and have weekly or fortnightly visits until the child was aged two. The government was 'prepared to single out babies still in the womb to break cycles of deprivation and behaviour' (*The Guardian*, 16 May 2007, p1). The shift to cycles of disadvantage, by Rutter and Madge, had been reversed.

Conclusion

In this chapter, and in order to trace continuities and changes, the focus has been on the way that New Labour has chosen to tackle social exclusion and child poverty. The chapter has therefore looked at policies on child poverty, relating these to CASE research and to work on poverty dynamics, and looking in particular at the Sure Start initiative. It has located these within the context of the concept of social exclusion explored in Chapter Seven, but has also looked at other pressures, most notably those around antisocial behaviour. In terms of the issue of child health, on the one hand, New Labour has made a commitment to ending child poverty, and shown a recognition of the role of structural factors. But on the other hand, the emphasis on the cycle of disadvantage in the Sure Start initiative, and the stress given to the transmission of poverty between generations, shows how the Blair government has drawn on aspects of the earlier cycle of deprivation debate. Powerful critiques of social exclusion have been mounted by Levitas and others. The chapter has argued that the emphasis on these, along with the focus on transmission mechanisms and intergenerational continuities, point to marked similarities with the 1970s' debate over transmitted deprivation.

Recent initiatives on social exclusion, as detailed in the chapter, now mean that these continuities are much stronger than ever before. They were most marked in the renewed push on social exclusion, from September 2006, where the key elements – the belief in the paradox of the persistence of deprivation in the midst of rising living standards and developing welfare services; the focus on intergenerational continuities; the enumeration of problem individuals and groups; the significance attached to early intervention; and the claim that these are supported by evidence and academic research – were all there in Joseph's speech of 34 years earlier. If the texts of the two speeches are placed alongside each other, it is very difficult to tell which was Joseph, and which is Blair. Blair's advisers could have saved themselves a good deal of trouble had they simply turned to the Joseph speech, or dusted off some of the books that came out of the Research Programme. In the final chapter, the Conclusion, we look again at the three parts of the book – the cycle of deprivation speech, the Research Programme itself, and more recent debates about child poverty and social exclusion – and attempt to draw these threads together.

Notes

[1] www.cabinet-office.gov.uk/seu (accessed 24 March 2000).

[2] www.cabinet-office.gov.uk/seu (accessed 24 March 2000).

[3] www.cabinet-office.gov.uk/seu (accessed 24 March 2000).

[4] www.cabinet-office.gov.uk/seu (accessed 24 March 2000).

[5] www.cabinet-office.gov.uk/seu (accessed 24 March 2000).

[6] www.cabinet-office.gov.uk/seu (accessed 24 March 2000).

[7] www.cabinet-office.gov.uk/seu (accessed 24 March 2000).

[8] *Sure Start: Making a difference for children and families*, pp 3–8. Available at www.surestart.gov.uk

[9] *Sure Start: Making a difference for children and families*, p 4. Available at www.surestart.gov.uk

[10] *National evaluation of Sure Start: Methodology report executive summary*, pp 1–2. Available at www.ness.org.uk (accessed 26 May 2006).

[11] www.news.bbc.co.uk (accessed 25 May 2005).

[12] www.respect.gov.uk (accessed 31 January 2007).

[13] www.cabinetoffice.gov.uk (accessed 16 June 2006).

[14] T. Blair, 'Interview with BBC on social exclusion', 31 August 2006, www.pm.gov.uk (accessed 6 September 2006).

[15] T. Blair, 'Our nation's future: social exclusion', 5 September 2006, www.pm.gov.uk (accessed 6 September 2006).

[16] T. Blair, 'Our nation's future: social exclusion', 5 September 2006, www.pm.gov.uk (accessed 6 September 2006).

[17] T. Blair, 'Our nation's future: social exclusion', 5 September 2006, www.pm.gov.uk (accessed 6 September 2006).

[18] T. Blair, 'Our nation's future: social exclusion', 5 September 2006, www.pm.gov.uk (accessed 6 September 2006).

Conclusion

This book has been framed by two speeches: the Joseph cycle speech in June 1972, and the Blair social exclusion speech in September 2006. The year 2006 also marked the 30th anniversary of the publication of Rutter and Madge's literature review (Rutter and Madge, 1976). The question is what links them, and what changes and continuities there have been over that 34-year period. This conclusion summarises five areas in which this intellectual history of the cycle speech and Research Programme has added significantly to existing knowledge. As we have seen, interest in the cycle speech and Research Programme has derived from one of the following perspectives: the career of Keith Joseph himself; an interest in the history of underclass stereotypes; research on approaches to poverty, including individualist or behavioural explanations; and arguments around the alleged neglect of agency in postwar social policy. Nevertheless, for the most part, these writers have focused on published sources, most obviously the two best-known products of the Research Programme: Rutter and Madge's literature review (1976) and Brown and Madge's final report (1982).

This book has been underpinned by a historical approach. The main sources available to the historian are the archival materials in the National Archives at Kew; the private papers of Keith Joseph himself and other significant actors; oral interviews with former civil servants and social scientists; published reports including the comparatively well-known Heinemann series; a range of other published documents including those by the SSRC; and contemporary newspapers, periodicals, and academic journals. A historical perspective throws up new and interesting questions, and it is these that this book has explored. First, what were the influences on Keith Joseph himself, in terms of both his own personal history, and the wider policy context, that help to explain the timing and content of the cycle speech? Second, how was the Research Programme set up, and why did it take the direction it did? Third, what was the attitude of the DHSS to the Research Programme, and how did this change as it developed? Fourth, what was the response of social scientists to the cycle hypothesis, and why did many social policy pundits take a deterministic position, which highlighted the relative importance of structural factors, and either ignored or downplayed the significance of behavioural, cultural, or personal characteristics? Fifth, what are the links between the 1970s' research, current interest in intergenerational continuities in poverty, policy initiatives such as Sure Start, and a refocusing of social exclusion on specific individuals and families?

Clearly Joseph was very closely identified with the cycle of deprivation hypothesis, through his famous speech to the Pre-School Playgroups Association, in June 1972, as Secretary of State for Social Services. In explaining its timing and content, Joseph's own background, his genuine concern with poverty, and the concept of the problem family all played a part. His biographers, Andrew Denham and Mark Garnett, provide numerous examples of his charity work and genuine concern with poverty and the homeless, which included the founding of the Mulberry Trust housing association and support for the CPAG. In interviews, Joseph admitted his sense of guilt over his privileged upbringing and affluent family background. When it came to the family, a further factor was his happy home life with his first wife and four children, and his traditional views over the respective roles of parents.

Nevertheless, while there is no doubt Joseph was genuinely concerned about poverty, and while he was sympathetic to the genteel poor, especially older people and those with disabilities, he regarded the low paid and the unemployed – the non-disabled poor – as problems. His speeches are peppered with arguments about the deserving and undeserving poor; cases of malingering and benefit fraud; and unemployables. In particular, Joseph's interest in low-income families was of a particular kind, and closely bound up with the concept of the problem family. This essentially behavioural explanation of poverty and deprivation, which emphasised household squalor and inadequate parenting, exercised an important influence over public health doctors, social workers, and voluntary organisations in the 1940-70 period. In 1966, for example, Joseph had included among categories of need, problem families whose poverty was not caused primarily by lack of income, but by difficulties in managing money and in using welfare services. However, while Joseph was influenced by the problem family literature, he was at the same time unaware of the important critiques that had been mounted against it. As Denham and Garnett (2001a, p xiv) have noted, Joseph was a man of academic enthusiasms, but showed little sign of the scepticism normally associated with the term 'intellectual'. In these ways, along with the better-known Edgbaston speech, Joseph's cycle hypothesis illustrates marked continuities between late 19th- and late 20th-century thought on poverty, placing it squarely within the longer-term history of recurring underclass stereotypes over the past 120 years.

While Joseph's personal history and view of poverty are clearly important, the broader policy context is also relevant. The timing of the cycle speech has been related to the rediscovery of poverty in both Britain and the US, and situated within a combination of reformist social engineering (evident in debates about educational disadvantage) and a more conservative 'social pathology' interpretation, which emphasised cultural deprivation. But contemporary documents reveal more explicit connections with the US Head Start programme. The work of Urie Bronfenbrenner, for example, was cited by Joseph in the cycle speech, and the American academic was involved in some of the early cycle seminars. Bronfenbrenner had played an important part in the setting up and subsequent evaluation of the Head Start projects. Moreover, in the autumn of 1972, the British team, which included Tessa Blackstone, Joan Cooper, and Geoffrey Otton, paid the visit to the US, sponsored by the Ford Foundation, to look at programmes for pre-school education, including Head Start. In the event, their report was tentative about the possible role of pre-school education and care in breaking an alleged cycle of deprivation (Blackstone, 1973). Nevertheless, these connections provide much evidence on processes of policy transfer that are themselves intriguing in light of Sure Start. Overall, the speech can be seen to have had complex origins in terms of Joseph's personality and the broader policy context, in the past and the present, in both Britain and the US.

The existing secondary accounts of the Research Programme, by Richard Berthoud (1983a) and Alan Deacon (2002a), have been based on the three published progress reports by the Joint Working Party, and on the studies from the Research Programme itself, notably Rutter and Madge's literature review (1976) and Brown and Madge's final report (1982). Arguably, attempting to find out 'what really happened' is an enterprise doomed to failure in a postmodernist age. Nevertheless, it is clear that a full understanding of the direction taken by the Research Programme, and in particular the shift from the behavioural focus of the cycle hypothesis to the structural emphasis of many of the researchers, is only possible through analysis of the available archival sources, supplemented by oral interviews. These materials shed new light on tensions within the DHSS–SSRC Joint Working Party, between the social scientists, and with the researchers and the DHSS civil servants. They also reveal the broader political context for the Research Programme, following the election of the Labour government in March 1974.

The archival sources make it possible to trace the setting up of the Research Programme, showing, for instance, that discussions between the DHSS and SSRC were under way in the spring of 1972, well before the cycle speech, and illustrating, through early working papers, differences about how deprivation might be defined. One question that the archival sources open up is that of the significance of the broader political context, in dictating the shift from the original behavioural emphasis of the cycle to the more structural focus of the Research Programme. The minutes of the meetings of the Joint Working Party and other materials illustrate important changes of personnel, such as the impact of the appointment to the Joint Working Party of Muriel Brown, Dennis Marsden, and Adrian Webb. Moreover, minutes and referees' reports indicate anxieties about the Research Programme that are largely glossed over in the final report. The internal report by the Organising Group, for instance, admitted that it had found it very hard to keep a clear view of the funding over the life of the Research Programme as a whole. The initial strategy of issuing an invitation to researchers had led to an imbalance where most of the proposed work emphasised familial processes and child development. While efforts had been made to correct that, it was still difficult to find good researchers interested in socioeconomic or social policy perspectives.

It is clear that the Research Programme departed dramatically from Joseph's original thesis. A cycle of deprivation that was essentially a behavioural interpretation of poverty, which stressed the importance of intergenerational continuities, became instead a cycles of disadvantage concept that was concerned more with structural factors and emphasised the discontinuities in the experiences of families. There were a variety of factors at work here, to do with the approach of the SSRC; differences between members relating to their disciplinary backgrounds; the influence of the literature review itself; and the broader political context after March 1974. What were the longer-term implications of the Research Programme? We noted earlier that, for the ESRC, the issue of childhood disadvantage was to an extent put aside, and the focus moved to inequalities in health, ultimately in the Health Variations Programme (1997-2001). Researchers such as Mildred Blaxter saw the Research Programme as one of the first to include qualitative methods, in an attempt at theory building and testing, and traced continuities in 'soft versions' of behavioural theories about the causes of inequality, in the work of Jocelyn Cornwall and Hilary Graham and others (Blaxter, 2004, p 56). Blaxter later reflected that 'it was more important for all the things that it did throw up that have been taken on in different ways, than what it actually concluded about transmitted deprivation'.[1] The ESRC certainly began to think increasingly in terms of directed programmes. Nevertheless, it is also arguable that insufficient attempts were made at evaluating the Research Programme at the time, with the result that the ESRC, aware of the weaknesses of the responsive mode, has perhaps gone too far in the opposite direction.[2]

If the Research Programme offers insights into the relationship between government and the management of social science research, its most severe critics were within the DHSS. It was a Joint DHSS–SSRC Working Party, with the DHSS providing the funding that organised the Research Programme. There were seven DHSS representatives on the Joint Working Party, including two each from the Local Authorities Social Services Division, the Social Work Services Division, and the Research Management Division. What is interesting is those divisions of the DHSS that were involved with the Research Programme: Social Services and Social Work, rather than Social Security. However, while the published reports show the composition of the Joint Working Party, the internal department files reveal the stance of the DHSS much more explicitly. Differences between the SSRC and the DHSS were apparent from the outset, particularly over the relevance of the Research Programme to policy. The DHSS was more inclined than the SSRC to see the Research Programme as both a major research exercise, and an experiment in post-Rothschild cooperation. Nevertheless, while individual DHSS members suggested that the SSRC should act as contractors, some shared Joseph's later antagonism to social science. As the research got under way, there is no doubt that day-to-day relationships between the DHSS and SSRC were difficult. The DHSS was concerned, for example, that the role of the Organising Group, and the procedures of the Chair, meant that some research had been funded that had not been subject to close scrutiny. There was also disquiet about the published progress reports. Yet DHSS civil servants were also scornful of attempts to give the Research Programme greater intellectual coherence. Moreover, in a period when there was increasing pressure on resources, there were doubts about the relevance of the cycle to policy. The result was that by the spring of 1977 the DHSS was playing a smaller part in the Working Party. These concerns came to a head over arrangements for the final report on the Programme as a whole. Many academics approached to help Muriel Brown and Nicola Madge with the final report had declined, and referees had been critical of several of the studies. Most strident, as we have seen, was Alice Sheridan.

As Richard Berthoud (1983a) has noted, the DHSS did see 'the problem' as one of individuals and the personal social services, whereas the SSRC saw it as one suitable for broader social scientific analysis. But the archival evidence reveals more deep-seated DHSS scepticism about the Research Programme as a whole, partly because it was more familiar with social surveys than with qualitative methodology or ethnographic fieldwork. Civil servants felt that Joseph's emphasis on the cycle of deprivation thesis was largely a personal crusade, and ministerial support evaporated following the election of the 1974 Labour government. Moreover, as already noted, it was not clear that the most appropriate parts of the DHSS were involved, since the Social Security Division remained outside the Research Programme. Perhaps most importantly, the DHSS members were essentially concerned throughout with the policy implications of the research, and saw the conclusions of the final report as being impractically broad and unrealistic. What were the long-term implications for DHSS involvement in research projects? As Chief Scientist, Sir Douglas Black was involved in discussions regarding DHSS misgivings about the value of the Research Programme. It seems highly probable, therefore, that the experience of the DHSS affected its involvement in the Black Report (DHSS, 1980) on inequalities in health.

Richard Berthoud has argued that the cycle hypothesis was fundamental to an understanding of the relationship between individuals and institutions in the social structure, and a test of the ability of social scientists to contribute to a real debate. Like Berthoud, Deacon (2003, p 132) argues that many social scientists did not respond to the challenge of the Research Programme, regarding Joseph's research agenda as at best a red herring and at worst a distraction from the much more important issue of the generation and persistence of inequalities. There is certainly evidence that many if not most social scientists favoured a structural explanation. The best-known examples are Bill Jordan and Bob Holman. However, adopting a collective biography approach to other social scientists who were hostile to the cycle hypothesis, or at best marginal to the Research Programme, reveals more about why they adopted the stance that they did. If we look at the work of Harriett Wilson, Adrian Sinfield, and Peter Townsend, for example, there are marked similarities in the approach that they took, along with direct personal links. First, many had taken the Diploma in Social Administration at the LSE in the early 1960s, along with placements with FSUs. They had been greatly attracted to, and deeply influenced by, the Fabian outlook of their teachers – Richard Titmuss, Peter Townsend, and Brian Abel-Smith – and for many this led to a lifelong commitment. Second, many were reacting against the emphasis in social work on casework, and attempting to counter the problem family stereotypes current in the 1950s and early 1960s. Third, through their research, whether on the socialisation of children, long-term unemployment, or different theories of the causes of poverty, they were concerned with the question of the relationship between behaviour and wider structural constraints. Fourth, Sinfield in particular had direct experience of the US 'War on Poverty', the impact of Oscar Lewis's culture of poverty theory, and the US literature on blaming the victim. Overall, their point of view was not that they regarded people in poverty as victims, whether passive or not, but that structural or simply external factors were the primary ones that explained their poverty, not their behaviour.

This was not the whole story of course, and the work of others, such as Herbert Gans in the US and A. H. Halsey in the UK, had shown a willingness to engage with both structural and cultural explanations. Ethnographic and anthropological fieldwork in the US had come to view culture as an adaptive response to environmental factors; and the experience of the EPAs had thrown these debates into relief. What appears to have happened is that this more subtle analysis became marginalised by the structural emphasis of much of the social policy community, especially after the famous Peter Townsend (1974) paper. There was a difference, of course, between hostility to ideology on the one hand, and the attractions of research funding on the other, and the literature review did help to draw social scientists in. It has been claimed that by then the die had largely been cast, and attitudes hardened in the late 1970s, with the publication of the early CDP reports, evidence of growing inequality, and rising unemployment. However, it is also important to look at what was going on in the early 1970s and in 1972 itself, when rising unemployment, the introduction of FIS, and broader policies on family planning all played a part in determining the response of some social scientists. While many authors argue that the cycle of deprivation hypothesis was tested in the Research Programme and found wanting, it would be more correct to say that it was ignored or subverted by many researchers, particularly those from social policy backgrounds. It was left to others to grapple with what they termed personal and economic factors, and it is only more recently that the debate about agency and structure has become a major theme in social policy. Nevertheless, the year 1972 was as important in its own right as the late 1970s and early 1980s, the dating of ideological shifts needs to be moved earlier, to the early 1970s, and the idea of a quasi-Titmuss paradigm itself requires investigation.

In terms of the cycle of deprivation hypothesis, research by psychiatrists and psychologists since 1972 has revealed a much clearer sense of continuities and discontinuities, indicating that parental failure is only one component in psychosocial problems. Research has demonstrated that there is substantial intergenerational continuity, and that the continuities are more marked for the more severe problems than for the minor ones, but also that there are marked discontinuities. It has also demonstrated that resilience helps to explain individual differences, and that the continuities are greater looking backwards than looking forwards. Moreover, much more is known now about mediating processes, both within the family (such as poor parenting), and outside the family (such as overall living conditions), and these point to a synergistic interaction between them. Thus this research points to an interplay between risk and protective processes, and between different degrees of risk mechanisms, and is much more cautious about assigning causes to what are recognised as multifactorial disorders.[3]

Similarly, from the perspective of social policy, there have been major theoretical steps forward and methodological breakthroughs. The concept of social exclusion has been a major theoretical advance, deriving from European work on disadvantage, and recognising the value of a dynamic and relational approach to poverty. Critiques have been relatively slow to appear, but have focused on the privileging of paid work, the difficulties in operationalising the concept, and the wide-ranging indicators that have been chosen. The results of data from life-course perspectives, changes in income dynamics from one year to the next, and from intergenerational studies of the transmission of economic status have all had a major impact on understanding. Cohort studies such as the NCDS, for example, have demonstrated strong continuities and pervasive influences between childhood antecedents and adult outcomes. Moreover, this is an area of public policy where the links between academic research and policy initiatives seem particularly clear. What seems to have had the greatest impact on policy at the birth of Sure Start was the research on childhood disadvantage and intergenerational transmissions of economic status, which was quickly adopted in Treasury documents and the annual poverty reports (Machin, 1998).

In terms of knowing what works, in terms of policy initiatives, academics are helping to assess the impact of Sure Start, although the interim evaluation was critical. On the credit side, there are clearly major advances, in terms of the approach that the current government has taken to child poverty. Through an eclectic mix of earlier policies, New Labour has clearly arrived at an understanding of poverty that is both structural and behavioural. Major resources have been poured into changes to the tax and benefit system, to initiatives such as Sure Start, and to the creation of Children's Centres. The main problem has been that, as in the Research Programme of the 1970s, researchers still tend, for the most part, to study solely psychological factors, or solely economic ones. Dichotomies are more attractive to politicians and civil servants seeking solutions, and in terms of policy the picture is more mixed. Alongside these undoubted achievements, there have been more fundamental underlying continuities. The *Breaking the cycle* report by the SEU, for example, refers to an intergenerational cycle of deprivation, along with the transmission and inheritance of disadvantage (ODPM, 2004).

Moreover, alongside the focus on social exclusion has been the parallel rhetoric of antisocial behaviour, with its explicit problem family vocabulary. The SEU has been closed down, and its work transferred to a smaller taskforce in the Cabinet Office; social exclusion work is to be trained on the 'high harm, high risk and high lifetime cost families', with the aim of intervening in such families as soon as they appear at risk of exclusion, breakdown, or criminal behaviour. These continuities were most marked in Blair's social exclusion speech in September 2006, where the main elements – the focus on those left behind by growing affluence and government efforts to tackle poverty; the identification of problem individuals and families; the belief in early intervention; the focus on intergenerational continuities; and the reliance on health visitors – were indistinguishable from the Joseph cycle speech of 34 years earlier. What seems to have created the space in which these debates can occur, is the relatively early stage of knowledge about pathways and mechanisms, and the broader relationship between agency, structure, and behaviour.

The persistence of the vocabulary of problem family, cycle of deprivation, intergenerational continuity and transmitted deprivation offers an opportunity to take stock of the debate over the cycle of deprivation, to look backwards and to look forwards, and to think about what has really been achieved, in both the academic world and the policy arena, since 1972. Researchers have continued to deepen and refine our understanding of intergenerational continuities, and the role of mediating processes. Nevertheless, their understandable reluctance to offer answers around causal processes, or more specifically to do with pathways and mechanisms, has created a space in which alternative policy prescriptions can flourish. This means that alongside the focus on social exclusion, child poverty, and intergenerational continuities in economic status, there is a parallel and increasing emphasis on antisocial behaviour, parenting, and problem families. Arguably, what comes over most strongly from a review of the period 1972-2007 is the persistence of dichotomies – between continuity and discontinuity; between intra-familial and extra-familial factors; between social scientists and psychologists; between research and policy; and between individuals and institutions. If this book has documented and analysed the cycle speech and Transmitted Deprivation Research Programme, and has helped to place current policies on social exclusion in historical perspective, it will have served its purpose.

Notes

[1] Interview between the author and Mildred Blaxter, Bristol, 12 September 2006.

[2] Interview between the author and Tony Atkinson, Paris, 18 April 2006.

[3] Michael Rutter, 'Keith Joseph's claim on transmitted deprivation and what followed from it', paper given at the 'Cycles of disadvantage' conference, St Catherine's College, Oxford, 21 July 2006.

References

Archives
National Archives, Kew, London
  BS 7/656–7
  BS 13/156, 163, 179, 183, 188–9, 229–30
  ED 207/100
  MH 152/72–90
  MH 166/997, 1515–18

ESRC, Polaris House, North Star Avenue, Swindon
  RB 2 series (mostly transferred to Kew)

Interviews
Tony Atkinson, Paris, 18 April 2006
Richard Berthoud, University of Essex, 2 May 2006
Tessa Blackstone, London, 6 July 2006
Mildred Blaxter, Bristol, 12 September 2006
Muriel Brown, Bristol, 7 July 2006
Alan Clarke, London, 24 May 2006
Frank Coffield, Newcastle upon Tyne, 8 April 2003
Raymond Illsley, Box Hill, Wiltshire, 13 September 2006
Nicola Madge, London, 3 May 2006
Robin Matthews, Cambridge, 25 May 2006
Geoffrey Otton, Bromley, Kent, 4 May 2006
Michael Rutter, London, 4 July 2006
Adrian Sinfield, Edinburgh, 26–27 May 2006
Olive Stevenson, Middleton Cheney, Oxfordshire, 20 July 2006
Peter Townsend, London, 3 July 2006
Robin Wendt, Chester, 22 May 2006

Private papers
Muriel Brown papers, Bristol
Keith Joseph papers, Conservative Party Archive, Bodleian Library,
  Broad Street, Oxford
  KJ 8/1–5
  KJ 11/3
Nicola Madge papers, London
Adrian Sinfield papers, Edinburgh (in the possession of the author)

Peter Townsend papers, Albert Sloman Library, University of Essex, Colchester, boxes 3, 6-11, 21-2, 33-4, 62-3, 69, 74

Harriett Wilson papers, Newcastle upon Tyne, 17 boxes and 1 file (currently in the possession of John Veit-Wilson)

Published sources

A framework for government research and development (1972), Cmnd 4814, London: HMSO.

Abel-Smith, B. and Townsend, P. (1965) *The poor and the poorest: A new analysis of the Ministry of Labour's family expenditure surveys of 1953-54 and 1960*, London: Bell.

Adelman, L., Middleton, S. and Ashworth, K. (2003) *Britain's poorest children: Severe and persistent poverty and social exclusion*, London: Save the Children.

Alcock, P. (2002) 'Editorial', *Benefits*, vol 10, no 3, pp 177-8.

Alcock, P. (2005) '"Maximum feasible understanding": lessons from previous wars on poverty', *Social Policy & Society*, vol 4, no 3, pp 321-9.

Allen, J., Cars, G. and Madanipour, A. (1998) 'Introduction', in A. Madanipour, G. Cars and J. Allen (eds) *Social exclusion in European cities: Processes, experiences and responses*, London: Jessica Kingsley, pp 7-19.

An enquiry into the Social Science Research Council by Lord Rothschild (1982), Cmnd 8554, London: HMSO.

Anonymous (1974) 'The exceptions', *New Society*, vol 28, 16 May, p 368.

Ashley, P. (1983) *The money problems of the poor: A literature review*, London: Heinemann.

Atkinson, A. B. (1969) *Poverty in Britain and the reform of social security*, Cambridge: Cambridge University Press.

Atkinson, A. B. (1972) *Unequal shares: Wealth in Britain*, London: Allen Lane The Penguin Press.

Atkinson, A. B., Maynard, A. K. and Trinder, C. G. (1983) *Parents and children: Incomes in two generations*, London: Heinemann.

Attlee, C.R. (1920) *The social worker*, London: Bell.

Bagguley, P. and Mann, K. (1992) 'Idle thieving bastards? Scholarly representations of the "underclass"', *Work, Employment & Society*, vol 6, no 1, pp 113-26.

Bane, M. J. and Ellwood, D. T. (1986) 'Slipping into and out of poverty: the dynamics of spells', *Journal of Human Resources*, vol 21, pp 1-23.

Barnes, M. (2002) 'Social exclusion and the life course', in M. Barnes, C. Heady, S. Middleton, J. Millar, F. Paradopoulis, G. Room and P. Tsakloglou, *Poverty and social exclusion in Europe*, Cheltenham: Edward Elgar, pp 1-23.

Barnes, M. (2005) *Social exclusion in Great Britain: An empirical investigation and comparison with the EU*, Aldershot: Ashgate.

Barnes, M., Heady, C., Middleton, S., Millar, J., Paradopoulis, F., Room, G. and Tsakloglou, P. (2002) *Poverty and social exclusion in Europe*, Cheltenham: Edward Elgar.

Becker, S. and Bryman, A. (eds) (2004) *Understanding research for social policy and practice: Themes, methods and approaches*, Bristol: The Policy Press.

Belsky, J., Melhuish, E., Barnes, J., Leyland, A. H. and Romaniuk, H. (2006) 'Effect of Sure Start local programmes on children and families: early findings from a quasi-experimental, cross sectional study', *British Medical Journal*, vol 332, pp 1476-8.

Berghman, J. (1995) 'Social exclusion in Europe: policy context and analytical framework', in G. Room (ed) *Beyond the threshold*, Bristol: The Policy Press, pp 10-28.

Berthoud, R. (1976) *The disadvantages of inequality: A study of social deprivation*, London: Macdonald and Jane's.

Berthoud, R. (1983a) 'Transmitted deprivation: the kite that failed', *Policy Studies*, vol 3, no 3, pp 151-69.

Berthoud, R. (1983b) 'Who suffers social disadvantage?', in M. Brown (ed) *The structure of disadvantage*, London: Heinemann, pp 14-48.

Beveridge, W. (1942) *Social insurance and allied services: Report by Sir William Beveridge*, Cmd 6404, London: HMSO.

Blackstone, T. (1971) *A fair start: The provision of pre-school education*, London: Allen Lane.

Blackstone, T. (1973) *Education and day care for young children in need: The American experience*, London: Bedford Square Press for the Centre for Studies in Social Policy.

Blair, T. (1999) 'Beveridge revisited: a welfare state for the 21st century', in R. Walker (ed) *Ending child poverty: Popular welfare for the 21st century?*, Bristol: The Policy Press, pp 7-18.

Blanden, J. (2006) 'Cycles of disadvantage', *Poverty*, vol 124, pp 15-17.

Blanden, J., Gregg, P. and Machin, S. (2005) *Intergenerational mobility in Europe and North America: A report supported by the Sutton Trust*, London: Centre for Economic Performance.

Blaxter, M. (1981) *The health of the children: A review of research on the place of health in cycles of disadvantage*, London: Heinemann.

Blaxter, M. (2004) 'Understanding health inequalities: from "transmitted deprivation" to "social capital"', *International Journal of Social Research Methodology*, vol 7, pp 55-9.

Blaxter, M. and Paterson, E. (1982) *Mothers and daughters: A three-generational study of health attitudes and behaviour*, London: Heinemann.

Board of Education and Board of Control (1929) *Report of the Mental Deficiency Committee*, London: HMSO.

Bottoms, A. E. (1974) 'On the decriminalization of English juvenile courts', in R. Hood (ed) *Crime, criminology and public policy: Essays in honour of Sir Leon Radzinowicz*, London: Heinemann, pp 319-45.

Bradshaw, J. (2001) 'Child poverty under Labour', in G. Fimister (ed) *An end in sight? Tackling child poverty in the UK*, London: CPAG, pp 9-27.

Bronfenbrenner, U. (1970, 1972 edn) *Two worlds of childhood: US and USSR*, New York, NY: Simon and Schuster.

Bronfenbrenner, U. (1975) 'Is early intervention effective?', in M. Guttentag and E. L. Struening (eds) *Handbook of evaluation research*, vol 2, Beverly Hills, CA: Sage Publications, pp 519-603.

Brown, M. (1983a) 'Deprivation and social disadvantage', in M. Brown (ed) *The structure of disadvantage*, London: Heinemann, pp 1-13.

Brown, M. (ed) (1983b) *The structure of disadvantage*, London: Heinemann.

Brown, M. and Madge, N. (1982a) *Despite the welfare state: A report on the SSRC–DHSS programme of research into transmitted deprivation*, London: Heinemann.

Brown, M. and Madge, N. (1982b) 'Which way for the welfare state?', *New Society*, vol 61, 8 July, pp 52-4.

Brown, M. and Payne, S. (1969, 7th edn 1990) *Introduction to social administration in Britain*, London: Unwin Hyman.

Burchardt, T. (2000) 'Social exclusion: concepts and evidence', in D. Gordon and P. Townsend (eds) *Breadline Europe*, Bristol: The Policy Press, pp 385-405.

Burchardt, T., Le Grand, J. and Piachaud, D. (1999) 'Social exclusion in Britain 1991–1995', *Social Policy & Administration*, vol 33, no 3, pp 227-44.

Burchardt, T., Le Grand, J. and Piachaud, D. (2002a) 'Introduction', in J. Hills, J. Le Grand and D. Piachaud (eds) *Understanding social exclusion*, Oxford: Oxford University Press, pp 1-12.

Burchardt, T., Le Grand, J. and Piachaud, D. (2002b) 'Degrees of exclusion: developing a dynamic, multidimensional measure', in J. Hills, J. Le Grand and D. Piachaud (eds) *Understanding social exclusion*, Oxford: Oxford University Press, pp 30-43.

Burgess, S. and Propper, C. (1999) 'Poverty in Britain', in P. Gregg and J. Wadsworth (eds) *The state of working Britain*, Manchester: Manchester University Press, pp 259-75.

Burgess, S. and Propper, C. (2002) 'The dynamics of poverty in Britain', in J. Hills, J. Le Grand and D. Piachaud (eds) *Understanding social exclusion*, Oxford: Oxford University Press, pp 44-61.

Burney, E. (2005) *Making people behave: Anti-social behaviour, politics and policy*, Cullompton: Willan.

Byrne, D. (1997) 'Social exclusion and capitalism: the reserve army across time and space', *Critical Social Policy*, vol 17, pp 27-51.

Byrne, D. (1999) *Social exclusion*, Buckingham: Open University Press.

Cabinet Office, Social Exclusion Taskforce (2007) *Reaching out: Progress on social exclusion*, London: Cabinet Office.

CASE (Centre for Analysis of Social Exclusion) and HM Treasury (1999) *Persistent poverty and lifetime inequality: The evidence*, CASEreport 5, HM Treasury Occasional Paper 10, London: CASE/HM Treasury.

Castle, B. (1974) 'The cycle of deprivation – the political challenge', in BASW, *The cycle of deprivation: Papers presented to a national study conference, Manchester University, March, 1974*, Birmingham: BASW, pp 1-7.

Castle, B. (1993) *Fighting all the way*, London: Macmillan.

CDP (Community Development Projects (1977) *Gilding the ghetto: The state and the poverty experiments,* London:CDP.

Central Advisory Council for Education (England) (1967) *Children and their primary schools*, London: HMSO.

Clarke, A. D. B. (1973) 'The prevention of subcultural subnormality: problems and prospects', *British Journal of Subnormality*, vol 19, no 1, pp 7-20.

Clarke, A. D. B. and Clarke, A. M. (1953) 'How constant is the IQ?', *Lancet*, no ii, pp 877-80.

Clarke, A. D. B. and Hermelin, B. F. (1955) 'Adult imbeciles, their abilities and trainability', *Lancet*, no ii, pp 337-9.

Clarke, A. M. and Clarke, A. D. B. (eds) (1958, 3rd edn 1974) *Mental deficiency: The changing outlook*, London: Methuen.

Clarke, J. (1980) 'Social democratic delinquents and Fabian families: a background to the 1969 Children and Young Persons Act', in National Deviancy Conference (ed) *Permissiveness and control: The fate of the sixties legislation*, London: Macmillan, pp 72-95.

Clasen, J., Gould, A. and Vincent, J. (1997) *Long-term unemployment and the threat of social exclusion: A cross-national analysis of the position of long-term unemployed people in Germany, Sweden and Britain*, Bristol: The Policy Press.

Coffield, F. (1975) 'Deprivation in detail', *New Society*, vol 32, 24 April, p 206.

Coffield, F. (1982) *Cycles of deprivation*, Durham: Durham University.

Coffield, F. (1983) '"Like father like son": the family as a potential transmitter of deprivation', in N. Madge (ed) *Families at risk*, London: Heinemann, pp 11–36.

Coffield, F., Robinson, P. and Sarsby, J. (1980) *A cycle of deprivation? A case study of four families*, London: Heinemann.

Colley, H. and Hodkinson, P. (2001) 'Problems with *Bridging the Gap*: the reversal of structure and agency in addressing social exclusion', *Critical Social Policy*, vol 21, no 3, pp 335–59.

Committee on Local Authority and Allied Personal Social Services (1968) *Report of the Committee on Local Authority and Allied Personal Social Services*, the 'Seebohm Report', Cmnd 3703, London: HMSO.

Cook, T. (1983) 'Recycling deprivation', *Social Work Today*, vol 14, no 44, p 20.

Cooper, J. (1983) *The creation of the British personal social services 1962-1974*, London: Heinemann.

Davie, R., Butler, N. and Goldstein, H. (1972) *From birth to seven: A report of the National Child Development Study*, London: Longman/National Children's Bureau.

Deacon, A. (1993) 'Richard Titmuss: 20 years on', *Journal of Social Policy*, vol 22, no 2, pp 235–42.

Deacon, A. (1996) 'The dilemmas of welfare: Titmuss, Murray and Mead', in S. J. D. Green and R. C. Whiting (eds) *The boundaries of the state in modern Britain*, Cambridge: Cambridge University Press, pp 191–212.

Deacon, A. (2000) 'Learning from the US? The influence of American ideas upon "New Labour" thinking on welfare reform', *Policy & Politics*, vol 28, no 1, pp 5–18.

Deacon, A. (2002a) *Perspectives on welfare: Ideas, ideologies and policy debates*, Buckingham: Open University Press.

Deacon, A. (2002b) 'Echoes of Sir Keith? New Labour and the cycle of disadvantage', *Benefits*, vol 10, no 3, pp 179–84.

Deacon, A. (2003) '"Levelling the playing field, activating the players": New Labour and the "cycle of disadvantage"', *Policy & Politics*, vol 31, no 2, pp 123–37.

Deacon, A. (2004) 'Review article: different interpretations of agency within welfare debates', *Social Policy & Society*, vol 3, no 4, pp 447-55.

Deacon, A. and Mann, K. (1999) 'Agency, modernity and social policy', *Journal of Social Policy*, vol 28, no 3, pp 413-35.

Dean, H. and Taylor-Gooby, P. (1992) *Dependency culture: The explosion of a myth*, Hemel Hempstead: Harvester Wheatsheaf.

Dearden, L., Machin, S. and Reed, H. (1997) 'Intergenerational mobility in Britain', *Economic Journal*, vol 107, pp 47-66.

Denham, A. and Garnett, M. (2001a) *Keith Joseph*, Chesham: Acumen.

Denham, A. and Garnett, M. (2001b) 'From "guru" to "godfather": Keith Joseph, "New" Labour and the British Conservative tradition', *Political Quarterly*, vol 72, no 1, pp 97-106.

Denham, A. and Garnett, M. (2002) 'From the "cycle of enrichment" to the "cycle of deprivation": Sir Keith Joseph, "problem families" and the transmission of disadvantage', *Benefits*, vol 10, no 3, pp 193-8.

DES (Department of Education and Science) (1965) *Report of the Committee on Social Studies*, Cmnd 2660, London: HMSO.

Devereux, E. C., Bronfenbrenner, U. and Rodgers, R. R. (1969) 'Child-rearing in England and the United States, a cross-national comparison', *Journal of Marriage and the Family*, vol 31, no 2, pp 257-70.

DHSS (Department of Health and Social Security) (1974a) *The family in society: Preparation for parenthood: An account of consultations with professional, voluntary and other organisations October 1972–February 1973*, London: HMSO.

DHSS (1974b) *The family in society: Dimensions of parenthood: A report of a seminar held at All Souls College, Oxford 10-13 April 1973*, London: HMSO.

DHSS (1976) *Prevention and health – everybody's business: A reassessment of public and personal health*, London: HMSO.

DHSS (1977) *Priorities in the health and social services: The way forward*, London: HMSO.

DHSS (1980) *Inequalities in health: Report of a research working group*, London: DHSS.

Dolowitz, D. P. (2000) 'Policy transfer: a new framework of policy analysis', in D. P. Dolowitz with R. Hulme, M. Nellis and F. O'Neill, *Policy transfer and British social policy: Learning from the USA?*, Buckingham: Open University Press, pp 9-37.

Donald, D., Hutton, A. and Taylor, P. (1978) 'The temporal stability of deprivation in West Central Scotland: a feasibility study,' London: SSRC (unpublished).

Donnison, D. (1982) *The politics of poverty*, Oxford: Martin Robertson.

Donovan, C. (2001) 'Government policy and the direction of social science research', DPhil thesis, University of Sussex.

Driver, S. and Martell, L. (1998) *New Labour: Politics after Thatcherism*, Cambridge: Polity Press.

DSS (Department of Social Security) (1999) *Opportunity for all: Tackling poverty and social exclusion*, Cm 4445, London: HMSO.

Duncan, G. J. (1984) *Years of poverty years of plenty: The changing economic fortunes of American workers and families*, Ann Arbor, MI: Institute for Social Research.

Duncan, G. and Hill, D. (1974) 'Attitudes, behavior, and economic outcomes: a structural equations approach,', in G. J. Duncan and J. N. Morgan, *Five thousand American families: Patterns of economic progress*, vol 3, Ann Arbor, MI: Institute for Social Research, University of Michigan, pp 61-100.

DWP (Department for Work and Pensions) (2001) *Opportunity for all: Making progress*, Cm 5260, London: HMSO.

EC (European Commission) (1993) *Growth, competitiveness, employment: The challenges and ways forward into the 21st century*, White Paper COM(93) 700, Luxembourg: EC.

Empson, J. (1977) 'Cycles of disadvantage', *British Journal of Psychology*, vol 68, pp 393-4.

ESRC (Economic and Social Research Council) (2005) *SSRC–ESRC: The first forty years*, Swindon: ESRC.

Essen, J. and Wedge, P. (1982) *Continuities in childhood disadvantage*, London: Heinemann.

Etzioni, A. (1993, 1995 edn) *The spirit of community: Rights, responsibilities, and the communitarian agenda*, London: Fontana.

Eysenck, H. (1977) 'Ghostly throng', *New Society*, vol 39, 20 January, pp 138-9.

Fairclough, N. (2000) *New Labour, new language?*, London: Routledge.

Falkingham, J. and Hills, J. (eds) (1995a) *The dynamic of welfare: The welfare state and the life cycle*, Hemel Hempstead: Prentice Hall/Harvester Wheatsheaf.

Falkingham, J. and Hills, J. (1995b) 'Introduction', in J. Falkingham and J. Hills (eds) *The dynamic of welfare: The welfare state and the life cycle*, Hemel Hempstead: Prentice Hall/Harvester Wheatsheaf, pp 1-5.

Field, F. (1974) *Unequal Britain: A report on the cycle of inequality*, London: Arrow Books.

Field, F. (1995) *Making welfare work: Reconstructing welfare for the millennium*, London: Institute of Community Studies.

Field, F. (1996) *Stakeholder welfare*, London: IEA Health and Welfare Unit.

Field, F. (1998) *Reflections on welfare reform*, London: Social Market Foundation.

Flather, P. (1987) '"Pulling through" – conspiracies, counterplots, and how the SSRC escaped the axe in 1982', in M. Bulmer (ed) *Social science research and government: Comparative essays on Britain and the United States*, Cambridge: Cambridge University Press, pp 353-72.

Fuller, R. and Stevenson, O. (1983) *Policies, programmes and disadvantage: A review of literature*, London: Heinemann.

Gazeley, I. (2003) *Poverty in Britain, 1900-1965*, Basingstoke: Palgrave Macmillan.

George, V. N. (1968) *Social security: Beveridge and after*, London: Routledge & Kegan Paul.

Ghate, D. and Hazel, N. (2002) *Parenting in poor environments: Stress, support and coping*, London: Jessica Kingsley.

Giddens, A. (1998) *The third way: The renewal of social democracy*, Cambridge: Polity Press.

Giddens, A. (2000) *The third way and its critics*, Cambridge: Polity Press.

Glennerster, H. (ed) (1983a) *The future of the welfare state: Remaking social policy*, London: Heinemann.

Glennerster, H. (1983b) 'The need for a reappraisal', in H. Glennerster (ed) *The future of the welfare state: Remaking social policy*, London: Heinemann, pp 1-9.

Gordon, D. and Pantazis, C. (1997) 'Measuring poverty: breadline Britain in the 1990s', in D. Gordon and C. Pantazis (eds) *Breadline Britain in the 1990s*, Aldershot: Ashgate, pp 5-47.

Gordon, D. and Spicker, P. (eds) (1999) *The international glossary on poverty*, London: Zed Books.

Graham, H. (ed) (2001) *Understanding health inequalities*, Buckingham: Open University Press.

Gregg, P. and Machin, S. (2001) 'Childhood experiences, educational attainment and adult labour market performance', in K. Vleminckx and T.M. Smeeding (eds) *Child well-being, child poverty and child policy in modern nations: What do we know?*, Bristol: The Policy Press, pp 129-50.

Halcrow, M. (1989) *Keith Joseph: A single mind*, London: Macmillan.

Halsey, A. H. (2004) *A history of sociology in Britain: Science, literature, and society*, Oxford: Oxford University Press.

Haworth, A. and Manzi, T. (1999) 'Managing the "underclass": interpreting the moral discourse of housing management', *Urban Studies*, vol 36, no 1, pp 153–65.

Higgins, J. (1978) *The poverty business: Britain and America*, Oxford: Blackwell.

Hills, J. (2002) 'Does a focus on "social exclusion" change the policy response?', in J. Hills, J. Le Grand and D. Piachaud (eds) *Understanding social exclusion*, Oxford: Oxford University Press, pp 226–43.

Hills, J. (2004) *Inequality and the state*, Oxford: Oxford University Press.

Hills, J. and Stewart, K. (eds) (2005) *A more equal society? New Labour, poverty, inequality and exclusion*, Bristol: The Policy Press.

Hills, J., Le Grand, J. and Piachaud, D. (eds) (2002) *Understanding social exclusion*, Oxford: Oxford University Press.

HM Government (2006) *Reaching out: An action plan on social exclusion*, London: Cabinet Office.

HM Treasury (1999) *Tackling poverty and extending opportunity: The modernisation of Britain's tax and benefit system: Number four*, London: HM Treasury.

Hobcraft, J. (1998a) *Intergenerational and life-course transmission of social exclusion: Influences of childhood poverty, family disruption, and contact with the police*, London: CASE.

Hobcraft, J. (1998b) 'Intergenerational and life-course transmission of social exclusion', in CASE and HM Treasury, *Persistent poverty and lifetime inequality: The evidence*, CASEreport 5, HM Treasury Occasional Paper 10, London: CASE/HM Treasury, pp 115–19.

Hobcraft, J. (2002) 'Social exclusion and the generations', in J. Hills, J. Le Grand and D. Piachaud (eds) *Understanding social exclusion*, Oxford: Oxford University Press, pp 62–83.

Holman, A. (1983) 'Continuities in childhood disadvantage', *British Journal of Social Work*, vol 13, pp 358–9.

Holman, B. (1982) 'After the research', *Community Care*, vol 435, 28 October, pp 22–3.

Holman, R. (1970) *Socially deprived families in Britain*, London: Bedford Square Press.

Holman, R. (1973) 'Poverty: consensus and alternatives', *British Journal of Social Work*, vol 3, no 4, pp 431–46.

Holman, R. (1978) *Poverty: Explanations of social deprivation*, London: Martin Robertson.

Home Office (1960) *Report of the Committee on Children and Young Persons*, Cmnd 1191, London: HMSO.

Home Office (1965) *The child, the family and the young offender*, Cmnd 2742, London: HMSO.

Home Office (1968) *Children in trouble*, Cmnd 3601, London: HMSO.

Home Office/Scottish Education Department (1972) *Report of the Departmental Committee on the Adoption of Children*, Cmnd 5107, London: HMSO.

Hope, K. (nd) 'Intelligence and social mobility', London: SSRC (unpublished).

Howard, A. (1990, 1991 edn) *Crossman: The pursuit of power*, London: Pimlico.

Howarth, C., Kenway, P., Palmer, G. and Miorelli, R. (1999) *Monitoring poverty and social exclusion 1999*, York: Joseph Rowntree Foundation.

Howarth, C., Kenway, P., Palmer, G. and Street, C. (1998) *Monitoring poverty and social exclusion: Labour's inheritance*, York: Joseph Rowntree Foundation.

Howe, G. (1994) *Conflict of loyalty*, London: Macmillan.

Hutton, W. (1995) *The state we're in*, London: Jonathan Cape.

IILS (International Institute for Labour Studies) (1996) *Social exclusion and anti-poverty strategies: Project on the patterns and causes of social exclusion and the design of policies to promote integration: A synthesis of findings*, Geneva: International Labour Organization.

Jarman, B. (1983) 'Identification of underprivileged areas', *British Medical Journal*, vol 286, pp 1705-9.

Jarvis, S. and Jenkins, S. P. (1998a) 'How much income mobility is there in Britain?', *Economic Journal*, vol 108, pp 428-43.

Jarvis, S. and Jenkins, S. P. (1998b) 'Income and poverty dynamics in Great Britain', in L. Leisering and R. Walker (eds) *The dynamics of modern society: Poverty, policy and welfare*, Bristol: The Policy Press, pp 145-60.

Jenkins, S. P. (2000) 'Modelling household income dynamics', *Journal of Population Economics*, vol 13, pp 529-67.

Jensen, A. R. (1969) 'How much can we boost IQ and scholastic achievement?', *Harvard Educational Review*, vol 39, no 1, pp 1-123.

Jones, K. (1973) 'Introduction', in K. Jones (ed) *The year book of social policy in Britain 1972*, London: Routledge & Kegan Paul, pp vii-x.

Jordan, B. (1974) *Poor parents: Social policy and the 'cycle of deprivation'*, London: Routledge & Kegan Paul.

Joseph, K. (1966a) *Social security: The new priorities*, London: Conservative Political Centre.

Joseph, K. (1966b) 'Large families', *New Society*, vol 30, p 7.

Joseph, K. (1974) 'Foreword', in M. Kellmer Pringle, *The needs of children: A personal perspective prepared for the Department of Health and Social Security*, pp 9-10, London: Hutchinson.

Joseph, K. (1859, 1986 edn) 'Introduction', in S. Smiles, *Self-help*, London: Sidgwick & Jackson, pp 7-16.

Joseph, K. and Sumption, J. (1979) *Equality*, London: John Murray.

Joseph, Lord (1990) *Rewards of parenthood? Towards more equitable tax treatment*, London: Centre for Policy Studies.

Joseph, Lord (1991) *The importance of parenting*, London: Centre for Policy Studies.

Kellmer Pringle, M. (1974, 2nd edn 1980) *The needs of children: A personal perspective prepared for the Department of Health and Social Security*, London: Hutchinson.

Kogan, M., Korman, N. and Henkel, M. (1980) *Government's commissioning of research: A case study*, Uxbridge: Brunel University, Department of Government.

Kolvin, I., Miller, F. J. W., Scott, D. McI., Gatzanis, S. R. M. and Fleeting, M. (1990) *Continuities of deprivation? The Newcastle 1000 family study*, Aldershot: Avebury.

Lait, J. (1983) 'Problems of social science', *SSRC Newsletter 48*, p 13.

Le Grand, J. (1997) 'Knights, knaves or pawns? Human behaviour and social policy', *Journal of Social Policy*, vol 26, no 2, pp 149-69.

Le Grand, J. (2003) *Motivation, agency and public policy: Of knights & knaves, pawns & queens*, Oxford: Oxford University Press.

Leadbeater, C. (1999) 'New Labour's secret godfather', *New Statesman*, vol 128, 10 May, pp 13-14.

Leathard, A. (1980) *The fight for family planning: The development of family planning services in Great Britain*, London: Macmillan.

Lee, A. and Hills, J. (1998) *New cycles of disadvantage? Report of a conference organised by CASE on behalf of ESRC for HM Treasury*, London: CASE.

Lee, P. and Murie, A. (1997) *Poverty, housing tenure and social exclusion*, Bristol: The Policy Press.

Leisering, L. and Leibfried, S. (1999) *Time and poverty in western welfare states: United Germany in perspective*, Cambridge: Cambridge University Press.

Leisering, L. and Walker, R. (eds) (1998a) *The dynamics of modern society: Poverty, policy and welfare*, Bristol: The Policy Press.

Leisering, L. and Walker, R. (1998b) 'New realities: the dynamics of modernity', in L. Leisering and R. Walker (eds) *The dynamics of modern society: Poverty, policy and welfare*, Bristol: The Policy Press, pp 3-16.

Leisering, L. and Walker, R. (1998c) ' Making the future: from dynamics to policy agendas', in L. Leisering and R. Walker (eds) *The dynamics of modern society: Poverty, policy and welfare*, Bristol: The Policy Press, pp 265-85.

Levitas, R. (1996) 'The concept of social exclusion and the new Durkheimian hegemony', *Critical Social Policy*, vol 46, pp 5-20.

Levitas, R. (1998) *The inclusive society? Social exclusion and New Labour*, London: Macmillan.

Levitas, R. (2000) 'What is social exclusion?', in D. Gordon and P. Townsend (eds) *Breadline Europe*, Bristol: The Policy Press, pp 357-83.

Levitas, R. (2006) 'The concept and measurement of social exclusion', in C. Pantazis, D. Gordon and R. Levitas (eds) *Poverty and social exclusion in Britain*, Bristol: The Policy Press, pp 123-60.

Lidbetter, E. J. (1933) *Heredity and the social problem group: Volume 1*, London: Edward Arnold.

Liebow, E. (1967) *Tally's corner: A study of negro streetcorner men*, Boston, MA: Little, Brown and Company.

Lister, R. (1982) 'A policy of deprivation', *Health Services*, 17 September.

Lister, R. (ed) (1996) *Charles Murray and the underclass: The developing debate*, London: IEA Health and Welfare Unit.

Lister, R. (2004) *Poverty*, Cambridge: Polity Press.

Littlewood, P. and Herkommer, S. (1999) 'Identifying social exclusion: some problems of meaning', in P. Littlewood, I. Glorieux, S. Herkommer and I. Jonsson (eds) *Social exclusion in Europe: Problems and paradigms*, Aldershot: Ashgate, pp 1-21.

Loney, M. (1983) *Community against government: The British Community Development Project 1968–78 – a study of government incompetence*, London: Heinemann.

Lowe, R. (1996) 'The social policy of the Heath government', in S. Ball and A. Seldon (eds) *The Heath government 1970-1974: A reappraisal*, Harlow: Addison Wesley Longman Group, pp 191-214.

Lowe, R. (2005) *The welfare state in Britain since 1945* (3rd edn), Basingstoke: Palgrave Macmillan.

Lowe, R. and Nicholson, P. (eds) (1995) 'The formation of the Child Poverty Action Group', *Contemporary Record*, vol 9, no 3, pp 612-37.

Macgregor, S. (1981) *The politics of poverty*, Harlow: Longman.

Machin, S. (1998) 'Childhood disadvantage and intergenerational transmissions of economic status', in CASE and HM Treasury, *Persistent poverty and lifetime inequality: The evidence*, CASEreport 5, HM Treasury Occasional Paper 10, London: CASE/HM Treasury, pp 17-21.

Mack, J. and Lansley, S. (1985) *Poor Britain*, London: George Allen & Unwin.

McLaughlin, E. (1996) 'Researching the behavioural effects of welfare systems', in J. Millar and J. Bradshaw (eds) *Social welfare systems:Towards a research agenda*,Bath: University of Bath/ESRC, pp 57-82.

Macnicol, J. (1987) 'In pursuit of the underclass', *Journal of Social Policy*, vol 16, no 3, pp 293-318.

Macnicol, J. (1999) 'From "problem family" to "underclass", 1945-95', in R. Lowe and H. Fawcett (eds) *Welfare policy in Britain: The road from 1945*, London: Macmillan/Institute of Contemporary British History, pp 69-93.

MacQueen, I. A. G. (1969) 'Community education in birth control', *Medical Officer*, 5 December, pp 301-2.

Madanipour, A., Cars, G. and Allen, J. (1998) (eds) *Social exclusion in European cities: Processes, experiences and responses*, London: Jessica Kingsley.

Madge, N. (1978) 'A description and comparison of sub-contracts listed as "familial processes"', London: SSRC (unpublished).

Madge, N. (ed) (1983) *Families at risk*, London: Heinemann.

Mandelson, P. (1997) *Labour's next steps:Tackling social exclusion*, London: Fabian Society.

Mann, K. (1994) 'Watching the defectives: observers of the underclass in the USA, Britain and Australia', *Critical Social Policy*, vol 14, no 2, pp 79-99.

Marquand, D. (1996) 'Moralists and hedonists', in D. Marquand and A. Seldon (eds) *The ideas that shaped post-war Britain*, London: Fontana, pp 5-28.

Marsden, D. (1969) *Mothers alone: Poverty and the fatherless family*, London: Allen Lane.

Marsden, D. (1970) 'Fatherless families on National Assistance', in P. Townsend (ed) *The concept of poverty: Working papers on methods of investigation and life-styles of the poor in different countries*, London: Heinemann, pp 220-35.

Marsden, D. and Duff, E. (1975) *Workless: Some unemployed men and their families*, Harmondsworth: Pelican Books.

Matthews, R. (1975) 'Rothschild and after: 1972-75', *SSRC Newsletter 29*, pp 8-10.

Matthews, R. (1982) 'Rothschild on the Social Science Research Council: some reflections', *Policy Studies*, vol 3, no 1, pp 1-11.

Meredith, S. (2006) 'Mr Crosland's nightmare? New Labour and equality in historical perspective', *British Journal of Politics and International Relations*, vol 8, pp 238-55.

Mishra, R. (1989) 'The academic tradition in social policy: the Titmuss years', in M. Bulmer, J. Lewis and D. Piachaud (eds) *The goals of social policy*, London: Unwin, pp 64-83.

Morgan, J. N., Dickinson, K., Dickinson, J., Benus, J. and Duncan, G. (1974) *Five thousand American families – patterns of economic progress*, vol 1, Ann Arbor, MI: Institute for Social Research, University of Michigan.

Morris, P. (1969) *Put away: A sociological study of institutions for the mentally retarded*, London: Routledge & Kegan Paul.

Mortimore, J. and Blackstone, T. (1982) *Disadvantage and education*, London: Heinemann.

Moynihan, D. P. (1965) *The negro family: The case for national action*, Washington, DC: US Department of Labor.

Murie, A. (1983) *Housing inequality and deprivation*, London: Heinemann.

Murray, C. (1984) *Losing ground: American social policy, 1950-1980*, New York, NY: Basic Books.

Newson, J. and Newson, E. (1968) *Four years old in an urban community*, London: George Allen & Unwin.

O'Connor, A. (2000) 'Poverty research and policy for the post-welfare era', *Annual Review of Sociology*, vol 26, pp 547-62.

O'Connor, A. (2001) *Poverty knowledge: Social science, social policy and the poor in twentieth century US history*, Princeton, NJ: Princeton University Press.

ODNB (*Oxford Dictionary of National Biography*) (2004) Oxford: Oxford University Press.

ODPM (Office of the Deputy Prime Minister) (2004) *Breaking the cycle: Taking stock of progress and priorities for the future: A report by the Social Exclusion Unit*, London: ODPM.

Olds, D. L. (2006) 'The Nurse–Family Partnership: an evidence-based preventive intervention', *Infant Mental Health Journal*, vol 27, no 1, pp 5-25.

Oliver, J. E. (1985) 'Successive generations of child maltreatment: social and medical disorders in the parents', *British Journal of Psychiatry*, vol 147, pp 484-90.

Oliver, J. E. and Cox, J. (1973) 'A family kindred with ill-used children: the burden on the community', *British Journal of Psychiatry*, vol 123, pp 81-90.

Oliver, J. E. and Taylor, A. (1971) 'Five generations of ill-treated children in one family pedigree', *British Journal of Psychiatry*, vol 119, pp 473-80.

Ormerod, P. (2005) 'The impact of Sure Start', *Political Quarterly*, vol 76, no 4, pp 565-7.

Pahl, J. (1983) 'Muriel Brown and Nicola Madge, *Despite the welfare state*', *Journal of Social Policy*, vol 12, pp 548-50.

Papps, P. (1998) 'Anti-social behaviour strategies – individualistic or holistic?', *Housing Studies*, vol 13, no 5, pp 639-56.

Parry, W. H., Wright, C. H. and Lunn, J. E. (1967) 'Sheffield problem families – a follow up survey', *Medical Officer*, vol 118, pp 130-2.

Paterson, A. and Inglis J. (1976) 'Inherited problems (2): the inter-generational cycle of deprivation', *Social Work Today*, vol 8, no 8, pp 13-15.

Paugam, S. (1996) 'Poverty and social disqualification: a comparative analysis of cumulative social disadvantage in Europe', *Journal of European Social Policy*, vol 6, no 4, pp 287-303.

Percy-Smith, J. (2000) 'Introduction: the contours of social exclusion', in J. Percy-Smith (ed) *Policy responses to social exclusion: Towards inclusion?*, Buckingham: Open University Press, pp 1-21.

Philp, A. F. and Timms, N. (1957) *The problem of 'the problem family': A critical review of the literature concerning the 'problem family' and its treatment*, London: FSU.

Piachaud, D. (1981) 'Peter Townsend and the holy grail', *New Society*, vol 57, 10 September, pp 419-21.

Piachaud, D. (2001) 'Child poverty, opportunities and quality of life', *Political Quarterly*, vol 72, pp 446-53.

Piachaud, D. and Sutherland, H. (2002) 'Child poverty', in J. Hills, J. Le Grand and D. Piachaud (eds) *Understanding social exclusion*, Oxford: Oxford University Press, pp 141-54.

Platt, L. (2005) *Discovering child poverty: The creation of a policy agenda from 1800 to the present*, Bristol: The Policy Press.

Putnam, R. D. (2000) *Bowling alone: The collapse and revival of American community*, New York: Simon & Schuster.

Quinton, D. and Rutter, M. (1988) *Parenting breakdown: The making and breaking of inter-generational links*, Aldershot: Avebury.

Raban, C. (1982) 'A cycle of deprivation?', *Critical Social Policy*, vol 2, no 1, pp 118-20.

Raison, T. (1990) *Tories and the welfare state: A history of Conservative social policy since the Second World War*, Basingstoke: Macmillan.

Rapoport, R., Rapoport, R. N. and Strelitz, Z. with Kew, S. (1977) *Fathers, mothers and others: Towards new alliances*, London: Routledge & Kegan Paul.

RCDIW (Royal Commission on the Distribution of Income and Wealth) (1978) *Report no 6: Lower incomes*, Cmnd 7175, London: HMSO.

Respect Task Force (2006) *Respect action plan*, London: Home Office.

Richardson, L. and Le Grand, J. (2002) 'Outsider and insider expertise: the response of residents of deprived neighbourhoods to an academic definition of social exclusion', *Social Policy & Administration*, vol 36, no 5, pp 496-515.

Ridge, T. (2002) *Childhood poverty and social exclusion from a child's perspective*, Bristol: The Policy Press.

Rigg, J. and Sefton, T. (2004) *Income dynamics and the life cycle*, CASEpaper 81, London: CASE.

Robinson, D. (1975) 'Looking forward from 1975', *SSRC Newsletter 29*, pp 11-12.

Rodger, J. J. (2006) 'Antisocial families and withholding welfare support', *Critical Social Policy*, vol 26, no 1, pp 121-43.

Room, G. (1995a) (ed) *Beyond the threshold: The measurement and analysis of social exclusion*, Bristol: The Policy Press.

Room, G. (1995b) 'Poverty and social exclusion: the new European agenda for policy and research', in G. Room (ed) *Beyond the threshold*, Bristol: The Policy Press, pp 1-9.

Room, G. (1995c) 'Conclusions', in G. Room (ed) *Beyond the threshold*, Bristol: The Policy Press, pp 233-47.

Rowntree, B. S. (1901, 1902 edn) *Poverty: A study of town life*, London: Macmillan.

Runciman, W. G. (1966) *Relative deprivation and social justice: A study of attitudes to social inequality in twentieth-century England*, London: Routledge & Kegan Paul.

Rutter, M. (1972, 2nd edn 1982) *Maternal deprivation reassessed*, Harmondsworth: Penguin.

Rutter, M. (1998) 'Introductory lecture: new cycles of disadvantage', in A. Lee and J. Hills, *New cycles of disadvantage? Report of a conference organised by CASE on behalf of ESRC for HM Treasury*, London: CASE, pp 1-7.

Rutter, M. and Madge, N. (1976) *Cycles of disadvantage: A review of research*, London: Heinemann.

Ryan, W. (1971) *Blaming the victim*, New York, NY: Pantheon Books.

Scrivens, E. (1983a) 'Mildred Blaxter: *The health of the children*', *Journal of Social Policy*, vol 12, p 138.

Scrivens, E. (1983b) 'Mildred Blaxter and Elizabeth Paterson: *Mothers and daughters*', *Journal of Social Policy*, vol 12, pp 561-2.

Seabrook, J. (1977) 'Ghostly throng', *New Society*, vol 39, 6 January, pp 28-9.

Seldon, A. and Lowe, R. (1996) 'The influence of ideas on social policy', *Contemporary British History*, vol 10, no 2, pp 160-77.

Seldon, A. and Pappworth, J. (1983) *By word of mouth: Elite oral history*, London: Methuen.

Sen, A. (1983) 'Poor, relatively speaking', *Oxford Economic Papers*, vol 35, pp 153-69.

Sen, A. (1985) 'A sociological approach to the measurement of poverty: a reply to Professor Peter Townsend', *Oxford Economic Papers*, vol 37, pp 669-76.

Sennett, R. (2003, new edn 2004) *Respect: The formation of character in a world of inequality*, Harmondsworth: Penguin.

SEU (Social Exclusion Unit) (1998a) *Rough sleeping: Report by the Social Exclusion Unit*, Cm 4008, London: The Stationery Office.

SEU (1998b) *Bringing Britain together: A national strategy for neighbourhood renewal*, Cm 4045, London: The Stationery Office.

SEU (1998c) *Truancy and school exclusion: Report by the Social Exclusion Unit*, London: The Stationery Office.

SEU (1999a) *Teenage pregnancy*, Cm 4342, London: The Stationery Office.

SEU (1999b) *Bridging the gap: New opportunities for 16-18 year olds not in education, employment or training: Report by the Social Exclusion Unit*, Cm 4405, London: The Stationery Office.

Shearer, A. (1981) 'Labelling the poor', *New Society*, vol 55, 26 March, p 559.

Sheffield Health Committee (1956) *Annual report of the MOH, 1955*, Sheffield: Sheffield Health Committee.

Sheffield Health Committee (1960) *Annual report of the MOH, 1959*, Sheffield: Sheffield Health Committee.

Sheffield Health Committee (1970) *Annual report of the MOH, 1969*, Sheffield: Sheffield Health Committee.

Shonfield, A. (1975) 'Politics and policy: 1969-71', *SSRC Newsletter 29*, pp 6-8.

Showler, B. and Sinfield A. (1981) (eds) *The workless state: Studies in unemployment*, Oxford: Martin Robertson.

Silburn, R. (1978) 'A report summarising and comparing the sub-contracts of the "socio-economic" group', London: SSRC (unpublished).

Silver, H. (1994) 'Social exclusion and social solidarity: three paradigms', *International Labour Review*, vol 133, pp 531-78.

Silver, H. (1996) 'Culture, politics and national discourses of the new urban poverty', in E. Mingione (ed) *Urban poverty and the underclass: A reader*, Oxford: Blackwell, pp 105-38.

Silver, H. and Silver, P. (1991) *An educational war on poverty: American and British policy-making, 1960-1980*, Cambridge: Cambridge University Press.

Sinfield, A. (1968a) 'Poverty rediscovered', *Race*, vol 2, pp 202-9.

Sinfield, A. (1968b) *The long-term unemployed: A comparative survey*, Paris: OECD.

Sinfield, A. (1969) *Which way for social work?*, London: Fabian Society.

Sinfield, A. (1970) 'Poor and out of work in Shields: a summary report', in P. Townsend (ed) *The concept of poverty: Working papers on methods of investigation and life-styles of the poor in different countries*, London: Heinemann, pp 220-35.

Sinfield, A. (1974) 'Poverty and the social services department', in M. J. Brown (ed) *Social issues and the social services*, London: Charles Knight, pp 57-78.

Sinfield, A. (1975) 'We the people and they the poor: a comparative view of poverty research', *Social Studies*, vol 4, no 1, pp 3-25.

Sinfield, A. (1976) 'Income transfers and transmitted deprivation: some preliminary comments for the fourth conference on socio-economic factors in transmitted deprivation, 28 September 1976', Essex: Sociology Department, University of Essex, pp 1-7 (unpublished).

Sinfield, A. (1981a) *What unemployment means*, Oxford: Martin Robertson.

Sinfield, A. (1981b) 'Unemployment in an unequal society', in B. Showler and A. Sinfield (eds) *The workless state: Studies in unemployment*, Oxford: Martin Robertson, pp 122-66.

Smith, D. and Macnicol, J. (2001) 'Social security and the informal economy: survival strategies on a South London estate', in R. Edwards and J. Glover (eds) *Risk and citizenship: Key issues in welfare*, London: Routledge, pp 142-56.

Smith, D. M. (2005) *On the margins of inclusion: Changing labour markets and social exclusion in London*, Bristol: The Policy Press.

Spicker, P. (2007) *The idea of poverty*, Bristol: The Policy Press.

Squires, P. (2006) 'New Labour and the politics of antisocial behaviour', *Critical Social Policy*, vol 26, no 1, pp 144-68.

SSRC (Social Science Research Council) (1972) 'SSRC submission to government on "A framework for government research and development" (Cmnd 4814)', *SSRC Newsletter 14*, pp 2-6.

SSRC (1978) 'Experience of commissioning research', *SSRC Newsletter 36*, pp 18-20.

SSRC–DHSS (Social Science Research Council–Department of Health and Social Security) (1974) *Transmitted deprivation: First report of the DHSS/SSRC Joint Working Party on Transmitted Deprivation*, London: SSRC.

SSRC–DHSS (1975) *Transmitted deprivation: Second report of the DHSS/SSRC Joint Working Party on Transmitted Deprivation*, London: SSRC.

SSRC–DHSS (1977) *Transmitted deprivation: Third report of the DHSS/SSRC Joint Working Party on Transmitted Deprivation*, London: SSRC.

Stevenson, O. (1963) 'The understanding case worker', *New Society*, vol 44, 1 August, pp 9-12.

Stewart, K. (2005) 'Towards an equal start? Addressing childhood poverty and deprivation', in J. Hills and K. Stewart (eds) *A more equal society? New Labour, poverty and exclusion*, Bristol: The Policy Press, pp 143-65.

Stewart, K. and Hills, J. (2005) 'Introduction', in J. Hills and K. Stewart (eds) *A more equal society? New Labour, poverty and exclusion*, Bristol: The Policy Press, pp 1-19.

Such, E. and Walker, R. (2002) 'Falling behind? Research on transmitted deprivation', *Benefits*, vol 10, no 3, pp 185-92.

Such, E. and Walker, R. (2005) 'Young citizens or policy objects? Children in the "rights and responsibilities" debate', *Journal of Social Policy*, vol 34, no 1, pp 39-57.

Taylor, L. (1982) 'Journey into crime', *New Society*, vol 61, 12 August, p 271.

Taylor-Gooby, P. (1981) 'The empiricist tradition in social administration', *Critical Social Policy*, vol 2, pp 6-21.

Timmins, N. (1995, paperback edn 2001) *The five giants: A biography of the welfare state*, London: HarperCollins.

Tisdall, E. K. M. (2006) 'Antisocial behaviour legislation meets children's services: challenging perspectives on children, parents and the state', *Critical Social Policy*, vol 26, no 1, pp 101-20.

Titterton, M. (1992) 'Managing threats to welfare: the search for a new paradigm of welfare', *Journal of Social Policy*, vol 21, pp 1-23.

Townsend, P. (1952a) 'Poverty: ten years after Beveridge', *Political and Economic Planning*, no 344, pp 21-40.

Townsend, P. (1952b) 'Social security and unemployment in Lancashire', *Political and Economic Planning*, no 349, pp 113-36.

Townsend, P. (1957) *The family life of old people: An inquiry in East London*, London: Routledge & Kegan Paul.

Townsend, P. (1958) 'A society for people', in N. Mackenzie (ed) *Conviction*, London: MacGibbon and Kee, pp 93-120.

Townsend, P. (1962a) *The last refuge: A study of residential institutions and homes for the aged in England and Wales*, London: Routledge & Kegan Paul.

Townsend, P. (1962b) 'The meaning of poverty', *British Journal of Sociology*, vol 13, no 3, pp 210-27.

Townsend, P. (ed) (1970) *The concept of poverty: Working papers on methods of investigation and life-styles of the poor in different countries*, London: Heinemann.

Townsend, P. (1974) 'The cycle of deprivation: the history of a confused thesis', in BASW, *The cycle of deprivation: Papers presented to a national study conference, Manchester University, March, 1974*, Birmingham: BASW, pp 8-22.

Townsend, P. (1979) *Poverty in the United Kingdom: A survey of household resources and standards of living*, Harmondsworth: Penguin.

Townsend, P. (1981) 'Foreword', in B. Showler and A. Sinfield (eds) *The workless state: Studies in unemployment*, Oxford: Martin Robertson, pp xi–xvii.

Townsend, P. (1985) 'A sociological approach to the measurement of poverty – a rejoinder to Professor Amartya Sen', *Oxford Economic Papers*, vol 37, pp 659-68.

Townsend, P. (1987) 'Deprivation', *Journal of Social Policy*, vol 16, pp 125-46.

Townsend, P. (1993) *The international analysis of poverty*, Hemel Hempstead: Harvester, Wheatsheaf.

Townsend, P. (1997) 'Redistribution: the strategic alternative to privatisation', in A. Walker and C. Walker (eds) *Britain divided: The growth of social exclusion in the 1980s and 1990s*, London: CPAG, pp 263-78.

Townsend, P. and Bosanquet, N. (eds) (1972a) *Labour and inequality: Sixteen Fabian essays*, London: Fabian Society.

Townsend, P. and Bosanquet, N. (1972b) 'Introduction: the need for radical policy', in P. Townsend and N. Bosanquet (eds) *Labour and inequality: Sixteen Fabian essays*, London: Fabian Society, pp 5-11.

Townsend, P., Phillimore, P. and Beattie, A. (1988, new edn 1989) *Health and deprivation: Inequality and the North*, Beckenham: Croom Helm.

Toynbee, P. and Walker, D. (2001) *Did things get better?*, Harmondsworth: Penguin.

Triseliotis, J. and Russell, J. (1984) *Hard to place: The outcome of adoption and residential care*, London: Heinemann.

UNICEF (2007) *Child poverty in perspective: An overview of child well-being in rich countries*, Florence: UNICEF Innocenti Research Centre.

Utting, D. (1995) *Family and parenthood: Supporting families, preventing breakdown: A guide to the debate*, York: Joseph Rowntree Foundation.

Valentine, C.A. (1968) *Culture and poverty: Critique and counter-proposals*, Chicago, IL: University of Chicago Press.

Vinovskis, M.A. (2005) *The birth of Head Start: Preschool education policies in the Kennedy and Johnson administrations*, Chicago, IL: University of Chicago Press.

Waldfogel, J. (1999) *Early childhood interventions and outcomes*, CASEpaper 21, London: CASE.

Walker, A. (1996) 'Blaming the victims', in R. Lister (ed) *Charles Murray and the underclass: The developing debate*, London: IEA Health and Welfare Unit, pp 66-74.

Walker, A. and Walker, C. (eds) (1997) *Britain divided: The growth of social exclusion in the 1980s and 1990s*, London: CPAG.

Walker, R. (1995) 'The dynamics of poverty and social exclusion', in G. Room (ed) *Beyond the threshold: The measurement and analysis of social exclusion*, Bristol: The Policy Press, pp 102-28.

Watt, P. and Jacobs, K. (2000) 'Discourses of social exclusion: an analysis of *Bringing Britain together: A national strategy for neighbourhood renewal*', *Housing, Theory and Society*, vol 17, no 1, pp 14-26.

Webb, S. (1995) *Poverty dynamics in Great Britain: Preliminary analysis from the British Household Panel Survey*, London: Institute for Fiscal Studies.

Webster, C. (1996) *The health services since the war: Volume II: Government and health care: The British National Health Service 1958-1979*, London: The Stationery Office.

Weir, S. (1981) 'The SSRC and its family', *New Society*, vol 58, 26 November, pp 365-6.

Weir, S. (1982) 'Sentence of death on the SSRC?', *New Society*, vol 59, 7 January, pp 11-12.

Welshman, J. (2002) 'The cycle of deprivation and the concept of the underclass', *Benefits*, vol 10, no 3, pp 199-205.

Welshman, J. (2004) 'The unknown Titmuss', *Journal of Social Policy*, vol 33, no 2, pp 225-47.

Welshman, J. (2005) 'Ideology, social science, and public policy: the debate over transmitted deprivation', *Twentieth Century British History*, vol 16, no 3, pp 306-41.

Welshman, J. (2006a) *Underclass: A history of the excluded 1880-2000*, London: Hambledon/Continuum.

Welshman, J. (2006b) 'From the cycle of deprivation to social exclusion: five continuities', *Political Quarterly*, vol 77, no 4, pp 475-84.

Welshman, J. (2007a) 'Knights, knaves, pawns, and queens: attitudes to behaviour in postwar Britain', *Journal of Epidemiology and Community Health*, vol 61, pp 95-7.

Welshman, J. (2007b) 'The cycle of deprivation: myths and misconceptions', *Children & Society*.

Welshman, J. (2007c) 'Social science, housing, and the debate over transmitted deprivation', in M. Jackson (ed) *Health and the modern home*, London: Routledge.

West, D. J. (1969) *Present conduct and future delinquency*, London: Heinemann.

West, D. J. (1982) *Delinquency: Its roots, careers and prospects*, London: Heinemann.

Whelan, B. J. and Whelan, C. T. (1995) 'In what sense is poverty multidimensional?', in G. Room (ed) *Beyond the threshold: The measurement and analysis of social exclusion*, Bristol: The Policy Press, pp 29-48.

Williams, F. and Pillinger, J. (1996) 'New thinking on social policy research into inequality, social exclusion and poverty', in J. Millar and J. Bradshaw (eds) *Social welfare systems: Towards a research agenda*, Bath: University of Bath/ESRC, pp 1-32.

Williams, F. and Popay, J. (1999) 'Balancing polarities: developing a new framework for welfare research', in F. Williams, J. Popay and A. Oakley (eds) *Welfare research: A critical review*, London: UCL Press, pp 156-83.

Williams, F., Popay, J. and Oakley, A. (1999b) 'Changing paradigms of welfare', in F. Williams, J. Popay and A. Oakley (eds) *Welfare research: A critical review*, London: UCL Press, pp 2-16.

Williams, R. (1976, 1983 edn) *Keywords: A vocabulary of culture and society*, New York, NY: Oxford University Press.

Wilson, H. (1958) 'Juvenile delinquency in problem families in Cardiff', *British Journal of Delinquency*, vol IX, pp 94-105.

Wilson, H. (1959) 'Problem families and the concept of immaturity', *Case Conference*, vol 6, no 5, pp 115-18.

Wilson, H. (1962) *Delinquency and child neglect*, London: George Allen & Unwin.

Wilson, H. (1966) 'The plight of the large family', *New Society*, vol 30, 7 April, pp 8-11.

Wilson, H. (1970) 'The socialisation of children', in R. Holman, *Socially deprived families in Britain*, London: Bedford Square Press, pp 109-41.

Wilson, H. (1974a) 'Parenting in poverty', *British Journal of Social Work*, vol 4, no 3, pp 241-54.

Wilson, H. (1974b) 'The life and death of the cycle of deprivation and some unresolved problems', *Poverty*, vol 30, pp 3-8.

Wilson, H. and Herbert, G. (1972) 'Hazards of environment', *New Society*, vol 20, 8 June, pp 508-11.

Wilson, H. and Herbert, G. W. (1978) *Parents and children in the inner city*, London: Routledge & Kegan Paul.

Wilson, W. J. (1987) *The truly disadvantaged: The inner city, the underclass and public policy*, Chicago, IL: University of Chicago Press.

Wootton, B. (1959) *Social science and social pathology*, London: Allen & Unwin.

Wright, C. (1955) 'Problem families: a review and some observations', *Medical Officer*, vol 94, pp 381-4.

Wright, C. H. and Lunn, J. E. (1971) 'Sheffield problem families: a follow up study of their sons and daughters', *Community Medicine*, vol 126, no 22, 3304, pp 301-7, 315-21.

Wynn, M. and Wynn, A. (1974) 'Can family planning do more to reduce child poverty?', *Poverty*, vol 29, pp 17-20.

Young, M. (1975) 'The first years: 1965-68', *SSRC Newsletter 29*, pp 3-6.

Young, M. and Willmott, P. (1957) *Family and kinship in East London*, London: Routledge & Kegan Paul.

Zigler, E. and Valentine, J. (eds) (1979) *Project Head Start: A legacy of the War on Poverty*, New York, NY: The Free Press.

Index

'reserve army of labour' 244–5
resources, lack of 181
Respect Task Force 250–1
responsibility
  and New Labour policies 244
  behaviour/ anti-social behaviour 249
  and social exclusion 210
  and social policy 13, 214–15, 234
  vs choice 228–9
  vs opportunity 233
  and welfare state 237
Revenu Minimum d'Insertion
  (RMI)(France) 208
rewards, influence on behaviour 214
Room, Graham 209, 211
Rothschild Reports (1972, 1982)
  10–11, 81, 154
Rowntree study (York) 110, 128–9,
  165, 218–19
Royal Commission on the Distribution
  of Income and Wealth 128–9
Runciman, W G 196
Rutter, Michael 45–6, 64–5, 83–4
  JWP discussion paper 87–8
  JWP Literature Review (1976) 94–8,
  145, 164–200

S

school meals, free 60, 182
Second Report (JWP)(1975) 110,
  124–5, 189
Seebohm Committee on Local
  Authority and Allied Personal Social
  Services (1968) 27–8, 51
selectivists 62
self-improvement, and welfare 214
self-infliction and deprivation 56
seminars
  Dimensions of Parenthood (1973) 64
  Implications for Policy and Practice
  159
  Mechanics of Transmission 159
  Multiple Deprivation (1975) 127–8
  New Cycles of Disadvantage(1997)
  15–16, 236–8
  at Sunningdale 119
SEU, *see* Social Exclusion Unit
Sheffield Problem Family Studies 37,
  39–41, 110, 183
Sheridan, Alice 82–4, 153
Silburn, Richard 156
Silver, Hilary 208, 212–13
Sinfield, Adrian 187–92
'situational' deprivation 143
social capital 207, 214, 215
social control, and poverty 191
social deprivation 181, 197

social disqualification, *see* social
  exclusion
social disqualification, indicators
  209–10
social environment, relevance of 86–7
social exclusion
  and behaviour 248–9
  and child poverty 227
  and citizenship 7, 211–13, 216, 234
  and cultural factors 211
  and cycle of deprivation hypothesis
  217–18
  and disability 208
  EC policy 209–12
  emphasis on paid work 245, 248
  in France 208–12
  indicators of 209–10
  and insertion 208–10
  and juvenile delinquency 245
  and lack of power 209
  and minimum income 208
  and moral responsibility 210
  New Labour policies on 17–18,
  208–12, 214–18, 244–9
  obscuring inequalities 245–6
  and poverty 198–9, 210–11
  and relative deprivation 213–14, 245
  and social integration/ participation
  209
  and solidarity 212
  and underclass 213, 244, 248–9
  and unemployment, long term 211
Social Exclusion Unit (SEU)
  focus on transmitted deprivation 252
  research 247–8
  role/ focus of 235–6, 253–4
  transfer of functions 253–4
'social handicap' 185
social integration, *see* social exclusion
social isolation, *see* social exclusion
social mobility, and transmitted
  deprivation 226–7
social pathology 7, 12–13
social science research
  approaches to 175–201 (*see also*
  behaviour; deprivation; poverty;
  structure)
Social Science Research Council
  (SSRC)
  debates/ differences of opinion with
  DHSS 80–3, 154, 265
  on Final Report (JWP) 147
social work
  Labour policies on 144–5 (*see also*
  deprivation; poverty; welfare)
socially deprived families, definition 177
solidarity, and social exclusion 212